TELEVISION AND SOCIAL BEHAVIOR

REPORTS AND PAPERS, VOLUME II:

TELEVISION AND SOCIAL LEARNING

A TECHNICAL REPORT TO THE SURGEON GENERAL'S SCIENTIFIC ADVISORY COMMITTEE ON TELEVISION AND SOCIAL BEHAVIOR

Edited By
John P. Murray, Eli A. Rubinstein, and George A. Comstock
Editorial Coordination: Susan Lloyd-Jones

U.S. DEPARTMENT OF HEALTH, EDUCATION, AND WELFARE
Health Services and Mental Health Administration

National Institute of Mental Health
5600 Fishers Lane
Rockville, Maryland

Staff Members

Eli A. Rubinstein	Vice Chairman, Surgeon General's Scientific Advisory Committee
George A. Comstock	Senior Research Coordinator
John P. Murray	Research Coordinator
Michael Adler	Staff Assistant
Eileen Marchak	Research Assistant
Susan S. Lloyd-Jones	Editor
Joseph D. Reckley	Administrative Officer
Margaret D. Salladay	Secretary
Laura A. De Lisi	Secretary

Former Staff Members

Douglas A. Fuchs	Senior Research Coordinator (through 6/70)
John P. Robinson	Research Coordinator (through 9/70)
Harold Leigh	Administrative Officer (through 10/70)
Thomas Brubeck	Information Officer (through 5/71)
Deborah Cutler	Research Assistant (through 8/70)
Jan W. Lipkin	Secretary (through 4/70)

Advisory Committee Members

Ira H. Cisin	Charles A. Pinderhughes
Thomas E. Coffin	Ithiel de Sola Pool
Irving L. Janis	Alberta E. Siegel
Joseph T. Klapper	Anthony F. C. Wallace
Harold Mendelsohn	Andrew S. Watson
Eveline Omwake	Gerhart D. Wiebe

Preface

This document is one of five volumes of technical reports resulting from a broad scientific inquiry about television and its impact on the viewer. In the spring of 1969, by Congressional request, the DHEW initiated a special program under the general auspices of a Surgeon General's Scientific Advisory Committee on Television and Social Behavior. The major emphasis was to be on an examination of the relationship between televised violence and the attitudes and behavior of children. During the ensuing two years, more than fifty scientists participated directly in this program of research and produced over forty scientific reports.

The reports which are included in these five volumes are the independent work of the participating researchers. These results have all been made available to the Scientific Advisory Committee as evidence which the Committee could then evaluate and draw its own conclusions in the preparation of its own report. However, this work is of significance in its own right and is being published independently as source material for other researchers and for such interest as the general public may have in these technical reports.

In any broad scientific undertaking of this nature, where many individuals are involved, a careful balance between collaboration and independence of responsibility must be established. During the two and half years that this program of research was active, a constant effort was made to protect the scientific independence of the individual investigators and, at the same time: 1) to foster both cooperation and exchange among the researchers, 2) to develop as much of a total program structure as possible, and 3) to permit maximum communication and feedback among the researchers, the full-time staff responsible for planning and implementing the total research program, and the Scientific Advisory Committee responsible for the final assessment and evaluation of the research.

This is not the place to describe in detail how that balance of collaboration and independence was established and maintained. I believe, however, that these five volumes of technical reports provide an accurate and meaningful indication of our success in achieving the goal. The reports themselves are the products of the respective authors. They have been edited only to insure some comparability of format and to delete any excessive redundancies in review of the literature or introductory material. In some instances, where a report seemed initially too long the author was requested to reduce the report without deleting any critical material. All editing done by staff was submitted for the author's approval. We believe the result has made each of these five volumes a more readable and integrated totality than would otherwise be expected from a collection of research reports produced under the time constraints of this program.

In each instance, the integration of the five volumes was further established by the inclusion of an overview paper which attempts to summarize and relate the papers in that volume. These overview papers are also the independent work of the respective authors.

It would be difficult to convey to the reader the extraordinary efforts required by all participants in this research program to bring the endeavor to its published conclusion within the time allotted. Despite that time pressure, these volumes demonstrate an unusually high level of both productivity and quality for an area of research which has had more than its share of complexity and controversy.

In addition to the work of all persons directly engaged in this program, a very large number of individuals at one time or another provided advice and guidance to the researchers, to the staff, and to the Scientific Advisory Committee. It would be impossible to provide a complete list of these additional consultants. The total count is in the hundreds. While their names are not visible in these products, their counsel was often a very significant factor in the course of an individual piece of research or in a decision on the direction of the research program. To all those individuals, this program owes a special debt of gratitude for the collective wisdom made available to us.

And finally, on behalf both of the members of the Scientific Advisory Committee and of the staff who served the program, I wish especially to express much appreciation to the participating researchers who did the work and wrote the reports that contributed the new knowledge contained in these volumes.

Eli A. Rubinstein
Vice-Chairman, Surgeon General's
Scientific Advisory Committee on
Television and Social Behavior

Contents

Television and Social Learning: Some Relationships Between Viewing Violence and Behaving Aggressively (Overview)

Robert M. Liebert

What are the effects upon children of observing violent television programs? The question is one which has been continually posed since the advent of television sets as a common fixture in the American home almost two decades ago. Answers to it, based both on simple opinion and on research which reflects varying degrees of sophistication and appreciation of the complexity of the phenomenon, have ranged from confident statements that the medium's influence is uniformly pernicious to equally glib assertions that merely watching entertainment fare can do little to shape children's social behavior.

1

Although literally hundreds of studies have been focused directly or indirectly on television and its effects upon youngsters since the 1950s, the series of investigations recently commissioned by the Television and Social Behavior program of the National Institute of Mental Health constitutes one of the first systematic and purposefully coordinated attempts to employ the efforts of a large group of researchers with relevant expertise and diverse viewpoints. Five of these commissioned papers—four experimental reports and a literature review—appear in the subsequent chapters of this book. The purpose of the present paper is to provide a relatively brief overview of the research from which these contributions grew, and to identify and consider both the points of agreement and the inconsistencies that exist among them.[1] This task can best be served by beginning with synopses of the theoretical and methodological questions which relate to the study of television and aggression.

The scientific issue most fundamentally related to the particular question of the effects of television revolves around the nature of *observational learning*, i.e., the way in which the behavior of children (and adults) changes as a function of exposure to the behavior of others. Thus, it is to basic and applied research and theory in this area that we will first turn our attention.

Regardless of their particular theoretical affiliations, investigators interested in socialization have virtually all acknowledged that a child's values, knowledge, and behavior may be developed and molded, at least in part, by observational learning. Specifically, research studies have shown that the simple observation of others can be very potent in changing such widely varied aspects of social behavior as a child's willingness to aid others (e.g., Rosenhan and White, 1967), his ability to display self-control (e.g., Bandura and Mischel, 1965), and his learning of language rules (e.g., Liebert, Odom, Hill, and Huff, 1969). Young children's observation of others *on film* has been shown to produce an impressive level of learning of unfamiliar behaviors (Coates and Hartup, 1969), to increase children's sharing (Bryan and Walbek, 1970), and to markedly reduce phobic reactions (Bandura and Menlove, 1968; Hill, Liebert, and Mott, 1968).

This list represents only a few examples from the impressive body of evidence which suggests that learning by observation is a critical aspect of the social learning processes through which the child is informed about the world around him and molded into an adult member of his society (Bandura, 1969; Bryan and Schwartz, 1971; Liebert and Spiegler, 1970). It is therefore understandable that professionals and laymen alike have become increasingly interested in and concerned about determining the nature and extent to which such social learning occurs as a function of television viewing by children.

Definitions and distinctions

A number of different types of phenomena may, and have been, subsumed under the general classification of observational learning. Thus, in order to avoid confusion regarding the terms used, a series of definitions is provided below (cf. Liebert and Spiegler, 1970). These definitions will be employed consistently in the remainder of this paper and may prove helpful in clarifying both the factual and the theoretical issues which must be addressed periodically as we proceed.

Modeling. Modeling refers to the observed behavior of others, whether presented through direct demonstrations or through films, television, or stories which are heard or read. When modeling cues are presented by direct exposure to other persons, the phenomenon has typically been referred to as *live modeling,* while the behavior of others as observed in movies, television, and other representative media is usually considered to fall in the general category of *symbolic modeling.*

Observational learning. Any and all of the demonstrated consequences of exposure to modeling will be subsumed under the term *observational learning.* Observational learning can take several different forms and may therefore be measured in a number of different ways, depending upon the interests of a particular investigator or the nature of a particular issue.

Acquisition vs. acceptance. The broadest distinction among the various forms of observational learning, introduced by Albert Bandura and Richard Walters (1963) almost a decade ago, is between acquisition or the *ability* to reproduce previously unfamiliar acts as a function of observational learning and the subsequent acceptance and spontaneous *performance* of behaviors that are the same as, or similar to, those which have been observed. A child may observe and remember a particular adult's manner of speech, the particular expressions which he uses, or the novel forms of helping (or hurting) others which the exemplar displays without necessarily *adopting* any of these characteristics. Nonetheless, if the observer can reproduce or describe the behavior he has witnessed (for example, when asked to do so), then the most basic form of observational learning, the *acquisition* of new behaviors, has occurred.

The possibility that behavior can be acquired observationally and retained, without necessarily being performed immediately, has important implications for our understanding of the effects of both television and other observational learning opportunities. If a child has learned some new behavior, then he clearly possesses the potential to produce it if (or when) he finds himself in a situation in which such a performance appears to be desirable, useful, or likely to serve his own purposes. Thus, although learning does not necessarily lead to action, it does make possible the performance of otherwise unavailable forms of social responses. Exposure to novel modeling cues therefore changes the potential range of activities which a child may display when stressed, for example, or provoked, or called upon to act in a situation where these otherwise dormant skills appear to become potentially useful.

Finally, it should be noted that acceptance of another's behavior as a guide for one's own does not necessarily imply an increase in similarity between the behavior of the model and that of the observer. The child who sees a peer burned by a hot stove will typically become *less* likely to touch the dangerous appliance than previously; he accepts the exemplar's actions and consequences as a guide for what he should *not* do.

Direct imitative effects vs. inhibition-disinhibition. Many observationally learned behaviors do lead to acceptance, either immediately or when environmental conditions are conducive. Researchers have noted two related but distinguishable kinds of imitative performance: *direct imitative effects* and *inhibition* or *disinhibition effects*. The concept of direct imitation refers to whether the observer endeavors to exactly reproduce or mimic the behavior which he has observed. A child who repeats exactly some of the expressions used by his father, and a child who precisely matches the kicking, hitting, and other forms of attack against a plastic Bobo doll which he has seen displayed in a brief movie, are both showing direct imitative effects. Likewise, the child in our earlier example who now *avoids* the stove is engaging in direct *counter* imitation.

In contrast, the inhibition-disinhibition dimension refers to the performance of behaviors which fall in the same general *class* as those observed, but may be different in virtually all particulars.[2] Thus, for example, a child who sees his parent donate money to a charity and subsequently becomes more likely to share chocolate cake with his little sister is showing a disinhibition (or response facilitation) regarding the *class* of sharing.

Inhibition as a function of observational learning represents the other side of the coin from disinhibition. For example, the child who, on the first day of class in the third grade, sees that the new teacher punishes one of his classmates sharply for adamantly announcing his refusal to comply with a particular request, may subsequently become *less* likely to turn in his first homework assignment late. Failing to turn in homework on time and speaking out inappropriately in class are hardly identical behaviors in terms of the particular acts which they involve. However, they fall into a common class of behavior—disobedience to the dictates of the teacher—and thus the behavior of the observer may be traced to the behavior of (and subsequent consequences to) the model.

Integration of processes: the three stages of observational learning

The processes of observational learning outlined above may now be seen to involve three stages: 1) the observer must be exposed to modeling cues; 2) he must acquire and be able to reproduce what he has seen or heard; 3) he may or may not accept the model's behavior as a guide for his own actions. Thus, step 3 may be manifested in imitative effects (i.e., the observer's behavior becomes more like that of the model than previously), which can involve either direct imitation, or disinhibition, or both. Alternatively, the effects of modeling may produce counterimitative effects (direct counterimitation or inhibition). Finally, exposure and acquisition can occur without leading to acceptance, a result which may be thought of as nonimitation. These steps, and the alternatives involved at each of them, are shown graphically in Figure 1.

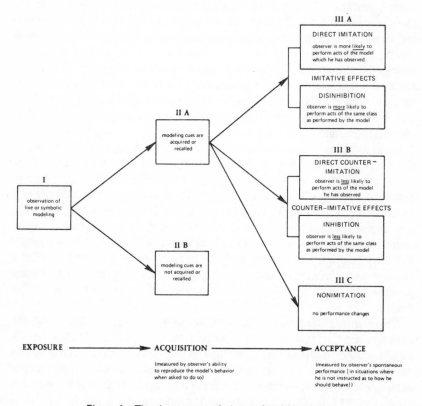

Figure 1. The three stages of observational learning

Figure 1 also suggests that children's exposure to aggressive television programming, a situation in which observational learning may potentially occur, may have a number of different effects. Evidence of each of the possibilities shown is available. However, before we consider these substantive findings, it will be helpful to distinguish among the methods which have been employed to obtain them.

Research approaches to the study of television and aggression

Three somewhat different research strategies, each with strengths and weaknesses, have been employed to explore the question of the effects of television upon children: *survey techniques, correlational studies,* and *experimental investigations.*

Surveys. The survey technique typically involves identifying a relatively large sample of persons (usually several hundred respondents or more), preferably representative of the population at large in terms of age socioeconomic and ethnic backgrounds, and systematically obtaining questionnaire information about such things as the frequency with which they (or their children) watch television, an indication of favorite programs, and so on. Surveys can also be used to determine the nature and contents of television's offerings. In the latter category falls the extensive and sophisticated surveys of George Gerbner (1968, 1971), which have provided valuable information on the amount and nature of current television.

Like all other research efforts, surveys vary in sophistication and in the degree to which we can be confident that their samples reflect the larger population (of children, of programs) which they are designed to probe. A paper by LoSciuto (1971) provides some excellent comments on the criteria and difficulties which characterize this approach. Briefly, it is important that the sample surveyed should be appropriately representative of the population, large enough that descriptions of the sample will closely approximate those of the population, and tapped in such a manner as to minimize the probability that the information-gathering process will bias the information obtained (cf. Neale and Liebert, in press).

Correlational studies. Correlation, as the name implies, deals with the co- or joint relationship between two or more variables. The method is ideally suited to answering questions of the form: "Do variable X and variable Y go together or vary together?" Such questions have often been asked about television and aggression. Are children who watch a lot of violent television more aggressive than those who watch less? Is the social class of the child's parents related to the amount or kind of programs he watches? Are boys more likely to be influenced by aggressive television programs than girls?[3]

The correlational method is characterized by the fact that all subjects are observed under identical (or nearly identical) conditions. The measurements themselves involve preexisting characteristics of the participants, so that no effort is made to manipulate or control the events to which they are exposed. While this last characteristic appears, at first blush, to be an advantage, it is, in fact, the method's most serious drawback. Without systematically varying the conditions to which subjects are exposed, it is usually not possible to draw causal inferences. A substantial correlation between two variables means that each can be "predicted" from the other statistically, but it does not tell us whether either is the cause of the other. There is, for example, a high positive correlation between the number of churches in a city and the number of crimes committed in that city; the more churches a city has, the more crimes are committed. Does this mean that religion fosters crime? Certainly not. That crime fosters religion? Unlikely. The correlation is due to a third variable—population—which leads to an increase in both churches and crime. Or consider the possibility of a positive relationship between the amount of aggressive television which a child watches and the degree to which he behaves aggressively in life situations. From such a correlation it might be argued that youngsters who observe aggressive television become more likely to aggress as a result of the television fare to which they are exposed—that is, that the television programs cause the aggressive behavior to some degree. This argument *may* be true, but not as a logical inference from the observed relationship.

It is possible that some children are *both* more likely to be aggressive in their own behavior *and* more likely to enjoy watching aggressive programs than others, due to some unidentified "third variable." If this were the case, aggressive children would not be expected to become less aggressive by a change in their television diets, nor would relatively unaggressive children become more aggressive as a function of increased exposure to such programming. It is therefore vital that correlational results be supplemented by research which permits logical inferences about causal relationships in order to determine whether a consistent pattern emerges. For this purpose, the researcher and critic must turn to experimental investigations.

Experimental investigations. In an experimental investigation all subjects are treated alike except for differential exposure to one or more manipulated events or independent variables. They are subsequently tested on one or more measures (referred to as dependent variables which are expected to be controlled by or to depend upon the independent variable. If the subjects are assigned to groups randomly (so that each person had an equal chance of being in any treatment group) or if possible initial differences are otherwise controlled or cancelled out, then the investigator can conclude that the differences in the independent variable (or treatment) caused or produced differences on the dependent variable(s). For this reason, experimental research is widely considered to be the most powerful research tool in the social sciences.

Exposure to aggressive modeling through television

The question of children's exposure to aggressive modeling through television may be considered in terms of two components: 1) How much of available television fare provides such modeling? 2) How much time do children spend in exposure to such content? Excellent survey research conducted under the auspices of NIMH appears to provide relatively clear answers to both these questions.

Frequency of violent content on the commercial networks. Gerbner (1971) studied the frequency of overt physical violence during prime time and Saturday morning network programs during the fall of 1969 and compared these data with similar 1967 and 1968 studies which he had conducted for the National Commission on the Causes and Prevention of Violence. He found that in 1969, as in earlier years, "about eight in ten plays still contained violence, and the frequency of violent episodes was still about five per play and nearly eight per hour." The violence index (Gerbner's overall measure of the frequency with which violent acts are portrayed) actually rose for one of the networks, NBC, from 1968 to 1969.

Further, since our primary concern is in programs which are likely to be of particular interest to children, it is especially important to note that cartoons, the most violent of programs in 1967, increased their lead in 1969.

Frequency with which children are exposed to violent content. Lyle and Hoffman (1971) conducted an extensive survey of media use among more than one thousand children from widely varied backgrounds. They concluded that "television saturation was almost total; only two percent of the students stated that there was not a working TV set in their home." Their data also show that more than one-third of the first graders are still watching television at 8:30 p.m. on weeknights, and more than one-half of the sixth graders are doing so. Likewise, Stein and Friedrich (1971, this volume) report that, in their sample, television watching was reported to be among the children's most frequent waking activities. Lesser (1970) has argued that a child born today will, by the age of 18, have spent more of his life watching television than in any other single activity except sleep.

The pervasiveness of television can be seen even more clearly by moving from percentage figures to absolute numbers. McIntyre and Teevan (1971), citing the Violence Commission staff reports of 1969, remind us that "on one Monday during the period covered, over five million children under the age of 12 . . . were still watching between

10:30 and 11:00 p.m. . . ." They also point to the commission's observations that "there is a great deal of violent content available, at all times of the day, for all manner of intended audience," that "the presentation of violence is typically as a means of achieving virtually any type of goal," and that "the use of violence, whether sanctioned or not, is likely to be a successful means of obtaining such goals."

Moreover, high-violence programs are among young children's favorites. In the Lyle and Hoffman report, for example, first grade children were found to prefer programs of the sort heavily saturated with violence. Twenty-four percent of the children said that cartoons were their favorite type of program, while another 13 percent selected detective and "hip adventure" programs as their favorites. A similar pattern was found in Stein et al.'s (1971) study of preschoolers, whose parents reported that they watched cartoons an average of more than seven hours per week. Even adult violent programs were watched more than a full hour per week by these three- to five-year old children.

Clearly, the first stage of the observational learning of aggression from television, *exposure,* does occur. At this writing, there appears to be no question that violent television fare is available in overwhelming abundance and that children do watch these programs both frequently and regularly. It is to the second stage, acquisition, that we must turn next.

Acquisition

No one would doubt that children can learn novel forms of behavior—both words and actions—from simply watching others. It is, however, only through systematic research that we are able to see the degree to which this form of learning is effectively mediated by television and television-like formats.

As Stevenson (1971, this volume), in his review of the effects of television on preschool children has observed, the Ball and Bogatz (1970) evaluation of the instructional effectiveness of *Sesame Street* provides one of the most comprehensive demonstrations of young children's acquisition of knowledge from television. The conclusion drawn by these writers is one with implications both for the learning of aggression from television and also for the more appetizing prospect of using positive television fare for instructional purposes: ". . . television has been shown to work extremely well as a teaching medium. It achieved this result [referring to *Sesame Street*] not only in learnings that involve simply association (for example, naming letters) but also in learning that involves complex cognitive processes (sorting and classifying) . . ."

Studies designed to show that brief exposure to novel *aggressive* behaviors can lead to their acquisition by quite young children have uniformly shown that this influence is potent indeed (Bandura, 1965; Bandura, Ross, and Ross, 1963a; Hicks, 1965). In one such study, for example, 88 percent of the subjects (3-5 year old boys and girls) displayed imitative aggression of novel modeled acts even though they had not been asked to do so and were free to play with attractive, nonaggressive toys such as a tea set, crayons, cars and trucks, plastic farm animals, and the like.

Particularly striking is the degree to which some of the subjects appeared to be virtually "carbon copies" of the aggressive models whom they had observed. Photographs taken by Bandura and his associates illustrating these imitative effects are shown in Figure 2. The topmost frames show the female model's performance of four novel aggressive responses while the middle and bottom frames respectively depict a male and a female subject spontaneously reproducing the behaviors which they had seen earlier on film.

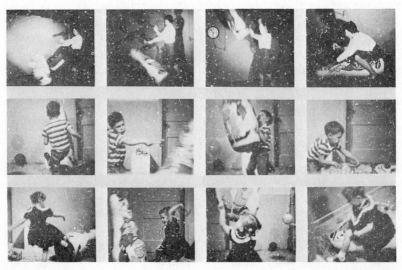

Courtesy of Dr. Albert Bandura

Figure 2: Photographs from the film *Social Learning of Aggression Through Imitation of Aggressive Models,* illustrating children's acquisition of aggressive responses through observational learning.

Further, there is evidence that behavior acquired in this way may be recalled for long periods of time, as evidenced by delayed retests of acquisition. Hicks (1965) found that subjects shown a simulated television program similar to those used by Bandura and his associates showed substantial acquisition of these behaviors after a single viewing; this acquisition was still in evidence when they were tested again, without further exposure, six months later. In a second study by the same author (Hicks, 1968), about 40 percent of the aggressive responses were found to be retained for a period of eight months. On the basis of these data, it is relatively easy to concur with Goranson's (1969) conclusion that novel aggressive behaviors can be learned from television and, with even limited practice, be retained for impressively long periods of time.

Since these studies typically involved inanimate rather than human victims, and have been mistakenly criticized for employing this strategy, it may be helpful to note their rationale explicitly. Bandura (1969) has explained the strategy this way:

> A social-learning theory of aggression distinguishes the acquisition of instrumental responses that have destructive or pain-producing potential from the conditions governing their subsequent performance. Aggressive response patterns are characteristically acquired under nonfrustrating conditions in the absence of injurious intent and often toward inanimate objects. Thus, for example, military recruits acquire and perfect combat skills through many hours of target practice and simulated skirmishes; boxers develop hurtful pummeling abilities by using punching bags and sparring partners whom they do not necessarily intend to hurt; and huntsmen acquire the basic rudiments of hunting by shooting at inanimate targets before they go out in search of game. Indeed, if aggressive repertoires were taught only while individuals were hostilely aroused and entertained injurious designs, many of the tutors and learners would probably be maimed during the acquisition phase.

Recall of particular physical acts must, however, be distinguished from the acquisition and recall of the somewhat more subtle plot themes and relationships which characterize televised stories. In order to explore an aspect of this latter issue, Leifer and Roberts (1971, in this volume) studied age differences in children's understanding of aggression which they observed on television. Almost 300 subjects served in their experiment, including kindergarteners, third graders, sixth graders, ninth graders, and twelfth graders. The primary purpose of this study was to identify age differences in children's understanding of the motives and consequences which attended aggressive acts. Striking age differences were obtained, showing that understanding of motives and consequences increases with age. Specifically, as Leifer and Roberts note: "Kindergarteners could answer only about one-third of the questions about either motives or consequences, third graders only about one-half, and twelfth graders about 95 percent. Hence the younger subjects, by our measures, are not taking in, or retaining, much of the information about motives and consequences in a television program."

The Leifer and Roberts data are consistent with the findings of Stein (1971, in this volume), which show that preschool children were able to remember some of the characters and details of the programs which they were shown in her experimental field study (to be discussed in detail in a later section) but that their recall was very far from perfect. These data seem to show that children will fail to recall much of the "nonaction" detail in a particular sequence which they have observed only once.

Stevenson (1971, in this volume) has noted that enduring recall of such materials would probably be most likely for young children if the material to which the child is exposed produces emotional responses, if the observed content is discussed with others, or if a common theme is shown repeatedly. Are these conditions met when children watch aggressive television?

Osborn and Endsley (1971) have explored the relationship between emotional reactions and program content. They had four- and five-year-old children observe a variety of programs, including one containing human violence and one containing cartoon violence, as well as cartoon and human programs with no violent episodes. Galvanic skin responses (a measure of emotional reactivity) revealed that the violent programs, and particularly the one containing human violence, produced more emotional responses than did the nonviolent programs. Moreover, (and of particular interest in terms of the acquisition issue), the children showed quite good recall of the contents of the violence programs. In fact, recall of the human violence or cartoon violence programs was significantly better than that of the program showing nonviolent human interaction.

With respect to the second point, Lyle and Hoffman (1971) found that television programs were subordinate only to school as a topic of dicussion among youngsters.

Finally, regarding Stevenson's third point, we may ask, "To what repeated themes and lessons are viewers of violent programs exposed?" Gerbner (1971) has answered lucidly:

> To be able to hit hard and to strike terror in the hearts of one's opponents—that makes one count when the chips are down. The battered hero triumphs over evil by subduing the bad guy in the end. The last man to hit the dust confirms his own flaw of character and cause. Hurting is a test of virtue, and killing is the ultimate measure of man. Loss of life, limb, or mind, any diminution of the freedom of action, are the wages of weakness or sin in the symbolic shorthand of ritual drama. . . .The typical plot ends by reaching a reassuring and usually foregone conclusion . . ."

The data reviewed in this section suggest that children are likely to acquire, with the level of repeated exposure which takes place, a good deal of the aggressive repertoire that they see in televised violence. In fact, by virtue of their popularity and their ability to evoke emotional responses, programs containing violence appear particularly likely to be learned and retained from televised observational experience. Thus it is not surprising that what Goranson (1969) has referred to as the "response forms" of aggression can be reproduced by observers easily and with a remarkable degree of fidelity.

The degree to which children are attentive to or learn from the complex and occasionally sophisticated nuances of plot, intrigue, and verbal aggression in the more "adult" type of crime dramas is not yet well understood. A full grasp of these procedures would require systematically varying the characteristics of otherwise unfamiliar inputs and then exploring their recall and retention across various time periods. Research of this type would be extremely valuable theoretically and could play an important subsequent role in the development of television programs which are designed to teach substantive material and prosocial lessons, an appetizing possibility hinted at both in Stevenson's paper and in the findings of Stein and Friedrich about the facilitation of prosocial and self-control behavior by *Misterogers Neighborhood*

However, notwithstanding the preceding qualifications, it is clear that children can and do acquire aggressive behaviors from the type of television fare which is currently available. But the question of whether they accept this material as a guide for their own actions remains.

Acceptance

Results reviewed in the foregoing sections clearly show that children in our society are exposed to a substantial amount of modeled aggression on television, and that repeated exposure to this fare is likely to lead to acquisition of both novel aggressive responses and the perception that aggression is often a potent interpersonal technique for serving one's own ends. The remaining, and perhaps most important, question is the degree to which children accept and utilize information which they have gathered in this way in a variety of performance situations.

Direct imitative and counterimitative effects. Following the theoretical distinctions advanced earlier, our discussion begins with studies of direct imitative and counterimitative effects. There are at least a few instances of direct imitation in naturalistic situations which have been truly unfortunate, such as a lad who was stabbed while he and his friends reenacted scenes from the movie *Rebel Without a Cause* which they had seen on a television rerun (*San Francisco Chronicle*, 1961), or the youngster who doctored the family dinner with ground glass after observing this tactic used successfully on a television crime show (Schramm, Lyle, and Parker, 1961). A more general (if less dramatic) influence of televised aggression upon direct imitation can be seen from experimental studies conducted in the laboratory.

A study by Bandura (1965) is among the most important for a theoretical understanding of the nature of direct imitative effects. Bandura had children watch a model perform a series of aggressive acts against a plastic Bobo doll clown. One group observed the model rewarded for this behavior, one observed the model receive no consequences, and one observed the model punished. When the children were subsequently put in a play situation, those who saw the model rewarded or perform without consequences showed a high level of direct imitation. Not surprisingly, those who observed the punished model, in contrast to the other groups, showed relatively few imitative aggressive responses (that is, showed counterimitation). Nonetheless, when children in all groups were subsequently asked by the experimenter to reproduce as many of the model's aggressive acts as they could, and were offered attractive incentives for doing so, the previously observed effects of vicarious consequences were entirely eliminated and all groups showed a remarkably high and uniform degree of learning.

Data like the foregoing suggest that when conditions favor activating observationally learned responses into performance, the likelihood of this performance's occurring will not be diminished by the presence of vicarious punishment at the time of observational learning. This evidence may successfully rebut the argument, made by spokesmen for the mass media, that the depiction of violence has no harmful effects on young observers as long as it is ultimately punished. In the light of repeated demonstrations that vicarious punishment does not impede the learning or recall of aggressive acts (cf. Liebert and Fernandez, 1970), it appears that these violent offerings can still have profound effects on the behavior of the viewers by teaching more aggressive responses.

Equally impressive are children's responses to questions regarding direct imitation. When Lyle and Hoffman (1971) asked first graders whether they had ever copied what they had seen on television, more than 60 percent said they had done so. Moreover, when they were asked to indicate the type of program which they imitated in play activities, adventure shows (such as *Batman*) led the list. Not surprisingly, these imitative activities were largely interpersonal in character; the children were much more likely to use television programs as a guide for their play activities when playing with friends than when playing alone.

A recent experiment by Martin, Gelfand, and Hartmann (1970) suggests why adults may often not be witness to the direct imitation of aggressive modeling. These investigators exposed children to an aggressive model and then put them in a situation where aggressive play was possible. Some children performed in the presence of adults, some in the presence of peers, and some alone. The general pattern of results disclosed that *the presence of an adult reduced the amount of aggression* but that the presence of a *same-sexed peer* increased aggression, relative to the control group. Thus, in life situations, the most powerful effects of aggressive modeling may occur under circumstances where they cannot be observed by parents or other adults. Goranson (1969), citing earlier studies, reached a similar conclusion: ". . . parental evaluation or instruction regarding the permissibility of aggression seen in media can be effective in controlling aggression imitation, but this communication may be irrelevant when adults are not later present to monitor the child's behavior."

That direct imitative effects after observing aggression may occur for more than just the type of *play* activities described above, is indicated by the results of several recent experiments. In the first of these (Hanratty, Liebert, Morris, and Fernandez, 1969), four- and five-year-old boys from a Sunday school kindergarten served as subjects. Half the subjects observed a two-and-one-half-minute color sound film in which an adult male model aggressed against a human clown. The behavior displayed by this symbolic model included sharp and unprovoked verbal insults to the clown, shooting at the clown with a toy machine gun, and beating the clown vigorously with a plastic mallet. Half the group saw no such film.

Thereafter, half of the subjects in each of these groups were permitted to play in a research room, where they found a human clown standing idly, as well as a mallet and a toy gun. The remaining children were placed in a comparable situation, except that they found a plastic Bobo doll rather than a human. The children were left in this situation for ten minutes, during which time their aggressive responses toward the clown, plastic or human, were recorded. Not surprisingly, the brief film did increase children's aggression against the inflated Bobo. However, regardless of whether the children had seen the aggressive film or not, the majority of those who were placed with the plastic toy exhibited some aggressive action. In contrast, of the children who had not observed the movie, none engaged in any sort of aggressive behavior toward the human clown. There are, of course, strong inhibitions for aggressing against a human being, even one who is attired as a clown, and there was no provocation for doing so. Nonetheless, observation of the aggressive movie did elicit physical assaults against the human clown, including at least one swat with the mallet which was hard enough that the victim showed a red mark on her arm several hours later.

In a second experiment (Hanratty, 1969), it was again found that a film of this type, without other provocation, would lead children to physically assault a human victim. Moreover, such aggression was displayed by both boys and girls (only boys had participated in the first experiment) and for films in which both an eight-year-old boy and an adult served as models. This finding has been essentially replicated a third and a fourth time with somewhat older boys (Hanratty, O'Neal, and Sulzer, 1971; Savitsky, Rogers, Izard, and Liebert, 1971), although in the Hanratty et al. (1971) study, frustration did interact with modeling for these older and perhaps more inhibited observers.

Since direct imitative effects definitionally require a circumstance virtually identical to the one observed, it has been argued that they are less important, from a social point of view, than inhibitory and disinhibitory effects. However, it is precisely in this last category that the greatest controversy has raged regarding the adequacy and interpretation of research results. This is also the area in which greatest research emphasis has recently been placed—as evidenced by the fact that all four original studies appearing in the present volume, and almost half of all of the studies sponsored by NIMH, sought evidence about the inhibitory or disinhibitory effects of observing aggressive television in terms of a willingness to aggress against other persons.

Inhibitory and disinhibitory effects: correlational studies. Several recently completed correlational studies bear directly on the possibility of
a relationship between the amount of violence a child observes and the
amount of aggressive behavior which he displays in naturalistic situations.

Working with adolescent subjects, McIntyre and Teevan (1971) found
a relatively small but consistent relationship between objective ratings
of the amount of violence on programs which youngsters reported
watching and deviant behavior as measured by a variety of indices.
Interestingly, this relationship becomes somewhat stronger if the degree
of violence of the television programs is assessed by the subject's own
perceptions than if it is assessed by objective ratings. Likewise, these
investigators found a positive relationship between the violence rating
of the subject's favorite programs and the degree to which they
expressed approval of violence. Further, while violence was more likely
to be approved if it had been rewarded than if it had been punished,
McIntyre and Teevan point out that "whether the characters were
viewed as behaving the way people ought to act has no effect on the
frequency of approval." They specifically note:

> Those adolescents whose favorite programs are more violent more frequent-
> ly approve of a teenage boy punching or knifing another teenage boy. If the
> favorite program is described as depicting violence as a means to an end, or
> violence rewarded, teen violence is approved more often than if the program
> were not so described. Whether or not the program "shows the way people
> ought to act" does not influence frequency of approval.

In another NIMH-sponsored correlational study, Dominick and
Greenberg (1971) determined, through the use of a questionnaire technique, the amount of exposure to television violence for 434 fourth-,
fifth-, and sixth-grade boys enrolled in Michigan public schools during
the spring of 1970. Evaluation of the violent content of the programs
themselves was based on earlier analyses of newspaper and magazine
critics (see Greenberg and Gordon, 1971). Exposure was then related to
the boys' approval of and willingness to use violence, as measured by
the items drawn from the Sears Antisocial Aggression scale (1961) and
the Buss-Durkee Hostility Inventory (Buss, 1957) respectively. Measures were also obtained of the degree to which the boys perceived violence as effective and the degree to which they suggested violent solutions to conflict situations when presented with open-ended questions.
In this investigation, specific predictions regarding interactions between family attitudes and social class on the one hand, and exposure to
violent content on television on the other hand, had been advanced.
Consistent with predictions, exposure to aggressive television was related to the boys' stated willingness to use violence and to their perceptions of its effectiveness when used. The direction of these influences
was consistent with hypotheses; higher exposure was associated with
greater approval.

As Dominick and Greenberg note, one of the most intriguing aspects of their findings is the tendency for violent exposure to be more often associated with violent attitudes for middle-class than for lower-class youngsters. It is the case, however, that when the home environment is weak in efforts to control the development of aggressive attitudes, then the relationship between exposure to violence on television and the child's own attitudes become stronger. In the investigators' own words: ". . . for relatively average children from average home environments, continued exposure to violence is positively related to acceptance of aggression as a mode of behavior. When the home environment also tends to ignore the child's development of aggressive attitudes, this relationship is even more substantial and perhaps more critical."

Dominick and Greenberg used the same methods to relate television violence and aggressive attitudes for girls. The results closely paralleled those for boys, with exposure to such aggressive fare making a "consistent independent contribution to the child's notions about violence. The greater the level of exposure to television violence, the more the child was willing to use violence, to suggest it as a solution to conflict, and to perceive it as effective."

In yet another correlational study conducted for the Television and Social Behavior program, McLeod, Atkin, and Chaffee (1971) examined the relationship between viewing of televised violence and a variety of measures of aggressive behavior in two relatively large samples of adolescents, one in Maryland and another in Wisconsin. The study is noteworthy for its careful consideration of multiple correlations among a variety of predictor variables and for reports of internal consistency among all the measures employed. The outcome of these correlational studies may be summarized in the authors' own words:

> Our research shows that among both boys and girls at two grade levels [junior high and senior high] the more the child watches violent television fare, the more aggressive he is likely to be as measured by a variety of self-report measures. . . .Partialing out (total) viewing time slightly reduces the positive correlations of violence viewing and aggressive behavior in most cases, but the basic result is the same as for the raw correlations . . . .Similarly, the partialing out of socioeconomic status and school performance does not alter the basic pattern of raw correlations. . . .We may conclude, then, that adolescents viewing high levels of violent content on television tend to have high levels of aggressive behavior, regardless of television viewing time, socioeconomic status, or school performance. These partials appear to rule out as alternative explanations simple television exposure, social status and general competence as a student.

A particularly sophisticated correlational study of television and aggression was undertaken by Lefkowitz, Eron, Walder, and Huesmann (1971). The Lefkowitz et al. report is based on a longitudinal study of the entire population of children of a particular age in a rural New York county and involved approximately 900 youngsters. Designed from the outset to relate children's aggressive behavior to various familial, social, and experimental factors which might influence it, these investigators employed a peer measurement technique of aggression (focusing exclusively upon acts which would harm or irritate other persons). The measurement instrument has been amply researched (Walder, Abelson, Eron, Banta, and Laulicht, 1961) and accepted by investigators of different theoretical persuasions (e.g., Feshbach and Singer, 1971).

The first measures obtained in this study of television and aggression revealed a significant relationship, for male subjects, between the amount of television violence which they watched in the third grade and independently assessed peer ratings of aggression in the classroom at that time (Eron, 1963). This correlational finding was later replicated with a different sample—eighth-grade boys and girls in an urban city in the South.

Lefkowitz et al. recently completed the longitudinal phase of their study by obtaining data from more than 400 of the youngsters whom they had studied ten years earlier. The measures obtained included peer ratings of aggression at this age, self-reports of aggression in an interview, and self-reports of various aspects of television viewing. The results of this ten-year followup showed that (but again only for boys) amount of aggression watched in the third grade was significantly related to peer ratings of aggression at age 19.

Additionally, using a sophisticated approach technically referred to as a *cross-lagged panel design*, Lefkowitz et al. showed that their findings provide stronger evidence for a causal relationship than is usually available from correlational studies. To understand the basic logic behind this approach,[4] consider the possibility, raised in our earlier discussion of correlation studies, that a relationship will appear between overt aggression and preferences for aggressive television simply because persons who are more willing to use aggression themselves are also more likely to enjoy seeing it used by others in television dramas. This is an important "rival hypothesis" to the notion that seeing aggressive television *causes* aggressive behavior. However, if the rival hypothesis were correct, preferences for aggressive television at age 19 in the Lefkowitz et al. study should "go together" with overt aggression in the third grade as closely as preferences for aggressive programs in the third grade go with aggression at age 19. In other words, the relationships, if accounted for by a constant third variable, should go both ways in time.

In contrast, if television aggression does cause aggressive behavior later, it would be plausible to find a link between earlier television watching and later aggression but not vice versa. This is exactly what was disclosed by the Lefkowitz et al. data. Third-grade preferences for aggressive television predicted later aggression, but later television preferences did *not* relate to the youngsters' earlier aggressive behavior at all. For this reason, it is reasonable to agree with the investigators' interpretation of their findings: that, for boys, ". . .on the basis of the cross-lagged correlations, the most plausible single causal hypothesis would appear to be that watching violent television in the third grade leads to the building of aggressive habits" and ". . .that a substantial component of aggression at all three grade levels and a particularly large component at the thirteenth grade can be predicted better by the amount of television violence which the child watched in the third grade than by any other causal variable measured and reinforces the contention that there is a cause and effect relation between the violence content of television and overt aggressive behavior."

The possibility that many of the effects of viewing aggressive television are cumulative over many years, as suggested by Lefkowitz et al., is also raised by the Stein and Friedrich report. These latter investigators did not find a relationship between interpersonal aggression during the first few weeks of nursery school and home viewing of aggression for their very young (3-5-year-old) subjects, although such a relationship has been repeatedly found for older children and adolescents. (There are of course, other possibilities, and Stein and Friedrich list several.)

The correlational studies of Dominick and Greenberg (1971), of Lefkowitz et al. (1971), of McIntyre and Teevan (1971) and of McLeod et al. (1971) uniformly show an association between exposure to aggressive television and aggressive attitudes and/or behavior for elementary school-age and adolescent subjects. The fact that the Lefkowitz et al. study shows such an effect only for boys is less inconsistent than it appears at first blush, since the measure focused on the actual performance of aggressive acts, negatively sanctioned for girls in our culture, while the other studies focused on approval for aggression or other attitudinal measures. This last study is also best able to stand in its own right, because it uses the longitudinal cross-lagged correlational approach.

All these correlational studies may be legitimately challenged as not firmly showing causation; they should, however, increase our confidence in the external validity (the applicability beyond the laboratory) of experimental studies designed to elucidate causal relationships and underlying processes if a consistent pattern emerges.

Disinhibitory effects: experimental studies

A number of studies conducted during the 1960s showed that observation of filmed or televised aggression would disinhibit children's willingness to aggress on a variety of measures.

In a relatively early experiment, Lovaas (1961) showed that nursery school children's aggressive behavior would be increased following exposure to symbolic aggressive stimuli. One group of subjects saw sequences from an aggressive film entitled *Rassling Match,* which provided an almost continual display of one cartoon figure aggressing against another by hitting, biting, and the like. A second group of children saw a film depicting three baby bears and a mother bear engaging in gentle play activity. Following the film, subjects were presented with two large toys, and their play activities were observed. Depressing the lever on the aggressive toy mechanism automated a doll who turned and hit a second doll on the head with a stick. Depressing the lever on the nonaggressive toy apparatus triggered a wooden ball, enclosed in a cage, to jump through obstacles. The subjects were presented with the doll toy and the ball toy side by side, so that they could operate either toy or both simultaneously, if they wished. Children engaged in significantly more play with the hitting dolls after exposure to the aggressive film than after the nonaggressive film.[5]

In view of the fact that most television programs appear to depict aggression as a potent technique for power and achievement, studies which have focused upon the inhibiting and disinhibiting effects of consequences accruing to a model for aggression are of particular importance. In one such study, Bandura, Ross, and Ross (1963) exposed one group of nursery school boys and girls to a television program in which one character, Johnny, refuses another, Rocky, the opportunity to play with some toys. The program goes on to show a series of aggressive responses by Rocky, including hitting Johnny with a rubber ball, shooting darts at Johnny's cars, hitting Johnny with a baton, lassoing him with a hula-hoop, and so on. At the end of this sequence, Rocky, the aggressor, is playing with all of Johnny's toys, treating himself to sweet beverages and cookies, and finally departs with Johnny's hobby horse under his arm and a sack of Johnny's toys over his shoulder. At this point, a commentator announces that Rocky was victorious. In a second group, the program was rearranged so that after Rocky's initial aggression, Johnny retaliated in kind by administering a sound thrashing to the aggressor.

Two other groups served as controls; in one, a nonaggressive but highly expressive television program was observed, and in the second no television program was seen. Children's subsequent aggressive responses while playing for twenty minutes in a special test room constituted the primary dependent measure. The results clearly showed that children who observed a rewarded aggressor showed far more aggression themselves than children in the other groups. Moreover, at the conclusion of the experiment the children were asked to state which of the characters, Rocky or Johnny, they would prefer to emulate. Sixty percent of those who observed Rocky rewarded for his behavior indicated that they would select him as a model; only 20 percent of those who saw him punished indicated that they would choose to emulate him. Additionally, the authors noted a classic example of how socially reprehensible but successful modeled aggressive acts may influence children. One of the girls, who had expressed marked disapproval of Rocky's aggressive behavior as it occurred, later exhibited many of his aggressive responses. Finally, in an apparent effort to make her emulation of the ruthless but successful Rocky complete, she turned to the experimenter and inquired, "Do you have a sack here?"

Like research in direct imitative effects, investigations of disinhibitory effects have not been limited to the study of play activities. For example, in a series of three experiments, Walters and Llewellyn-Thomas (1963) evaluated the influence of film-mediated aggressive models upon hospital attendants, high school boys, and young female adults. In these studies subjects in experimental groups watched the knife fight scene from the movie *Rebel Without a Cause*, while control subjects watched a sequence which showed adolescents engaging in constructive activities. Both before and after exposure to the film all subjects were asked to participate in what was ostensibly a "conditioning" experiment which required them to administer electric shocks to another person for making "errors" on a learning task. The difference in the intensity of shocks which the subjects administered in the two sessions served as the primary dependent measure. In all three experiments, subjects exposed to the aggressive film significantly raised the shock levels which they administered relative to the controls. It is important to note that this heightened aggression was manifested in a situation entirely different from the one depicted in the film, and by subjects drawn from three rather different subcultures.

A particularly well-designed study of the effects of observing aggression was conducted by Hartmann (1969). In this investigation, delinquent adolescent boys were either angered or treated neutrally and then showed one of three films, two of which were aggressive in content. Regardless of whether they were angered or not, seeing an aggressive film produced more subsequent aggression (ostensible electric shocks to another person) than did the neutral film. Moreover, and of particular importance, boys with a past history of aggressive behavior were more aggressive than other boys. This finding, and a similar finding by Wolf and Baron (1971) [comparing college students and convicts with records of assaultive crimes] provide validation for the assertion that laboratory measures involving button pressing which (ostensibly) inflects harm are related to interpersonal aggression in naturalistic situations.

A study reported by Feshbach and Singer (1971a), also involving adolescent boys, is directly at odds with both the findings of the Walters and Thomas and Hartmann studies and with the preponderance of research in the area. The study was conducted with approximately 400 boys who were enrolled either in residential private schools or in boys' homes serving youngsters who are either mildly disturbed or whose families are unable to care for them. Approximately half the subjects in each institution were permitted to watch a predominantly "aggressive" diet of television programs while the remaining subjects were permitted to watch a diet containing primarily nonaggressive programs.

Among the subjects from the four boys' care homes, significant differences between the groups were found on measures of aggressive behavior in three of them (as rated by institutional personnel) during the six weeks of the experiment. Specifically, in these institutions, boys exposed to the predominantly aggressive diet were *less* aggressive than those exposed predominantly to nonaggressive programs. In contrast, the data reveal virtually no significant differences between the aggressive and the control program groups for boys in the private schools. However, although limited to lower-class institutionalized males of a particular age range, the results reported by Feshbach and Singer remain an anomalous outcome. Unfortunately, there are a number of fundamental design problems in this study which cast doubt on both the internal and the external validity of the outcome. For example, in two of the three institutions in which significant results were obtained the control ("nonaggressive diet") subjects objected very strongly because *Batman* was not available to them. The experimenters then acceded to the demand by adding this program to the control diet. Another problem is that the data themselves were collected by untrained institutional employees rather than by trained personnel, but no adequate reliability checks appear to have been made nor was the probability of rater bias dealt with systematically. Additionally, the control group boys may have behaved more aggressively because of being deprived of some of their favorite programs. A more complete discussion regarding the Feshbach and Singer study appears in Volume 5 in this series.

In a more recent study, Liebert and Baron (1971, in this volume) sought to investigate the question of whether exposure to aggression, as modeled in actual television fare, would disinhibit younger children in terms of their willingness to hurt another child. The investigators exposed children of both sexes and two age groups (5-6, 8-9 years) to brief excerpts taken directly from publicly broadcast television shows. For children in one group, these excerpts depicted instances of aggression (a brutal fist fight, a shooting, and the like), while for children in a second condition, exciting but nonaggressive sporting events were shown. Following exposure to one of these two programs, children in both groups were provided with a series of opportunities to either *hurt* or *help* another child by pushing, respectively, either a red or a green button. The children were told that pushing the green button would help this child (who was not actually present during the study) to win a prize, but that pushing the red button would hurt him. In addition, they were informed that the longer they pushed either button, the more the other child would be helped or hurt. Results indicated that children who had observed the violent scenes pushed the red button for a significantly longer period of time than those who had observed the nonaggressive scenes.

In another study concerned with disinhibitory effects, Leifer and Roberts (1971, in this volume) obtained information on the subsequent willingness to aggress of children and adolescents (kindergarteners through twelfth graders) after they watched television programs which differed in the amount of violent content displayed. The programs were taken directly from the air, without editing. The children were first tested on their recall and understanding of the motives and consequences of the violent acts which they had seen and were then tested on a specially designed response hierarchy of their willingness to aggress. The child was presented with a series of real-life situations ("You're standing in line for a drink of water. A kid comes along and just pushes you out of line. What do you do?") and asked to choose between a pair of alternative responses. One of the alternatives was typically aggressive ("Push them"), while the other was not ("Go away").

In addition to finding that children chose physical aggression on the response hierarchy described above more often at older than at younger ages, they also found an important relationship between the amount of violence in the program a child viewed and his subsequent willingness to select physically aggressive responses after television viewing.

Specifically, the more violent programs reliably produced higher levels of aggressive responding than the less violent ones. It is of further interest that, in this experiment, understanding the motivations for and consequences of violence in a program did not account to a significant degree for the aggression scores. It appears that the instigating effect of viewing violence is not reduced by an increased understanding of the motivations and consequences which surround it, at least for this measure and these age groups. It is also of interest to note that the differential effects of program content upon willingness to aggress tended to vary with age, although these differences are not significant. The nature of the tendency is that the relationship between amount of violence and subsequent physical aggression on the response hierarchy measure tended to be greater for kindergarteners and third grade children than for children in the sixth, ninth, or twelfth grades.

In interpreting their results and correctly identifying the study's major methodological weaknesses, Leifer and Roberts note:

> Whatever analysis was performed, the amount of violence in the program affected the amount of aggression subsequently chosen. Nothing else about the program—the context within which violence was presented—seemed to influence subsequent aggression. Furthermore, our measures of understanding of the cues hypothesized to control aggression—motivations and consequences—did not relate at all to aggression choices. These results are not encouraging in their implications; however, they should be interpreted with some caution. All children were tested on their understanding of the motivations and consequences in the programs before they were tested on the response hierarchy.

Leifer and Roberts also report six other studies, varying in their major purposes, in which the effects of televised aggression upon children's aggressive choices could be assessed. Three of these provide further evidence for a disinhibitory effect while none suggests a decrease in aggressiveness after exposure to aggression. This latter negative finding is of some interest. Even observing aggression which had both bad motives and bad consequences (in programs produced by special editing) did not reduce aggression relative to a nonaggressive program.

While television and film programs, as typically observed in both naturalistic and laboratory situations, do not formally state whether they are real or fictional in character, the provision of such specific introductions and descriptions may potentially play an important role in their effects. For example, Orson Welles's radio play version of H. G. Wells's *War of the Worlds* was apparently perceived as reality rather than fiction by many adult listeners, some of whom went into the streets armed in order to defend themselves against invading Martians. Parents who observe that their children are becoming upset by stories, movies, and television plays often provide reassurance that what is being seen or heard is "just a story" or "not real." Do such reminders, explanations, or "identifying statements" moderate the influence of observing aggression on television?

A series of experiments conducted by Feshbach (1971, this volume) was designed to determine if the effects of film-mediated violence upon children varies as a function of whether the material was said to be taken from "real life" or was specifically identified and labeled at the outset as fictional or fantasy material.

Feshbach advanced the hypothesis that ". . .aggressive tendencies should be lessened or unaffected to the extent that dramatic content functions as fantasy in the larger, cognitive sense and is perceived as fantasy in the narrower, fictional sense. If the dramatic content is perceived as 'real,' the possibility of facilitating aggression through such processes as imitation, instruction, and disinhibition should be considerably enhanced." He reported three experiments related to this hypothesis. In the first of these, in which the subjects were 9-11-year-old boys from either lower- or middle-class families, three experimental conditions were used: real aggression, fantasy aggression, and control. Among those in the aggression conditions, half the subjects in each group witnessed a war sequence and the other half saw a police action sequence. Control children were shown either a circus film or no television whatsoever. The dependent measure was a response box designed as an "aggression machine" and was similar to the widely accepted type of apparatus used by Mallick and McCandless (1966) and by Liebert and Baron (1971) in their report in this volume.

In addition to the fact that actual newsreels or movie scenes from Hollywood were used, subjects in each of the groups were specifically "set" by the experimenter in terms of what they were about to see. Thus, for example, boys exposed to the reality-army film were told that they were ". . .going to see a war film made by a Hollywood studio." Following observation of one of the films, the subjects were administered an adjective checklist to assess their moods. Subsequently, they performed on the aggression machine. While some interesting changes both in mood and in program evaluations were noted, no significant overall differences were obtained on the measure of aggression against another person.

In his second experiment, Feshbach employed the same violent film for both fantasy and reality groups, but, as he notes, ". . .under clearly different set conditions. In one experimental treatment, the subject believed he was seeing a film of a real event; in another treatment, the subject was shown the same film but was led to believe that it was fictional." In the fantasy set condition, the subjects were told: "We are going to show you a film that was made in a Hollywood studio. The story is about a student riot. You might have seen some of the actors on television before." The aggressive film was a combination of the campus riot reality and fantasy films of his first experiment.

The adjective mood list was again presented prior to the opportunity to aggress, so the study shares the methodological problem of an "intervening test" that also weakens the Leifer and Roberts investigation. Results clearly indicated that children exposed to the aggressive reality film are more aggressive than those exposed either to no film or to the fantasy one. Likewise, as Feshbach had expected, children in the fantasy set condition showed less aggression than children who had not observed a film at all. No important changes in mood, as measured by a questionnaire, were detected. It is unfortunate that this experiment did not include a control group in which no "set" at all was given. Thus, especially since many young children may perceive fictional television drama as presenting real-life situations, it would be difficult to extrapolate from the data as they stand to naturalistic television viewing by children. Nonetheless, the finding is potentially quite important, and the hypothesis clearly merits further research.

In a third experiment, Feshbach endeavored to determine the differential effects of reality vs. fantasy set on aggression machine behavior when subjects were told that the aggression machine was to be disconnected so that they would only be "imagining" the consequences of pushing various buttons. No statistically significant differences were obtained in that small, exploratory study.

Laboratory studies of the sort described above provide the best source of information about basic processes and causal relationships. However, to assure generality of such findings to the more complex natural environment, such investigation must be supplemented by correlational studies (such as those considered in the preceding section) and, if possible, also by experimental field studies.

The investigation conducted by Stein and Friedrich (1971) employed the experimental method in a relatively naturalistic situation in order to determine some of the cumulative or longer-range effects of observing television upon children. The subjects in the Stein experiment were 97 children (52 boys and 45 girls) between three and one-half and five and one-half years of age, who were systematically exposed to television programs of differing content during the course of their participation in a summer nursery school.

This carefully designed experiment involved an initial measurement period in which the free play of children in the nursery school was observed and rated according to a variety of categories; a four-week experimental period in which children were systematically exposed either to aggressive cartoons (*Batman* and *Superman*), neutral television programming (children working on a farm and the like), and prosocial programming (episodes from the program *Misterogers Neighborhood*); and a two-week postviewing period in which effects could be observed and assessed.

The children were exposed to the programs or films for approximately 20 minutes per day, three times a week during a four-week period. During this time, and during the two-week postviewing period, the children's behavior was again systematically observed in the naturalistic preschool situation. Behavior ratings included measures of aggression, prosocial behavior, and self-control.[6] They were checked carefully for reliability and collected by raters who were "blind" to the children's treatment. Analyses of data were based on four observation periods, because the first and second two weeks of the experimental period were separated so as to identify changes during this time in the effects of the programs.

Stein and Friedrich found that children who were initially in the upper half of the sample in interpersonal aggression subsequently showed greater interpersonal aggression if they were exposed to the aggressive programming than if they were exposed to either the neutral or prosocial programming; but children who were initially low in aggression did not respond differentially to these treatments. Children exposed to the prosocial and neutral television programs did not differ from each other on these measures of interpersonal aggression. The investigators appropriately described their findings on this measure as follows:

> These results suggest that children who initially are high in aggression respond to aggressive television programs with higher levels of aggression than they would under neutral conditions. These effects occurred in naturalistic behavior that was removed both in time and in environmental setting from the viewing experience. They occurred with a small amount of exposure, particularly in relation to the amount the children received at home, and they endured during the postviewing period.

In contrast to the effects detected for interpersonal aggression, the television programs did not have a systematic effect upon either fantasy aggression or aggression toward inanimate objects.

A second measure on which the programs were shown to have differential effects upon children was prosocial self-control. This term refers to measures of rule obedience, tolerance of delay, and task persistence which the children showed in a variety of nursery school situations. Results showed clearly that children exposed to the prosocial television programs subsequently displayed higher levels of self-control on each of these measures than did children exposed to the aggressive programs, while those observing the neutral programs generally showed self-control which fell between the other two groups. These findings were particularly true for children with relatively high IQs. Moreover, the direction of the changes in the two groups appeared to have been antithetical; that is, children who observed the aggressive programs decreased on these measures of self-control relative to the baseline, while those who observed prosocial programs generally increased. Thus, as Stein and

Friedrich note: "following the procedure of using the Neutral group as the comparison point for evaluating the effects of the experimental treatments, it appears that the aggressive programs have a deleterious effect on children's willingness to tolerate delay, and to a lesser extent, on rule obedience."

The effects of the programs on children's prosocial behavior were somewhat more complicated, because they interacted with the socioeconomic background of the children. Specifically, exposure to the prosocial television programs produced an increase in prosocial interpersonal behavior among the lower-class children, while exposure to the aggressive programs resulted in a similar increase among the children from higher socioeconomic backgrounds. Thus, the investigators note that for the latter group, the reduction in self-control produced by aggressive programs was accompanied by:

> increased social interaction that was primarily cooperative. It appears, therefore, that the aggressive programs had a general stimulating effect for the higher SES children that led to higher social interaction and lower levels of personal control. For those who were already aggressive, it led to aggression as well.

EVALUATION AND SUMMARY OF RESULTS

Recent research on the relationship between children's viewing of television violence and their aggressive behavior was reviewed in the light of theoretical and methodological issues. The data suggest consistently that children are exposed to a heavy dose of violence on television. It is also clear that they can and do retain some of the aggressive behaviors which they see, and are often able to reproduce them. Differences in recall as a function of age are in the expected direction (better recall with increasing age). Differences in recall as a function of content are less clearly understood, but violent content appears to be learned and remembered at least as well as nonviolent fare.

Children often accept and directly imitate observed aggression in their play activities if the observed performances have been rewarded or have reaped no consequences. They also report copying actual televised sequences in play. Punishment to an aggressive model leads children to avoid reproduction of the exemplary behavior, but does not prevent learning or subsequent performance under more favorable circumstances.

Correlational studies show a regular association between aggressive television viewing and variety of measures of aggression. For measures of attitudes and approval of aggression, such a result often appears for both sexes. When measures of aggressive behavior are considered, the relationship may be limited to boys. These correlational studies have employed impressively broad samples in terms of range of economic backgrounds and family characteristics.

It is important to note that the correlational results, while generally consistent, point to a moderate (rather than a strong) relationship between watching television violence and subsequent aggressive attitudes and behavior. Further, the relationship is attenuated by the presence of certain family and cultural characteristics. Just as a child's food diet or exercise are related to his health but do not predict it exclusively or even predominantly, children's exposure to television violence is related to some measures of aggression. Correlational studies support, but do not prove, the hypothesis of a causal relationship between exposure to television violence and aggression.

Experimental studies of disinhibitory and inhibitory effects preponderantly show that observing violence can lead to an increase in a child observer's willingness to aggress. These findings are also consistent with the correlational data. But, as Berkowitz has noted, it is important to distinguish between the statement that observation of violence *can* have such effects and that it *will* have them for any particular child or program, since ". . .a good many situational and personal factors influence the relationship between witnessed violence and the likelihood of aggressive actions by observers, including the observers' attitudes toward the violent event, the extent to which they are set to act aggressively, their aggressive habits, etc."

Recent studies provide support for each of the qualifiers mentioned above. For example, Stein and Friedrich found that naturalistic aggression was increased by watching aggressive cartoons only for children who were relatively aggressive initially; Feshbach found that a specific fantasy set actually reversed the usual impact of having aggression; and Ekman, Liebert, Friesen, Harrison, Zlatchin, Malmstrom, and Baron (1971) found that the 5-6-year-old boys in the Liebert and Baron study were instigated by observing aggression only if they displayed positive facial affects while viewing.

Evidence supporting the assertion that televised violence can reduce aggression is scant and is directly at odds with correlational data based on widely varied samples as tapped by many different researchers.

Almost all experimental studies have some methodological flaws. The Leifer and Roberts (1971) study injected an intervening test between exposure to violence and their measures of aggression; the stimulus materials employed by Liebert and Baron (1971) preserved a story line in the aggressive program but not in the nonaggressive one; Stein and Friedrich's control group observed films while the other groups watched actual television programs. An extended list would encompass almost all the other experimental studies cited in this paper. It is important, however, that each of these flaws tends to be unique rather than shared by all of the investigators. The studies are quite consistent in the overall direction of their findings and, in the aggregate, may be defended soundly against charges of confounded effects.

While it is possible to thoughtfully analyze any given investigation regarding the question of adequacy of design, there is no easy answer to the question of their external applicability. In fact, sophisticated researchers have long ago forsaken the concept of the "critical experiment" regarding any sort of final knowledge about general processes in the social sciences. Instead, it is widely agreed that the best solution lies in considering the accumulated weight of evidence on a particular issue, coming variously from surveys, correlational studies, and experiments conducted both in the laboratory and in the field. If the balance is sufficiently tipped when a variety of methods, approaches, and laboratories are considered, then the researcher can draw conclusions of social applicability with some confidence.

The present writer believes that the findings discussed here, in conjunction with the considerable body of earlier research, warrant formally advancing some tentative conclusions into the arena of public debate. Specifically, the following summary is suggested by the data in aggregate:

1. It has been shown convincingly that children are exposed to a substantial amount of violent content on television, and that they can remember and learn from such exposure.

2. Correlational studies have disclosed a regular association between aggressive television viewing and a variety of measures of aggression, employing impressively broad samples in terms of range of economic background and geographic and family characteristics.

3. Experimental studies preponderantly support the hypothesis that there is a directional, causal link between exposure to television violence and an observer's subsequent aggressive behavior.

It has been repeatedly shown in experimental studies of observing aggression in film and television formats that, under some circumstances, disinhibitory effects can occur in samples covering the age gamut from preschool children to mature adults. At almost every age range, such findings have been found by at least two or more independent research teams. These results generally mesh with the now numerous correlational studies which are able to approach more closely the situations in which viewing, and aggression, occur naturalistically. Studies failing to produce statistically reliable results are a distinct minority, and those suggesting that seeing aggression reduces aggression are rare enough to be called anomalous.

If a probabilistic view of the accumulated evidence is taken, as it typically is in the health sciences, the weight of the evidence to date would seem to represent real progress in determining the effects of violence on television upon youngsters. Specifically, there is more than a trivial basis for a "best guess" conclusion which is central to the major question: *At least under some circumstances, exposure to televised aggression can lead children to accept what they have seen as a partial guide for their own actions. As a result, the present entertainment offerings of the television medium may be contributing, in some measure, to the aggressive behavior of many normal children. Such an effect has now been shown in a wide variety of situations.*

FOOTNOTES

1. Sincere thanks are due to Emily Davidson, Diane Liebert, John Neale, Jacqueline Portnoy, Rita Poulos, and Michael Sobol for their assistance in the preparation of this paper. The opinions expressed herein remain the responsibility of the author, not of the staff of the Television and Social Behavior program nor necessarily of the investigators whose work is described.

2. According to the usage of Bandura and Walters, inhibitory and disinhibitory effects may include responses which are dissimilar to those displayed by the model, but the emphasis is placed upon the fact that a class of behaviors can be affected. Thus, for these theorists, dissimilarity is not a *defining* property of the processes.

3. It may not be immediately obvious that this last question is a correlational one. It is, however, merely an alternate form of the question: Do the effects of television go together with the sex of the observer?

4. It should be emphasized that this explanation is intended only to illustrate the reasoning involved in this technique, and does not fully reflect its complexities. A complete discussion may be found in Neale and Liebert (in press).

5. An analogous experiment conducted by Larder (1962) showed a similar increase in preference for an aggressive toy by children who had merely *heard* an aggressive story, as compared with children who had been exposed to a nonaggressive story.

6. While many interesting correlations reported by Stein and Friedrich will not be reviewed in this paper, it is of some interest that overall measures of interpersonal aggression and interpersonal prosocial behavior were positively related; i.e., they tended to go together. Thus, children who were more aggressive were also more likely to engage in prosocial types of activities. It is extremely important to note that this result does *not* mean that the two categories will be similarly susceptible to such additional influences as the effects of television. For example, in adults, height and weight (as measures of body size) are also positively related. Nonetheless, if we consider the effects of a change of diet (in this case nutritional diet rather than television diet), it is clear that three milkshakes daily would readily increase the weight of most people but would not influence the height of any of them. Thus, positive relationships between two measures do not mean that both of them will be equally influenced by the presence or absence of some sort of treatment.

REFERENCES

Ball, S., and Bogatz, E. A. *The first year of Sesame Street. An evaluation.* Princeton: Educational Testing Service, 1970.

Bandura, A. Influence of models' reinforcement contingencies on the acquisition of imitative responses. *Journal of Personality and Social Psychology*, 1965, **1**, 589-95.

Bandura, A. *Principles of behavior modification.* New York: Holt, Rinehart & Winston, 1969.

Bandura, A., and Menlove, F. L. Factors determining vicarious extinction of avoidance behavior through symbolic modeling. *Journal of Personality and Social Psychology*, 1967, **5**, 16-22.

Bandura, A., and Mischel, W. Modification of self-imposed delay of reward through exposure to live and symbolic models. *Journal of Personality and Social Psychology*, 1965, **2**(5), 698-705.

Bandura, A., Ross, D., and Ross, S. Imitation of film-mediated aggressive models. *Journal of Abnormal and Social Psychology*, 1963, **66**(1), 3-11.

Bandura, A., Ross, D., and Ross, S. Vicarious reinforcement and imitative learning. *Journal of Abnormal and Social Psychology*, 1963, **67**(7), 601-07.

Bandura, A., and Walters, R. H. *Social learning and personality development.* New York: Holt, Rinehart & Winston, 1963.

Berkowitz, L. Experimental investigations of hostility catharsis. *Journal of Consulting and Clinical Psychology*, 1970, **35**(1), 1-7.

Bryan, J. and Schwartz, T. Effects of film material upon children's behavior. *Psychological Bulletin*, 1971, **75**(1), 50-59.

Bryan, J., and Walbek, N. Preaching and practicing generosity. Children's actions and reactions. *Child Development*, 1970, **41**, 329-53.

Coates, B., and Hartup, W. Age and verbalization in observational learning. *Developmental Psychology*, 1969, **1**, 556-62.

Dominick, J. R., and Greenberg, B. S. Attitudes toward violence: the interaction of television exposure, family attitudes, and social class. *Television and Social Behavior:* a report to the Surgeon General's Scientific Advisory Committee, Vol. 3. Washington, D. C.: U. S. Government Printing Office, 1971.

Ekman, P., Liebert, R. M., Friesen, W. V., Harrison, R., Zlatchin, C., Malmstrom, E. J., and Baron, R. A. Facial Expressions of emotion while watching televised violence as predictors of subsequent aggression. *Television and Social Behavior*, Vol 5. Washington, D. C.: U. S. Government Printing Office, 1971.

Eron, L. Relationship of TV viewing habits and aggressive behavior in children. *Journal of Abnormal and Social Psychology*, 1963, **67**(2), 193-96. 1963.

Feshbach, S. Effects of reality versus fantasy in filmed violence. *Television and Social Behavior*, Vol. 2 (this volume).

Feshbach, S., and Singer, R. *Television and Aggression.* San Francisco, California: Jossey-Bass, Inc., 1971.

Gerbner, G. Violence in television drama: a study of trends and symbolic functions. *Television and Social Behavior*, Vol. 1. Washington, D. C.: U. S. Government Printing Office, 1971.

Goranson, R. E. A review of recent literature on psychological effects of media portrayals of violence. Report to the National Commission on the Causes and Prevention of Violence, 1969.

Greenberg, B. S., and Gordon, T. F. Children's perceptions of television violence: a replication. *Television and Social Behavior*, Vol. 5. Washington, D. C.: U. S. Government Printing Office, 1971.

Hanratty, M. A. Imitation of film-mediated aggression against live and inanimate victims. Unpublished master's thesis, Vanderbilt University, 1969.

Hanratty, M. A., Liebert, R. M., Morris, L. W., and Fernandez, L. E. Imitation of film-mediated aggression against live and inanimate victims. Proceedings of the 77th Annual Convention of the American Psychological Association, 1969, pp. 457-58.

Hanratty, M. A., O'Neal, E., and Sulzer, J. L. The effect of frustration upon imitation of aggression. *Journal of Personality and Social Psychology*, in press.

Hartman, D. P. Influence of symbolically modeled instrumental aggression and pain cues on aggressive behavior. *Journal of Personality and Social Psychology*, 1969, **11**(3), 380-88, 1969.

Hicks, D. J. Imitation and retention of film-mediated aggressive peer and adult models. *Journal of Personality and Social Psychology*, 1965, **2**(1), 97-100.

Hicks, D. J. Effects of co-observer's sanctions and adult presence on imitative aggression. *Child Development*, 1968, **38**(1), 303-09.

Hill, J. E., Liebert, R. M., and Mott, D. E. Vicarious extinction of avoidance behavior through films: an initial test. *Psychological Reports*, 1968, **22**, 192.

Larder, D. L. Effect of aggressive story content on nonverbal play behavior. *Psychological Reports*, 1962, **11**, 14.

Lefkowitz, M. M., Eron, L. D., Walder, L. O., and Huesmann, L. R. Television violence and child aggression: a followup study. *Television and Social Behavior*, Vol. 3, Washington, D. C.: U. S. Government Printing Office, 1971.

Leifer, A., and Roberts, D. Children's responses to television violence. *Television and Social Behavior*, Vol. 2 (this volume).

Lesser, G. S. Designing a program for broadcast television. In Korten, F. F., Cook, S. W., and Lacey, G. L. (Eds.) *Psychology and the problems of society.* Washington: American Psychological Association, 1970, 208-14.

Liebert, R. M., and Baron, R. A. Short-term effects of televised aggression on children's aggressive behavior. *Television and Social Behavior,* Vol. 2 (this volume).

Liebert, R. M., and Fernandez, L. E. Imitation as a function of vicarious and direct reward. *Developmental Psychology*, 1970, **2**(2), 230-32.

Liebert, R. M., Odom, R. D., Hill, J. H., and Huff, R. L. Effects of age and rule familiarity on the production of modeled language constructions. *Developmental Psychology*, 1969, **1**(2), 108-12.

Liebert, R. M., and Spiegler, M. D. *Personality: an introduction to theory and research.* Homewood, Ill.: The Dorsey Press, 1970.

Lövaas, O. Ivar. Effect of exposure to symbolic aggression on aggressive behavior. *Child Development*, 1961, **32**, 37-44.

Lyle, J., and Hoffman, H. R. Children's use of television and other media. *Television and Social Behavior*, Vol. 4.

McIntyre, J. J., and Teevan, J. J. Television and deviant behavior. *Television and Social Behavior*, Vol. 3.

McLeod, J. M., Atkin, C. K., and Chaffee, S. H. Adolescents, parents, and television use. *Television and Social Behavior*, Vol. 3.

Mallick, S. K., and McCandless, B. R. A study of catharsis of aggression. *Journal of Personality and Social Psychology*, 1966, **4**, 591-96.

Martin, M. F., Gelfand, D. M., and Hartmann, D. P. Effects of adult and peer observers on children's responses to an aggressive model. *Child Development*, 1971, in press.

Mussen, P., and Rutherford, E. Effects of aggressive cartoons on children's aggressive play. *Journal of Abnormal and Social Psychology*, 1961, **62**(2), 461-64.

Neale, J. M., and Liebert, R. M. *Science and social behavior: An introduction to methods of research.* Englewood Cliffs, New Jersey: Prentice-Hall, in press.

Osborn, D. K., and Endsley, R. C. Emotional reactions of young children to TV violence. *Child Development*, 1971, **42**, 321-31.

Reid, J. B. Reliability assessment of observation data: a possible methodological problem. *Child Development*, 1970, **41**, 1143-50.

Rosenhan, D., and White, G. M. Observation and rehearsal as determinants of pro-social behavior. *Journal of Personality and Social Psychology*, 1967, **5**, 424-31.

Rosenthal, R. *Experimenter effects in behavioral research.* New York: Appleton, 1966.

Rosenthal, R., and Gaito. The interpretation of levels of significance by psychological researchers. *Journal of Psychology*, 1963, **55**, 33-38.

Savitsky, J. C., Rogers, R. W., Izard, C. E., and Liebert, R. M. The role of frustration and anger in the imitation of filmed aggression against a human victim. *Psychological Reports*, 1971, **29**, 807-810.

Schramm, W., Lyle, J., and Parker, E. *Television in the lives of our children.* Stanford: Stanford University Press, 1961.

Stein, A. H., and Friedrich, L. K. Television content and young children's behavior. *Television and Social Behavior*, Vol. 2 (this volume).

Stevenson, H. W. Television and the behavior of preschool children. *Television and Social Behavior*, Vol. 2 (this volume).

Walder, L. O., Abelson, R., Eron, L. D., Banta, T. J., and Laulicht, J. H. Development of ·a peer-rating measure of aggression. *Psychological Reports*, 1961, **9**, 497-556.

Walters, R. H., and Llewellyn-Thomas, E. Enhancement of punitiveness by visual and audiovisual displays. *Canadian Journal of Psychology*, 1963, **17**, 244-55.

Appendix A:
TV and Social Learning:
A Summary of the Experimental Effects
of Observing Filmed Aggression

Gloria D. Strauss and Rita W. Poulos

This appendix presents the major results of studies appearing in *Television and Social Behavior: an annotated bibliography of research focusing on television's impact on children* (Atkin, Murray, and Nayman, 1971), prepared under the auspices of the National Institute of Mental Health. All research reports included here are experimental in nature and were designed to explore the effects of filmed aggression on the attitudes and/or behavior of the audience. Additionally, each report met the following requirements:

1. One or more groups of subjects were exposed to films or television programs displaying violence or aggression.

2. At least one group of subjects was not exposed to film or television aggressive content, thereby constituting a control condition.

3. At least one dependent variable was examined which might tap subjects' aggression, whether measured behaviorally or through attitude questionnaires.

4. A statistically significant result was obtained.

The material is presented in two lists. The first includes those studies which lend support to the hypothesis that observing filmed violence can instigate aggression by the viewer. The second group of studies includes those which support the hypothesis that observing filmed violence can reduce aggressive behavior by the viewer.

It should be noted that this is *not* an independent literature search, since even studies conducted more recently for the Television and Social Behavior program or many cited in Liebert's review are not included. Rather, it is an attempt to summarize the findings of experiments included in the Atkin, Murray, and Nayman bibliography according to their relevance to a particular pair of opposing hypotheses.

The following studies provide support for the hypothesis that viewing aggression can instigate aggression:

Reference	Subjects	Independent variables	Main dependent variable	Results
1A. Bandura, Ross, and Ross (1963a)	Nursery school children	Four conditions: 1) human aggressive model—live 2) human aggressive model—film 3) cartoon aggressive model—film 4) no treatment	Behavioral rating in play situation	$\underline{S}$s who observed aggressive models exhibited more aggression than did those who did not. Filmed instances of aggression were as effective as real-life sequences.
2A. Bandura, Ross and Ross (1963b)	Nursery school children	Four conditions: 1) aggressive model—rewarded 2) aggressive model—punished 3) active but non-aggressive model 4) no exposure to model	Behavioral rating in play situation	$\underline{S}$s who observed the aggressive model rewarded displayed more aggression than children in the other three groups. $\underline{S}$s who observed the aggressive model punished did not differ from those who viewed the nonaggressive model or who were not exposed to a model.
3A. Berkowitz, Corwin, and Heironimus (1963)	College males	Three factors: 1) angered vs. neutrally treated $\underline{S}$s 2) aggressive vs. neutral film 3) justified vs. unjustified filmed aggression	Attitude measures	$\underline{S}$s who were angered and viewed a film involving justified aggression indicated greater hostility toward their tormenter than $\underline{S}$s who viewed the neutral film. $\underline{S}$s who viewed the neutral film displayed more "indirect aggression" than did those who viewed a film including a sequence of relatively unjustified aggression.
4A. Berkowitz and Geen (1966)	College males	Three factors: 1) angered vs. neutrally treated $\underline{S}$s	Electric shock administered to confederate	Angered $\underline{S}$s who viewed the aggressive film and who interacted with the cue-valenced confederate were more aggressive than $\underline{S}$s in any other group.

The following studies provide support for the hypothesis
that viewing aggression can instigate aggression: (Continued)

Reference	Subjects	Independent variables	Main dependent variable	Results
		2) aggressive vs. neutral film 3) confederate did or did not have cue value		
5A. Berkowitz and Geen (1967)	College males	Three factors: 1) aggressive vs. neutral film 2) justified vs. unjustified filmed aggression 3) confederate did or did not have cue valence	Electric shock administered to confederate	Ss who saw the justified aggressive film and interacted with a cue-valenced confederate were more aggressive than those who saw the neutral film and interacted with the cue-valanced confederate.
6A. Geen and Berkowitz (1967)	College students	Three factors: 1) frustrated vs. insulted vs. neutrally treated Ss 2) aggressive vs. neutral film 3) confederate did or did not have cue value	Electric shock administered to confederate	Ss who were insulted prior to observing an aggressive film behaved more aggressively than did Ss who were insulted prior to observing the neutral film.
7A. Hanratty, Liebert, Morris, and Fernandez (1969)	4 and 5 year-old males	One factor: 1) film in which an adult aggressed against a clown vs. no film	Behavioral rating in a play situation	Children who viewed the film were more aggressive than those who did not.
8A. Hartmann (1969)	Adolescent males (delinquent)	Two factors: 1) angered vs. neutrally treated Ss.	Administration of electric shock	Ss who witnessed the aggressive film administered more shock than those who saw the neutral film.

The following studies provide support for the hypothesis
that viewing aggression can instigate aggression: (Continued)

Reference	Subjects	Independent variables	Main dependent variable	Results
		2) film involving a neutral game vs. film of a boy's aggressive behavior vs. film of the pain reactions of a victim of aggression		
9A. Heinrich (1961)	Children, aged 12 to 16	One factor: 1) aggression-arousing vs. appeasing vs. ambivalent films	Attitude measures	Aggressive attitudes were stimulated by some aggression-arousing films, reduced by one of the appeasing films, and not influenced by the ambivalent films.
10A. Lovaas (1961)	Nursery school children	One factor: 1) aggressive vs. nonaggressive cartoon	Choice of aggressive vs. neutral toy	Ss who had seen the aggressive film preferred the aggressive toy.
11A. Mussen and Rutherford (1961)	Six- and seven-year-old children	Two factors: 1) frustrated vs. neutrally treated Ss 2) aggressive cartoon vs. nonaggressive cartoon vs. no cartoon	Desire to destroy an inanimate object	Ss who saw the aggressive film expressed more aggressive impulses than those in other groups.
12A. Walters and Parke (1964)	Preschool males	Four conditions: 1) disobedient model—rewarded 2) disobedient model—punished 3) disobedient model—no consequences 4) no film	Resistance to temptation to disobey	Ss who saw the model punished and those who saw no film exhibited little disobedience. Children who saw disobedience rewarded or receive no consequences disobeyed more.

The following studies provide support for the hypothesis
that viewing aggression can instigate aggression : (Continued)

Reference	Subjects	Independent variables	Main dependent variable	Results
13A. Walters and Llewellyn-Thomas (1963)	High school males and adults	One factor: aggressive film vs. neutral film	Administration of electric shock	Ss who had seen the aggressive film administered more shocks than they had done previously.
14A. Walters and Willows (1968)	7-11 year-old males (emotionally disturbed and normal)	Three conditions: 1) aggressive model— film 2) nonaggressive model— film 3) neutral film	Behavioral rating in a play situation	Ss who observed the aggressive model displayed more aggression than did Ss who were exposed to the nonaggressive model or neutral film.
15A. Walters, Leat, and Mezei (1963)	Kinder-garten males	Three conditions: 1) disobedient model— rewarded 2) disobedient model— punished 3) no film	Resistance to temptation to disobey	Ss who saw the model rewarded were more aggressive than those who saw the model punished; Ss who saw the model punished aggressed less than those who did not see a film.
16A. Walters, Llwellyn-Thomas, and Acker (1962)	Adult males	Two conditions: 1) aggressive film 2) neutral film	Shock to confederate	Ss who viewed the aggressive film were more aggressive.

The following studies provide support for the hypothesis
that viewing aggression can reduce aggression

Reference	Subjects	Independent variables	Main dependent variable	Results
1B. Feshbach (1961)	College males	Two factors: 1) insulted vs. neutrally treated Ss 2) aggressive vs. neutral film	Attitude measures	Ss who had been insulted prior to viewing the aggressive film showed less aggression than similar Ss who viewed the neutral film.
2B. Feshbach (1969)	Preadolescent and adolescent males	One factor: steady diet of aggressive TV vs. steady diet of neutral TV shows	Daily behavior rating by institutional personnel; personality tests; attitude scales.	Exposure to aggressive television content reduced or controlled expression of aggression.

REFERENCES (APPENDIX A)

Atkin, C. K., Murray, J. P., and Nayman, O. B. *Television and social behavior: An annotated bibliography of research focusing on television's impact on children.* National Institute of Mental Health, Public Health Service Publication, No. 2099, 1971.

Bandura, Albert, Ross, Dorothea, and Ross, Sheila A. Imitation of film-mediated aggressive models. *Journal of Abnormal and Social Psychology*, 1963, **66**(1), 3-11.

Bandura, Albert, Ross, Dorothea, and Ross, Sheila A. Vicarious reinforcement and imitative learning. *Journal of Abnormal and Social Psychology*, 1963, **67**(6), 601-07.

Berkowitz, Leonard, Corwin, Ronald, and Heironimus, Mark. Film violence and subsequent aggressive tendencies. *Public Opinion Quarterly*, 1963, **27**, 217-29.

Berkowitz, Leonard, and Geen, Russell G. Film violence and the cue properties of available targets. *Journal of Personality and Social Psychology*, 1966, **3**(5), 525-30.

Berkowitz, Leonard, and Geen, Russell G. Stimulus qualities of the target of aggression: a further study. *Journal of Personality and Social Psychology*, 1967, **5**(3), 364-68.

Feshbach, Seymour. Stimulating versus cathartic effects of a vicarious aggressive activity. *Journal of Abnormal and Social Psychology*, 1961, **63**(2), 381-85.

Feshbach, Seymour. The catharsis effect: research and another view. In D. L. Lange, R. K. Baker, and J. S. Ball (Eds.), *Violence and the media.* Washington, D. C. National Commission on the Causes and Prevention of Violence, 1969, pp. 461-472.
(See also Feshbach, S., and Singer, R. *Television and aggression.* San Francisco: Jossey Bass, 1971.)

Geen, Russell G., and Berkowitz, Leonard. Some conditions facilitating the occurrence of aggression after the observation of violence. *Journal of Personality*, 1967, **35**, 666-76.

Hanratty, M. A., Liebert, R. M., Morris, L. W., and Fernandez, L. E. Imitation of film-mediated aggression against live and inanimate victims. Proceedings of the 77th Annual Convention of the American Psychological Association, 1969, pp. 457-58.

Hartmann, Donald P. Influence of symbolically modeled instrumental aggression and pain cues on aggressive behavior. *Journal of Personality and Social Psychology*, 1969, **11**(3), 280-88.

Heinrich, Karl. *Filmerleben, Filmwirkung, Filmerziehung: Der Einfluss des Films auf die Aggressivitaet bei Jugendlichen; Experimentelle Untersuchungen und ihre lern-psychologischen Konsecuenzen. (Film experience, film effects, film education: the influence of films on aggressiveness of youth; experiments and consequences for the psychology of learning.)* Berlin: H. Schroedel, 1961.

Lovaas, O. Ivar. Effect of exposure to symbolic aggression on aggressive behavior. *Child Development*, 1961, **32**, 37-44.

Mussen, Paul, and Rutherford, Eldred. Effects of aggressive cartoons on children's aggressive play. *Journal of Abnormal and Social Psychology*, 1961, **62**(2), 461-64.

Walters, Richard H., and Parke, Ross D. Influence of response consequences to a social model on resistance to deviation. *Journal of Experimental Child Psychology*, 1964, **1**, 269-80.

Walters, Richard H., and Llewellyn-Thomas, Edward. Enhancement of punitiveness by visual and audiovisual displays. *Canadian Journal of Psychology*, 1963, **17**, 244-55.

Walters, Richard H., and Willows, Donna C. Imitative behavior of disturbed and nondisturbed children following exposure to aggressive and nonaggressive models. *Child Development*, 1968, **39**, 79-89.

Walters, Richard H., Leat, Marion, and Mezi, Louis. Inhibition and disinhibition of responses through empathetic learning. *Canadian Journal of Psychology*, 1963, **17**, 235-43.

Walters, Richard H., Llewellyn-Thomas, Edward, and Acker, C. William. Enhancement of punitive behavior by audiovisual displays. *Science*, 1962, **136**(3519), 872-73.

Children's Responses to Television Violence

Aimée Dorr Leifer and Donald F. Roberts

Institute for Communication Research
Stanford University

✗   Television is an important contributor to the socialization of our children. It is certainly not the only socializer, nor is it necessarily the most potent;but given the nature of the medium (cf., Siegel, 1969), the large amount of time children devote to viewing (cf., Schramm, Lyle, and Parker, 1961), and the fact that children learn a great deal through simple observation of behavior (cf., Bandura, 1965b, 1969; Flanders, 1968), it is difficult not to believe that television has a significant impact on children's social behavior. Moreover, considering that a large part of what television portrays can be characterized as violent behavior (Catton, 1969; Gerbner, 1969), it is difficult not to be concerned about this impact.

Research over the past decade has shown that children can and do learn an extensive range of behaviors through observation of models; that a modeled performance may influence (inhibit or disinhibit) similar, as well as identical, behavior on the part of observers; that it makes little difference whether the modeled performance is live or film-mediated; and that a wide variety of cues in both the modeled behavior and the subsequent performance situation may mediate both an observer's learning and his performance. (For discussion of theory and reviews of research see Bandura, 1965b, 1969; Bandura and Walters, 1963; Flanders, 1968; Hartup and Coates, 1970; Roberts, 1971). Thus, a child observing a modeled performance, whether live or film-mediated (cf. Bandura, Ross and Ross, 1963a), may learn specific new behaviors (like judo techniques) and/or he may learn whether the newly acquired behavior or a similar class of behaviors already in his response repertoire (e.g., other aggressive acts) is appropriate in situations more or less similar to those in which the model appeared (Bandura and Walters, 1963; Berkowitz, 1962a).

The distinction between a symbolic presentation's effect on learning and its effect on performance is important. Cues in the modeling stimuli may affect learning or performance or both (Bandura, 1965b; 1969). For example, observation of contingent reinforcement delivered to a model may serve to sensitize the child to the behavioral or situational contingencies which led to the observed reinforcement (vicarious reinforcement leading to an increase in the probability of learning) and/or it may serve to increase the child's expectation of similar reinforcement for similar behavior (vicarious reinforcement leading to an increase in the probability of performance).

Performance also depends on cues in the subsequent behavioral situation. Thus, failure to perform an observed behavior need not imply failure to learn (Bandura and Walters, 1963; Mischel, 1968). Bandura (1965a) found that children who witnessed a model being punished for aggressive behavior initially failed to perform the behavior they viewed; but later, when supplied with sufficient incentives, they were able to reproduce the behavior accurately. Apparently they simultaneously learned the behavior and became sensitized to sanctions which inhibited performance of what was learned. Cues in the symbolic presentation (e.g., reward or punishment contingent on the behavior) interacted with cues in the subsequent behavioral situation (e.g., presence or absence of incentives) to influence the child's actions.

The learning/performance distinction is particularly crucial when we consider observational learning of aggressive behavior. On the one hand, North American society socializes such that there is early inhibition of much aggression (Whiting and Child, 1953); on the other hand, it teaches how, when, and where aggressive acts can or should be performed (Sears, Maccoby, and Levin, 1957). It is in this teaching of "why," "when," and "where" that television may be most influential. Various aggressive responses are not foreign to most children's behavior repertoires, and the commonly used ones are easily learned. However, children must also learn our society's rather complicated norms for why, where, and when to use these responses. They are often and repeatedly exposed to such norms through television and may learn much from such exposure.

Norms are often transmitted through models' *motivations* for aggression and the *consequences* of their aggression. This information is particularly suited to provide the child with cues about sanctions for and against aggression—about when aggression is justified and when unjustified, when rewarded and when punished, when to be admired and when condemned. To the extent that a child perceives modeled aggressive behavior to be justified, rewarded, useful, or admirable in various situations, to that extent we might expect an increase in the probability of his subsequently aggressing.

There is some experimental evidence that these two variables do influence performance of observed aggression. Several investigators have found that, in general, positive, negative, or neutral consequences to a model for aggressive behavior (reward or punishment, success or failure, etc.) respectively increase, decrease, or do not effect subsequent performance of imitative and nonimitative aggression (Bandura, 1965a; Bandura, Ross, and Ross, 1963b; Brodbeck, 1955; Rosekrans and Hartup, 1967). Similarly, other studies have shown that observed aggression which is perceived to be justified increases the probability of an observer's subsequent aggressive responses (Albert, 1957; Berkowitz and Rawlings, 1963).

Depiction of these two variables, *motivation* for aggression and *consequences* of aggression, is common to many dramatic television programs which portray aggressive behavior. Indeed, following the guidelines of the National Association of Broadcaster's *Television Code* (1969), television usually portrays criminal behavior, which is often violent, as unjustified and as leading to some kind of "inevitable" retribution. Following the experimental evidence, then, one could hope that television's portrayal of negative motives for and negative consequences of aggression would result in inhibiting subsequent aggression among children in much the same way that such inhibition seems to occur in laboratory experiments.

There are, however, several dangers inherent in attempting to generalize laboratory findings to nonlaboratory settings. One of these has to do with the nature of the symbolic stimuli used in the two settings. Modeling stimuli used in laboratory experiments are usually short and focused on the behaviors being studied—behaviors which are often chosen to be novel and attention-getting. They manifest little of the character development, richness of setting, and display of roles and behaviors found in most television drama. The complexity of television programs as stimuli is further increased in that they usually portray many acts with many different messages. For example, a detective program might depict a number of violent episodes, each with different motivations and different consequences. Television's portrayal of unjustified aggression leading to negative consequences usually involves an enforcer of laws or standards who engages in *justified* aggression, usually with *positive* consequences, in order to punish the villains.

Moreover, within television programs, motives for and consequences of aggression may be widely separated from the aggressive act, both in temporal terms (e.g., aggression modeled early in the program may not be punished until near the end of the program) and in terms of interpolated information (e.g., subplots, character development, commercials, etc., which often occur between motive and act and/or between act and consequences). Clearly, a relevant question is whether children even associate justifications for or consequences of aggression with the acts themselves—a question which becomes especially important when we consider possible age differences in effects of television violence.

Another problem in generalizing laboratory findings, then, has to do with the lack of studies of developmental differences in observational learning and disinhibition. Hartup and Coates (1970), after a thorough search, were able to find only nine such studies. These studies indicate no age-related differences in performance of simple model behaviors without explicit instructions to imitate, but clear increases with age in performance of complex model behaviors with explicit instructions to imitate. In addition, Leifer (1966) found that with increasing age children imitated more of a series of complex play behaviors even without explicit instructions to imitate. Undoubtedly the learning/performance distinction is relevant to these findings, in that older children may learn more of any modeled performance but may be more selective in what they choose to perform.

Evidence that increases in age might lead to increases in learning and retention of what is learned, and to differences in which aspects of a complex stimulus are attended to, comes from studies of the development of children's intellectual functioning (e.g., Bruner, Olver, and Greenfield, 1966; Flavell, 1963), studies of the development of verbal mediation (e.g., Flavell, Beach, and Chinsky, 1966; Kendler, 1963; Marsh and Sherman, 1966), and studies of age-related differences in attention to symbolically mediated behavior (e.g., Collins, 1970; Hale, Miller, and Stevenson, 1968; Roberts, 1968). Such findings imply age-related differences in the impact of cues related to motivations and consequences. For example, Leifer and her students (1972) found age differences in comprehension of cues inherent in complex behavioral sequences in an entertainment film, with older children superior to younger children in sequencing main events and in understanding such things as feelings and motivations of characters. To the extent that "feelings and motivations" function as cues, we might expect differences across age in learning and subsequent performance of television-mediated behavior.

There is also reason to suggest that motivations may not function as effectively as consequences as controlling cues for young children. Young children pay relatively little attention to motivation in judging the morality of another's act (Flavell, 1963; Hoffman, 1970; Kohlberg, 1964; Piaget, 1962) when both motivation and consequences are presented. Moreover, they are willing to judge morality solely on the basis of amount of damage done, adult sanctions, and acts of God. They also do not use motivation as a basis for judging kindness of another's act (Baldwin and Baldwin, 1970).

A final area in which developmental differences in observational learning might be expected is in discount of the modeling stimulus as a source of imitation or disinhibition. Dysinger and Ruckmick (1933) reported clear increases with age in adult discount of the material presented in feature films. If this finding also pertains to the entertainment fare of current television, one might expect less impact of the depicted aggression, motivations, and consequences among older children and adults than among younger children, even though older children are better able to understand and apply what they have seen. Some effect of exposure exists, since there is a substantial body of work indicating that entertainment films and videotapes will disinhibit aggressive responses in adolescents and adults (e.g., Berkowitz, 1970; Walters and Thomas, 1963).

Some of the important, unanswered questions, then, have to do with developmental changes in perception and comprehension of cues depicting motivations and consequences, with age-related changes in the influence of these cues on both learning and subsequent performance of observed aggression, and with age-related relative differences in the impact of these two variables. For example, in order to make valid production decisions it would be important to know whether children first respond to cues pertaining to motives or to cues pertaining to consequences, whether these two variables have differential impact at different ages, and what happens when the two cues are incongruent (e.g., when justified motives for aggression leads to negative consequences).

A final problem in generalizing from laboratory experiments is the dependent variables used. Experimental studies, in order to compare various independent variables, facilitate performance of observed aggression by removing the usual sanctions against aggression and then concentrating on manifested behavior. Outside the laboratory, however, sanctions against aggression are usually operative. Hence, behavioral manifestations of observed aggression may occur infrequently. This does not mean, however, that observing aggression has no effect.

Rather, it may simply mean that the influence of observed aggression is not strong enough to overcome operating sanctions in a particular situation—even though observation may well have increased the probability of aggressive behavior under some conditions. This is particularly true in the situations social scientists can directly observe and measure. For example, observation of television violence could increase the probability of subsequent aggression from five percent to 20 percent—certainly a significant change but still not enough to provide many overt aggressive acts to analyze as data. It seems, then, that some measure of change in the perceived acceptability of aggression, in the position of aggressive responses in a hypothetical response hierarchy, after viewing television violence, is called for.

The work reported in the following pages attempts to deal with some of the problems raised above.[1] First, the research attempted to use as stimuli either complete television programs or edited programs as close to the original as possible. Further, our concern has been to study the effects *across age* of exposure to television-mediated violence. Particular emphasis is placed on the motivations for and consequences of violence, how these cues are learned, and their role in modifying the effects of exposure to violence *per se*. For these purposes, we have developed a paper and pencil measure of aggressive response which is conceptually close to the child's everyday life and which enables us to judge whether viewing television-mediated violence changes the probability of aggressing in day to day conflicts.

CONSTRUCTION AND VALIDATION OF RESPONSE HIERARCHY INSTRUMENT

Rationale

The response hierarchy measure was developed to estimate aggressive behavior in day-to-day conflicts, rather than aggressive behavior within a laboratory setting. It was designed for rapid administration to individual young children and to groups of older children.

Most experimental studies of the effects of exposure to modeled aggression employ contrived measurement situations. They are frequently arranged to facilitate performance of the observed aggressive behaviors or of other aggressive behaviors. A child may be placed in a situation similar to that in which the model performed and/or in one where the usual sanctions against aggression are removed. Such procedures are perfectly appropriate: they increase the probability of aggressive behavior to a level at which the effects of the independent variables may be assessed.

However, under most circumstances in children's and adults' lives, sanctions against aggression are operative: conditions subsequent to viewing modeled aggression are not arranged to facilitate aggressive responses. Thus, behavioral manifestations of aggression after viewing may occur relatively infrequently; yet it is these manifestations which are of particular interest in estimating the effects of television viewing.

Viewing violent television programs may make infrequent aggressive behavior relatively less infrequent in any given situation. However, this still may not create a statistically significant change in overt behavior in nonlaboratory settings (e.g., Siegel, 1956), since behavior depends upon the situation in which the child finds himself and on the relative strength of various responses in his behavioral repertoire, as well as on exposure to modeled aggression.

Therefore, it is desirable to have a measure of the effect of viewing violence which does not rely solely on overt aggressive behavior. This measure should represent, as nearly as possible, behavior in daily encounters in which aggression is possible. It should measure changes in the probability of performing aggression—of aggressive responses being more likely to be performed, viewed as more acceptable, or viewed as acceptable in more situations, even though the probability of aggressive behavior might not increase beyond a performance threshold.

We conceived of aggressive responses as one class of behaviors in a response repertoire similar to Hull's habit-family hierarchy (cf., Hilgard and Bower, 1966) or White's (1965) hierarchical arrangement of learning processes. When faced with a stimulus such as a conflict situation, the child has available to him a number of behavioral responses or classes of responses which he may perform, as shown in Figure 1. Some of these would be aggressive responses.

Possible behavior structure before viewing aggression		Possible behavior structure after viewing aggression
Run away	Performance	Run away
Yell for help	threshold	Judo chop
Smile		Yell for help
Judo chop		Smile
Persuade		Persuade

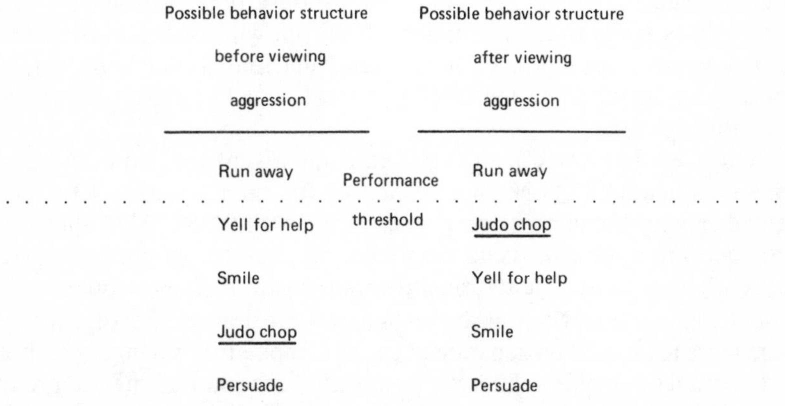

Figure 1: Possible responses in a hypothetical response hierarchy

The likelihood that any given response will be performed is a function of many variables, including the child's socialization and the way he perceives the conflict situation and its contingencies; these factors influence the relative strength of responses in the repertoire.

To the extent that television content performs a socializing function or is capable of changing the child's perception of various contingencies in a conflict situation, then, observations of television-mediated violence may influence the position of aggressive responses in his response hierarchy. For example, an aggressive response might start out low in a child's hierarchy (that is, it would have a low probability of performance in most situations), as indicated in the first column of Figure 1. It then might move upward in the hierarchy as a consequence of exposure to television-mediated violence, as indicated in the second column of Figure 1. One can then argue that the child has been affected by television viewing, even though overt aggressive behavior is unlikely because the response is still below his performance threshold.

Development

Our aim was to develop a paper and pencil instrument based on conflict situations and responses to them (including aggressive responses) which were conceptually close to the child's life experiences. To obtain the situations and responses, boys and girls from three to sixteen years old responded to an open-ended interview about what made them angry, what they did about the situations that made them angry, how one could hurt people, and when hurting people was justified. From these answers a set of typical situations which made children angry and four characteristic types of response to such situations—physical aggression, verbal aggression, leaving the field, and positive coping with the frustrator (including appeal to authority)—were developed. An item consisted of one situation and four responses, one per response type. Responses were randomly assigned to each situation. The result was a pretest instrument of 36 items, 12 appropriate for children from four to ten years old, 12 appropriate for children ten to 16 years old, and 12 appropriate across the entire age range.

Items were presented using a paired comparisons technique. All possible combinations of the four responses for each situation were presented, giving six pairs of responses to each situation. This approach provided the option of using data from all subjects and/or from only those who had a consistent (transitive) ranking of the four responses.

Stick figure illustrations of the responses were drawn. The appropriate pairs were presented on separate pages of a booklet for younger children and on slides for older children. Young children marked the picture of the response they preferred and older children marked the letter (A or B) of the response they preferred. Two very simple practice items were provided. Appendix A illustrates one complete item in the instrument.

The 36 pretest items were administered to 91 boys and girls four, seven, ten, 13, and 16 years of age. All subjects responded to the 12 items appropriate for the entire age range; four-, seven-, and ten-year-olds received the 12 items appropriate for younger children; another group of ten-year-olds and all thirteen- and sixteen-year-olds received the 12 items appropriate for older children. Order of presentation of items and of the six pairs of responses within items were randomized. The subjects were asked to consider each situation as one they had encountered and to choose the response they would actually perform when in that situation (see Appendix B for instructions).

Items on which many children failed to give herarchical responses were eliminated. For the remaining items, a simple count was made of the number of times each response was chosen. Thus, on any item a physical aggression score could range from 0 (physical aggression never chosen) to 3 (physical aggression chosen every time it was presented). Verbal aggression was similarly scored. Combined aggression scores (physical + verbal aggression) could be obtained by counting choice of both physical and verbal aggression, and they ranged from 1 to 5.

Items were then *ranked* by frequency of choice of physical aggression and frequency of choice of physical plus verbal aggression. Items which elicited similar rankings for aggressive responses within each grade were selected. There were nine such items: three appropriate for younger

Table 1: Mean frequency of choice
of physical aggression by age and sex*

			Given items for ages 4-10 and 4-16			Given items for ages 10-16 and 4-16		
Item number in final version			Four years	Seven years	Ten years	Ten years	13 years	16 years
	1	Boys	1.0	0.6	1.6	2.2	2.0	2.5
Items from pretest set		Girls	1.2	0.3	1.0	1.0	0.8	1.8
for ages 4-16	2	Boys	1.5	1.0	1.3	2.3	2.3	2.2
		Girls	0.9	0.7	1.1	2.3	1.2	1.0
	3	Boys	0.9	0.5	0.8	1.4	1.1	0.9
		Girls	1.2	0.4	0.5	0.7	0.6	0.6
	4	Boys	1.4	0.4	1.0	2.4	2.4	2.8
Items from pretest set		Girls	1.8	0.3	0.8	1.7	1.5	2.2
for ages 4-10 and	5	Boys	1.2	0.6	1.2	1.8	1.4	2.1
10-16		Girls	1.4	0.0	0.6	0.7	1.0	0.8
	6	Boys	1.2	0.4	0.6	1.6	1.1	1.5
		Girls	1.5	0.3	0.5	0.7	0.4	0.5

*possible range = 0 to 3.0

children, three appropriate for older children, and three appropriate across the entire age range. By this procedure in any developmental study, the same data would be available over all ages for three items, and comparable data for younger and for older children would be available for three more items. The final instrument is in Appendix C.

Mean frequency of choice for each of the items in the final instrument is summarized in Table 1 for physical aggression and Table 2 for physical plus verbal aggression. The consistent age-related pattern in these tables—high aggression scores for four-year-olds, dropping to low scores for seven-year-olds, then rising again among older children—illustrates both the importance of investigating aggressive behavior across ages and the rationale for selecting final items on the basis of comparability of item *rankings* rather than on comparability of response hierarchy scores themselves.

Table 2: Mean frequency of choice of physical
plus verbal aggression by age and sex*

			Given items for ages 4-10 and 4-16			Given items for ages 10-16 and 4-16		
	Item number in final version		Four years	Seven years	Ten years	Ten years	13 years	16 years
	1	Boys	3.0	1.6	2.6	3.3	4.2	4.6
Items from		Girls	2.3	1.4	2.9	2.3	2.9	3.6
pretest set for	2	Boys	3.1	2.0	2.7	4.1	4.3	4.1
ages		Girls	2.5	1.8	2.9	3.8	2.8	3.0
4-16	3	Boys	2.4	1.6	2.0	2.8	2.6	2.4
		Girls	2.2	1.1	2.0	1.8	1.9	1.8
	4	Boys	2.4	1.5	3.0	4.1	3.9	4.8
Items from		Girls	3.2	1.4	2.4	3.4	3.7	4.0
pretest set for	5	Boys	2.1	1.6	2.3	3.8	3.7	4.1
ages		Girls	2.8	1.3	2.7	1.9	3.0	3.2
4-10 and 10-16	6	Boys	3.0	1.6	1.9	3.6	3.4	3.9
		Girls	2.8	1.5	1.7	2.7	2.8	3.0

*possible range = 1.0 to 5.0

Test-retest reliability

Test-retest reliability of the instrument was assessed using a sample of 18 four-year-old boys and girls, with a time interval of one month between initial and final testing. The correlation coefficient for physical aggression was .72; for verbal aggression, .57; for physical plus verbal aggression, .84. Test-retest reliability was judged acceptable, at least at this age, given the small N and the obtained correlations.

Validation

Although the final version of the response hierarchy instrument appeared to have good face validity, data on its correlation with actual behavior were judged desirable. Several validation studies were conducted.

An experiment by Bandura, Ross, and Ross (1963b) was chosen as a validation model for younger children. Three videotapes with two twelve-year-old male models were constructed paralleling three of Bandura, Ross, and Ross's four experimental conditions. In two of the tapes Rocky aggressed at length against a wide assortment of toys and finally against Jamie to gain access to Jamie's toys. In one version Rocky was rewarded for his aggression, the final scene depicting Jamie cowering in a corner and Rocky seated stage center, eating a cookie and drinking a coke with most of the toys gathered around him. In the other version Rocky was punished for his aggression, with Jamie walloping him and reclaiming all his toys and Rocky retreating to the corner in tears. The third videotape showed the two boys playing together with the same set of toys, actively but not aggressively.

Nursery school boys and girls were taken individually from their classroom to the nurses' lounge which contained a television monitor. Each subject was "allowed" to watch television while the experimenter completed "some work" she had to do. After viewing, the experimenter (E) and the subject (S) proceeded to the experimental room.

Half of the Ss, all of whom were run first, found the room full of toys, some of which had appeared in the videotape and some of which had not. S was told to play while E remained in the room absorbed in her "work." Play behavior was scored particularly for imitative and nonimitative aggression for 20 minutes, in five-second intervals, by an observer (O) behind a one-way mirror. O was blind as to which videotape S had viewed. Three Ss, all in the aggression rewarded condition, were scored jointly by two Os. Percent agreement over all 240 five-second intervals was .96 for one female S and .99 and .90 for two male Ss.

For the remaining half of the Ss, the room contained not toys, but a second E, also blind as to which videotape S had viewed, who administered the response hierarchy items. The first E again remained in the room "working."

Results for the behavioral half of the study were analyzed in terms of imitative and nonimitative aggression scores. Results for the response hierarchy half of the study were analyzed in terms of the number of times physical aggression, verbal aggression, and physical plus verbal aggression responses were chosen. Group means for both the behavioral and the physical and verbal aggression response hierarchy scores are presented in Table 3 and plotted in Figure 2.

Table 3: Mean behavioral and response hierarchy
scores for four-year-old validation by sex and
videotape condition (all Ss, raw scores)

	Imitative aggressive behavior*			Nonimitative aggressive behavior*		
	Aggression rewarded	Aggression punished	Non-aggressive active	Aggression rewarded	Aggression punished	Non-aggressive active
Girls-mean	0.60	0.40	1.00	28.20	67.80	16.40
S D	1.20	0.80	2.00	10.78	34.78	15.81
Boys-mean	7.80	3.20	1.20	76.00	46.40	43.80
S D	8.61	5.91	1.47	33.46	64.70	14.66

*N = 5 per cell

	Physical aggression response hierarchy**			Verbal aggression response hierarchy**		
	Aggression rewarded	Aggression punished	Non-aggressive active	Aggression rewarded	Aggression punished	Non-aggressive active
Girls-mean	8.12	9.37	6.75	9.75	8.00	7.62
S D	1.69	2.50	3.11	2.90	2.55	1.93
Boys-mean	9.25	9.62	5.12	9.50	7.50	7.25
S D	3.77	2.83	2.93	1.66	2.40	2.77

**N = 8 per cell

For imitative aggressive behavior, a 3 x 2 analysis of variance (ANO-VA) (conditions by sex) and a Kruskal-Wallis one-way ANOVA showed no significant differences between conditions, although the Kruskal-Wallis analysis was significant in the Bandura study with more Ss. Mann-Whitney analyses of the three groups by pairs yielded differences significant at $p < .001$, with rewarded more aggressive than punished, rewarded more aggressive than active, nonaggressive, and punished more aggressive than active, nonaggressive, replicating Bandura's results.[2]

Inspection of nonimitative aggression scores revealed one aberrant score in each of three cells (rewarded boys; punished boys; punished girls). This resulted in notable nonhomogeneity of variance across cells. Two different techniques were used to correct for this: (1) the three Ss were deleted and a 3 x 2 ANOVA performed on the remaining raw

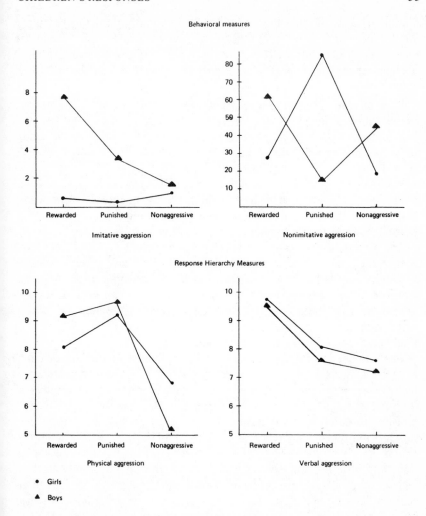

Figure 2:   Comparability of behavioral and response hierarchy measures in validation with four-year-olds

scores, and (2) variance stabilizing transformations were applied to the
raw scores for all Ss prior to performing the 3 x 2 ANOVA. The results
were the same for both analyses and will only be reported for the first.
There was a significant effect of conditions (F=3.77; df=2,21; p < .05)
with more nonimitative aggression in the rewarded than in the punished
condition and more in the punished than in the active, nonaggressive
condition. Although there was no main effect for sex, a significant condition by sex interaction (F=28.84; df=2,21; p < .01) was due to the differential effects of the punished condition on boys, who displayed little
nonimitative aggressive behavior, and on girls, who displayed much

nonimitative aggressive behavior. Both boys and girls displayed more nonimitative aggressive behavior in the rewarded condition than in the nonaggressive condition. These results replicate those of Bandura in all respects except that of girls' nonimitative aggression in the punished condition.

Each of the three response hierarchy scores (physical aggression, verbal aggression, physical plus verbal aggression) was analyzed in a two-factor ANOVA (conditions by sex). F values for the effect of conditions reached significance in each analysis ($F = 5.91$; $df = 2,42$; $p < .01$, $F = 3.37$; $df = 2,42$; $p < .05$, and $F = 5.73$; $df = 2,42$; $p < .01$, respectively), with choice of aggression about the same for the rewarded and punished conditions and greater than that for the active, nonaggressive condition. F values for the main effect of sex and for the condition by sex interaction did not approach significance in any of the analyses.

The pattern of results using the response hierarchy scores differs from that of the behavior scores, as is apparent in Figure 2, where response hierarchy scores increase in aggression after viewing punished aggression and behavioral scores decrease. However, the two sets of findings are not necessarily in conflict. Detailed analysis of the aggression punished videotape suggests that the different obtained patterns of results might be expected from the two measures.

The punished condition is the most complicated of the three scenarios: Rocky asks to play with Jamie's toys and is refused—a reprehensible refusal on the part of Jamie. Rocky then aggresses against many of the toys and against Jamie—also reprehensible. Finally, Jamie asserts himself (in defense of his rights in a frustrating situation?), aggresses rather brutally against Rocky, and reclaims all his toys. Rocky's aggression is clearly punished, and one would expect little imitation of his actions and little nonimitative aggression with the toys he used—both of which comprised a major portion of the behavioral measure. However, Jamie's aggression is quite useful and perhaps even considered justified in our society. It follows that since the response hierarchy measure consists of situations which are frustrating, and since children in the aggression-punished condition in fact see aggression demonstrated to be quite useful in such a situation, one might expect them to respond *more* aggressively to the response hierarchy measure. Thus, this difference between the two patterns of results does not appear to invalidate the response hierarchy measure, and the remaining data seem to validate it for four-year-olds.

The initial effort to validate the response hierarchy instrument among older children was unsuccessful and will be summarized briefly. The validation model was an experiment reported by Walters and Thomas (1963). Stimuli were either a videotape of a knife fight from *Rebel Without a Cause* (aggressive) as used by Walters and Thomas, or an excerpt from the television series *Make Room for Daddy* (nonaggressive) in place of the art film used by Walters and Thomas. Seventy-two 13-year-old boys and girls were Ss. For almost half of them from each condition, the dependent variable was intensity of shock administered to a male confederate during a subsequent "learning" experiment; the remaining Ss completed the response hierarchy instrument. Ss were run individually for the shock measure and in pairs for the response hierarchy measure by a male or female E, counterbalanced across conditions, sex of S, and type of dependent measure. Es were blind as to condition of each S. Measures were obtained both before and after viewing.

Mean shock intensity scores and physical aggression response hierarchy scores are shown in Table 4. For shock intensity, a 2 x 2 x 2 analysis of covariance (condition by sex of S by E, covarying on before scores) showed that the aggressive condition elicited slightly higher intensity shocks ($F = 3.50$; $df = 1,23$; $p < .10$), but no other effects. Similar analysis of the response hierarchy scores revealed no effect for condition, but showed an unexpected and largely uninterpretable effect for E on physical aggression scores ($F = 9.91$; $df = 1,31$; $p < .01$).

In order to increase the N per cell using the response hierarchy measure, an additional 19 boys and 19 girls, with a third E (male), saw the

Table 4: A. Mean change scores for shock intensity
by sex, experimenter, and videotape condition*

	Aggressive videotape		Nonaggressive videotape	
	E 1	E 2	E 1	E 2
Girls-mean	.58	1.13	.20	.15
S D	1.60	1.75	.69	.32
Boys-mean	.12	.30	.32	−.17
S D	.68	1.97	1.30	.58

*N = 4 Ss per cell

B. Mean change scores for response hierarchy
physical aggression by sex, experimenter, and
videotape condition**

	Aggressive videotape		Nonaggressive videotape	
	E 1	E 2	E 1	E 2
Girls-mean	.47	.73	.43	.63
S D	.14	.25	.42	.48
Boys-mean	.47	.57	.13	1.07
S D	.25	.51	.48	.34

**N = 5 Ss per cell

videotapes and completed the response hierarchy in an after-only design. Physical aggression after-scores from this second wave of Ss were combined with after-scores from the first wave, transformed, to stabilize the variances, and submitted to a three factor ANOVA (condition by sex of S by E). (See Appendix D for mean scores and ANOVA table.) There was no effect for condition. There was an effect of sex ($F=8.79$; $df=1,66$; $p < .01$), with boys giving more aggressive responses than girls. The effect for experimenter did not approach significance. Scores for verbal aggression and physical and verbal aggression were similarly analyzed. Again there was no effect for condition. Since the remainder of the results of these analyses are either uninterpretable or uninteresting in light of the failure to obtain an effect for condition, they are not reported here.

Finally, a second experiment attempted to increase the differential impact of the aggressive and nonaggressive stimuli by using a prize fight scene from *The Champion* and a rather dull travelogue. Forty-two 13-year-old boys and girls were run in groups, by a single male E, using an after-only design. Mean response hierarchy scores are presented in Appendix D. A 2 x 2 ANOVA (sex by condition) for each of the three types of response hierarchy score revealed only a tendency for the aggressive videotape to elicit slightly higher verbal aggression scores ($F=3.28$; $df=1,38$; $p < .10$) than the nonaggressive tape did. There were no other significant main or interaction effects for any of the three scores.

These two studies failed to validate the response hierarchy instrument among 13-year-olds, but, given the lack of difference between conditions on the behavioral measure (i.e., shock intensity), they do not necessarily invalidate it. The failure to obtain differences between the aggressive and the nonaggressive tapes may be due to the age of the participating Ss. Walters and Llewellyn-Thomas's significant results with shock intensity were obtained using groups of adult males, adult females, and 15-year-old males. It may be that the two-year age difference between the present subjects and the youngest subjects tested by Walters and Thomas locates a difference in responsiveness to aggressive displays or in sensitivity to situations in which aggressive responses (behavioral or verbal) are measured. Comparison of the groups on shock intensity measures indicates that something like this might be the case. The one expected result that was found with the response hierarchy instrument was the sex difference in aggressiveness, although it appeared in only one of the preceding validation attempts with 13-year-olds.

In light of the failure to find differences among 13-year-olds in response to aggressive presentations on either dependent variable, one more validation with older children was attempted using a nonexperimental approach.

The response hierarchy instrument was administered via slides to fifth grade Ss. Two fifth grade teachers independently rated each S on overt aggressive behavior in the school environment.[3] Teachers were asked to conceive of aggressive behavior in terms of "hitting, shoving, name calling, etc." Ratings were obtained on a seven-point scale ranging from very unaggressive (=1) to "very aggressive" (=7) (see Appendix E). Only those 34 Ss who responded to the response hierarchy instrument and who were rated by both teachers were included in the analyses reported here.[4]

The correlation between response hierarchy scores for physical aggression and teacher ratings of aggressive behavior was significantly different from zero for both teachers (Teacher 1: $r=.49$; $Z=3.15$; $p <$ .005 and Teacher 2: $r=.33$; $Z=2.02$; $p < .05$). Correlations between response hierarchy scores for verbal aggression and teacher ratings of aggressive behavior were low (Teacher 1: $r=.10$; Teacher 2: $r=.04$), probably indicating that teachers based their ratings almost entirely on children's physical behavior.

ANOVAs were performed for those high and low in rated aggression. The two teachers' ratings were simply averaged since there was high homogeneity of variance between them. Those students who obtained an average score of less than 5 were assigned to the low aggressive behavior group ($N=15$); those students whose average score was 5 or more were assigned to the high aggressive behavior group ($N=19$). The mean physical aggression scores for boys and girls rated high and low in aggressive behavior are presented in Table 5 and Figure 3. A two-factor ANOVA (behavior rating by sex of S) revealed a significant effect of teacher rating of aggressive behavior ($F=4.69$; $df=1,30$; $p <.05$), with Ss rated high in aggressive behavior choosing more physical aggression responses than Ss rated low in aggressive behavior. There was no significant effect of sex, nor was there a behavior rating by sex interaction.

These relationships between response hierarchy scores and independent ratings of aggressive behavior appear to validate the response hierarchy instrument for fifth graders. It does discriminate, for both boys

Table 5: Mean response hierarchy scores for
fifth graders by sex and teacher
rating of aggressiveness in the
school environment

	High aggressive behavior	Low aggressive behavior
Girls-mean	1.07	0.35
S D	0.94	0.36
N	12	11
Boys-mean	0.88	0.67
S D	0.90	0.25
N	7	4

and girls, among children who are rated by teachers as manifesting either more or less aggressive behavior in the normal school environment.

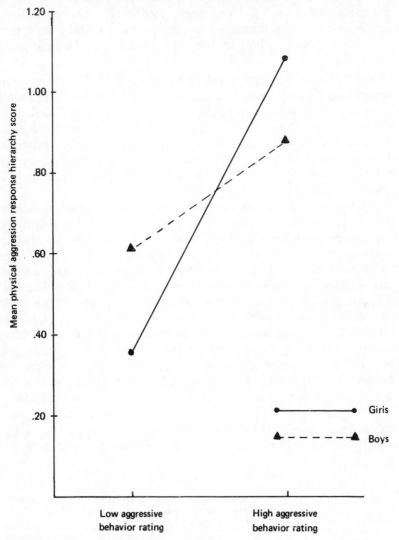

Figure 3: Mean response hierarchy scores for fifth graders by sex and teacher rating of aggressiveness in the school environment

Thus, based on the preceding work, the response hierarchy measure was judged valid enough for further use. This is not to say that further validation work, particularly among older children, is not called for. However, given: (1) that construction of the instrument was based on interviews with children ranging in age from three to 16; (2) that the situations and responses comprising it have a good deal of conceptual or face validity; (3) that no study invalidated the instrument; (4) that an experiment with preschoolers and a field study with fifth graders both demonstrated the discriminative power of the measure; and (5) that the exigencies of time demanded that we turn to other phases of the research, it was decided to continue using the instrument in the studies reported in the following pages.

All subsequent administrations and scorings of the response hierarchy were quite similar to that presented in this section. Children seven or under were tested individually on the three items appropriate for younger Ss and the three items appropriate across the entire age range. Responses were in a booklet; Ss pointed to the picture representing their choice, and E recorded the choice. Older Ss worked in groups on the six items designed for them (three appropriate for older children and three appropriate across the entire age range), viewing slides of the response alternatives and circling the letter representing their choice. Instructions were minimally altered to take account of differences in experimental procedures and surroundings.

Mean choices of physical, verbal, and physical plus verbal aggression were computed for each S. Many of the subsequent analyses revealed high correlations between physical or verbal aggression and physical plus verbal aggression, as one would expect, and also between physical and verbal aggression. Because of this, and because physical and verbal aggression scores could not be independent, most of the analyses to be reported in succeeding sections will be for physical aggression only.

EXPERIMENT 1: UNDERSTANDING OF CONTEMPORARY PROGRAMS

The work reported in this section was designed primarily to chart age changes in understanding the motivations for and consequences of violent acts in current television programs. In addition, children's evaluations of characters and actions portrayed in these programs were assessed. Originally, the effects of justified/unjustified aggression and good/bad consequences for aggression were to be studied also. However, because contemporary television programs do not present a uniform set of motives or consequences for aggressive acts, clear prediction of effects of exposure to different types of programs was not possible. Because of these difficulties, the study reported here was followed by further work (see section on "Motivations and consequences. . .") in which videotapes of current programs were edited to produce the desired uniform set of motivations and consequences. However, in order to provide exploratory data, the tendency to aggress was measured in this first study after exposure to the unedited videotape and administration of the understanding measure.

This section, then, describes selection of television programs and construction of comprehension and evaluation tests, administration and analysis of the comprehension and evaluation tests, and analysis of the exploratory response hierarchy data.

The theoretical and experimental rationale for the comprehension study has already been presented. It suggested the following hypotheses:

1. Understanding of the motivations for and consequences of television-mediated violence will increase with age.
2. Younger children will understand consequences better than motivations, but this difference in understanding will decrease with age.
3. With increasing age, evaluation of the motivations and consequences for violent acts will approximate that of adults within the surrounding communities.

Method

Stimuli. Six half-hour television programs, including commercials, were recorded on black and white videotape. The programs were selected for their clarity of presentation, interest, and violence from tapes of fifteen different programs. Each program contained numerous incidents of violence, both justified and unjustified, with both good and bad consequences. Table 6 presents the programs employed.

Programs were classified into three types which appeal to and are typically viewed by children of different ages (cf., Schramm, Lyle, and Parker, 1961). Presumably they would be understood by the age groups for which they were designed. Adult judges from surrounding communities agreed that the two programs classed as primarily for young children were appropriate for children from four or five years of age on, that the westerns were appropriate for children from 10 to 12 on, and that the crime programs were appropriate for teenagers. It should be noted, however, that a substantial proportion of the adult judges felt the programs were not appropriate for children of any age, even though they were judged typical of what was available on television.

Construction of the understanding test. Each program was viewed by adults from nearby communities. They were members of PTAs, church groups, recreational groups, and similar organizations. Given the demographics of their communities, their judgments are probably representative of a middle-class view of what constitutes violence, the morality of it, and the desirability of its consequences.

The information and evaluation questionnaire was similar to parts of those used by Gerbner (1969) in his content analysis of contemporary television programs. The following information was requested: list of all violent episodes in the program, initiator and receiver of violence in

Table 6: Characteristics of programs
(including program type, program, number violent episodes, percent
of viewers listing each episode, episodes where receiver
was violent, and episodes included in understanding test)

Violent episodes (In temporal order)	Children's programs		Western programs		Crime programs	
	Rocket Robin Hood	Batman	Rifleman	Have Gun	Adam 12	Felony Squad
	% Rate	% Rate	% Rate	% Rate	% Rate	% Rate
1	39*	[65]	15	[92]	[92]	[79] *
2	43	[82]	32	38	33	[60] *
3	21	[94] *	2*	[92] *	[53]	[70] *
4	43	[82] *	[55]	8	3	[84] *
5	39	[71] *	30	53*	25	[88] *
6	[54]	6	[47]	69	39	54
7	29		[47] *	[100]	[56]	3
8	[89] *		13	69*	[64]	25
9	[54]		30	8		[60] *
10	[54]		30	[92] *		55*
11	25		[40] *	69		[48] *
12	36		4	53*		
13			30*	30		
14			26*	61*		
15			[36] *			
16			17*			
17			6*			

☐ Included in primary set of questions

⌐ ¬ Included in secondary set of questions

* Receiver responded violently

each episode, violence of receiver's response, justifiability of each violent act, "goodness" of the immediate and final consequences for each participant in the violence, and a character evaluation of both initiator and receiver of violence. Respondents were also asked to give a general, overall rating of the program for the "goodness" of the motivations and of the consequences. Finally, as previously noted, they were asked how typical the program was, the age child for which it was appropriate, and to give any other comments they wished. Appendix F contains the questionnaire and the various definitions given to all respondents.

Ratings were analyzed separately for each episode. From Table 6, which presents the proportion of adults who rated each episode as violent and the perceived violence of the receiver's response to the initial aggression, it is apparent that the programs differed considerably in the frequency and clarity of violent episodes and in whether or not the receiver's response was violent. Variability in presentation of motivations, consequences, and character type will be presented when age changes in these are considered in the results section. Suffice it to say here that the variability in these evaluations is indeed great, both within and across programs.

For each program, the three violent episodes listed by the greatest proportions of adult viewers were chosen for testing with all child subjects. One to four additional episodes—those rated by the next largest proportions of adults—were added when testing older children. These two sets of episodes will hereafter be referred to as primary and secondary sets, respectively. The episodes in the primary and secondary sets for each program are identified in Table 6.

A multiple choice test was constructed utilizing the information from the adult ratings. Either three or four questions were formulated for each of the three to seven violent episodes in each program. Two questions presented the violent action and asked what the immediate consequences were for the characters identified by the adult raters as initiator and receiver. A third question asked why the violent action was performed, and a fourth asked why the receiver responded violently (if he did aggress in return). Questions eliciting evaluation of the motives and consequences for each violent action as either good, bad, or in-between were also included. Finally, for each character who participated in a violent episode, either as initiator or as receiver, there was a question about the final consequences for him in the program and about the goodness of his character.

Each multiple choice question contained four alternatives. All alternatives represented information presented in the program either visually or verbally or both. Two of the alternatives were judged to be good consequences or motives, and two were judged to be bad. The order of presentation of the alternatives for each question was randomized, and the questions for all episodes combined and randomized. When adults who had not seen a program took the test for it, their scores ranged from 20 percent to 37 percent correct, with four of the six programs under 30 percent. Appendix G contains all the questions for one violent episode. Cartoons were used for testing young children on these questions.

Subjects. Two hundred seventy-one children served as Ss: 40 kindergarteners, 54 third graders, 56 sixth graders, 51 ninth graders, and 70 twelfth graders, with approximately equal numbers of boys and girls at each grade. The community in which they live is low-middle to middle class, with a substantial Chicano population. The particular schools Ss attended were from 15 to 40 percent Chicano. Subjects within each grade and sex were randomly assigned to programs; no attempt has been made to analyze the data by ethnic group.

Procedure. Subjects in the four older age groups were tested in mixed-sex groups of eight to ten by either of two female Es. Es were counterbalanced across groups, and Ss were randomly assigned to programs. The situation was as informal as possible within the school environment (e.g., ordinarily not in the regular classroom). Ss were told we were interested in what children of different ages thought about different types of television programs. They were asked to relax and view the program as they would at home, then we would ask them some questions about what they thought of it.

At the conclusion of the program, Ss answered the multiple choice questions about what they had seen. The entire test was read aloud to third graders, while older Ss worked on their own. All Ss were tested on the four to seven episodes per program, primary and secondary sets combined, shown in Table 6.

Following the multiple choice test, all Ss were administered the response hierarchy instrument. This was presented as a separate task (the results of which we were interested in), which was given to fill up the remainder of the class session. The four older age groups saw the response alternatives on slides and circled on an answer sheet the letter that corresponded to the response they chose.

The procedure with kindergarten Ss was the same as that for the older Ss, with the following exceptions. Children were run in mixed-sex groups of three rather than eight or ten. The four alternatives for each multiple choice question were presented with stick-figure cartoons; S pointed to his response. The alternative responses in the response hierarchy were also presented as stick-figure cartoons. Testing was done individually with one of four possible female Es.

Results

Understanding. Answers to the questions about motivations for and consequences of violence in each program were scored as correct or incorrect. The number correct was computed for motivations, immediate consequences, and final consequences. Computations—performed separately for the primary and secondary sets of episodes—were converted to a percentage of the maximum possible correct for each category for each program, in order to make the scores comparable across programs and across categories. Percentage scores were converted to arcsin scores prior to analysis to stabilize variance across cells (e.g., 25%=0.524; 50%=0.785; 75%=1.047, and 100%=1.539).

Figure 4 presents age changes in understanding of the motives for violence, immediate consequences of violence, and final consequences to all characters who participated in violence over all programs combined. The data are for the primary episodes. The pattern of results with the secondary episodes for the four older groups was quite similar.

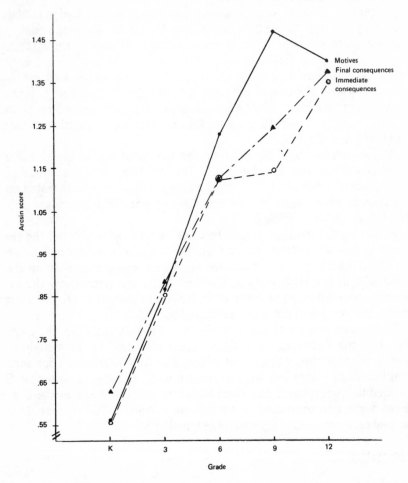

Figure 4:   Understanding of motivations for and immediate and final consequences of violence by grade for three primary episodes

The arcsin scores for motives, immediate consequences, and final consequences were each subjected to a nested factors analysis of variance.[5] Independent variables were grade, sex, type of program, and specific program nested under program type. In order to equalize cell

Ns, 91 Ss were randomly discarded until a total of three Ss per cell remained. (Subsequent three-way analyses of variance included all Ss and will be reported later.)

In the nested factors ANOVA there is a clear and highly significant age effect for all three measures ($F=60.81$; $F=40.74$; and $F=29.13$ respectively with $df=4,120$; $p < .001$). Although an age effect was predicted, the magnitude of the age differences found is still striking. Kindergarteners could answer only about one-third of the questions about either motives or consequences, third graders only about one-half, and twelfth graders about 95 percent. Hence, the younger Ss, by our measures, are not taking in, or not retaining, much of the information about motives and consequences in a television program.

There is general, continued improvement in learning motives and consequences through the twelfth grade. This is reflected in a highly significant linear trend for grade for each measure ($F=217.45$; $f=153.11$; and

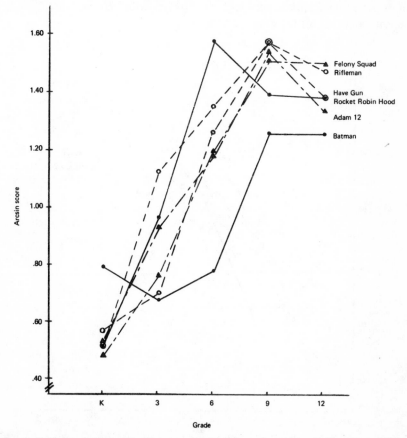

Figure 5: Understanding of motivations for violence by grade and program for three primary episodes

F=113.01 respectively, with df=1,120; p < .001). A much smaller, but significant, portion of the variance attributable to age in understanding of motivations and of immediate consequences is accounted for by a quadratic trend (F=23.01; df=1,120; p < .001; F=5.18; df=1,120; p < .05, respectively).

There was no significant sex difference in performance on any of the three dependent variables, nor was there any significant effect for *type* of program. There was a significant effect for programs for both motivations and final consequences (F=3.81; df=3,120; p < .05; F=9.25; df=3,120; p < .01, respectively). These results are apparent in Figures 5, 6, and 7, which present arcsin scores by grade and program for motivations, immediate consequences, and final consequences, respectively. The only significant interaction term in any of the analyses was a grade by program interaction for understanding of motivations (F=2.47; df=12,120; p < .01). The exact interpretation of this interaction is not clear, but Figure 5 indicates that it is probably due to the age pattern for understanding *Batman*, and perhaps *Rocket Robin Hood*, which is different from that for the other programs.

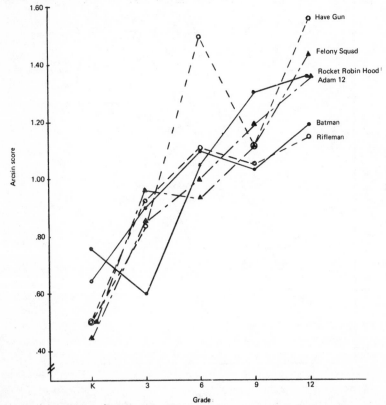

Figure 6:   Understanding of immediate consequences of violence by grade and program for three primary episodes

The additional one to four episodes (secondary set) that Ss from third, sixth, ninth, and twelfth grades responded to were subjected to identical analyses. The same increases with age in understanding were found, although the effect is quite weak for immediate consequences ($F=15.56$; $df=3,96$; $p < .001$; $F=2.21$; $df=3,96$; $p < .10$; $F=9.84$; $df=3,96$; $p < .001$, respectively). The linear trend for grade was also significant for each of the three dependent variables ($F=34.35$; $df=1,96$; $p < .001$; $F=5.02$; $df=1,96$; $p < .05$; $F=24.17$; $df=1,96$; $p < .001$). There remains a significant quadratic trend ($F=5.95$; $df=1,96$; $p < .05$) and a significant residual ($F=6.36$; $df=1,91$; $p < .05$) for understanding motivations.

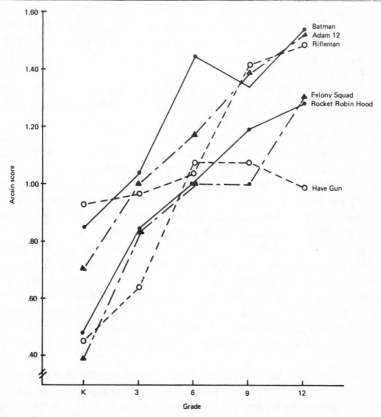

Figure 7: Understanding of final consequences for violence by grade and program for three primary episodes

Again there was no significant effect of sex in any of the analyses. However, there were significant effects of program type for immediate and final consequences ($F=8.91$ and $F=5.06$ with $df=2,96$; $p < .01$). For immediate consequences the order from most to least understood was westerns, crime, and children's programs. For final consequences it was children's programs, crime programs, and westerns. For all three measures there was a significant effect of programs ($F=4.26$, $F=7.11$, and

$F = 4.71$ with $df = 3,96$ ad $p < .01$ for all three). There were no significant interaction terms in the analyses of motivations and immediate consequences, but there were two significant interactions for final consequences (for grade by program $F = 2.53$; $df = 9,96$; $p < .05$; for grade by sex by program type $F = 2.69$; $df = 6,96$; $p < .05$). The effects are weak, significant (due to the large number of degrees of freedom), and largely uninterpretable. In summary, the analyses of the additional episodes tested with older Ss largely confirm the results reported for three episodes tested with all Ss.

Additional three-way ANOVAs for unequal Ns[6] were performed to be certain that the results reported above remained when all Ss were included. Two analyses were performed for each of the three dependent variables: grade by sex by program, and grade by sex by program type. The results will not be reported in detail here since they largely repeat those already reported.

For all three measures there was a highly significant effect for grade, and again the linear trend was highly significant. There was a significant effect for motivations and for final consequences, but not for immediate consequences. Program type was significant when it was the third independent variable in the analyses of motivations and final consequences. However, this result is probably largely due to differences in the programs, since these differences are not separately accounted for in the three-way ANOVAs as they are in the nested factors ANOVAs. Thus, one may probably conclude that the results reported from the nested factors ANOVAs represent the data for all Ss tested.

Inspection of all data showed no differences in younger Ss' understanding of motivations and consequences. If there are any differences in such understanding, they occur at the sixth and ninth grades, with motivations better understood than consequences. Because of the visible lack of predicted results, no analyses were performed to test hypothesis 2 (that younger children will understand consequences better than motivations and that this difference in understanding will decrease with age).

Evaluations. Answers to the questions evaluating the character of all those who participated in violence, their motivations, the immediate consequences to them, and the final consequences to them were scored as good, good and bad, bad, and don't know or no answer. The percentage of viewers giving each of these four ratings was calculated separately for each question in the comprehension tests by program and grade level. Character evaluations of each character who participated in the three primary episodes of violence are presented graphically in Figure 8 by grade and program; adult ratings are included for comparison. Comparable figures for evaluation of motivations, immediate consequences, and final consequences are presented in Appendix I.

Rocket Robin Hood

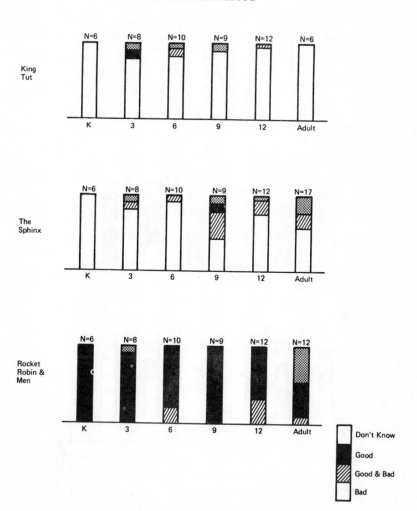

Figure 8: Character Evaluation — *Rocket Robin Hood*

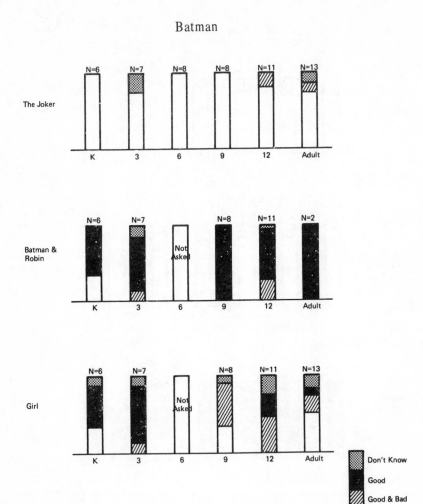

Figure 8 (cont.)

Rifleman

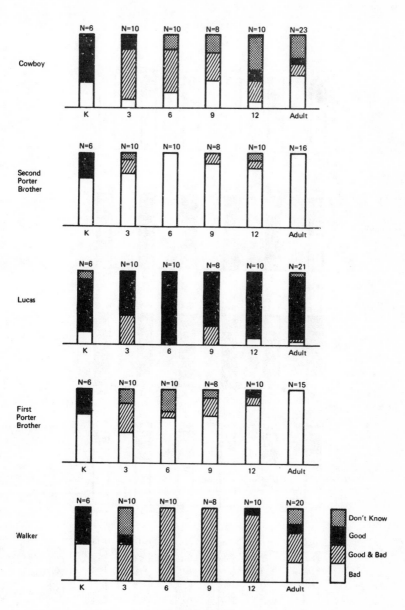

Figure 8 (cont.)

Have Gun

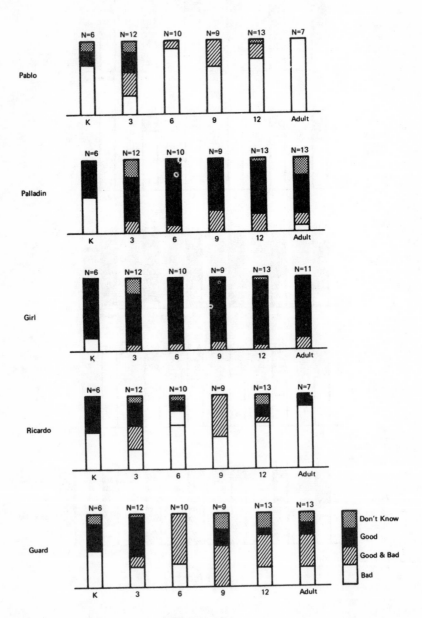

Figure 8 (cont.)

Adam 12

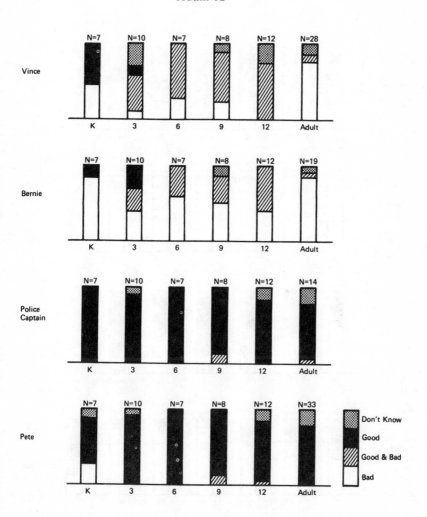

Figure 8 (cont.)

Felony Squad

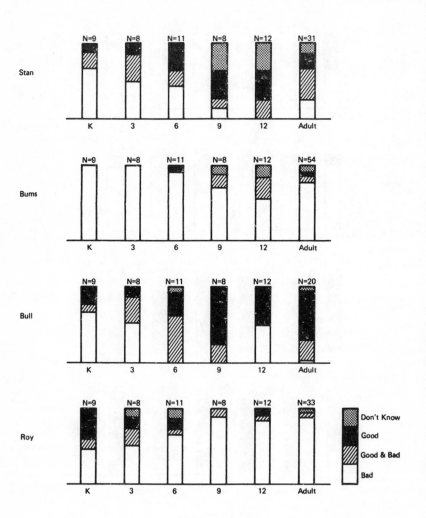

Figure 8 (cont.)

For character evaluation, all Ss who viewed a program were included in its evaluation data set. For motivations, immediate consequences, and final consequences, only those Ss who correctly answered the relevant question about motivation or consequences were included. The data for some of the evaluations are probably not very reliable, since the number of subjects upon which it is based is quite small. The N for each evaluation has been included in the figures, so that the reader may make his own estimate of the stability of the data.

The evaluations of adults and kindergarteners are not directly comparable to those of third, sixth, ninth, and twelfth graders. The latter four grades were asked to choose among good, good and bad, bad, and don't know for their evaluations, while kindergarteners were asked to choose only between good or bad. If a kindergartener said he didn't know or that the character was both good and bad, he was scored accordingly, but Es did not suggest such options to Ss of this age. Adults were given all four ratings as options; however, their evaluations were made in the context of evaluating all violent episodes in the program and did not follow a question about the relevant program content.

Inspection of the data presented in Figure 8 and Appendix I indicates that a majority of Ss at each age usually agree with Ss at other ages in their evaluations. If the majority of the twelfth graders thought a character was bad, the majority of the kindergarteners, third, sixth, and ninth graders were also likely to think he was bad. There is not, however, a consistent trend over age in the pattern of evaluation; children's evaluations as they mature do not successively and smoothly approximate those of twelfth graders or adults.

To better summarize the evaluation data over age, characters from all programs were combined and then divided into good and bad major characters and minor characters (see Figure 8). The four sets of ratings (character, motivations, immediate consequences, and final consequences) were then tallied for each grade. Each rating was counted as a unit, so that the total N corresponded to the total number of ratings given rather than to the number of Ss giving the ratings. For each grade the percentages of all ratings that were good, bad, and good and bad were then calculated. As before, all Ss were included in the data on evaluation of character, while only those Ss who correctly answered the relevant question about motivation, immediate consequences, or final consequences were included in those evaluations. The results presented here are for the primary episodes only.

Table 7 presents percentages of evaluations of good and bad major characters and minor characters for each of the five grades; adult ratings are included for comparison purposes. There were seven good major characters, eleven bad major characters, and six minor characters included (respectively) in the three types of ratings. The majority of Ss at all ages agree in their evaluation of the three types of characters: the good major characters are good, the bad major characters are bad, and the minor characters are diverse. Kindergarteners are more likely to be confused about a character's nature than are any of the other Ss. Fully one-third of kindergarten ratings for the good major characters were bad. By third grade this had dropped to 15.9 percent, with further decreases at older ages. 28.6 percent of the kindergarten ratings of the bad characters were good, with this percentage decreasing rapidly at older ages. The adult ratings were generally more polarized than the children's; however, this is probably an artifact of the differing techniques for eliciting the ratings rather than a true age difference. Testing adults with the same instruments used for children would clarify the nature of these apparent differences between child and adult responses.

Table 7: Percentage of responses for evaluation of character by grade and character type

	Good major character			Bad major character			Minor character		
Rating	Bad	Good-bad	Good	Bad	Good-bad	Good	Bad	Good-bad	Good
Grade									
K	34.1	2.3	63.6	70.0	1.4	28.6	53.6	4.9	41.5
3	15.9	17.5	66.7	50.0	34.9	15.1	30.8	25.0	44.2
6	0.0	17.5	82.5	71.9	26.0	2.1	41.7	33.3	25.0
9	0.0	16.7	83.3	63.2	35.6	1.1	32.5	37.5	30.0
12	8.9	16.4	74.7	66.7	29.9	3.4	21.6	39.2	39.2
Adult	3.3	12.0	84.8	86.1	10.3	3.6	59.8	23.8	16.4

The evaluations of the final consequences to the three types of characters who participated in violence are shown in Table 8. This table was constructed similarly to the table for character evaluation. Again, the majority of Ss at each age tend to agree in their evaluations of the final consequences to each character. However, there are two notable exceptions.

Table 8: Percentage of responses for evaluation of final consequences by grade and character type

	Good major character			Bad major character			Minor character		
Rating	Bad	Good-bad	Good	Bad	Good-bad	Good	Bad	Good-bad	Good
Grade									
K	47.4	0.0	52.6	65.6	0.0	34.4	70.0	0.0	30.0
3	10.0	13.3	76.7	37.9	34.5	27.6	28.6	35.7	35.7
6	6.1	18.4	75.5	21.2	28.2	50.6	28.6	28.6	42.8
9	3.7	22.2	74.1	11.2	30.0	58.8	33.3	20.8	45.8
12	5.5	17.8	76.7	14.9	31.6	53.5	34.2	21.1	44.7
Adult	17.5	8.7	73.8	73.4	5.7	20.9	64.4	22.1	13.5

First, adults and children appeared not to have rated the consequences to bad characters on the same basis. Adults apparently evaluated the consequences in relation to the character, while children evaluated them in relation to society. Thus, going to jail was a bad consequence in an adult rating and a good consequence in a child's rating—except for kindergarteners who rated consequences to bad characters similarly to adults. (Perhaps very young children are not able to take the good of society into account in providing their evaluations.) These problems do not arise for good characters. They are good, the consequences to them are good, and their fates are good for society. Ss of all ages agreed in rating the final consequences to good characters as good, although kindergarteners were less uniform in their evaluations than are older Ss.

Second, kindergarteners apparently view negatively everything associated with violence. Of their ratings for the final consequences to good major characters, 47.4 percent were bad; the next closest percentages were 10.0 percent for third graders and 17.5 percent for adults. For bad major characters, 65.6 percent of the kindergarten ratings were bad, with the next closest ratings being 73.4 percent for adults and 37.9 percent for third graders. A similar pattern holds for the final consequences to minor characters. This jaundiced view of everything associated with violence is least apparent in the character evaluations (see Table 7), becomes somewhat apparent in the evaluations of final consequences, and is more apparent in the two succeeding tables for evaluations of immediate consequences and motivations (Tables 9 and 10).

Evaluations of the immediate consequences to three types of characters are presented in Table 9. The ratings are based upon 11 instances of immediate consequences for good major characters, 16 instances for bad major characters, and nine for minor characters. Again there is general agreement among all the children in evaluation of immediate consequences to the good and bad major characters. However, their evaluations do not agree with those of the adult raters. Most adults felt that the immediate consequences to good and bad major characters and to minor characters were bad, while children evaluated them as good for the major characters and confused for the minor characters. Whether this difference is due to the different techniques for eliciting evaluations or to

Table 9: Percentages of responses for
evaluation of immediate consequences
by grade and character type

Rating	Good major characters			Bad major characters			Minor characters		
	Bad	Good-bad	Good	Bad	Good-bad	Good	Bad	Good-bad	Good
Grade									
K	54.8	0.0	45.2	44.4	3.7	51.9	38.9	0.0	61.1
3	21.2	26.9	51.9	16.9	19.7	63.4	47.2	19.4	33.3
6	7.2	25.3	67.5	21.2	23.2	55.6	28.9	28.9	42.2
9	12.3	24.6	63.0	23.5	18.6	57.8	41.7	22.9	35.4
12	14.0	23.4	62.6	21.0	28.0	51.0	40.6	26.6	32.8
Adult	45.2	18.1	36.7	58.6	21.2	20.3	66.0	21.8	12.2

real differences in evaluating immediate consequences is unknown. Since the consequence which children were evaluating was written in such a way that an evaluation of it in relation to the character would agree with the adult evaluation, there is a suggestion of real differences in the evaluation of immediate consequences.

As with final consequences, kindergarteners are more likely than older children to evaluate immediate consequences as bad for both good and bad major characters. The interpretation of this as a general displeasure with violence is tempered here by the fact that the immediate consequences for minor characters are more likely to be judged good than judged bad. However, the evaluations of immediate consequences for minor characters show considerable shift from age to age and probably reflect the inconclusive handling of these characters.

Further support for the assertion that kindergarteners generally disapprove of violence is found in the evaluation of motivations for all violent acts. These data are presented in Table 10 and are based on nine motivations for good major characters, 11 for bad major characters, and five for minor characters. Kindergarteners uniformly disapprove of the motivations for violent acts, whether the character is a good or bad major character or a minor character. This is in sharp contrast to older children and adults, who evaluated the motivations of good major characters as generally good and of bad major characters as bad. As with character evaluation, adults are more skewed in their evaluations than are any of the child Ss.

Table 10: Percentage of responses for evaluation of motivations
by grade and character type

	Good major character			Bad major character			Minor character		
Rating	Bad	Good-bad	Good	Bad	Good-bad	Good	Bad	Good-bad	Good
Grade									
K	80.0	0.0	20.0	75.0	0.0	25.0	90.9	0.0	9.1
3	20.0	20.0	60.0	51.1	27.6	21.3	50.0	13.6	36.4
6	30.6	16.7	52.8	56.4	30.8	12.8	51.2	29.3	19.5
9	17.4	23.2	59.4	61.6	23.3	15.1	28.9	26.3	44.7
12	21.6	30.9	47.4	48.5	27.2	24.3	48.2	37.5	14.3
Adult	7.6	26.7	65.6	84.7	12.1	3.2	71.1	7.4	21.5

These data on the evaluation over age of motivations for, consequences of, and characters who participate in violence demonstrate that all subjects—except perhaps kindergarteners—understand whether an actor or the motivation for or consequence of an action was good or bad. Even kindergarteners understand which characters are good and bad, although they are apparently more confused about the portrayal than are older children; they also appear to generally disapprove of violence. The data provide some indication that the technique used to elicit evaluations will influence the pattern of obtained evaluations and that children may identify with society in evaluating consequences to those who participate in violence rather than judging from the participant's point of view.

Finally, a few comments on the variability in presentation of motivations, consequences, and characterization among the six programs are in order. Table 11 presents a summary of adult ratings for the three primary episodes of each program. The entries are simply counts of the rating (good, good and bad, bad) chosen by the majority of adults each time a rating was asked for. For example, for *Rocket Robin Hood* three character evaluations were requested; for one character the majority of evaluations was good, while for the other two the majority was bad.

Table 11: Summary of adult ratings: number of times majority of adults rated characters, final consequences, motivations, and immediate consequences as good, good and bad, or bad

| | Children's programs | | Western programs | | Crime programs | |
	Rocket Robin Hood	Batman	Rifleman	Have Gun	Adam 12	Felony Squad
Characters						
Good	1	1	1	2	2	1
Bad	2	2	3	2	2	2
Mixed	0	0	1	1	0	1
Final consequences						
Good	1	2	1	2	2	0
Bad	2	0	3	2	2	4
Mixed	0	1	1	1	0	0
Motivations						
Good	2	2	1	2	1	1
Bad	2	2	3	2	2	4
Mixed	0	0	0	0	0	1
Immediate consequences						
Good	3	2	2	2	2	0
Bad	3	3	1	2	2	5
Mixed	0	1	3	2	2	1

It is apparent from Table 11 that the two children's programs present the fewest characters, all of whom are viewed primarily as either good or bad, but not both. Their motivations for violence are either good or bad, and the consequences to them are either good or bad (except in one instance). The two westerns appear to be the most complicated of the programs. They have the largest number of characters, with both good and evil often seen embodied in one character. Consequences to those participating in violence are seen more as bittersweet than are consequences to characters in the other two program types. The two crime programs differ considerably from each other. *Felony Squad* is a program filled with bad characters, whose motivations for violence are bad and for whom the consequences of violence are bad. *Adam 12* is a simpler story that pits good guys against bad and distributes the motivations and consequences accordingly.

It was not the intent of this study to content-analyze a set of contemporary television programs. Gerbner (1971) has supplied such data for the body of work of which this report is one part. However, the diversity in presentation across programs—even programs of one designated type—was great in the sample of programs used here, and we wished to indicate this fact in Table 11. Such diversity in presentation has implications for the results we could obtain and for the inferences one might wish to make about the effects on children of viewing contemporary television programs.

Response hierarchy. Mean scores on the response hierarchy measure were calculated as described early in this paper. Analyses were performed on both physical and verbal aggression scores. However, only the results for physical aggression will be reported, since the two scores are neither conceptually nor statistically independent ($r = .40$ in this study).

The six stimulus programs differed in the amount of violence they presented and in the portrayal of the motivations for and consequences of violence. Table 12 presents the program characteristics as judged by the adult raters. The children's programs are the least violent and also present the best consequences for aggression. The other two types of programs are more violent and contain more varied presentations of motivations and consequences. In general, the more violent programs were rated as presenting less good motivations ($r = -.42$) and

Table 12: Adult raters' judgments of portrayal of amount
of violence and of overall motivations for and overall
consequences of violence in each television program

	Rocket Robin Hood	Batman	Rifleman	Have Gun	Adam 12	Felony Squad
Violence rating*	3	1	5	7	2	7
Percent raters saying motivations for violence were "good"	.26	.33	.49	.29	.38	.09
Percent raters saying consequences of violence were "good"	.46	.50	.38	.33	.28	.03

*1 = least violence portrayed; 7 = most violence portrayed

consequences (r= -.64). Acceptability of the motivations and consequences within each program was relatively similar (r= .66 between
motivations and consequences).

Although it is apparent from Table 12 that an independent assessment
of the influence of violence, motivations and consequences on later aggression was not possible, *best estimates* of the influence of each of
these variables, in interaction with age and understanding, follow.
Figure 9 shows the number of physical aggression responses made by Ss
at each grade level for each of the six programs. In conjunction with the
program characteristics (Table 12) and the three understanding measures (Figures 5, 6, and 7) they represent the data included in the analyses
that follow.

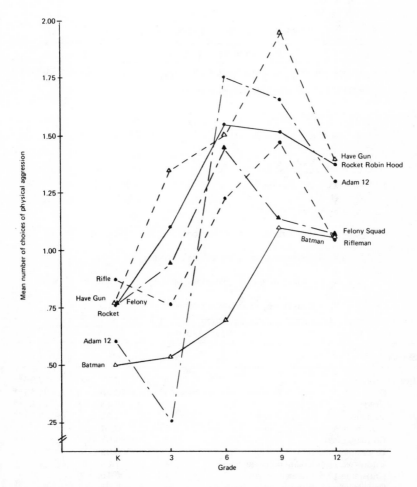

Figure 9:   Choice of physical aggression following viewing of entire television program by grade and program

Our general model postulates that the probability of aggression following exposure to television programming at least depends upon the amount of violence in the program, the motivations for it, the consequences for it, how well the motivations are understood, and how well the consequences are understood. In order to test this model, we performed a regression analysis using physical aggression as the dependent variable and the following independent variables: sex of S, grade of S, amount of violence in program, goodness of motivations for violence, goodness of final consequence of violence, understanding of motivations, understanding of immediate consequences, understanding of final consequences, and consistency-inconsistency of the response hierarchies for all six situations. In the first analysis, all Ss and all programs were combined into one regression equation. In six subsequent

Table 13: Results of regression analysis

Regression equation

$$Y = 0.53X_1 + 0.04X_2 + 0.08X_3 - 0.37X_4 + 0.76X_5 + 0.20X_6 - 0.22X_7 + 0.07X_8 + 0.03X_9 - 0.52$$

Where Y = Choice of physical aggression

X_1 = Sex

X_2 = Grade

X_3 = Violence

X_4 = Motivations

X_5 = Consequences

X_6 = Understanding of motivations

X_7 = Understanding of immediate consequences

X_8 = Understanding of final consequences

X_9 = Consistency of response hierarchies

ANOVA Table

Source	df	MS	F
Regression	9	3.97	7.56**
Sex	1	18.26	34.45**
Grade	1	10.43	19.67**
Violence	1	3.83	7.22**
Motivations	1	0.14	
Consequences	1	1.01	
Understand motives	1	0.85	
Understand immediate consequences	1	1.05	
Understand final consequences	1	0.16	
Consistency of response hierarchy	1	0.05	
Residual	1261	0.53	

**$p < .01$

analyses, each program was analyzed separately, with sex, grade, understanding of motivations, immediate consequences, and final consequences as the five independent variables.

The results of the regression analysis including all Ss and all programs are presented in Table 13. Only three variables contributed significantly to prediction of physical aggression. Sex is the most powerful predictor of choice of physical aggression after viewing television programs, with boys more aggressive than girls. Grade significantly predicts physical aggression; children chose more physical aggression with increasing age. Finally, the amount of violence in the program a child views predicts how aggressively he or she will respond after viewing it, with the more violent programs producing more aggressive responses in viewers. Neither the motivations for violence, the consequences of violence, nor the understanding of these variables predicted later aggressive responses. Finally, the consistency of S's response hierarchy is not related to the amount of physical aggression he chooses.

Similar analyses were performed on each program separately to better assess the role of understanding of motivations and consequences in determining subsequent aggression. Sex and grade of Ss again predicted physical aggression. Understanding of the motivations for and consequences of violence in each program never accounted for a significant proportion of the variability in the aggression scores. The regression analyses for each program separately were performed once with all Ss and once with only those Ss who were consistent on all six items of the response hierarchy. There were no differences in the results of these two analyses.

However, it is interesting to note the differences across the six programs in percentage of Ss whose hierarchies were all consistent:

Rocket Robin Hood	20%
Batman	51%
Rifleman	28%
Have Gun	55%
Adam 12	50%
Felony Squad	21%

There is no obvious reason for these differences. The possibility was examined that *Rocket Robin Hood, Rifleman,* and *Felony Squad* present motivations and consequences not consonant with the amount of violence presented. It was not apparent, however, that the portrayals in these programs are any more confusing in their message about the desirability of physical aggression than are the portrayals in the other programs. It is unlikely that the program differences are due to S differences, since assignment to programs was random. The explanation awaits more data.

It had been predicted that the effects of exposure to different television portrayals of motivations and consequences would become more discriminable with increasing age. Such an interaction is not implied by

Figure 9, but it cannot be directly tested with regression analysis. To test for interactions between grade level and various presentation variables, three three-factor ANOVAs were performed on physical aggression scores. In all three analyses, sex and grade comprised two of the factors, with the third factor either amount of violence portrayed (low, moderate, high), evaluation of motivations for violence (bad, moderately bad, moderately good, good), or evaluation of consequences of violence (bad, bad/good, good). Figures 10, 11, and 12 chart mean physical aggression scores for each grade by each of these latter three categories.

The analyses in which the third factor was amount of violence portrayed revealed a significant main effect for sex ($F=32.77$; $df=1,241$; p

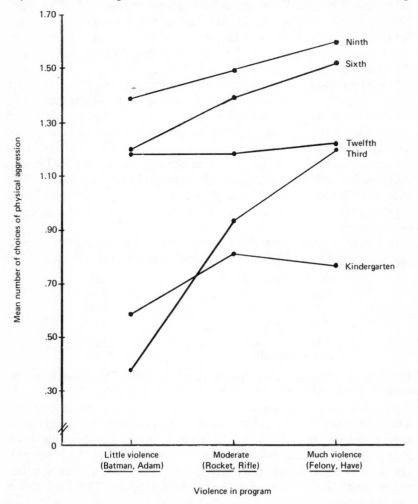

Figure 10:   Choice of physical aggression following viewing of entire television program by grade and amount of violence

< .01), with boys responding more aggressively than girls. There was also a significant effect for grade ($F = 10.76$; df = 4,241; $p < .01$), with older children generally responding more aggressively than younger children, although twelfth graders failed to maintain the pattern (see Figure 10). Finally, and most important, there was a significant main effect for amount of violence portrayed in the program, with the two most violent programs producing the most subsequent physical aggression and the two least violent programs producing the least subsequent physical aggression ($F = 4.61$; df = 2,241; $p < .05$).

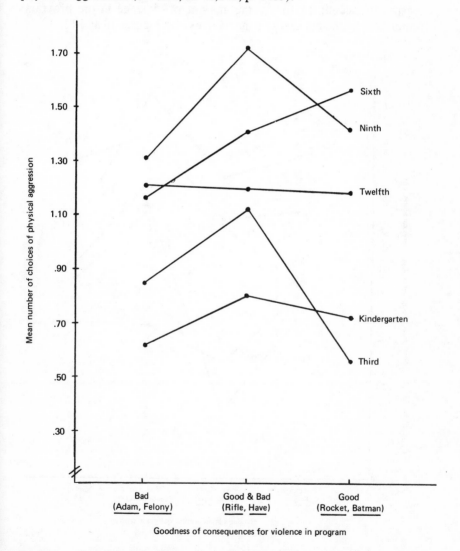

Figure 11: Choice of physical aggression following viewing of entire television program by grade and consequences for violence

In the two analyses using motivations and consequences for violence as the third factors, sex and grade are again significant, as they should be since their mean square terms are the same and the error term changes only slightly. There was no main effect for consequences. There was, however, a main effect for evaluation of motivations (F=5.58; df=2,231; p <.01), with the order of conditions from most to least physical aggression being,: moderately bad, bad, good, and moderately good. Although one might wish to explain these latter results in terms of the mediating influence of portrayed motivations, they are probably most reasonably accounted for by the amount of violence in the programs rather than by the motivations themselves (see Figures 10 and 12).

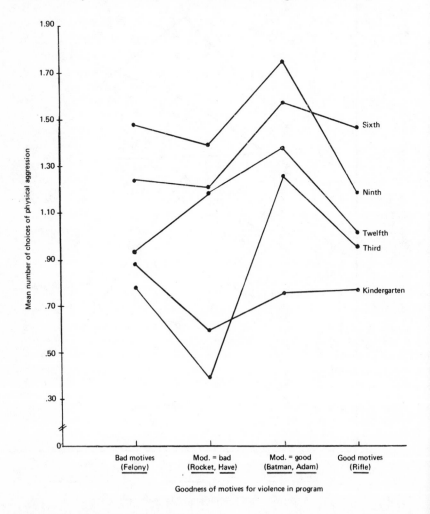

Figure 12:   Choice of physical aggression following viewing of entire television program by grade and motivations for violence

There were no significant or nearly significant interactions in any of the three ANOVAs. This lack of significant interactions is important in that it demonstrates no statistical support for the hypothesis that the effects of violent programming will change with the child's level of development and the context within which violence is displayed.

No further analyses were performed on the response hierarchy scores. Whatever analysis was performed, the amount of violence in the program affected the amount of aggression subsequently chosen. Nothing else about the program—the context within which violence was presented—seemed to influence subsequent aggression. Furthermore, our measures of understanding of the cues hypothesized to control aggression—motivations and consequences—did not relate at all to aggression choices. These results are not encouraging in their implications; however, they should be interpreted with some caution. All children were tested on their understanding of the motivations and consequences in the programs *before* they were tested on the response hierarchy. This may confound the results for the response hierarchy. Work by Collins (see Experiment 4) suggests that such confounding might, in fact, possibly have occurred.

Discussion

The study reported in this section was designed to provide information about how much is understood of the motivations for and the consequences of violence in contemporary television programs. Children between kindergarten and twelfth grade were tested. Ninth and twelfth graders understood most of the motivations for violent acts and the immediate and final consequences to characters participating in violence. Kindergarteners apparently understood very little about the motivations and consequences for violence, performing at the level of chance on items dealing with motivations and immediate consequences and slightly better than chance for items about final consequences. Third and sixth graders understood a moderate amount about motivations and consequences. It is possible that the poor results with young children were due to the testing technique. Yet in pretesting, it was adjudged the best of several techniques, providing children with verbal and pictorial descriptions of all answers and requiring them only to recognize the one correct alternative out of four.

Although older children understood motivations better than they understood consequences, there was no indication that younger children understood consequences better than motivations or vice versa. Whether these results are primarily determined by the clarity of presentation of the motivations and consequences in television programs or whether they truly reflect relatively equal understanding of motivations and consequences can only be determined by further work.

The amount children understood about motivations and consequences depended heavily on the specific program being tested. Even though programs could be reliably divided into children's programs, westerns, and adult crime programs, this categorization did not predict how well any program would be understood by children of a given age. For example, kindergarteners understood quite a bit about the final consequences in three of the programs and not much about final consequences in the other three programs—and there was one children's program, one western, and one adult crime program in each group. The two programs whose motivations for violence were understood best and worst were both children's programs. The lack of congruence between the apparent intended audience of a program and how well that audience actually understands the program was notable. It should cause parents and producers to ponder their ability to predict what their children understand about contemporary television programs.

If the messages presented in television programs about the motivations for and consequences of violence are received, then the viewer's evaluation of these motivations and consequences and the characters associated with them should correspond to that intended by the program. The results of this study suggest that this is the case. The majority of tested children of all ages tended to agree in their evaluations of characters, motivations, and consequences. These evaluations, with one exception, also usually agreed with those of adults, which were elicited under different conditions from the children's. Children did, however, tend to evaluate consequences from society's point of view, while adults evaluated from the individual character's point of view.

Unfortunately, whether or not children understand the motivations for and consequences of violence does not predict the results of exposure to these motivations and consequences when they are associated with violent actions. If one measures aggression subsequent to viewing contemporary television programs containing violence, one finds that it is the amount of violence in the program, not the motivations and consequences for it, and not how much is understood about these motivations and consequences, that predicts subsequent aggression. In this instance children were given equally plausible nonaggressive or even prosocial activities that could be chosen in place of aggression, yet the more violent the program they watched, the more aggression they chose. The results suggest that these effects are strongest at third, sixth, and ninth grades, weaker at kindergarten and weakest at twelfth grade. However, there is no statistical support for the suggestion that the effects of exposure to violent television programs differ with the age of the viewer.

One might then conclude that when television violence influences subsequent choice of aggressive and prosocial actions in situations in which one is angered or annoyed, it is the amount of violence one has been exposed to rather than the motivations for or consequences of this violence that will affect how aggressive one is. The more one has been exposed to violence, the more aggressive one is likely to be. This conclusion must, of course, be tempered by informed evaluation of the context within which these results were obtained.

EXPERIMENT 2:
MOTIVATIONS AND CONSEQUENCES FOR VIOLENCE AND SUBSEQUENT AGGRESSIVE RESPONSES ACROSS AGE

The experiment reported in this section examines the role of the motivations for and consequences of violence in contemporary television programs in modifying the effects of exposure to such violence. It allows better inferences about the effects of motivations and consequences *per se* than were possible in Experiment 1, but in doing so sacrifices the use of entire, unedited contemporary television programs.

The experimental and theoretical rationale for the work reported in this section has already been presented. The original hypotheses were as follows:

1. Exposure to violence committed with good motivations will elicit more frequent selection of aggressive responses in anger-provoking situations than exposure to violence committed with bad motivations.

2. Exposure to violence concluding with good consequences will elicit more frequent selection of aggressive responses in anger-provoking situations than exposure to violence concluding with bad consequences.

3. Differences in the effects of exposure to violence with good and bad motivations or consequences will increase with age.

4. For young children differences in the effects of exposure to violence with good and bad consequences will be greater than they will be in the effects of exposure to violence with good and bad motivations.

The results of Experiment 1 suggest that hypothesis 4 will not be supported. Young children did not show any evidence of understanding motivations better than consequences, and older children understood motivations better than consequences. Hence one would predict either no differences at any age between the effects of motivations and consequences or perhaps a greater effect for motivations than for consequences, especially at older ages.

However, Experiment 1 also suggested that the motivations for and/or consequences of aggression—and what is understood about them—do not modify aggressive tendencies after exposure to televised aggression and the motivations and consequences associated with it. This implies that hypotheses 1, 2, and 3 would receive little support in the present study. However, due to the problems of (1) nonindependent testing of aggressive preference and understanding and (2) nonindependence of depicted aggression, motivations, and consequences, hypotheses 1, 2, and 3 were considered viable.

For subsidiary analyses, a nonviolent television program was included in the experimental design. It provides some estimate of both the effect of exposure to violence regardless of the motivations and consequences associated with it and the extent to which motivations and consequences do in fact modify the effect of exposure to violence.

Method

Stimuli. Five different television programs were taped off the air and edited to provide one program containing no violence and little action and four programs containing violence and action. The four violent programs were *McCloud, Mod Squad, Gunsmoke,* and *Silent Force*[7] and respectively filled the following categories in relationship to all violent actions within the program: good motivations—good consequences; good motivations—bad consequences; bad motivations—good consequences; and bad motivations—bad consequences. The categorizations of these four tapes were agreed upon by graduate students, research assistants, and faculty members, but they were not independently assessed by a group of adults from the community. The nonviolent, low active program was a *Wide World of Adventure* travelogue on Austria. All tapes were 20 to 30 minutes long, black and white, with all commercials removed and program titles and credits left in.

Subjects. Ss were 62 preschoolers, 40 fifth graders, and 30 twelfth graders, with about equal numbers of boys and girls at each grade. Fifth and twelfth grade Ss attended schools in a nearby community while preschoolers attended Stanford University Nursery School.

Procedure. Ss were tested twice, approximately 14 days apart for fifth and twelfth graders and 21 days apart for preschoolers. At the first session, during regular school hours, the response hierarchy was administered by one of three possible female Es. For fifth and twelfth graders, Ss were in mixed sex groups of five to ten; preschoolers were tested individually.

The second session, also during regular school hours, was again directed by one of three possible female Es. Es were counterbalanced over groups for both the before and the after test, with the same E administering the response hierarchy for both the before and after tests and a different E presenting the television program. All Ss viewed the television program in mixed-sex groups. Fifth and twelfth graders were tested in the same groups, and preschoolers were tested individually. The two forms of the response hierarchy for older children were counterbalanced across groups for fifth and twelfth graders; the two forms for younger children were counterbalanced within groups of preschoolers. Ss were randomly assigned to conditions.

Ss were told that we were interested in what children of different ages thought about different types of television programs. They were asked to relax and view the program. Afterwards we would fill time with the response hierarchy, which they were familiar with, for two reasons: we wanted the results of it to compare with the previous administration; and the opinion questionnaire would be more representative of their true opinions if some time elapsed between television viewing and completion of the questionnaire. Preschoolers were not given any rationale for activities except the E's desire to know what children thought about different types of television programs. Ss then viewed one program, completed the response hierarchy, and filled out a short questionnaire about the program. The questionnaire asked for their evaluations of the motivations for and consequences of all aggressive acts within the program, an evaluation of how violent the program was, whether they had seen this particular program or programs like it, whether it was like television they watched, and whether what they saw actually occurred in real life.

Subject loss. The attrition rate from the before test to the after test was quite high. Table 14 presents the number of boys and girls tested both times for each grade and program and the number of other children who completed only the before test. There were three such children in the fifth grade; all were absent from school on the unannounced days of testing. There were 27 such children in preschool: 18 did not return to

Table 14: Number of subjects begun and completed
by sex, grade, aggressive content, and depicted motivations
and consequences for aggression

		Before and after test					Before test only
		Aggressive content				Nonaggressive content	
Motivations		Good	Good	Bad	Bad	- -	
Consequences		Good	Bad	Good	Bad	- -	
Preschool	Girls	3	3	3	3	3	16
	Boys	5	3	3	5	4	11
	Total	8	6	6	8	7	27
Fifth	Girls	5	6*	4	2	5*	2
	Boys	4	2	3	4	2	1
	Total	9	8	7	6	7	3
Twelfth	Girls	3	1	3	2	3	4
	Boys	0	3	2	0	2	7
	Total	3	4	5	2	5	11

*Includes one girl who was angry about missing P.E. to participate in the experiment and whose change score was considerably greater than any other S's. This girl was excluded from all data analyses.

summer session although they had preregistered for it (the before test was at the end of spring session and the after test at the beginning of summer session); six were not tested because their parents did not allow them to watch the type of programs we were showing, and three were consistently absent or resistant to testing. The 11 twelfth graders who did not show up for the after test are not easily accounted for. The after test was administered during the period of semester final examinations, and many students elected to attend only those classes for which they had exams. The experiment was unannounced, so perhaps these Ss were diligently studying rather than attending the class in which the experiment was to take place.

Table 15: Evaluation of perceived motivations and consequences by good-bad depiction and grade*

A. Perceived motivations

			Portrayed motivations	
			Good	Bad
Grade	Preschool	x̄	3.57	4.00
		sd	1.92	1.65
		N	14	14
	Fifth	x̄	2.38	2.38
		sd	1.22	1.00
		N	16	13
	Twelfth	x̄	2.71	3.43
		sd	1.03	0.90
		N	7	7

*Larger number equals worse motivations

B. Perceived consequences

			Portrayed consequences	
			Good	Bad
Grade	Preschool	x̄	4.29	3.29
		sd	1.44	1.98
		N	14	14
	Fifth	x̄	2.81	3.08
		sd	0.81	1.09
		N	16	13
	Twelfth	x̄	3.38	4.33
		sd	1.22	0.75
		N	8	6

*Larger number equals worse consequences

Results

The analyses for this study were carried out primarily with the pre-schoolers and fifth graders, since data were available for only a few twelfth graders. Where appropriate in tables and figures, the data for the twelfth graders have been included to give an indication of the probable direction of the results if more Ss were run. However, all results should be interpreted with some caution since even the number of preschool and fifth grade subjects in each cell is small.

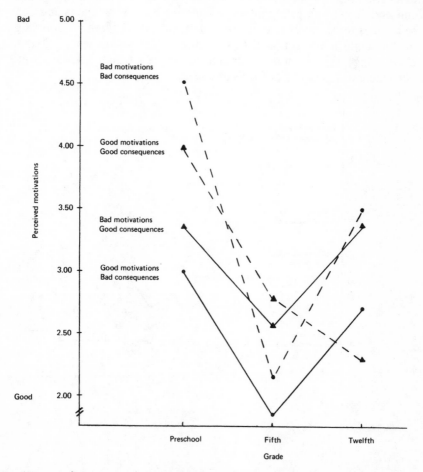

Figure 13: Evaluation of perceived motivations for violence by depiction of motivations and consequences and grade level

Scores on the two questions about the motivations for and consequences of aggression in each of the programs were analyzed to test the success of the motivation and consequence manipulations. Mean scores on these questions, presented in Table 15 and graphed in Figures 13 and 14, indicate that the manipulations were only partially successful. Preschoolers apparently understood the motivations and not the consequences, fifth graders the consequences and not the motivations, and twelfth graders both motivations and consequences.

Preschool and fifth grade Ss' scores on the motivations and consequences questions were analyzed in three-way ANOVAs (grade by depiction of motivation by depiction of consequence).[8] In both analyses there was a significant effect for grade (F = 12.08; df = 1,49; p < .01 for evaluation of motivation and F = 4.77; df = 1,49; p < .05 for evaluation of consequences), with fifth graders considering both motivations and consequences to be better than preschoolers did. There were no other significant main or interaction effects in either analysis—suggesting, among other things, that the motivation and consequence manipulations were not successful for all Ss or for Ss of any one age.

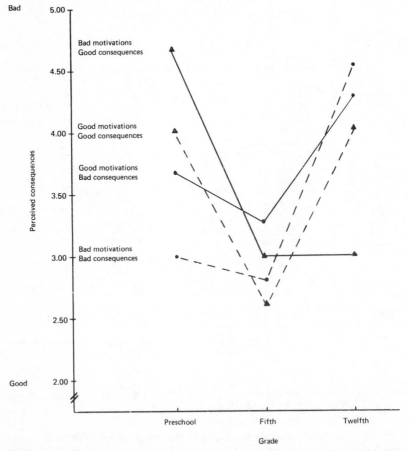

Figure 14: Evaluation of perceived consequences of violence by depiction of motivations and consequences and grade level

A similar analysis was carried out on Ss' perception of the amount of violence in each program. These data are presented graphically in Figure 15. The perceived aggression in the travelogue has been included for comparison and indicates that all Ss may have considered it less violent than the other four programs, although it is not until twelfth grade that there is a clear differentiation between ratings for violent and nonviolent programs. There are no obvious differences between the perceived violence ratings of the four violent programs. Analysis of variance with the preschool and fifth grade Ss for the four violent programs (grade by motivation by consequence) revealed no significant main or interaction terms whatsoever. One can probably conclude that the four violent programs do not differ in the perceived amount of aggression they contain and certainly do not differ in perceived aggression by virtue of the depicted motivations and consequences.

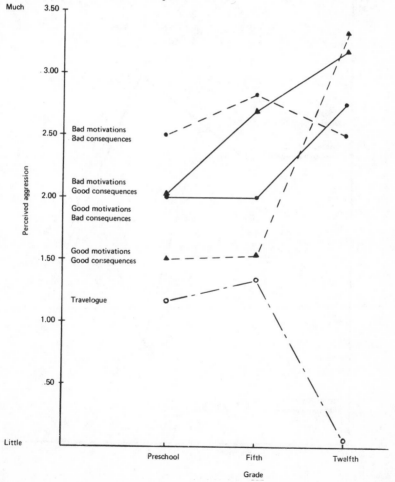

Figure 15: Amount of perceived aggression by depiction of motivation and consequences and grade level

Response hierarchy scores were coded as in Experiment 1, and analyses were performed on the physical aggression scores. Most analyses employed a change score (physical aggression after viewing minus physical aggression at least two weeks prior to viewing). These data are presented graphically in Figure 16. A three-way ANOVA for the preschool and fifth grade Ss' scores revealed only one significant main effect and no significant interactions, providing support for hypothesis 1 and no support for hypotheses 2, 3, and 4. Those programs whose depicted motivations for aggression were bad produced a slight decrease in aggres-

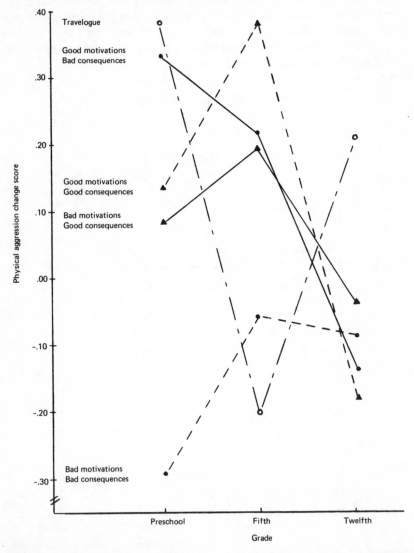

Figure 16:   Response hierarchy change scores by depiction of motives and consequences and by grade level

sion from the before to the after test, while those programs whose motivations were good produced a slight increase in aggressive responses ($F = 4.10$; $df = 1,49$; $p < .05$). Figure 16 suggests that this effect is due almost entirely to the program with bad motivations and bad consequences (*Silent Force*). However, t-tests between physical aggression change scores for this program and the next closest program (bad motivation and good consequences) did not approach significance ($t < 1$). Moreover, t-tests indicated that none of the change scores was significantly different from zero ($t < 1$).

Figure 16 includes the physical aggression change score for Ss who viewed the nonaggressive travelogue. The aggressiveness of these Ss relative to those who viewed the aggressive tapes varies with the age of the Ss. Although t-tests revealed no significant differences between the travelogue and any of the programs at any grade level generally for preschool Ss, exposure to the travelogue produced about as much change in aggressive choices as did three of the violent programs. For fifth graders it produced less change in aggressive choices than did three of the violent programs, and for twelfth graders it produced more change than any of the four violent programs.

Regression analyses were also performed on the physical aggression change scores to test for the effects of (1) exposure to aggressive content *per se* and (2) individual differences in perceived aggression, motivation, and consequences. Independent variables were sex, grade, depicted aggression, depicted motivation for aggression, depicted consequences for aggression, perceived aggression, perceived motivation, and perceived consequences. Scores from all five programs were included in the analysis. There were no significant predictors and no significant regression equation. There is a slight suggestion of the same effect for depicted motivation as that previously found in the ANOVA. Because regression analyses may be performed with missing data, a second analysis that included twelfth-grade Ss was run. Again there were no significant predictors and no significant regression equation.

Similar regression analyses were run using the physical aggression score immediately after television viewing as the dependent variable, and including the physical aggression score obtained in the before test as an additional independent variable. In these analyses the aggressiveness of a child on the before test was a good predictor of his aggressiveness after television viewing ($F = 61.27$; $df = 1,79$; $p < .01$ for all three grades and $F = 50.35$; $df = 1,60$; $p < .01$ for preschool and fifth grade Ss only). Boys were more aggressive than girls ($F = 5.93$; $df = 1,79$; $p < .05$ for all three grades and $F = 2.97$; $df = 1,60$; $p < .10$ for preschool and fifth-grade Ss only). There was also the suggestion that children who were more aggressive on the after test perceived the depicted consequences of aggression to be worse than children who were less aggressive ($F = 3.17$; $df = 1,79$; $p < .10$ for all three grades and $F = 3.68$; $df = 1,60$; $p < .10$ for preschool and fifth-grade Ss only).

These regression analyses suggest that there is no effect of exposure to aggressive and nonaggressive content that is consistent over age. (The regression analyses performed here cannot reflect interactions such as suggested by Figure 15.) They also provide no indication that an S's conception of the depicted aggression, motivations, or consequences is related to his subsequent aggressive behavior.

Discussion

The results of this study provide only scant support for the hypothesis that the type of motivations and consequences associated with aggressive behavior will modify the effects of exposure to such aggressive behavior. The data suggest that aggression performed with good motives may lead to greater subsequent aggression on the part of the viewer than aggression performed with bad motivations. There was no support for a similar effect of good and bad consequences for aggressive behavior, nor was there any indication statistically of a differential effect of motivations, consequences, or aggression on children of widely different ages.

These results, however, must be viewed with caution. Graphically they suggest that exposure to aggressive content—whatever the motivations and consequences associated with it—may have different effects (when compared with exposure to nonaggressive content) on children between the ages of four and 18. Moreover, the type of motivations and consequences associated with aggressive content may influence the subsequent aggressive behavior of young children and not that of older children. Yet a comfortable acceptance or rejection of these statements must rest on data from many more children and other programs.

EXPERIMENT 3:
JUSTIFICATION FOR AGGRESSION AND SUBSEQUENT AGGRESSIVE RESPONSES ACROSS AGE

In conjunction with this research contract, M. J. Nolan (1971) explored the relationship over age between portrayed justification for an aggressive display and the amount of subsequent aggression. Berkowitz and Rawlings, using college age males as Ss, have reported (1963) that aggression presented to adults as justified produced greater subsequent aggression than aggression presented as unjustified. Nolan sought to extend these findings to younger children. The theoretical and experimental rationale for the work has already been presented. The hypotheses were:

1. Exposure to justified aggression will elicit more frequent selection of aggressive responses in anger-provoking situations than exposure to less justified aggression.

2. Differences in the effects of exposure to justified and less justified aggression will increase with age.

Method

The same stimulus used by Berkowitz and Rawlings—a nine-minute 25-second prize fight scene from the movie *The Champion* (1949)—was selected for presentation. The Berkowitz and Rawlings introductions, which manipulated justification for the portrayed aggression, were used with some alterations. Language was simplified enough to make the content understandable to the youngest subjects in this study. Additionally, some aspects of the justification were altered.[9]

Thus in the aggression-justified condition in the present study, the loser was presented as a scheming manipulator who used friends and acquaintances to his own benefit. In the aggression-less-justified condition he was presented as an average fellow who only wanted to succeed as a boxer. The action in both conditions was identical: Midge Kelly, played by Kirk Douglas, was defeated in a bloody boxing match.

In order to mediate the stimulus via television, videotape recordings were made from the original film. A professional announcer recorded the two justification stories over the film sound track; this served as introduction to the action. This procedure differs from Berkowitz and Rawlings's procedure in which the stories were read to Ss before they began to view the film. For the fight itself, the original sound track was used.

Subjects. Ss were 51 fourth graders, 56 seventh graders, and 53 tenth graders, with about equal numbers of boys and girls at each grade. All attended parochial schools in nearby communities. Ss were assigned as an entire class to one of the two justification conditions. One male graduate student served as E throughout; however, a double-blind procedure was successfully maintained so that he remained unaware of condition assignments until the completion of the entire project.

Procedure. Ss were tested as a class during regular school hours. The situation was informal and, with one exception, outside regular classrooms. Ss were told they would be participating in two separate studies —one study of attitudes of children of different ages toward types of television movies, and the other a study of situation-specific behavior. E explained that attitude questionnaires were more effective if some time were allowed to elapse between seeing the movie and answering the questions about it. This time would be filled by the situation-specific behavior study.

With E out of the room, Ss watched the tape with one of the two justifications for the beating. At the conclusion of the tape E returned and administered the response hierarchy, using slides to portray the response pairs. After this a questionnaire about the film was administered. It consisted of several filler items and three items designed to measure

S's opinion about the character of the loser and whether he deserved to be beaten. Ss were then asked about the true nature of the experiment, which no one seemed to have divined. Finally, Ss were debriefed and all questions were answered.

Results

Scores on the two questions asking for evaluation of the loser's character and the one question asking whether he deserved to lose were analyzed to test success of the justification manipulation. Mean scores on these questions, presented in Table 16, indicate that Ss in all three grades understood the manipulation.

Table 16: Mean scores for perceived character of victim
and justification for loss
by justification condition and grade

Grade	Good person Aggression:		Fair in dealings Aggression:		Deserve to lose Aggression:	
	Justified	Less Justified	Justified	Less Justified	Justified	Less Justified
4	11.88	16.85	11.25	16.85	18.13	15.19
7	12.04	15.34	10.74	15.17	19.63	16.72
10	10.42	16.03	10.21	12.41	16.67	14.66
	High score means more desirable character		High score means more desirable character		High score means more deserving of beating	

Scores on each question were submitted to a three factor ANOVA (grade by sex by justification condition) which revealed a highly significant effect for justification in each case (first character evaluation question: $F=66.09$; second character evaluation question: $F=52.39$; deserve to lose question: $F=19.59$; with $df=1,148$ and $p < .001$ for all three).[10] Ss in the aggression-justified group were more likely to evaluate the loser's character as bad and more likely to feel that he deserved his beating than were Ss in the aggression-less-justified group. On the second character evaluation question there was also a grade by justification condition interaction ($F=3.14$; $df=2,148$; $p < .05$), due to greater between-condition differentiation among younger children.

Boys were more likely than girls to evaluate the character of the loser favorably on both character evaluation questions ($F=7.27$ and $F=4.36$ with $df=1,148$ and $p < .01$ and $p < .05$ respectively). There was greater between-condition differentiation among boys than among girls on the first character evaluation question ($F=10.19$; $df=1,148$; $p < .01$), and there was a significant effect for grade on the second character evaluation question ($F=8.34$; $df=2,148$; $p < .01$), with positive evaluation inversely related to grade. Grade was also significant on the question asking whether the loser deserved his beating ($F=6.26$; $df=2,148$, $p < .01$), but the order from most to least deserved was seventh, fourth, and tenth grades. There was no effect for sex on the latter question. In summary, then, there was clear evidence that the justification manipulation was successful.

Response hierarchy scores were coded as in previous experiments. Scores were transformed to stabilize variance across cells (Y^1 = arcsin $Y/18$). All analyses were then performed on both raw and transformed scores. Since results were the same regardless of which scores were used, only transformed data will be presented. Scores for choice of verbal aggression were also analyzed, but since they were neither conceptually nor statistically independent of those for physical aggression (r = -.82 for both fourth and seventh grade and -.89 for tenth grade), they too will not be reported.

Figure 17 presents mean physical aggression scores by justification, condition, and grade. These scores were submitted to a three-way

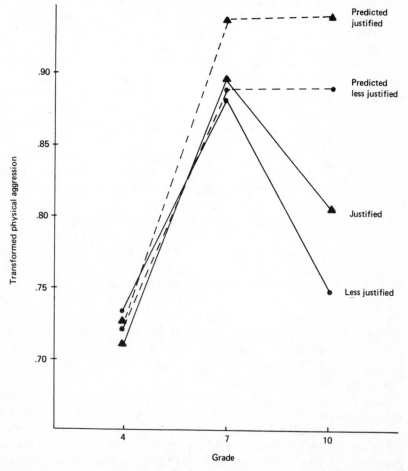

Figure 17: Mean transformed physical aggression scores and predicted physical aggression scores by justification condition and grade

ANOVA (sex by grade by justification). There was a significant effect for grade (F=4.56; df=2,148; p < .05), where order of grade from least to most aggressive was fourth, tenth, seventh. There was also an effect for sex (F=40.52; df=1,148; p < .001), boys consistently responding more aggressively than girls. There was no effect for justification condition (F< 1), nor were there any significant interactions.

These results failed to support either hypothesis 1 (that viewing justified aggression would lead to more aggressive responses than would viewing less justified aggression) or hypothesis 2 (that the justification manipulation would be more effective with older children than with younger). However, as Figure 17 illustrates, there was some indication of greater differentiation between conditions among the oldest Ss but not among the two younger groups. This differentiation was in the predicted direction.

In order to test for this effect, a planned comparison (Hays, 1963) embodying both hypotheses 1 and 2 was performed. The predicted results embodied by the planned comparison are superimposed upon the obtained results in Figure 17. The sum of squares for the planned comparison belongs to the sum of squares for grade, condition, and grade by condition. The planned comparison accounted for a significant proportion of this variability (F=6.55; df=1,148; p < .05). The F ratio for the residual was not significant, indicating that the planned comparison accounted for the major portion of the variability and providing some tentative support for hypothesis 2.

Finally, regression analyses were performed to test the effects of individual differences in understanding the justification manipulation. Four analyses, one for all Ss combined and one for subjects within each grade level, were performed, using choice of physical aggression as the dependent variable. For the combined analysis, independent variables were grade, sex, justification manipulation, S's rating of whether the loser deserved his beating, and S's evaluation of the loser's character (sum of two evaluation scores). With the exception of grade, the within-grade analyses contained the same independent variables.

Table 17 presents the results of all four regression analyses. Major emphasis should perhaps be put upon the ability of Ss' ratings of "deserved to lose" to predict subsequent aggression. Adult judges agreed that this variable was most related to the concept of justified or unjustified aggression. The loser's character was considered less central to evaluating justification for aggression.

In all four analyses, sex predicts choice of physical aggression, with boys more aggressive than girls at each grade. Justification manipulation never predicts choice of physical aggression. Ss' perceptions of whether the loser deserved his beating predicts physical aggression for all grades combined: Ss who see the aggression as more justified choose more aggressive responses themselves. This effect is greatest at fourth grade and nonexistent by tenth grade. The perceived character of the loser

Table 17: Results of regression analyses on physical aggression response hierarchy scores for three grades separately and combined

	All grades			Fourth grade			Seventh grade			Tenth grade		
	df	MS	F	df	MS	F	df	MS	F	df	MS	F
Regression	5	0.91	12.30**	4	0.40	4.17**	4	0.52	7.66**	4	0.26	4.72**
Grade	1	0.07	1.00	-	-	-	-	-	-	-	-	-
Sex	1	3.16	45.14**	1	0.94	9.40**	1	1.61	23.00**	1	1.00	20.00**
Condition	1	0.01	0.14	1	0.00	0.00	1	0.01	0.14	1	0.01	0.20
Deserves	1	0.77	11.00**	1	0.31	3.10[a]	1	0.17	2.43	1	0.02	0.40
Character	1	0.54	7.71**	1	0.36	3.60[a]	1	0.30	4.29*	1	0.00	0.00
Residual	154	0.07		46	0.10		51	0.07		48	0.05	

[a] $p < .10$
* $p < .05$
** $p < .01$

also predicts later choice of physical aggression, but surprisingly, those who rate the loser as a better person chose more physical aggression. As before, the effects of perception of character are strongest at fourth and seventh grades and not evident at tenth grade. In the overall analysis, grade is not a significant predictor of choice of physical aggression.

Discussion

The results suggest that the justification manipulations were effectively transmitted to all Ss regardless of their age, but that these manipulations did not influence Ss' later level of aggression. However, Ss' own evaluations of the justification and the character of the loser did influence their subsequent aggression. Ss who felt the beating was deserved were more likely to choose aggression to resolve their own conflicts; Ss who evaluated the loser's character more favorably also chose more aggression. These results are stronger with younger Ss; there are no such effects with the oldest Ss.

The positive relationship between favorable evaluation of the loser's character and subsequent physical aggression is puzzling. The justification manipulation produced the expected character evaluations at all grades: a less favorable evaluation in the justified condition and a more favorable in the unjustified. Yet a more favorable evaluation predicted more choices of physical aggression. An explanation should be sought through further research.

In summary, it appears that what is understood about the justification for observed aggression may influence subsequent aggression. However, in this study this was only true for younger children—perhaps those who do not discount television programs as fantasy. Finally, it should be noted that adult judgments about the justification that is being presented are not adequate for predicting the effect of the justification on children's subsequent aggression.

EXPERIMENT 4:
TEMPORAL SEPARATION OF MOTIVATIONS AND CONSEQUENCES FOR VIOLENCE AND SUBSEQUENT AGGRESSIVE RESPONSES ACROSS AGE

In conjunction with this research project, W. A. Collins investigated the effects over age of varying temporal separation between portrayals of aggression and the motivations for and consequences of it. In addition to measuring effects of varying temporal separation on understanding of motivations for and consequences of an aggressive sequence and on aggressive responses subsequent to viewing, he also attempted to correlate measures of understanding with measures of aggressive response. A detailed treatment of his research may be found in Collins

(1971). The previous work that relates to Collins's experiment was presented at the beginning of this paper. The hypotheses suggested by this work were:

1. Understanding of the motivations for and consequences of aggressive behavior will be greater when these events are contiguous in time than when they are separated in time by intervening events.

2. Differences in the effects of temporal separation on understanding will decrease with increasing age.

3. Temporal separation between negative motivations and negative consequences and the aggressive acts to which they pertain will increase the likelihood of subsequent aggressive behavior.

4. Differences in the effects of temporal separation on aggressive behavior will decrease with increasing age.

5. The better negative motivations and consequences for modeled aggression are understood the less likely is subsequent aggressive behavior to occur.

Method

Stimuli. One program from the then new (but now defunct) television series *Silent Force* was selected. It was edited for two purposes: to permit clear predictions about the behavioral effects of the aggressive content, and to provide two degrees of temporal separation (high and low) between motivations and aggression and between aggression and consequences. Adults viewed the program in its entirety and rated it as described in Experiment 1. In addition, viewers listed the motivations for and consequences of each aggressive act. All acts judged aggressive by the raters, except one at the end of the program, were removed. The remaining aggressive scene met two criteria: (1) both motivations and consequences for the aggression were judged to be negative; (2) neither the motivations nor consequences were themselves aggressive. Thus *all* aggressive behavior in the program was negatively motivated and led to negative consequences, thereby avoiding some of the problems encountered in our validation study with four-year-olds.

Temporal separation between motivations and aggression and between aggression and consequences was manipulated through placement of sequences of four one-minute commercials. In the high separation condition, one commercial sequence was placed between motivations and aggression and another commercial sequence between aggression and consequences. In the low separation condition, both sequences were placed near the beginning of the program, before portrayal of motivations, aggressive act, and consequences. The commercials were neither violent nor highly active, but their settings were similar to those in the program.

Final versions of the edited program were on black and white video-tape and lasted approximately 20 minutes. A black and white 8 mm. sound documentary film on California, also 20 minutes in duration, served as the stimulus for the control group.

Subjects. Ss were 99 third graders, 138 sixth graders, and 112 tenth graders, with about equal numbers of boys and girls at each grade. All attended parochial schools in nearby communities.

Procedure. Ss were tested twice, approximately eighteen days apart. At the first session, the response hierarchy was administered via slides by one female E to an entire class in its own classroom.

The second session occurred during regular school hours for third and sixth graders and right after school for tenth graders. Ss within each classroom were randomly assigned to one of five treatment groups, with boys and girls as equally distributed as possible. These groups are presented in Figure 18, along with a diagram of the entire procedure. Three male and four female Es were used. Es for the two groups who answered the comprehension questionnaire were blind to the program viewed and the hypotheses of the study. The E who administered the response hierarchy and items associated with it did not know which group any S was in.

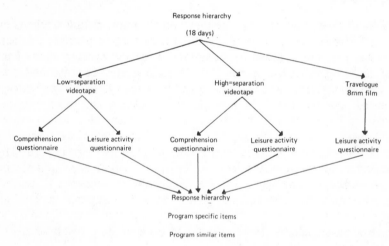

Figure 18: Five treatment groups with composition of subject groups at each point in the procedure

Ss in the four television groups were told that a coming development in home entertainment, the videotape recorder, was going to be demonstrated and that their opinions were desired. They were asked to relax and enjoy the program as they would at home. The appropriate tape of *Silent Force* was then shown. Ss in the control group were asked to look at the film on California in order to evaluate the film techniques used in it.

At the conclusion of the videotape half, the Ss in each separation condition completed the comprehension questionnaire, and half completed a questionnaire about leisure time activities. The latter questionnaire served as a control for the possible effects of the comprehension questionnaire on the response hierarchy and related items. All Ss in the control condition responded to the leisure time questionnaire. The comprehension questionnaire was similar to that employed in Experiment 1, although evaluations of motivation, consequences, and character were omitted. There were five questions about motivation, four about consequences, and one about the aggressive sequence in the final questionnaire. All items in both questionnaires were read to third graders; sixth and tenth graders worked on their own.

When the questionnaires were complete, all Ss returned to their classrooms, where they were administered the response hierarchy and six additional items. These additional items were in the same format as the response hierarchy items, with responses also presented in pairs on slides. Three situations presented conditions in which violence had occurred in the program (program-specific items). They were meant to test the likelihood that a child would advocate aggressive behavior under the conditions in which he had just seen it performed. The remaining three situations paralleled incidents which had contained aggression in the unedited program (program-similar items). The aggression had been edited out of the tapes the children had seen. These items were meant to test the likelihood that the depicted negative motivations and consequences would modify the advocacy of aggression in situations similar to the depicted ones and involving the same aggressor.

Results

Comprehension. 143 Ss viewed the high and low separation videotapes and also answered the comprehension questionnaire. The results over age are presented in Figure 19. The scores were subjected to a three-factor ANOVA (grade by sex by separation).[11] There was a significant main effect for grade ($F = 27.02$; $df = 2,131$; $p < .01$) with scores increasing with grade. There was no effect for sex ($F = 1.20$).

Contrary to hypothesis 1, there was no significant main effect of separation ($F = 1.27$; $df = 1,131$); understanding of motivations and consequences was no greater when these events were contiguous in time than when they were separated in time. Indeed, the results are in the opposite direction for the third and sixth graders. There were no significant interaction terms in the analysis of variance.

Hypothesis 2 (that the differences between the two conditions would decrease over grade) could not be tested in the standard analysis of variance because the predicted patterns of means would simultaneously reflect effects accounted for by separate terms in a three-way analysis of

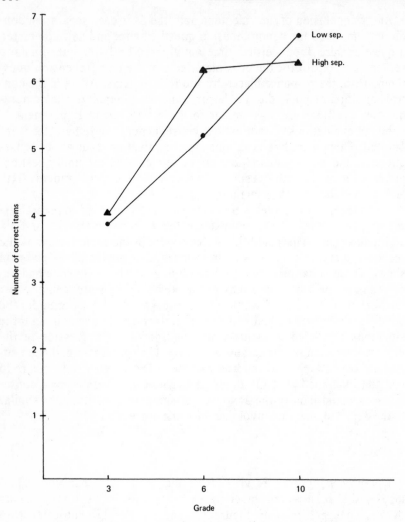

Figure 19: Mean comprehension scores by temporal separation and grade

variance. These terms are the main effects of grade and of separation and the interaction of grade and separation. The appropriate test for such a hypothesized pattern of means is a planned comparison (Hays, 1963). According to this procedure, a sum of squares with df = 1 is computed by associating observed cell means with coefficients which reflect the predicted pattern. These coefficients were -1, 2, 5 for third, sixth, and tenth graders in the low separation condition and -7, -2, 3 for the three grades in the high separation condition. The comparison accounted for a significant proportion of the between-group variance (F = 29.87; df = 1,131; p < .001), supporting hypothesis 2. However, the residual variance—that not accounted for by the predicted pattern—was also significant (F = 4.05; df = 10,131; p < .001).

Similar analyses were carried out separately for the five motivations and the four consequence questions. Results were quite similar to those just reported for the full score and will not be detailed here.

The results just reported were contrary to both prediction and pretest data. It was felt that differential attention to the two separation condition videotapes might provide an explanation. Es reported that third and sixth graders in the low separation condition lost interest when confronted with eight minutes of commercials (two sets of four minutes each) near the beginning of the program, and that their attention returned only when the aggressive sequence began. Such lack of attention during the early part of the program would mediate both against learning of characters' names (which was necessary to correctly respond to the questionnaire) and against learning much about motivations, which occurred prior to the aggressive sequence. Pretest Ss attended a different school and were attentive throughout both versions of the program.

In order to test this attention hypothesis, an additional group at each grade level viewed the videotape minus all commercials and then responded to the comprehension questionnaire. (Response hierarchy measures were not administered.) In all three grades, the no-commercial group scored higher on the comprehension test than did either of the two separation groups. However, t-tests between the no-commercial group and the higher of the two separation groups at each grade were never significant.

Response hierarchy and associated items. Figure 20 presents the before and after scores for the response hierarchy and the after scores for the program-specific and program-similar items. For the before scores, all Ss are combined at each grade, since there were no differences between any of the groups. The increasing aggressiveness with age on the before score corresponds to data reported elsewhere for the response hierarchy administered without exposure to aggressive stimuli. The curvilinear pattern for the after scores over age also corresponds to that reported after exposure to aggressive stimuli in Experiments 1 and 2.

Three physical aggression change scores were computed for each S by subtracting his preexposure response hierarchy mean from his postexposure mean for physical aggression, the response hierarchy items, the program-specific items, and the program-similar items. Change scores for verbal aggression were also computed, but since the stimulus aggression was primarily physical and since the physical and verbal scores are not independent, they will not be reported here. Results obtained in analyses of the verbal aggression scores were, however, similar to those reported here for physical aggression. Table 18 presents mean physical aggression change scores for each of the three measures.

The change scores were subjected to a four-factor ANOVA (grade by sex by separation condition by questionnaire type) in order to determine whether responding to the comprehension questionnaire influenced subsequent choices on the response hierarchy and related items. Control

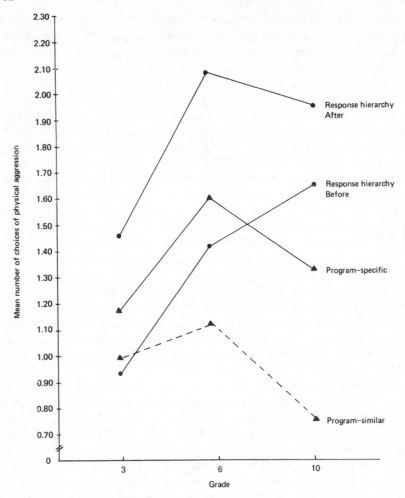

Figure 20:   Choice of physical aggression before and after treatment by item type and grade

group Ss, who responded only to the leisure time questionnaire, were excluded from this analysis.

While there was no significant effect for questionnaire in the response hierarchy change scores ($F<1$), there was an effect in both program-specific items ($F=13.62$; df=1,249; $p < .001$) and program-similar items ($F=4.61$; df=1,249; $p < .05$). Ss who completed the comprehension questionnaire responded more aggressively on program-related items than did Ss who completed the questionnaire unrelated to program content. While there was little indication of this effect on response hierarchy scores, the comprehension measure clearly sensitized Ss to program-related items.

Table 18: A. Mean physical aggression response hierarchy change scores by sex, grade, separation condition, and questionnaire type

| | | Comprehension questionnaire | | | Unrelated questionnaire | | |
| | | Grade | | | Grade | | |
Separation condition	Sex	3rd	6th	10th	3rd	6th	10th
Low	Boys	.92	.63	.48	.38	.78	.07
	Girls	.11	.90	.40	.12	.77	.52
High	Boys	.50	.80	.21	1.10	.51	.09
	Girls	.13	.67	.07	.56	.83	.10

B. Mean physical aggression program-specific change scores by sex, grade, separation condition, and questionnaire type

| | | Comprehension questionnaire | | | Unrelated questionnaire | | |
| | | Grade | | | Grade | | |
Separation condition	Sex	3rd	6th	10th	3rd	6th	10th
Low	Boys	.58	.48	.01	-.10	.18	-.23
	Girls	.11	.53	.54	-.10	.28	-.41
High	Boys	.65	.65	.11	-.62	.06	-.56
	Girls	.44	.27	.22	.02	.31	.00

C. Mean physical aggression program-similar change scores by sex, grade, separation condition, and questionnaire type

| | | Comprehension questionnaire | | | Unrelated questionnaire | | |
| | | Grade | | | Grade | | |
Separation condition	Sex	3rd	6th	10th	3rd	6th	10th
Low	Boys	.50	-.21	-.68	-.07	-.41	-1.10
	Girls	-.05	-.35	-.46	-.36	-.10	-.78
High	Boys	.48	.11	-.80	.05	-.32	-1.07
	Girls	.02	-.12	-.54	.06	-.22	-.54

The analyses also showed significant separation by questionnaire interactions for the program-related measures ($F = 27.41$ for program-specific and $F = 9.24$ for program-similar, with $df = 1,249$, $p < .001$ for both). Condition means for two measures showed that Ss who did not take the comprehension test changed markedly less in the low separation condition than in the high separation condition, while Ss who completed the comprehension test had change scores that were about the same in the two conditions. That is, taking the comprehension test appeared to wash out the effects of temporal separation. Although this interaction was not significant for the response hierarchy change scores, the means revealed a similar pattern in the low separation condition.

There were significant grade by questionnaire interactions for all three measures (F = 26.16 for response hierarchy, F = 14.60 for program-specific and F = 10.31 for program-similar; with df = 2,249 and p < .01 for all three), with the scores of third and tenth graders more affected by completing the comprehension questionnaire than the scores of sixth graders. There were also significant sex by questionnaire interactions for the two program-related measures (F = 27.45 for program-specific and F = 11.21 for program-similar; with df = 1,249 and p < .01 for both), with girls' change scores more affected by the comprehension test than boys' scores. There were no other significant interaction effects involving the questionnaires.

In summary, then, administration of the comprehension measure appeared to increase the likelihood of physically aggressive responses on the two program-related measures. This effect was more noticeable for Ss in the low separation condition than for Ss in the high separation condition. It also differed according to the age and sex of the S. Because of the contamination in change scores of Ss who had taken the comprehension questionnaire, subsequent analyses on response hierarchy and related scores were performed only with Ss who completed the leisure time questionnaire.

Mean change scores for the high and low separation and nonaggressive control conditions are presented in Figure 21 for all three grades and all three measures. The results for the response hierarchy will be presented in some detail here; then the results for the program-specific and program similar items will be presented briefly.

Response hierarchy change scores were submitted to a three-way ANOVA (grade by sex by condition). There was a significant effect for grade (F = 5.73; df = 2,188; p < .01), with the order from most to least change being sixth, third, and tenth. There was no significant effect for sex (F < 1). Girls and boys changed about the same amount, although boys chose more aggressive responses than did girls at each grade. There was a significant sex by grade interaction (F = 3.72; df = 2,188; p < .05) with third-grade girls showing less change than third-grade boys while girls in the other two grades changed more than the boys. There were no other significant interactions.

Contrary to hypothesis 3 (that temporal separation between negative motivation and consequences and aggression will increase subsequent aggression), there was no significant main effect for separation condition, nor was there a significant grade by condition interaction. However, t-tests between overall condition means showed that third graders' mean change score in the high separation condition was significantly higher than the mean in the low separation condition (t = 2.80; df = 188; p < .01). T-tests for differences between the film control group

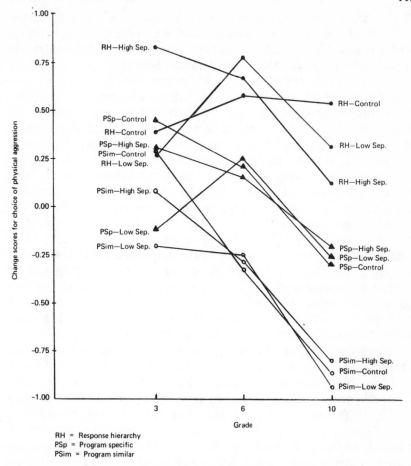

Figure 21:   Mean change scores for physical aggression by viewing condition, item type, and grade

and either of the two separation groups did not reach significance at any of the three grade levels. These t-test results provide tentative support for hypothesis 4 (that the effects of temporal separation on subsequent aggression will decrease with age).

Further support for this hypothesis comes from a planned comparison similar in conception to the one reported for comprehension scores. The coefficients for each grade in each condition were constructed to represent three aspects of the predicted pattern: (1) change scores would generally decrease over grade levels; (2) change scores would be greater in the high separation condition than in the low separation condition; and (3) the difference between the change scores in the two separation conditions would decrease over grades. The coefficients were 7, 2, -3 for grades 3, 6 and 10 in the high separation condition and 1, -2, -5 for Ss in the low separation condition. A significant proportion of the between-group variance was accounted for by this planned comparison (F=9.76;

df = 1, 188; p< .01). The residual sum of squares was not significant (F = 1.68; df = 16, 188). Thus the pattern of means representing hypothesis 4 accounted for most of the variability between the observed means in the experimental and control conditions at each age.

Results for the program-specific and program-similar items are presented in Figure 21. It is apparent that exposure to the videotaped programs did not influence the sixth and tenth graders' aggressive choices on the two sets of program-related items; the scores of the Ss in the high and low separation conditions are quite similar to the scores for Ss who had not even seen the program. However, among third graders, exposure to the videotaped program and temporal separation between motivation, aggression, and consequences do seem to matter. For program-specific items, third graders in the low separation condition change significantly less than third graders who saw the nonaggressive film (t = 2.33; df = 188; p < .02). As would be predicted, third graders in the high separation condition responded more aggressively than those in the low separation condition and less aggressively than those in the control condition, although neither difference was significant by t-test. For program-similar items and third-grade Ss, the order of the three groups from most to least change, is (again): control, high separation, low separation. None of the pairs of differences is significant.

Analysis of variance results for program-specific items showed that change scores decrease significantly with grade (F = 10.13; df = 2,188; p < .001). Third-grade girls change less than third-grade boys, while girls in the other two grades change more than the boys (F = 3.87; df = 2,188; p < .05). There were no other significant main or interaction effects.

Analysis of variance results for the program-similar items were identical to those for the program-specific items. There was a significant decrease in change scores with grade (F = 19.84; df = 2,188; p < .001), and girls changed less than boys in third grade and more in sixth and tenth grades (F = 5.10; df = 2,188; p < .001). There was no significant effect for sex and no other significant interaction.

Because of the previously reported evidence that completion of the comprehension test contaminated responses to program-related items, and because of some suggestion that response hierarchy scores might be similarly influenced, hypothesis 5 (that as understanding of negative motivation and consequences for depicted aggression increased subsequent aggression would decrease) was not tested.

One further, unplanned analysis was performed. This consisted of an examination of the effects of initial level of aggression on aggression after exposure to one of the three conditions. On the basis of response hierarchy before scores, Ss within each grade were divided at the median to form high and low initial aggression groups. Mean physical aggression change scores for Ss who were initially either high or low are presented in Figure 22 for all three grades and all three conditions.

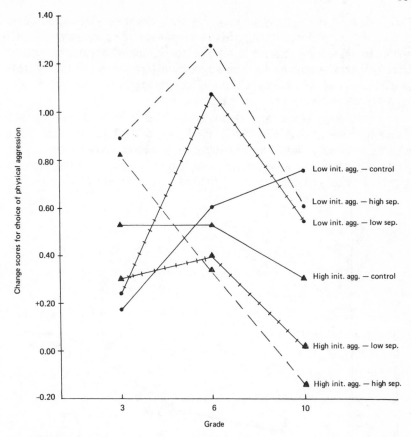

Figure 22: Mean change scores for physical aggression on the response hierarchy by viewing condition, initial aggression level, and grade

A four-way ANOVA (grade by sex by separation condition by aggression level) revealed a significant main effect for initial aggression ($F = 14.12$; $df = 1,170$; $p < .01$), with Ss who were initially low changing more than Ss who were initially high. A large part of this difference, however, is probably due to regression to the mean. There was also a grade by initial aggression level interaction ($F = 35.77$; $df = 3,170$; $p < .01$), with regression to the mean occurring in sixth and tenth grades but not in the third grade.

There was a significant condition by initial aggression level interaction ($F = 37.70$; $df = 2,170$; $p < .01$), which is presented graphically in Figure 23. High and low initial aggression Ss in the control group changed about the same amount; low aggression Ss in the low separation group changed somewhat more, and low aggression Ss in the high separation group changed much more. High initial aggression Ss in both separation groups changed about the same amount and less than the control group Ss.

Thus, viewing an aggressive program with negative motivations and consequences inhibited the aggressive responses of Ss who were initially high in aggression relative to high aggressive Ss who watched neutral fare; however, exposure to such aggressive fare increased the aggressive behavior of Ss who were initially low in aggression relative to low aggressive Ss who watched neutral fare.

The only other significant term was the interaction between sex and initial aggression level ($F = 29.97$; $df = 1,170$; $p < .01$). Girls and boys who were initially high in aggression showed about the same amount of postexposure change in aggression, while boys who were initially low in aggression changed more than did girls who were initially low.

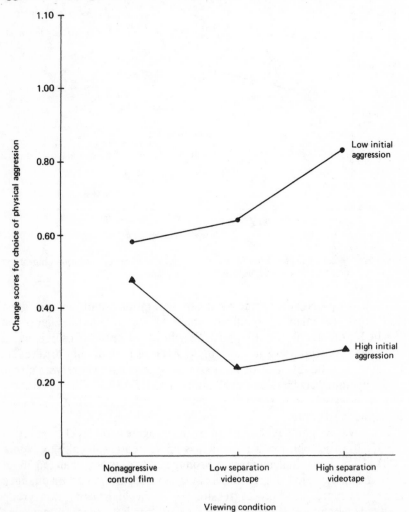

Figure 23: Mean change scores for physical aggression on the response hierarchy by viewing condition and initial aggression level

Discussion

Collins's work indicates that temporal separation between events adults perceive to be related to depicted aggressive behavior may make it difficult for young children to understand these relationships. Moreover, such temporal separation and the presumed consequent lack of understanding may result in increased aggressiveness, even if the intended message was that aggression does not pay and is not admired. For young children these effects may operate similarly for children both high and low in aggressive tendency. Such effects are considerably less pronounced or altogether absent among older children and adolescents.

DISCUSSION

The studies reported here were intended to explore the role of motivation for and consequences of aggressive acts in modifying the effects of exposure to such acts. The orientation has been developmental, with a continuous search for those variables that operate similarly regardless of age and those variables that operate differently upon children of different ages.

Throughout our work there has been only minimal evidence that motivations and consequences, as they are commonly depicted in television programs, modify the effects of exposure to the aggressive content of these programs. On the one hand, the validation experiment with four-year-olds demonstrated that depiction of highly salient, repeated consequences for aggressive behavior will influence both play behavior and verbal reports of behavioral solutions to fairly common situations involving interpersonal conflict. On the other hand, four studies which involved motivations and/or consequences for aggression, but in which the portrayal was considerably less blatant than that for the four-year-old validation and considerably closer to that of contemporary television, manifested little evidence that the observed motivations for or consequences of aggression modified subsequent aggression by the viewer.

Nolan (Experiment 3) presented children with a short aggressive sequence and with verbal information that made the beating of one of the aggressors either more or less justified. He found no evidence that the justification had much impact upon subsequent aggression by viewers, although there was some indication that the viewer's own interpretation of the justification influenced his subsequent aggression. Collins (Experiment 4) edited a tape of a current television program so that the motivations and consequences for all aggressive acts were bad. He found little support for the proposition that viewers of such a tape would be less aggressive than viewers of a nonaggressive tape (nor were they more aggressive). In our own study with tapes of current programs edited to vary the desirability of the motivations for and consequences of aggression, there was some evidence that the motivations for observed aggression influenced subsequent aggression (Experiment 2). This study suggested that children who viewed violence performed for socially acceptable reasons were subsequently more aggressive than were children who viewed violence performed for socially unacceptable reasons.

However, even this one effect of motivation for aggression vanished when children watched full, half-hour television programs (Experiment 1). These programs presented violent actions performed for both good and bad reasons and with good and bad consequences. Even though adults categorized the programs as generally portraying violence as rewarded, punished, well-motivated, or poorly motivated, such categorizations were not reflected in the subsequent aggression of viewers.

Although we found minimal evidence that the depicted motivations or consequences for violence influenced subsequent aggression by viewers of many ages, one might still expect such an influence at one or two ages. The work we have reported included children between the ages of three and eighteen, yet we did not find a clear developmental trend in the effects of exposure to aggression with different motivations and consequences.

There is evidence that such an effect can be found with specially constructed videotape sequences shown to four-year-olds and that the effect may remain for children of this age when the sequences are longer, edited versions of contemporary television programs (Experiment 2), but the effect disappears when the tapes are unedited, half-hour programs (Experiment 2). Combining the three studies that employed specially constructed or edited videotapes (Experiments 2, 3, and 4), one finds a slight effect for motivations and consequences at third grade, no effect for justification at fourth grade, a slight effect for motivations and consequences at fifth grade, no effect for motivations and consequences at sixth grade, no effect for justification at seventh grade, some effect for justification and for motivations and consequences at tenth grade, and no effect for motivations and consequences at twelfth grade. Only one program, however, produced very clear results—the one with both negative motivations and negative consequences (reported in Experiments 2 and 3). The one study that employed unedited tapes of current programs (Experiment 1) found no indication of an influence of motivations and/or consequences at kindergarten, third, sixth, ninth, and twelfth grades. Thus, there is little evidence for any developmental trend in the effects of motivations for and consequences of aggression on subsequent aggression.

The two most reasonable explanations for the general lack of effect for motivations and consequences are: that children do not understand the motivations and/or consequences as they are presented; and/or that they do not apply what they have seen isomorphically to their own behavior. We have not gathered direct evidence to support or refute the latter explanation, but we do have available evidence on the first (Experiment 1). Children as young as five apparently do not understand motivations and consequences as they are presented in current television programs. By about the third grade, they understand about half of the material they are tested on. From this age on there is steady improvement in understanding, such that twelfth graders understand almost all content they are tested on. Understanding did depend somewhat upon the specific program viewed, but it did not depend upon the type of program viewed (children's program, western, or adult crime program).

Collins (Experiment 4) has provided evidence that at least some of the lack of understanding of the motivations and consequences in contemporary television programs may be due to the mass of information presented and to the separation (both by time and by additional, irrelevant content) of the primary content of motivation, action, and consequence. Our hypothesis that younger children would understand less about motivations than consequences because they were not oriented toward evaluating actions on the basis of motivation received no support whatsoever.

Children from kindergarten onward apparently do understand the evaluative content of a program when they understand the behavioral content. In these studies, even kindergarteners who understood why an aggressive act was performed, or what the consequences of the act were, understood whether that motivation or consequence was good or bad. Moreover, all children understand whether a character is intended to be a "good guy" or a "bad guy." For the edited programs preschoolers understood whether the portrayed motivations for aggression were good or bad, although they did not understand the consequences. It should be noted here that evaluation data for all children at each age have not been examined for the study of unedited programs, and no measure of understanding the exact motivations or consequences was obtained in the study of edited programs. Thus, all the available data for estimating children's understanding of the evaluative aspects of a program have not been analyzed. However, there is sufficient data to suggest that preschool and kindergarten children understand only some of the evaluative content of a program, that by the age of eight children understand much of the evaluative message of a program, and that this understanding increases with age.

If children are only minimally affected by the motivations and consequences associated with current television portrayals of violence (even though by the age of eight they understand at least half of what is presented), are they any more affected by the portrayed violence itself? Within the body of work reported here are seven instances in which such a question might be answered by comparing aggressive behavior after exposure to aggressive content with aggressive behavior after exposure to nonaggressive content. In three of these instances there is no apparent effect of exposure to violence; in two there is a slight increase in aggressiveness after exposure to aggression; in two there is a notable increase in aggressiveness after exposure to aggression; and in none is there either a slight or notable decrease in aggressiveness after exposure to aggression.

There was no difference in verbal estimates of potential aggressive acts: (1) for children exposed to aggressive and nonaggressive content in Collins's study utilizing aggressive acts with bad motivations and consequences and a travelogue about California; (2) in the study utilizing four tapes edited to produce different combinations of good and bad motivations and consequences and a travelogue about Austria; or (3) in the 13-year-old validation utilizing a knife fight scene and a family life comedy. There was a nearly significant difference in (1) the tendency to give high intensity electric shock in the 13-year-old validation study utilizing the same knife fight scene and family life comedy and (2) in the tendency to choose verbally aggressive solutions to interpersonal conflict in the 13-year-old validation utilizing a boxing sequence and a travelogue about Austria.

Finally, there was a notable tendency (1) to play more aggressively with toys and to choose more aggressive solutions to interpersonal conflict after exposure to aggression with both positive and negative consequences than after exposure to active, nonaggressive play in the four-year-old validation study and (2) to indicate that one would resolve interpersonal conflict with physical aggression after viewing more violent programs than after viewing less violent programs in the study with full half-hour programs.

These overall findings include some fairly consistent differences with age in choice of aggressive solutions to interpersonal conflict; the pattern of differences depends upon the viewing stimulus. Without exposure to any television stimulus, the frequency of aggressive choices is a U-shaped function of age. This pattern was found in the pretesting of 24 items (from which the nine best were selected) and in the study involving edited tapes. In the first instance, the least aggressive children were the seven-year-olds; aggression increased from seven to 16 years of age, and preschoolers were about as aggressive as 16-year-olds. In the second instance, only three age points were measured; preschoolers and twelfth graders were about equally aggressive, while fifth graders were considerably less aggressive. Collins also measured aggressive choices without exposure to any television stimulus and found increasing aggressiveness from third through sixth and tenth grades (about eight to 16 years of age). This finding is quite consistent with the hypothesized U-shaped curve for aggressive choices over the ages three to 18.

Aggressive choices apparently increase with age after exposure to a nonaggressive television stimulus. Collins found increasing aggressiveness from third through tenth grade after the children viewed a travelogue about California, and the edited tapes study showed increasing aggressiveness from preschool through fifth and twelfth grades after viewing a travelogue on Austria.

Such increases were not found after viewing aggressive stimuli. Rather, an inverted U-shaped pattern was found for choice of physical aggression after exposure to aggressive content. Nolan found such a pattern using fourth, seventh, and tenth graders. Collins found such a pattern using third, sixth, and tenth graders. Such a pattern was found for kindergarteners, third, sixth, ninth, and twelfth graders after they viewed full-length television programs. Such a pattern was not, however, found in the study using tapes edited to manipulate motivations and consequences for aggression. In that instance, there was a decrease in aggressive choices from preschool to fifth to twelfth grades. The reason for this one disparity is not apparent, although it may be due to the inclusion of preschool children. The pattern of results for the fifth and twelfth graders corresponds to that of the other three studies. Since none of the other three studies includes children nearly as young as the preschoolers in the edited tapes study, the reliability of this exception to the inverted U-shaped pattern cannot be assessed.

These results suggest that aggressive displays, whatever their motivations or consequences, become increasingly effective in producing aggressive behavior as children mature from preschool to early adolescence, and that this effectiveness decreases from early adolescence on. This may be seen most clearly in three studies: Collins's study (Experiment 4), the edited tapes study (Experiment 2), and the unedited tapes study (Experiment 1). The Collins and edited tapes studies both used the *Silent Force* tape (bad motivations and bad consequences for aggression) and a travelogue. While the subject populations, the travelogues, and the *Silent Force* tapes differed somewhat, the results from the two studies may still be combined to examine the pattern of age differences in aggressiveness of children who watched the aggressive *Silent Force* tape and those who watched the nonaggressive travelogue. The difference between the means for these two groups increases from preschool through sixth grade and then decreases through tenth and twelfth grades. A similar pattern was found in comparisons over age of the difference in the number of aggressive choices of children who watched *Felony Squad*, the most violent program in the unedited tapes study, and those who watched *Batman*, the least violent program in the same study. Five grades were studied here; and once again the inverted U-shaped pattern with age holds for the difference in aggressiveness after viewing more and less violent programs, with the peak at sixth grade.

These effects hold for both boys and girls who have been included in all studies, although our work has not been directed at discovering sex differences in responses to aggressive stimuli and the motivations and consequences associated with it. Boys have, in almost all studies and at almost all ages, chosen aggression more often than girls, but the experimental stimuli apparently do not affect boys and girls differently. Rarely was there any interaction between the sex of the subject and any of the experimental manipulations employed, nor was there ever any significant effect for sex when change scores (after test minus before test) were used as dependent measures.

This use of both boys and girls as subjects in all studies is one of the positive aspects of the work reported here. There are other desirable features that should also be noted. We have used experimental stimuli that are either exact copies of current television programs (including commercials) or somewhat edited copies of current programs, rather than shorter excerpts or specially produced stimuli. We have used many different programs and types of programs. We have also used a dependent measure that is conceptually close to the everyday resolution of interpersonal conflict—the area that we hope to extrapolate to. Finally, we have carried out our work across a number of ages, utilizing similar stimuli, procedures, and measures wherever possible without totally sacrificing their meaningfulness for children of any age.

There are, however, a number of limitations in our work that should also be noted. The viewing situation was not that which a child experiences in his home, where most of his viewing is done. Effects of exposure were measured immediately after viewing and after only one exposure to the specified television content. Moreover, the dependent measure, while conceptually close to real-life behavior, was a verbal estimate of probable behavior rather than a measure of the actual behavior. This measure may not be equally sensitive for children of all the ages we studied. It was validated for preschoolers and fifth graders but not for 13-year-olds. Its validity for adolescents is still in question, because sex differences in aggressiveness in the measure were apparent with almost all the adolescent groups we studied, and behavioral measures of aggressiveness after exposure to aggressive and nonaggressive content showed little difference at thirteen.

Given these strengths and limitations, there are some conclusions that one might draw—at least tentatively—from the series of studies that has been reported here. While children, as they grow up, understand more and more about the television programs they view, there is little indication that the motivations and consequences for the aggression these programs portray influence the aggressive tendencies of children who have viewed them. It is reasonable to suggest that this is because of the nature of the portrayal rather than because of an inherent inability of children of any age to be influenced by the motivations for and consequences of aggressive acts they observe. There is rather clear evidence that exposure to current television programs that include aggressive acts produces greater subsequent aggression than one would find without such exposure. This effect increases as children mature to early adolescence and then decreases through adolescence. None of the results are, of course, in themselves the final proof-positive of anything. Yet, in conjunction with other evidence already available and that which may appear in the future, they may allow us to understand something of the effects on children of different ages of viewing contemporary television.

FOOTNOTES

1. The research upon which this report is based was performed pursuant to Contract No. HSM-42-70-54 with the National Institute of Mental Health, Health Services and Mental Health Administration, U. S. Department of Health, Education, and Welfare, to Nathan Maccoby, Aimee Dorr Leifer, and Donald F. Roberts.

We are grateful to numerous people who have provided the advice and assistance we needed to complete the work reported here. We wish especially to acknowledge those who played an integral part in the research, though we will still omit others who have helped when we needed it.

First, we owe thanks to Eleanor E. Maccoby, Department of Psychology, Stanford University, and to Nathan Maccoby and Wilbur Schramm, Institute for Communication Research, Stanford University, for their consultation and advice on various phases of the study.

We also acknowledge and appreciate those research assistants, Carolyn Clark, James Dillon, Henrietta Ferry, and Judy Juncker, and graduate students in Communication W. A. Collins (now on the faculty at the University of Minnesota), Bernadette Nelson-Shapiro, Michael Nolan, and L. Theresa Silverman, who worked with most of the children and adults as well as participating in all other phases of the project. Gordon Woodley, a Stanford University undergraduate, also participated on several parts of the study. Two other graduate students, Reginald McGhee and Bruce McKay, provided technical assistance. Mr. McGhee also recorded and edited the majority of our stimulus tapes and provided us with astute observations on the world view television content promotes. Finally, our thanks to Mr. Jurgen Wolff, the artist who provided the drawings which were an integral part of many of our dependent variables.

Our research required many subjects, ranging in age from preschool to adulthood, and we are indebted to them for their time, cooperation, and good humor. Particular thanks is owed to Dr. Edith Dowley and the faculty, staff, and students of Stanford University Nursery School, without whose unlagging assistance and excellent facilities most of our work with preschool children could never have been carried out. We also wish to thank the administrations, staffs, faculties, and students of the Mountain View School District and the Kenneth N. Slater School, Mountain View, California; The Mountain View-Los Altos Union High School District and Awalt High School, Mountain View, California; the San Jose Unified School District and the Willow Glen Elementary School, Hoover Junior High School, and Willow Glen High School, San Jose, California; Our Lady of the Rosary School, Palo Alto, California; St. Joseph's School, Holy Cross High School, and St. Francis High School, Mountain View, California; St. Joseph's School, Menlo Park, California; St. Nicholas School, Los Altos Hills, California; St. Lawrence the Martyr High School, Santa Clara, California; and Serra High School, San Mateo, California. Finally thanks are due the Directors and staffs of the Palo Alto Recreation Department and the Palo Alto Young Women's Christian Association, Palo Alto, California.

Various adult organizations assisted in establishing adult norms for several phases of our work. We especially wish to acknowledge St. Thomas Aquinas Church, St. Mark's Church, the First Lutheran Church, and the Church of Jesus Christ of Latter Day Saints; the Parent-Teacher Associations of the Addison, Barron Park, Greendell, Hoover, Ortega, and Van Auken Schools; and the Little House senior citizens center, all of Palo Alto, California, and the St. Athanasius Church, Mountain View, California.

Thanks are also due to Screen Gems, Inc., and to Leonard Berkowitz, University of Wisconsin, Albert Bandura, Stanford University, and Percy H. Tannenbaum, University of California at Berkeley, for the use of several stimulus films.

Finally, we salute Hester Berson and Jan Matthews for their skill in preparing and assembling this manuscript and their patience in the Sisyphean task of getting us to finish it once and for all.

2. For all analysis of variance tables reported in this section, see Appendix D.

3. A fourth-grade teacher in charge of several fifth graders also provided ratings. However, her ratings were omitted because she did not know more than half the students well enough to rate them, and the distribution of the ratings she did complete was significantly different from the distributions of the two fifth-grade teachers (probably due to her different comparison standard of fourth graders).

4. Of a population of 54 subjects, ten did not obtain parental permission to participate, five were absent during administration of the response hierarchy (which was unannounced), and five were not rated by at least one teacher because no teacher knew them well enough.

5. The analysis of variance tables for this experiment may be found in Appendix H.
6. Unless otherwise noted, all analyses of variance hereafter reported were for unequal Ns.
7. For further work with *Silent Force,* see Experiment 4.
8. The analysis of variance tables for this experiment may be found in Appendix J.
9. Berkowitz's justification for the loser's severe beating rested heavily on sexual conquests of the girl friends, fiancees, and wives of his male friends, relatives, and business associates. These exploits could only be alluded to with younger children—and hence also with older children in this study. It is doubtful, moreover, that younger children would be much disturbed by the sexual athletics of a middle-aged boxer.
10. For all analysis of variance tables for this experiment, see Appendix K.
11. For all analysis of variance tables in this section, see Appendix L.

REFERENCES

Albert, R. S. The role of the mass media and the effects of aggressive film content upon children's aggressive responses and identification choices. *Genetic Psychology Monographs,* 1957, **55**, 221-85.

Baldwin, C. P., and Baldwin, A. L. Children's judgments of kindness. *Child Development,* 1970, **41**, 29-47.

Bandura, A. Influence of models reinforcement contingencies on the acquisition of imitative responses. *Journal of Personality and Social Psychology,* 1965, **1**, 589-95. (a)

Bandura, A. Vicarious processes: a case of no-trial learning. In Berkowitz, L. (Ed.) *Advances in experimental social psychology,* Vol. 2. New York: Academic Press, 1965. (b)

Bandura, A. Social-learning theory of identificatory processes. In Goslin, D. A. (Ed.) *Handbook of socialization theory and research.* Chicago: Rand McNally, 1969.

Bandura, A., Ross, D., and Ross, S. A. Imitation of film-mediated aggressive models. *Journal of Abnormal and Social Psychology,* 1963, **66**, 3-11. (a)

Bandura, A., Ross, D., and Ross, S. A. Vicarious reinforcement and imitative learning. *Journal of Abnormal and Social Psychology,* 1963, **67**, 601-07. (b)

Bandura, A. and Walters, R. H. *Social learning and personality development.* New York: Holt, Rinehart and Winston, 1963.

Berkowitz, L. *Aggression: a social-psychological model.* New York: McGraw-Hill, 1962.

Berkowitz, L. The contagion of violence: An S-R mediational analysis of some effects of observed aggression. Paper presented at Nebraska Symposium on Motivation, March 12, 1970.

Berkowitz, L. and Rawlings, E. Effects of film violence on inhibitions against subsequent aggression. *Journal of Abnormal and Social Psychology*, 1963, **66**, 405-12.

Brodbeck, A. J. The mass media as a socializing agency. Paper read at American Psychological Association, San Francisco, 1955.

Bruner, J., Olver, R. R., and Greenfield, P. M. *Studies in cognitive growth.* New York: Wiley, 1966.

Catton, W. R. Jr., The worldview presented by mass media. In Baker, R. K., and Ball, S. J. (Eds.) *Mass media and violence: a report to the National Commission on the Causes and Prevention of Violence.* Washington, D. C.: U. S. Government Printing Office, 1969.

Collins, W. A. Learning of media content: A developmental study. *Child Development*, 1970, **41**, 1133-42.

Collins, W. A. Effects of temporal spacing on children's comprehension and behavior following exposure to media violence. Unpublished Ph.D. dissertation. Stanford University, 1971.

Dysinger, W. S., and Ruckmick, C. A. *The emotional responses of children to the motion picture situation.* New York: Macmillan, 1933.

Flanders, J. P. A review of research on imitative behavior. *Psychological Bulletin*, 1968, **69**, 316-37.

Flavell, J. H. *The developmental psychology of Jean Piaget.* Princeton: Van Nostrand, 1963.

Flavell, J. H., Beach, D. R., and Chinsky, J. M. Spontaneous verbal rehearsal in a memory task as a function of age. *Child Development*, 1966, **37**, 283-99.

Gerbner, G. Dimensions of violence in television drama. Report for the Mass Media Task Force: National Commission on the Causes and Prevention of Violence, 1969 (not for publication).

Hale, G. A., Miller, L. K., and Stevenson, H. W. Incidental learning of film content: a developmental study. *Child Development*, 1968, **39**, 69-78.

Hartup, W. W., and Coates, B. The role of imitation in childhood socialization. In Hoppe, R., Simmel, E., and Milton, G. A. (Eds.) *Early experiences and the processes of socialization.* New York: Academic Press, 1970.

Hays, W. L. *Statistics for psychologists.* New York: Holt, Rinehart and Winston, 1963.

Hilgard, E. R., and Bower, G. H. *Theories of learning.* New York: Appleton-Century-Crofts, 1966.

Hoffman, M. L. Moral development. In Mussen, P. H. (Ed.), *Manual of child psychology, Vol. 2.* New York: John Wiley and Sons, 1970.

Kendler, T. S. Development of mediating responses in children. In Wright, J. C., and Kagan, J. (Eds.) Basic cognitive processes in children. *SRCD Monograph*, 1963, **28**, No. 2.

Kohlberg, L. Development of moral character and moral ideology. In Hoffman, M. L., and Hoffman, L. W. (Eds.) *Review of child development research, Vol. 1.* New York: Russell Sage Foundation, 1964.

Leifer, A. D. The relationship between cognitive awareness in selected areas and differential imitation of a same-sex model. Unpublished Master's thesis, Stanford Univ., 1966.

Leifer, A. D., *et al.* Developmental aspects of variables relevant to observational learning. *Child Development,* 1972, in press.

Marsh, G., and Sherman, M. Verbal mediation of transposition as a function of age level. *J. Exp. Child Psychology,* 1966, **4,** 90-98.

Mischel, W. *Personality and assessment.* New York: Wiley, 1968.

National Association of Broadcasters. *The television code.* Washington, D. C.: NAB Code Authority, 1969.

Nolan, M. J. Effects of justified aggression upon children of different ages. Unpublished manuscript, Institute for Communication Research, Stanford University, 1971.

Piaget, J. *The moral judgment of the child.* London: Kegan Paul, 1932.

Roberts, D. F. A developmental study of opinion change: source-orientation versus content-orientation at three age levels. Unpublished doctoral dissertation, Stanford University, 1968.

Roberts, D. F. Communication and children: A developmental approach. In Schramm, W., Pool, I. DeS., et al. (eds.) *Handbook of communication.* Chicago: Rand McNally, 1971 (in press).

Rosekrans, M. A., and Hartup, W. W. Imitative influences of consistent and inconsistent response consequences to a model on aggressive behavior in children. *Journal of Personality and Social Psychology,* 1967, **7,** 429-34.

Schramm, W., Lyle, J., and Parker, E. B. *Television in the lives of our children.* Stanford, California: Stanford University Press, 1961.

Sears, R. R., Maccoby, E. E., and Levin, H. *Patterns of child rearing.* Evanston, Illinois: Row, Peterson and Company, 1957.

Siegel, A. E. Film-mediated fantasy aggression and strength of aggressive drive. *Child Development,* 1956, **27,** 365-78.

Siegel, A. E. The effects of media violence on social learning. In Baker and Ball (Eds.) *Mass media and violence.*

Walters, R. H., and Llewellyn-Thomas, E. Enhancement of punitiveness by audiovisual displays. *Canadian Journal of Psychology,* 1963, **17,** 244-55.

White, S. H. Evidence for a hierarchical arrangement of learning processes. In Lipsitt, L. P., and Spiker, C. C. (Eds.) *Advances in child development and behavior, Vol. 2.* New York: Academic Press, 1965.

Whiting, J. W. M., and Child, I. L. *Child training and personality.* New Haven: Yale University Press, 1953.

Appendix A: Sample of a complete response hierarchy item

"You're walking down the street. Some kid is mad at you and comes up and hits you. What do you do?"

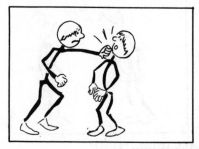

A. HIT THEM OR LEAVE THEM?

B. TELL A GROWN-UP OR CALL THEM "STUPID"?

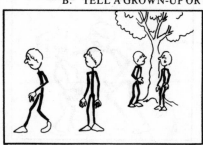

C. LEAVE THEM OR TELL A GROWN-UP?

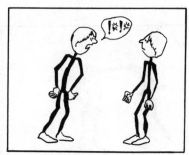

D. LEAVE THEM OR CALL THEM "STUPID"?

E.   HIT THEM OR CALL THEM "STUPID"?

F.   TELL A GROWN-UP OR HIT THEM?

Appendix B: Instructions for response hierarchy

(4 and 7 year-old Ss, pictures)

1. *Introduction (on way to room):*
   I'd like you both to help me finish some stories I have.

2. *Instructions:*
   This is what we'll do today. I'll read a short story. A story about something that could happen to you. Then, I want to know what you would do about it. When I've finished the story, I'll show you some pictures. You mark the picture that shows what you'd do if this happened to you.
   Open the test booklet to the first practice item and place it before each S.
   Here are some pictures for us to practice on.
   Give each S a color.
   And here are the colors for you to use when you mark the picture that shows what you would do.

3. *Practice Items:*
   Here's the story. You are standing outside. Someone comes along and asks you, "Are you a boy or a girl?" What do you do? Do you say, "I'm a boy" or "I'm a girl?" Take your color and mark the picture that shows what you would say.
   Let's look at the next pictures.
   Here's another story. You come home and your mother asks which is better for your health—a cookie or a cigarette. What do you say? A cookie or a cigarette? Take your color and mark what you'd do.
   That's interesting. I like that.

4. *Experimental Items:*
   Let's go on to some more stories. Remember, I'll read a story about something that might happen to you. You listen carefully. When I've finished, I'll show you some pictures. You mark the picture which shows what you'd do if this happened to you. You can only choose one picture each time, so choose carefully. Sometimes you won't want to choose either picture. But choose one anyhow, just to finish the story. Let's turn to the next page.

   NB: *If Ss want to change their responses, E crosses out first response and permits S to mark his second choice.*

5. *Thank Ss after completion of experimental session.*

(10 year-old Ss, pictures)

1. *Introduction:*
   I'd like to find out how you feel about different things that could
   happen to you.

2. *Instructions:*
   First of all, I need to know something about you. Take your booklet. On the back of the last page write your initials, your birthdate,
   and today's date. Also write an M or F for your sex.
   Good. Now turn your booklet over so that it is right-side-up again.
   This is what we'll do today. I'll read a short description of something that could happen to you. Then, I want to know what you
   would do about it. When I've read the description we'll look at sets
   of pictures in the booklet. Each page has two pictures on it. You
   mark one picture on each page that shows what you'd do if this happened to you.

3. *Practice Items:*
   There are some pictures for us to practice with.
   Here's the situation. You are standing outside. Someone comes
   along and asks you, "Are you a boy or girl?" What do you do? Do
   you say, "I'm a boy" or "I'm a girl?" Take a pencil and mark the
   picture that shows what you would say.
   Now, let's look at the next pictures. Turn your booklet to the second page. Here's the next situation. You come home and your
   mother asks you which is better for your health — a cookie or a cigarette. What do you say? A cookie or a cigarette? Take your pencil
   and mark what you'd do.
   That's good.

4. *Experimental Items:*
   Let's go on to some more situations. Remember, I'll read a description of something that could happen to you. Then I want to know
   what you would do about it. You look at the pictures and mark the
   one that shows what you'd do if it happened to you. You can only
   choose one picture at a time, so choose carefully. Sometimes you
   won't want to choose either picture. But choose one anyhow. There
   will be six pages of pictures for each situation. So you'll make six
   choices and then we'll go on to the next situation. Let's turn to the
   next page now.

   NB: *If Ss want to change their responses, E tells them to cross out
   their first response and mark their second choice.*

5. *At End:*
There, that finishes the booklet. Thank you for your help. Do you have any questions about what we did or why we're doing it? (Give straight explanations about what we're doing and why, but don't focus on violence.)

(10, 13, and 16 year-old Ss, slides)

1. *Introduction:*
I'd like to find out how you feel about different things that could happen to you.

2. *Instructions:*
First of all, I need to know something about you. Take your answer sheets. There should be two pages. On the upper right of each page, write your date of birth and your initials on the first line. Then write M or F for your sex. Where it says Card Set, write_____.
Where it says Experimenter, write_____.
This is what we'll do today. I'll read a short description of something that could happen to you. Then, I want to know what you would do about it. When I've read the description, I'll show you some slides. Each slide will have two pictures on it, one marked A and the other marked B. Take your answer sheet and circle A if it shows what you'd do in the situation. Circle B if it shows what you'd do.

3. *Practice Items:*
There are two items for us to practice with. They're labelled P1 and P2 on your answer sheet.
Here's the situation. You are standing outside. Someone comes along and asks you, "Are you a boy or a girl?" What do you do? Do you say, "I'm a boy" or "I'm a girl?" (Slide) Take your pencil and circle either A or B on the answer sheet.
Here's the next situation. You come home and your mother asks you which is better for your health — a cookie or a cigarette. What do you say? A cookie or a cigarette? Take your pencil and circle what you'd do.

4. *Experimental Items:*
Let's go on to some more situations. Remember, I'll read a description of something that could happen to you. Then, I want to know what you would do about it. You look at the slides and mark on the answer sheet the one that shows what you'd do if it happened to you. You can only choose one picture at a time, so choose carefully.

Sometimes you won't want to choose either picture. But please choose one anyhow. There will be six slides for each situation. So you'll make six choices and then we'll go on to the next situation.

NB: *If Ss want to change their responses, E tells them to cross out the first response and circle their second choice.*

5. *At End:*
There, that finishes all the slides. Thank you for your help. Do you have any questions about what we did or why we're doing it? (Give straight explanations about what we're doing and why, but don't focus on violence.)

Appendix C: Response hierarchy

(Final item set—4-10 years)

1. You're walking down the street. Some kid is mad at you and comes up and hits you. What do you do?
   a. Hit them
   b. Call them "Stupid"
   c. Leave them
   d. Tell a grown-up

2. You're standing in line for a drink of water. A kid comes along and just pushes you out of line. What do you do?
   a. Push them
   b. Call them a bad name
   c. Go away
   d. Say "That's all right"

3. You're playing a game with your friends. Someone takes your turn. What do you do?
   a. Push them
   b. Call them "Slob"
   c. Go into the house
   d. Tell them not to take your turn

4. You're playing a game and you keep making mistakes. Your friends start making fun of you. What do you do?
   a. Throw something at them
   b. Call them "Stupid"
   c. Go someplace else
   d. Say "That's all right"

5. You've just finished making something. Someone comes along and messes it up. What do you do?
   a. Hit them
   b. Call them a bad name
   c. Go away
   d. Say "That's all right"

6. Your friend promised to walk home with you. Then you see your friend walking home with somebody else. What do you do?
   a. Throw something at them
   b. Yell at them
   c. Go away
   d. Say "That's all right"

Final item set—10-16 years

1. You're walking down the street. Some kid is mad at you and comes up and hits you. What do you do?
   a. Hit them
   b. Call them "Stupid"
   c. Leave them
   d. Tell a grown-up

2. You're standing in line for a drink of water. A kid comes along and just pushes you out of line. What do you do?
   a. Push them
   b. Call them a bad name
   c. Go away
   d. Say "That's all right"

3. You're playing a game with your friends. Someone takes your turn. What do you do?
   a. Push them
   b. Call them "Slob"
   c. Go into the house
   d. Tell them not to take your turn

4. As you're leaving school you see two kids fighting with your best friend. What do you do?
   a. Push them
   b. Call them a bad name
   c. Leave them
   d. Tell the teacher

5. You've just heard that someone you thought was your friend has been making up stories behind your back. You encounter them after school. What do you do?
   a. Slap them
   b. Call them a bad name
   c. Go away
   d. Tell the teacher

6. You're playing a game and you're not doing so well. So somebody else starts taking over your plays. What do you do?
   a. Slap them
   b. Yell at them
   c. Go someplace else
   d. Tell the teacher

Appendix D: ANOVA Tables

Four-year-old validation

Imitative aggression

Source	df	MS	F
A − Videotape	2	26.43	< 2
B − Sex	1	86.70	3.55[a]
A B	2	31.30	< 2
Within	24	24.45	

Nonimitative aggression

	Three Ss deleted, raw scores			All Ss, transformed scores		
Source	df	MS	F	df	MS	F
A − Videotape	2	906.93	3.77*	2	.01	< 2
B − Sex	1	0.14	2	1	.01	< 2
A B	2	6944.94	28.84**	2	.08	6.17**
Within	21	240.78		24	.01	

[a]$p < .10$
*$p < .05$
**$p < .01$

Four-year-old validation

	Physical aggression			Verbal aggression			Physical + verbal aggression		
Source	df	MS	F	df	MS	F	df	MS	F
A − Videotape	2	55.77	5.91**	2	22.40	3.37*	2	106.08	5.73**
B − Sex	1	0.08	< 2	1	1.69	< 2	1	3.00	< 2
A B	2	7.90	< 2	2	0.06	< 2	2	7.75	< 2
Within	42	9.44		42	6.64		42	18.51	

*$p < .05$
**$p < .01$

Thirteen-year-old validation

	Shock intensity (Before test score as covariate)		
Source	df	MS	F
A — Sex	1	0.18	< 2
B — Videotape	1	4.23	3.50[a]
C — Experimenter	1	0.23	< 2
A B	1	1.38	< 2
A C	1	0.50	< 2
B C	1	0.04	< 2
A B C	1	0.07	< 2
Within	23	1.21	

	Physical aggression			Verbal aggression			Physical + verbal aggression		
				(Before test score as covariate)					
Source	df	MS	F	df	MS	F	df	MS	F
A — Sex	1	.001	< 2	1	.018	< 2	1	.012	< 2
B — Videotape	1	.000	< 2	1	.006	< 2	1	.003	< 2
C — Experimenter	1	.228	9.91**	1	.026	< 2	1	.059	< 2
A B	1	.006	< 2	1	.002	< 2	1	.000	< 2
A C	1	.036	< 2	1	.042	< 2	1	.002	< 2
B C	1	.060	2.61	1	.002	< 2	1	.084	< 2
A B C	1	.075	3.26[a]	1	.000	< 2	1	.055	< 2
Within	31	.023		31	.023		31	.051	

[a] $p < .10$
*$p < .05$
**$p < .01$

Thirteen-year-old validation (mean combined after scores for transformed response hierarchy physical aggression by sex, experimenter, and videotape condition)

	Aggressive Videotape				Non-Aggressive Videotape		
	E_1	E_2	E_3		E_1	E_2	E_3
Girls	1.44	3.39	.80		1.20	1.18	1.58
	N=5	N=5	N=10		N=5	N=5	N=9
Boys	2.97	1.59	2.59		3.10	3.36	2.74
	N=5	N=5	N=9		N=5	N=5	N=10

Transformed physical aggression score

Source	df	MS	F
A — Sex	1	29.10	8.79**
B — Videotape	1	0.74	< 2
C — Experimenter	2	1.46	< 2
A B	1	3.08	< 2
A C	2	5.48	< 2
B C	2	1.18	< 2
A B C	2	8.56	2.59
Within	66	3.31	

**$p < .01$

Thirteen-year-old validation (mean response hierarchy scores by sex and videotape condition for second thirteen-year-old validation using *The Champion*)

	Physical aggression		Verbal aggression		Physical + verbal aggression	
	Aggressive	Non-aggressive	Aggressive	Non-aggressive	Aggressive	Non-aggressive
Girls $\bar{x}$	8.33	9.77	12.92	11.00	21.25	20.77
sd	4.15	2.42	3.07	3.76	4.47	4.64
N	12	13	12	13	12	13
Boys $\bar{x}$	9.80	9.86	12.20	10.43	22.10	20.29
sd	2.98	2.23	1.99	2.87	3.67	3.84
N	10	7	10	7	10	7

ANOVA tables

	Physical aggression			Verbal aggression			Physical + verbal aggression		
Source	df	MS	F	df	MS	F	df	MS	F
A — Videotape	1	5.96	< 2	1	33.60	3.24[a]	1	11.25	< 2
B — Sex	1	6.51	< 2	1	2.04	< 2	1	1.26	< 2
A B	1	5.58	< 2	1	0.48	< 2	1	4.55	< 2
Within	38	10.70		38	10.37		38	19.97	

[a]$p < .10$

Fifth grade validation

Source	Physical aggression			Verbal aggression			Physical + verbal aggression		
	df	MS	F	df	MS	F	df	MS	F
A – Sex	1	0.03	< 2	1	0.41	< 2	1	0.22	< 2
B – Rated aggression	1	2.80	4.69*	1	0.17	< 2	1	4.36	3.33[a]
A B	1	0.41	< 2	1	0.01	< 2	1	0.38	< 2
Within	30	0.60		30	0.33		30	1.31	

[a] $p < .10$
* $p < .05$

Appendix E:
Teacher rating form for fifth grade validation

To: Fifth Grade Teachers, Slater School
From: Don Roberts, Stanford University
Re: Television and violence study: aggression ratings

On the following pages we have listed all of the 5th grade students at Slater School who took part in the study of television violence we are conducting. It will be of great help in the interpretation of our results if the teachers of these students would each give us an independent rating of how aggressively each participant generally behaves in the school environment, relative to his classmates. We will correlate your ratings with the responses given by the children in the experiment in order to check whether or not our measure has any relation to "real world" behavior.

We are interested in overt forms of aggression such as hitting, shoving, name calling, etc., rather than in more subtle, psychological forms of aggression.

These ratings will remain completely anonymous; individual names of the children will be destroyed as soon as the data are prepared for analysis.

The following pages list all of the students participating; each name is followed by a series of boxes ranging from "very aggressive" to "very unaggressive." Simply check the box which best describes the usual behavior of each child. The names are listed by class for the sake of convenience. However, we are asking each of you to rate *all* of the 5th grade students, regardless of whether or not they are in your class. Such multiple ratings should make the data more accurate. If you feel that you do not know enough about a student to make any judgment, simply mark the box at the far left of the page. Finally, we would like to request that you do not consult with the other teachers when making these ratings.

Thank you for your help.

Relative to other 5th grade students, _____ is:

	very aggressive	rather more aggressive than average	a bit more aggressive than average	about average in aggressive behavior	a bit less aggressive than average	rather less aggressive than average	very unaggressive	don't know well enough to rate
S_1*								
S_2								
S_3								
S_4								
S_5								
S_6								
S_7								
S_8								
S_9								
S_{10}								

* Students were listed alphabetically by name

Appendix F (Experiment 1):
Adult rating of television programs

Definitions for rating television programs

Violence is defined as a physical act that hurts some person, animal, or object—or as a physical act that could hurt some person, animal, or object if it were successfully carried out. Verbal threats, intimidation, or expressions of anger are not considered violent. Accidents, acts of God, or natural calamities such as lightning, hurricanes, faulty equipment, etc., may be violent.

A *violent episode* begins with an act of violence. It may include the violent act, what happens to the person who receives that act, the response of this person to the violence and what happens to him then, and what happens to the person who performed the first violent act. Usually all this will take place in one setting, and a change in setting is a good clue that the violent episode has ended. Occasionally one episode may be made up of a number of incidents that you feel should be coded separately. When this occurs give the whole episode one name and then fill out as many rating forms as there are significant incidents. You should not have to do this often.

A violent act may be performed by a person, animal, or cartoon character. Or it may have no individual who performs the act—like lightning striking a house, a bridge collapsing, a rock falling. The *person, animal, or object who was first violent* is the one who hits first, shoots a gun first, draws a gun first, etc.—even if he has a very good reason for doing so.

A violent act must be directed at or affect a person, animal, or object (including cartoon characters). The *person, animal, or object who received first violence* is the one who is hit first, shot at first, etc., — whether or not he deserves what he got.

Name of first violent episode	Name of person, animal or object who was first violent.	Name of person, animal or object who received first violence.
The reason for each person's action was	G N B ?	G N B ?
The immediate outcome of this episode for each person was	G N B ?	G N B ?
By the end of the program the fate of each person was	G N B ?	G N B ?
Each person's character could be described as	G N B ?	G N B ?
The response of the person who received the first violent act was violent		non-violent

Name of second violent episode	Name of person, animal or object who was first violent.	Name of person, animal or object who received first violence.
The reason for each person's action was	G N B ?	G N B ?
The immediate outcome of this episode for each person was	G N B ?	G N B ?
By the end of the program the fate of each person was	G N B ?	G N B ?
Each person's character could be described as	G N B ?	G N B ?
The response of the person who received the first violent act was violent		non-violent

Name of third violent episode	Name of person, animal or object who was first violent.	Name of person, animal or object who received first violence.
The reason for each person's action was	G N B ?	G N B ?
The immediate outcome of this episode for each person was	G N B ?	G N B ?
By the end of the program the fate of each person was	G N B ?	G N B ?
Each person's character could be described as	G N B ?	G N B ?
The response of the person who received the first violent act was violent		non-violent

Appendix G (Experiment 1):
Sample item from understanding test

1. Why did the Great Sphinx destroy Rocket Robin Hood's spaceship?
    a. Because King Tut asked him to
    b. Because Robin's spaceship attacked him
    c. Because Ezra was trapped inside
    d. Because the mummies ordered him to

    Good   Good and Bad   Bad
    Don't Know   (Evaluation of motive)

2. Why did Robin and his men fight with the Great Sphinx?
    a. Because the Sphinx tried to eat them
    b. Because the Sphinx had radioed King Tut to get them
    c. Because the Sphinx' gears were jammed
    d. Because the Sphinx was about to crush Ezra

    Good   Good and Bad   Bad
    Don't Know   (Evaluation of motive)

3. What happened to the Sphinx after it destroyed Rocket Robin
    Hood's spaceship?
    a. It was rewarded by the people of Nylor
    b. It was destroyed by Rocket Robin Hood's men
    c. It was destroyed by King Tut
    d. It flew into King Tut's palace

    Good   Good and Bad   Bad
    Don't Know   (Evaluation of consequence)

4. What happened to Robin and his men after the Sphinx destroyed
    their spaceship?
    a. They fell to the ground
    b. They were saved by Ezra
    c. They had to leave Nylor
    d. They managed to escape

    Good   Good and Bad   Bad
    Don't Know   (Evaluation of consequence)

5. What happended to the Great Sphinx at the end of the show?
    a. King Tut thanked it for a job well done
    b. It crashed to the ground

    c. The people of Nylor made it a national hero
    d. It was sent with King Tut to the caves of Nylor

        Good   Good and Bad   Bad
        Don't Know   (Evaluation of consequence)

        The Great Sphinx was . . . good   good and bad
        bad   don't know

6. What happened to Robin and his men at the end of the show?
    a. They took Ezra with them in the spaceship
    b. They had to get back to their old jobs
    c. They rode off in the tax wagon
    d. They sent King Tut to the caves of Nylor

        Good   Good and Bad   Bad
        Don't Know   (Evaluation of consequence)

        Robin and his men were . . .good   good and bad
        bad   don't know

Appendix H (Experiment 1): ANOVA Tables

Nested factors ANOVAs for arcsin understanding scores
primary set of episodes
Grades K, 3, 6, 9, 12

		Motivations			Immediate consequences			Final consequences	
Source	df	MS	F	df	MS	F	df	MS	F
A — Grade	4	5.24	60.17**	4	3.34	40.74**	4	3.12	29.13**
Linear	1	18.48	217.45**	1	12.56	153.11**	1	12.09	113.01**
Quadratic	1	1.96	23.01**	1	0.42	5.18*	1	0.34	3.18[a]
Rest	2	0.25	2.95[a]	2	0.19	2.34	2	0.02	< 1
B — Sex	1	0.26	3.07[a]	1	0.71	< 1	1	0.20	1.92
C — Program Type	2	0.17	2.00	2	0.36	< 1	2	0.13	1.22
Linear	1	0.04	< 1	1	0.01	< 1	1	0.10	< 1
Rest	1	0.30	3.53[a]	1	0.06	< 1	1	0.16	1.50
D in C — Program	3	0.32	3.81*	3	0.13	1.61	3	0.99	9.25**
A B	4	0.13	1.56	4	0.04	< 1	4	0.03	< 1
A C	8	0.07	< 1	8	0.16	1.99[a]	8	0.06	< 1
A D	12	0.21	2.47**	12	0.11	1.34	12	0.13	1.23
B C	2	0.08	< 1	2	0.05	< 1	2	0.06	< 1
B D	3	0.14	1.64	3	0.08	< 1	3	0.02	< 1
A B C	8	0.13	1.52	8	0.03	< 1	8	0.20	1.91[a]
A B D	12	0.10	1.12	12	0.14	1.65[a]	12	0.02	< 1
Within	120	0.08		120	0.08		120	0.11	

[a] $p < .10$
* $p < .05$
** $p < .01$

Nested factors ANOVAs for arcsin understanding scores
Secondary set of episodes
Grades 3, 6, 9, 12

		Motivations			Immediate consequences			Final consequences	
Source	df	MS	F	df	MS	F	df	MS	F
A — Grade	3	3.11	15.56**	3	0.50	2.21[a]	3	1.25	9.84**
Linear	1	6.87	34.35**	1	1.14	5.02*	1	3.10	24.17**
Quadratic	1	1.19	5.95*	1	0.25	1.08	1	0.23	1.77
Rest	1	1.27	6.36*	1	0.12	< 1	1	0.42	3.28[a]
B — Sex	1	0.54	2.70	1	0.69	3.04[a]	1	0.08	< 1
C — Program Type	2	0.16	< 1	2	2.03	8.91**	2	0.64	5.06*
Linear	1	0.25	1.25	1	1.95	8.54**	1	0.96	7.54**
Rest	1	0.07	< 1	1	2.12	9.28**	1	0.33	2.60
D in C — Program	3	0.85	4.26**	3	1.62	7.11**	3	0.60	4.71**
A B	3	0.31	1.55	3	0.17	< 1	3	0.14	1.08
A C	6	0.11	< 1	6	0.14	< 1	6	0.07	< 1
A D	9	0.36	1.80[a]	9	0.14	< 1	9	0.32	2.53*
B C	2	0.09	< 1	2	0.19	< 1	2	0.11	< 1
B D	3	0.03	< 1	3	0.24	1.04	3	0.02	< 1
A B C	6	0.28	1.40	6	0.12	< 1	6	0.34	2.69*
A B D	9	0.40	2.00[a]	9	0.13	< 1	9	0.16	1.23
Within	96	0.20		96	0.23		96	0.13	

[a] $p < .10$
* $p < .05$
** $p < .01$

Arcsin understanding scores for all Ss by program type
Primary set of episodes
Grades K, 3, 6, 9, 12

Source	df	Motivations MS	F	df	Immediate consequences MS	F	df	Final consequences MS	F
A – Sex	1	0.00	<1	1	0.04	<1	1	0.31	2.94[a]
B – Grade	4	6.71	64.93**	4	3.65	37.85**	4	4.18	39.32**
C – Program Type	2	0.39	3.73*	2	0.10	<1	2	0.48	4.51
A B	4	0.09	<1	4	0.02	<1	4	0.11	1.00
A C	2	0.23	2.24	2	0.07	<1	2	0.09	<1
B C	8	0.12	1.20	8	0.13	1.35	8	0.13	1.21
A B C	8	0.09	<1	8	0.07	<1	8	0.15	1.45
Within	241	0.10		241	0.10		241	0.11	

Arcsin understanding scores for all Ss by specific program
Primary set of episodes
Grades K, 3, 6, 9, 12

Source	df	Motivations MS	F	df	Immediate consequences MS	F	df	Final consequences MS	F
A – Sex	1	0.00	<1	1	0.04	<1	1	0.31	3.55[a]
B – Grade	4	6.71	75.26**	4	3.65	38.05**	4	4.18	47.41**
C – Program	5	0.49	5.50**	5	0.12	1.22	5	1.02	11.55**
A B	4	0.09	1.05	4	0.02	<1	4	0.11	1.20
A C	5	0.37	4.15**	5	0.04	<1	5	0.07	<1
B C	20	0.16	1.77*	20	0.11	1.10	20	0.17	1.90*
A B C	20	0.12	1.37	20	0.10	1.06	20	0.10	1.08
Within	211	0.09		211	0.10		211		

[a]p < .10
*p < .05
**p < .01

Physical aggression score after television viewing

Source	df	(1) Depicted violence MS	F	df	(2) Depicted motivations MS	F	df	(3) Depicted consequences MS	F
A – Sex	1	16.27	32.77**	1	16.27	32.59**	1	16.27	32.47**
B – Grade	4	5.34	10.76**	4	5.34	10.70**	4	5.34	10.66**
C – (1) Violence	2	2.29	4.61*						
(2) Motivations				3	2.79	5.58**			
(3) Consequences							2	1.04	2.08
A B	4	0.50	<1	4	0.50	<1	4	0.50	<1
A C	2	0.03	<1	3	0.37	<1	2	0.63	1.26
B C	8	0.49	<1	12	0.45	<1	8	0.51	1.02
A B C	8	0.54	1.08	12	0.34	<1	8	0.65	1.30
Within	241	0.50		231	0.50		241	0.50	

*p < .05
**p < .01

Appendix I (Experiment 1):
Evaluation of motivations

Rocket Robin Hood

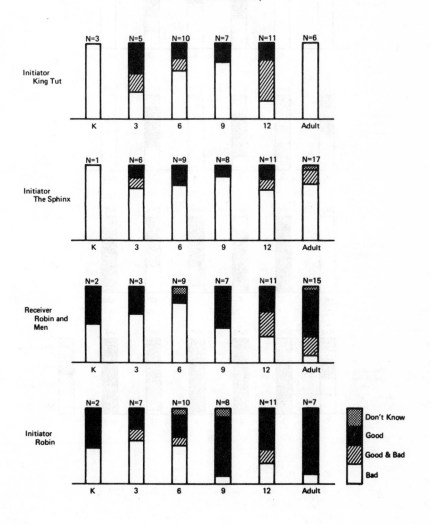

Batman

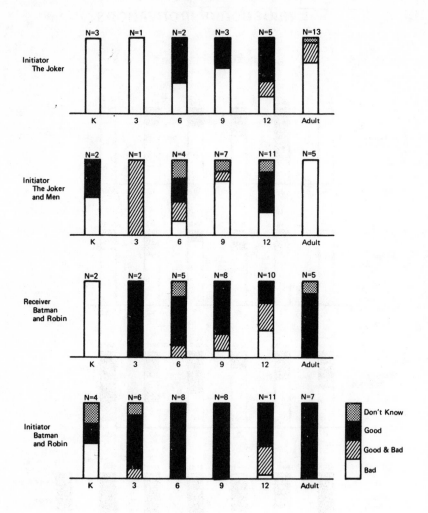

Rifleman

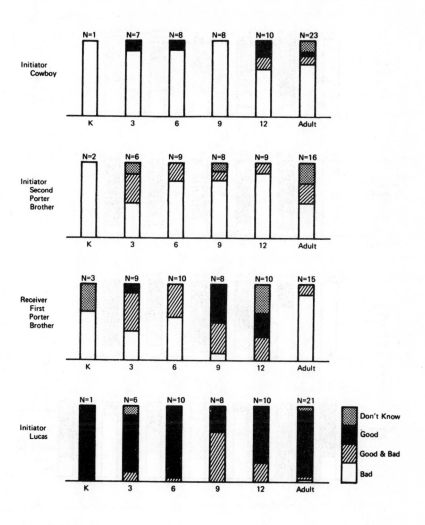

Have Gun

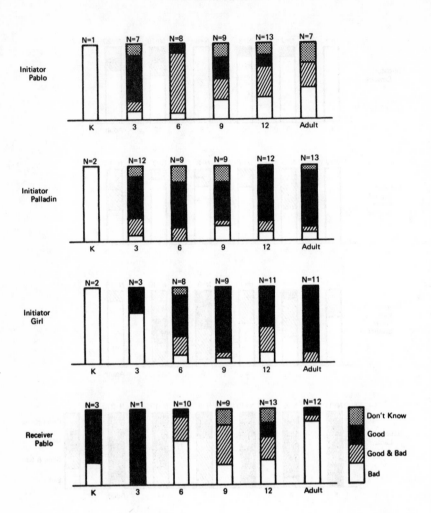

Adam 12

Initiator Vince

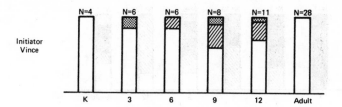

Initiator Bernie

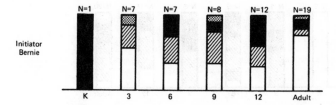

Initiator Police Captain

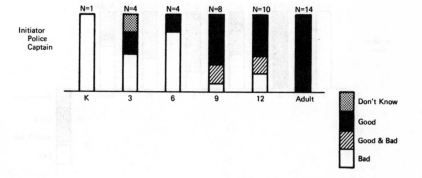

Don't Know

Good

Good & Bad

Bad

Felony Squad

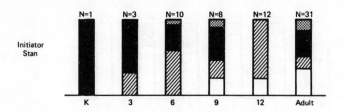

Initiator
Stan

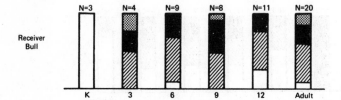

Receiver
Bull

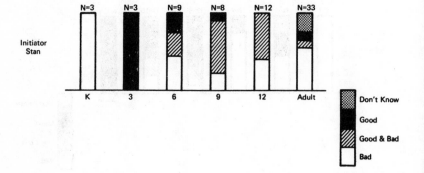

Initiator
Stan

Felony Squad (cont.)

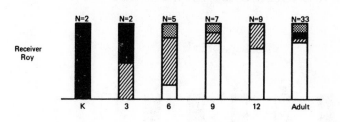

Receiver
Roy

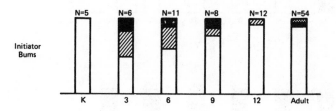

Initiator
Bums

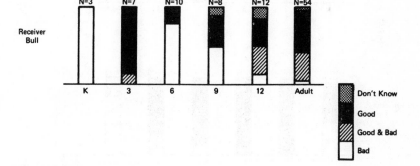

Receiver
Bull

Don't Know

Good

Good & Bad

Bad

Appendix I (Experiment 1): Evaluation of Immediate Consequences

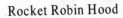

Rocket Robin Hood

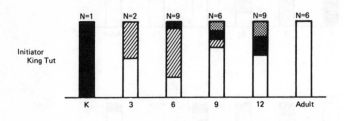

Initiator
King Tut

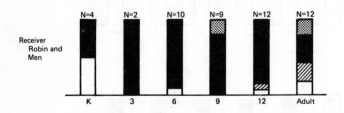

Receiver
Robin and
Men

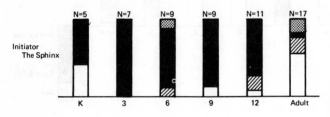

Initiator
The Sphinx

Rocket Robin Hood (cont.)

Receiver
Robin and
Men

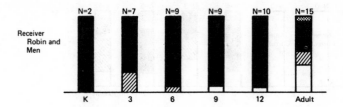

Initiator
Robin and
Men

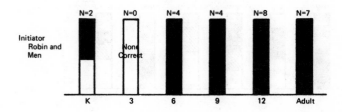

Receiver
King Tut

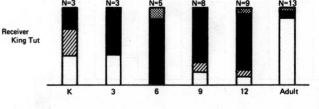

Don't Know

Good

Good & Bad

Bad

Batman

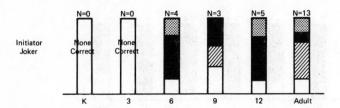

Initiator
Joker

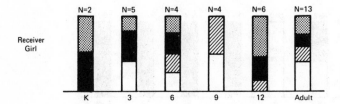

Receiver
Girl

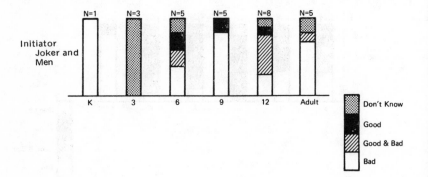

Initiator
Joker and
Men

Batman (cont.)

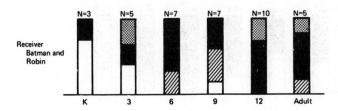

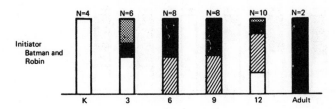

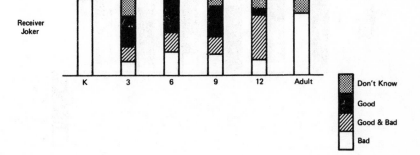

Rifleman

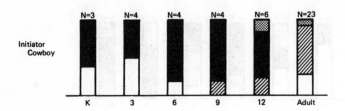

Initiator
Cowboy

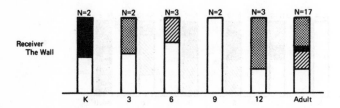

Receiver
The Wall

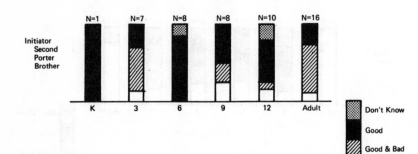

Initiator
Second
Porter
Brother

Don't Know
Good
Good & Bad
Bad

Rifleman (cont.)

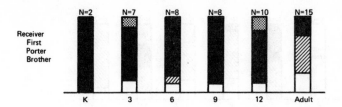

Receiver
First
Porter
Brother

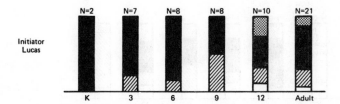

Initiator
Lucas

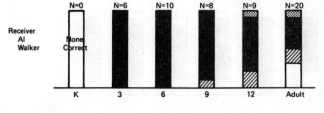

Receiver
Al
Walker

Don't Know
Good
Good & Bad
Bad

Have Gun

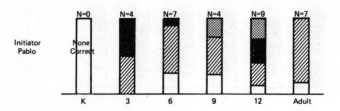

Initiator
Pablo

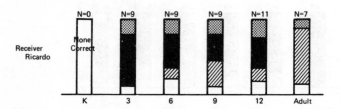

Receiver
Ricardo

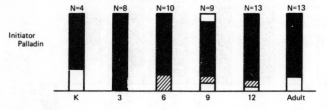

Initiator
Palladin

Don't Know

Good

Good & Bad

Bad

Have Gun (cont.)

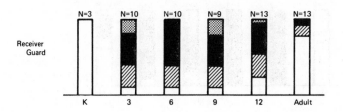

Receiver
Guard

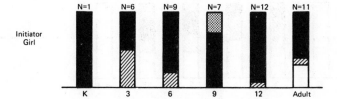

Initiator
Girl

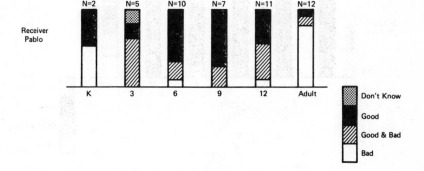

Receiver
Pablo

Adam 12

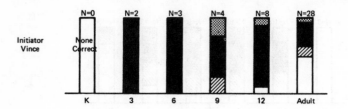

Initiator Vince

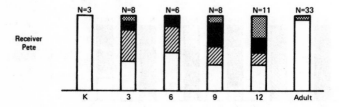

Receiver Pete

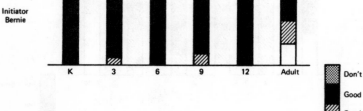

Initiator Bernie

Adam 12 (cont.)

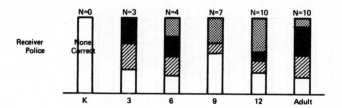

Receiver
Police

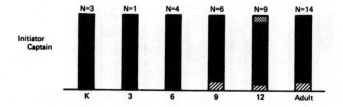

Initiator
Captain

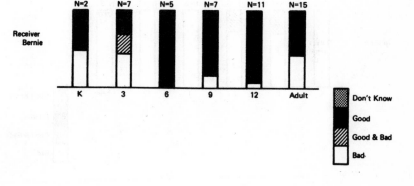

Receiver
Bernie

Don't Know

Good

Good & Bad

Bad

Felony Squad

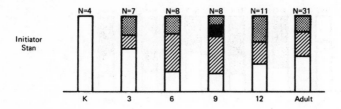

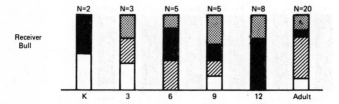

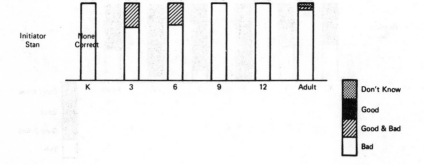

Felony Squad (cont.)

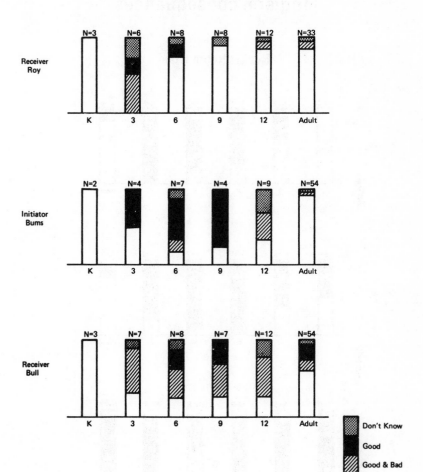

Appendix I (Experiment 1): Evaluation of longterm consequences

Rocket Robin Hood

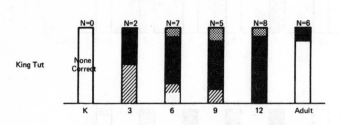

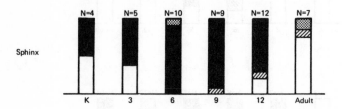

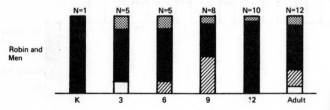

Batman

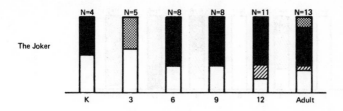

The Joker

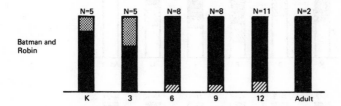

Batman and Robin

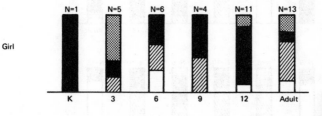

Girl

Don't Know
Good
Good & Bad
Bad

Rifleman

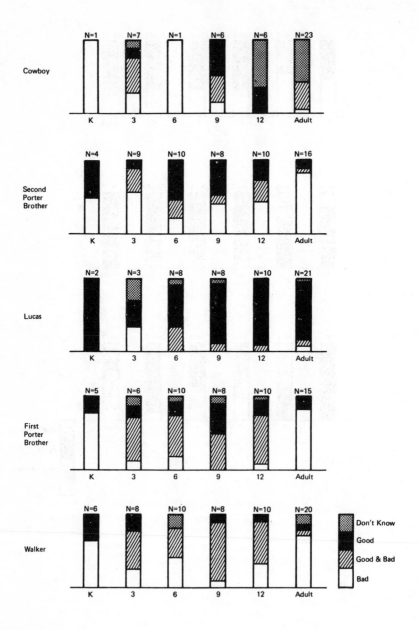

Have Gun

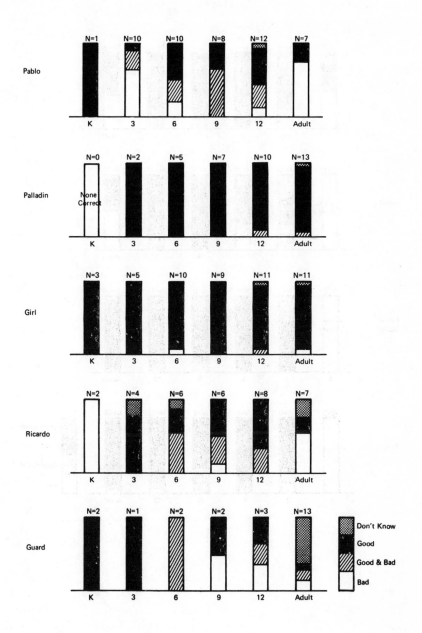

Adam 12

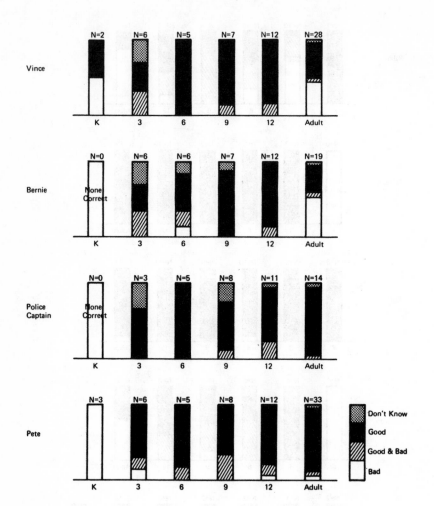

Felony Squad

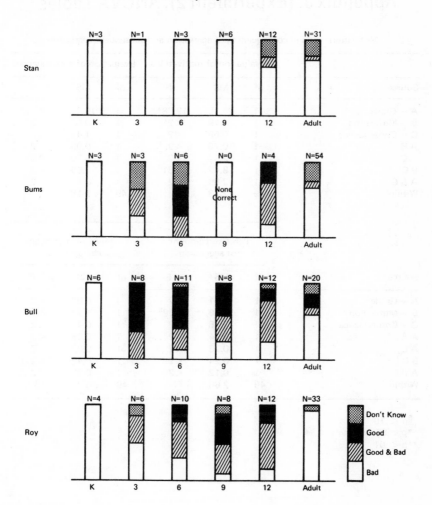

Appendix J: (Experiment 2): ANOVA Tables

Motivations for and consequences of aggression and subsequent aggression

	Evaluation of motivations			Evaluation of consequences		
Source	df	MS	F	df	MS	F
A — Grade	1	28.18	12.08**	1	10.41	4.77**
B — Motivation	1	1.19	<2	1	0.02	<2
C — Consequence	1	0.59	<2	1	1.41	<2
A B	1	0.70	<2	1	0.09	<2
A C	1	2.52	<2	1	5.70	2.61
B C	1	8.42	3.61[a]	1	3.59	<2
A B C	1	2.69	<2	1	0.46	<2
Within	49	2.33		49	2.18	

	Perceived amount of aggression			Physical aggression change score		
Source	df	MS	F	df	MS	F
A — Grade	1	0.61	<2	1	0.35	<2
B — Motivation	1	8.76	3.29[a]	1	1.22	4.10*
C — Consequence	1	2.76	<2	1	0.42	<2
A B	1	0.74	<2	1	0.05	<2
A C	1	0.23	<2	1	0.02	<2
B C	1	0.24	<2	1	0.42	<2
A B C	1	0.12	<2	1	0.23	<2
Within	49	2.66		49	0.30	

[a] $p < .10$
* $p < .05$
** $p < .01$

Motivations for and consequences of aggression and subsequent aggression

Physical aggression change score

Source	Preschool and fifth			Preschool, fifth, and twelfth		
	df	MS	F	df	MS	F
Regression	8	0.24	0.68	8	0.31	0.91
Sex	1	0.24	<2	1	0.41	<2
Grade	1	0.03	<2	1	0.00	<2
Depicted aggression	1	0.02	<2	1	0.27	<2
Depicted motivation	1	0.86	2.46	1	0.53	<2
Depicted consequence	1	0.11	<2	1	0.14	<2
Perceived aggression	1	0.21	<2	1	0.64	<2
Evaluation of motivations	1	0.14	<2	1	0.23	<2
Evaluation of consequences	1	0.31	<2	1	0.23	<2
Residual	61	0.35		80	0.33	

Physical aggression after score

Source	Preschool and fifth			Preschool, fifth, and twelfth		
	df	MS	F	df	MS	F
Regression	9	2.16	6.93**	9	2.46	8.27**
Sex	1	0.92	2.97[a]	1	1.78	5.93*
Grade	1	0.92	2.97[a]	1	0.18	<2
Depicted aggression	1	0.01	<2	1	0.38	<2
Depicted motivation	1	0.01	<2	1	0.06	<2
Depicted consequence	1	0.12	<2	1	0.13	<2
Perceived aggression	1	0.21	<2	1	0.01	<2
Evaluation of motivations	1	0.49	<2	1	0.23	<2
Evaluation of consequences	1	1.14	3.68[a]	1	0.95	3.17[a]
Physical aggression before score	1	15.61	50.35**	1	18.38	61.27**
Residual	60	0.31		79	0.30	

[a] $p < .10$
* $p < .05$
** $p < .01$

Appendix K (Experiment 3): ANOVA Tables

Justification for aggression and subsequent aggression

| | Understanding of manipulation | | | | | | | | |
| | Good person | | | Fair in dealings | | | Deserve to lose | | |
Source	df	MS	F	df	MS	F	df	MS	F
A — Grade	2	14.55	1.14	2	103.04	8.34**	2	90.85	6.26**
B — Sex	1	92.49	7.27**	1	53.84	4.36*	1	34.56	2.38
C — Justification condition	1	840.22	66.09**	1	647.54	52.39**	1	284.17	19.59**
A B	2	6.68	0.53	2	18.75	1.52	2	27.16	1.87
A C	2	19.63	1.54	2	38.87	3.14*	2	3.78	0.26
B C	1	129.49	10.19**	1	24.19	1.96	1	0.44	0.03
A B C	2	38.19	3.00[a]	2	24.91	2.02	2	4.44	0.31
Within cells	148	12.71		148	12.36		148	14.51	

[a]$p < .10$
*$p < .05$
**$p < .01$

Justification for aggression and subsequent aggression

ANOVA table for choice of physical aggression on response hierarchy

Source	df	MS	F
A — Grade	2	0.35	4.56**
B — Sex	1	3.14	40.52**
C — Justification condition	1	0.01	0.19
A B	2	0.04	0.57
A C	2	0.01	0.16
B C	1	0.07	0.86
A B C	2	0.07	0.85
Within cells	148	0.08	

Planned comparison and ANOVA table for choice of physical aggression on response hierarchy

Source	df	MS	F
A + C + AC (A = Grade, B = Justification condition)	5	0.75	9.38**
Contrast	1	0.52	6.55*
Residual	4	0.06	0.75
B + AB + BC + ABC (B = Sex)	6	3.43	42.88**
Within cells	148	0.08	

*$p < .10$
**$p < .01$

Appendix L (Experiment 4): ANOVA Tables

Total comprehension score

Source	df	MS	F
A – Sex	1	3.09	1.20
B – Separation	1	3.26	1.27
C – Grade	2	69.45	27.02**
A B	1	1.74	0.68
A C	2	7.19	2.80[a]
B C	2	6.14	2.39
A B C	2	3.65	1.42
Within	131	2.57	

Planned comparison for total comprehension score

Source	df	MS	F
Between	11	16.45	6.40**
Planned comparison	1	76.77	29.87**
Rest	10	10.41	4.05**
Within	131	2.57	

[a]$p < .10$
**$p < .01$

Physical aggression change scores

	Response hierarchy			Program-similar items			Program-specific items		
Source	df	MS	F	df	MS	F	df	MS	F
A – Sex	1	.48	1.07	1	.00	<1	1	.00	<1
B – Separation	1	.19	<1	1	.47	<1	1	.26	<1
C – Grade	2	5.75	12.84**	2	15.91	22.54**	2	3.65	5.00*
D – Questionnaire	1	.00	<1	1	3.25	4.61*	1	9.96	13.62**
A B	1	.46	1.04	1	.97	1.37	1	.53	<1
A C	2	11.43	25.53**	2	30.28	42.88**	2	6.90	9.44**
A D	1	.92	2.05	1	7.91	11.21**	1	20.07	27.45**
B C	2	10.11	22.59**	2	27.51	39.07**	2	6.27	8.58**
B D	1	1.06	2.37	1	6.53	9.24**	1	20.04	27.41**
C D	2	11.71	26.16**	2	7.28	10.31**	2	10.67	14.60**
A B C	2	.14	<1	2	.21	<1	2	.10	<1
A B D	1	.02	<1	1	.00	<1	1	.52	<1
A C D	2	.12	<1	2	.08	<1	2	.48	<1
B C D	2	1.39	3.10	2	.56	<1	2	.23	<1
A B C D	2	138.72	309.90**	2	48.54	68.75**	2	23.35	31.80**
Within	249	.45		249	.71		249		

*$p < .05$
**$p < .01$

Physical aggression change score

Source	Response hierarchy			Program-specific items			Program-similar items		
	df	MS	F	df	MS	F	df	MS	F
A – Sex	1	0.01	0.03	1	0.07	0.12	1	0.69	1.03
B – Condition	2	0.11	0.25	2	0.43	0.75	2	0.38	0.56
C – Grade	2	2.50	5.73**	2	5.72	10.13**	2	13.33	19.84**
A B	2	0.15	0.35	2	0.44	0.79	2	0.06	0.08
A C	2	1.63	3.72*	2	2.18	3.87*	2	3.43	5.10*
B C	4	1.47	3.37*	4	0.76	1.35	4	0.43	0.63
A B C	4	0.37	0.84	4	0.71	1.25	4	1.11	1.65
Within	188	0.44		188	0.56		188	0.67	

Response hierarchy planned comparison

	df	MS	F
Between	17	0.95	2.16**
Planned comparison	1	4.29	9.76**
Rest	16	0.74	1.68[a]
Within	188	0.44	

[a] $p < .10$
*$p < .05$
**$p < .01$

Physical aggression change score
response hierarchy

Source	df	MS	F
A – Sex	1	.01	<1
B – Condition	2	.11	<1
C – Grade	2	2.50	6.22**
D – Initial aggression	1	5.68	14.12**
A B	2	.42	1.05
A C	2	5.22	12.99**
A D	1	12.05	29.97**
B C	4	3.94	9.78**
B D	2	15.16	37.70**
C D	2	14.38	35.77**
A B C	4	.37	<1
A B D	2	.75	1.86
A C D	2	.47	1.17
B C D	4	.39	<1
A B C D	4	53.93	134.10**
Within	170	.40	

*$p < .05$
**$p < .01$

Short-Term Effects of Televised Aggression on Children's Aggressive Behavior

Robert M. Liebert and Robert A. Baron

In his review of the social and scientific issues surrounding the portrayal of violence in the mass media, Larsen (1968) noted that we may begin with two facts: "Mass media content is heavily saturated with violence, and people are spending more and more time in exposure to such content" (p. 115). This state of affairs has been used by both laymen and|professionals as the basis for appeals to modify the entertainment fare to which viewers, particularly children and adolescents, are exposed (Merriam, 1964; Schramm, Lyle, and Parker, 1961; Walters, 1966; Walters and Thomas, 1963; Wertham, 1966). Other writers, however, have argued that the kind of violence found on television or in

movies does not necessarily influence observers' "real-life" social behavior (Halloran, 1964; Klapper, 1968), and some have even characterized the portrayal of violence as potentially preventing the overt expression of aggression, at least under some circumstances (Feshbach, 1961;
Feshbach and Singer, 1971).

In view of the controversy, it is hardly surprising that recent years
have seen a substantial increase in the number of experimental studies
directed to this issue. An effort has been made to determine whether
children will learn and/or be disinhibited in their performance of aggressive acts as a function of exposure to *symbolic aggressive models* (for
example, in cartoons, movies, stories, and simulated television programs). This research has indicated consistently that children may indeed *acquire,* from even a very brief period of observation, certain mo-
toric and verbal behaviors which are associated with aggression in life
situations. More specifically, studies have repeatedly shown that after
viewing a film which depicts novel forms of hitting, kicking, and verbal
abuse, children can, when asked to do so, *demonstrate* this learning by
reproducing these previously unfamiliar behaviors with a remarkable
degree of fidelity (Bandura, 1965; Hicks, 1965). Taken together with the
large body of research on the observational learning of other behaviors
(Flanders, 1968), the available evidence appears to leave little doubt that
the learning of at least some aggressive responses can and does result
from television or movie viewing.

Equally important, however, is the question of whether the observation of violence will influence children's performance of aggressive acts
when they have|*not*|been specifically asked to show what they have seen
or learned. A relatively large number of experiments appear to provide
evidence relating to this issue (Bandura, Ross, and Ross, 1961, 1963,
1963b; Rosekrans and Hartup, 1967). In these studies, subjects have
typically been exposed to live or filmed aggressive scenes, then placed in
a free-play situation with a variety of toys or other play materials. Results obtained with these procedures have shown reliably that the exposure of young children to aggression produces increments in such play
activities as punching inflated plastic clowns, popping balloons, striking
stuffed animals, and operating mechanized "hitting dolls." However, it
has been argued by critics (Klapper, 1968) that these findings are not directly relevant to the question of whether exposure to symbolically
modeled aggression will increase children's willingness to engage in
behavior which might actually harm another human being. Since 1968 at
least four more recent experiments have been directed explicitly to this
question.

In the earliest of these studies, Hanratty, Liebert, Morris, and Fernandez (1969) investigated the effects of observing a two-and-one-half
minute film depicting physical and verbal aggression against a human
clown. A 2x2 factorial design was employed, in which preschool boys

drawn from a Protestant Sunday School either were or were not exposed to the aggressive film. Thereafter, half the viewers and half the nonviewers were permitted to play in a room containing a mallet, a toy gun, and a plastic (Bobo-doll) clown; the rest of the children were placed in an otherwise identical situation but in which a *human* clown replaced the familiar inanimate victim. The results of this experiment showed that the incidence of aggression was higher if the aggressive film had been seen than if it had not and that more aggression occurred against the inanimate than against the human victim. Additionally—and of greatest importance to the present discussion—physical aggression was directed against the human victim *only when the children had seen the aggressive film.*

A second experiment (Hanratty, 1969) again found that a film of this type, without other provocation, would lead children to physically assault a human victim. Moreover, in the second study, such aggression was displayed by both boys and girls and for films in which both an eight-year-old boy and an adult served as models. In a third experiment, by Savitsky, Rogers, Izard, and Liebert (1971), employing similar procedures, the finding that such a film would significantly increase aggression against a human victim was replicated with first and second grade boys from a rural public school.[1] In a fourth study within the same general paradigm, Hanratty, O'Neal, and Sulzer (in press) found that first grade boys from an urban parochial school were also significantly more likely to engage in interpersonal aggression if they had observed an aggressive film than they were if they had not. In contrast to the two previous studies, this study showed the modeling effect only for children who had been frustrated; whether the human victim had been the agent of frustration or not did not influence the frequency of aggression.

These previous investigations have demonstrated consistently that exposure to the behavior of filmed aggressive models may lead young children to directly imitate aggression against a human victim. However, all of these studies have employed specially prepared films depicting aggressive scenes which differ in several ways from those usually shown in standard television fare. Thus, the findings obtained are not directly relevant to answering the question of whether exposure to the type of violence generally depicted in regularly broadcast television shows will produce similar effects. Likewise, it is important to consider the possible *disinhibitory* effects (Lövaas, 1961; Siegel, 1956) rather than only the direct *imitative* effects of observing aggressive models. Although such effects have previously been observed with adult subjects and violent scenes taken from motion pictures (Berkowitz, 1965; Berkowitz and Rawlings, 1963; Walters and Llewellyn-Thomas, 1963), no previous investigation known to the authors has examined the influence of televised violence on interpersonal aggression among young children. It was with these latter questions that the present research was primarily concerned. We sought to determine whether exposure to violent scenes taken directly from nationally telecast programs would tend to increase the willingness of young children to engage in aggressive acts directed toward another child.[2]

METHOD

Participants

Population sampled. The sample was drawn both from Yellow Springs, Ohio, a small college town, and from a larger and more conservative neighboring community, Xenia. The participants were brought to Fels Research Institute in Yellow Springs by one of their parents in response to a newspaper advertisement and/or a letter distributed in local public elementary schools asking for volunteers to participate in a study of the effects of television on children. To assure that no potential participants were turned away because of scheduling inconveniences, parents were invited to select their own appointment times (including evenings or weekends), and transportation was offered to those who could not provide it for themselves.

Subjects. The subjects were 136 children, 68 boys and 68 girls. Sixty-five of the participants were five or six years of age; at the time of the study the remaining 71 subjects were eight or nine years of age. Within each age group and sex the children were assigned randomly to the treatment conditions. Approximately 20 percent of the children in this sample were black; virtually all of the remainder were white. The economic backgrounds from which these participants came was widely varied, as can be seen from the distribution shown in Appendix A. Further, although economic characteristics were not used as a basis for assignment to treatment groups, inspection suggested that the procedure of random assignment had adequately distributed them among the experimental groups (see Appendix B).

Experimental personnel. One of the investigators greeted the parent and child at the outset, served as the interviewer, and obtained informed parental consent for the child's participation. A 28-year-old white female served as experimenter for all the children, and two other adult females served as unseen observers throughout the experiment.

Design

A 2 x 2 x 2 factorial design was employed. The three factors were sex, age (5-6 or 8-9 years old), and treatment (observation of aggressive or nonaggressive television sequences.)

Procedure

Introduction to the situation. Upon the arrival of parent and child at the Institute, the child was escorted to a waiting room containing nonaggressive magazines and other play materials while the parent was interviewed in a separate room. During the interview, the nature of the experiment was disclosed to the parent, questions were invited and answered, and a written consent to the child's participation was obtained.[3]

Experimental and control treatment. After the interview, but without permitting the parent and the child to interact, the experimenter escorted each subject individually to a second waiting room containing children's furniture and a television videotape monitor. The television was turned on by the experimenter, who suggested that the child watch for a few minutes until she was ready for him. The experimenter left the child to watch television alone for approximately six and one-half minutes; the subjects were in fact continuously observed through a concealed camera and video monitor. For all groups, the first 120 seconds of viewing consisted of two one-minute commercials videotaped during early 1970. The first of these depicted the effectiveness of a certain paper towel, and the second advertised a humorous movie (rated "G"). The commercials were selected for their humor and attention-getting characteristics.

Thereafter, children in the experimental group observed the first three and one-half minutes of a program from a popular television series, *The Untouchables.* The sequence, which preserved a simple story line, contained a chase, two fist-fighting scenes, two shootings, and a knifing. In contrast, children in the control group viewed a highly active three-and-one-half minute videotaped sports sequence in which athletes competed in hurdle races, high jumps, and the like. For all subjects, the final 60 seconds of the program contained a commercial for automobile tires. Before the end of this last commercial, the experimenter reentered the room and announced that she was ready to begin.

Assessment of willingness to hurt another child. The subject was escorted by the experimenter from the television room to a second room and seated at a response box apparatus modeled after the one employed by Mallick and McCandless (1966). The grey metal response box, which measured approximately 17" wide x 6" high, displayed a red button on the left, a green button on the right, and a white light centered above these two manipulanda. The word HURT appeared beneath the red button, while the word HELP appeared beneath the green button. Several plastic wires led from the response box to a vent in the wall. The experimenter explained to the subject that these wires were connected to a game in an adjacent room and that "one of the other children is in the next room right now and will start to play the game in just a minute." She further explained that the game required the player in the other room to turn a handle and that the white light would come on each time the other child in the next room started to turn the handle, thus activating the red and green buttons.

The experimenter continued: "When this white light comes on, you have to push one of these two buttons. If you push this green button, that will make the handle next door easier to turn and will help the child to win the game. If you push this red button, that will make the handle next door feel hot. That will hurt the child, and he will have to let go of the handle. Remember, this is the *help* button, and this is the *hurt* button [indicating]. See, it says *help* and *hurt* . . . .You have to push one of these two buttons each time the light goes on, but you can push whichever one you want to. You can always push the same button or you can change from one button to the other whenever you want to, but just remember, each time the light goes on, you can push only one. So if you push this green button then you help the other child and if you push this red button then you hurt the other child. Now if you push this green button for *just a second,* then you *help the other child just a little,* and if you push this red button down for *just a second,* then you *hurt the other child just a little.* But if you push this green button down a little longer, then you help the other child a little more, and if you push this red button down a little longer, then you hurt the other child a little more, *The longer you push the green button, the more you help the other child* and *the longer you push the red button, the more you hurt the other child."*

This explanation, with slightly varied wording, was repeated a second time if the child did not indicate comprehension of the instructions. After being assured that the subject understood the task, the experimenter left the room.[4]

Although all the subjects were led to believe that other children were participating, there was, in fact, no other child; the entire procedure was controlled in the next room so as to produce 20 trials, with an intertrial interval of approximately 15 seconds. Each child's response to each trial (appearance of the white light) and the duration of the response recorded to the hundredth of a second was automatically registered. When the subject had completed 20 trials, the experimenter reentered the room and announced that the game was over.

Assessment of aggressive play. The influence of televised violence on the children's subsequent play activities was also explored, although this issue was of secondary interest in the present research (the study being primarily concerned with interpersonal aggression rather than aggression aimed at inanimate objects). After completing the button-pushing experiment, the child was escorted to a third room (designated the "play room") across the hallway. The room contained two large tables, on each of which appeared three attractive nonaggressive toys (for example, a slinky, a cook set, a space station) and one aggressive toy (a gun or a knife). Two inflated plastic dolls, 36 inches and 42 inches in height, also stood in the room. The child was told that he would be left alone for a few minutes and that he could play freely with any of the toys.

All the children were observed through a one-way vision mirror, and their aggressive behavior was recorded using a time sampling procedure. One point was scored for the occurrence of each of three predetermined categories of aggressive play (playing with the knife, playing with the gun, assaulting either of the dolls) during the first ten seconds of each of ten half-minute periods. In order to assess interobserver reliability for this measure, ten subjects were observed independently by the two observers. Their aggreement using the scoring procedures was virtually perfect ($r = .99$).

At the end of the play period, the experimenter reentered the room and asked the child to recall both the television program which he had seen and the nature of the game he had played. (All children included in the analyses were able to recall correctly the operation of the red and green buttons and the essential content of the television programs to which they had been exposed.)[5] The child was then escorted to the lounge where the parent was waiting, thanked for his or her participation, rewarded with a small prize, and asked not to discuss the experiment with his or her friends.

RESULTS

Willingness to hurt another child

The single overall measure which appears to capture the greatest amount of information in this situation is the total duration in seconds of each subject's aggressive responses during the 20 trials. Since marked heterogeneity of variance was apparent among the groups on this measure, the overall 2 x 2 x 2 analysis of variance was performed on square-root transformed scores (i.e., $x' = \sqrt{x} + \sqrt{x + 1}$ [Winer, 1962]). The means for all groups on this measure are presented in Table

Table 1: Mean total duration (transformed) of aggressive responses in all groups

Program shown	5-6 year olds		8-9 year olds	
	Boys	Girls	Boys	Girls
Aggressive	9.65	8.98	12.50	8.53
Number of subjects	15	18	20	17
Nonaggressive	6.86	6.50	8.50	6.27
Number of subjects	15	17	18	16

1. (The analysis of variance for this and all other measures reported appears in Appendix C). The analysis itself reveals only one significant effect—for treatment conditions ($F = 4.16$, $p<.05$). Children who had observed the aggressive program later showed reliably more willingness to engage in interpersonal aggression than those who had observed the neutral program.

Several supplementary analyses, which may serve to clarify the nature of this overall effect, were also computed. For example, a subject's total duration score may be viewed as the product of the number of times he aggresses and the average duration of each of these aggressive responses. Moreover, these two measures are only moderately, although reliably, related in the overall sample ($r = +.30$, $p<.05$). Analysis of variance for the average duration of the HURT responses reveals only a significant program effect that directly parallels the effects for total duration ($F = 3.95$, $p<.05$). The means for all groups on this measure are presented in Table 2. In contrast, analysis of the frequency measure fails to show any significant effects, although, as seen in Table 3, the tendency for the younger children is in the same direction.

In an exploratory internal analysis, restricted in this case to the 83 percent of the subjects who aggressed at least once, the latency in trials until the first aggressive response occurred was also computed. A child who aggressed on the initial trial received a score of 0, a child who aggressed for the first time on the eighth trial received a score of 7, and so on. These data are shown in Table 4. Analysis of variance revealed two

Table 2: Mean average durations (total duration/number of HURT responses)
of aggressive responses in all groups*

Program shown	5-6 year olds		8-9 year olds	
	Boys	Girls	Boys	Girls
Aggressive	3.42	2.64	5.18	3.07
Nonaggressive	2.55	2.09	2.07	1.57

*The number of subjects for each cell in this analysis is the same as that shown in Table 1.

Table 3: Mean number of aggressive responses in all groups*

Program shown	5-6 year olds		8-9 year olds	
	Boys	Girls	Boys	Girls
Aggressive	7.80	7.44	9.45	6.18
Nonaggressive	5.27	5.35	9.22	7.06

*The number of subjects for each cell in this analysis is the same as that shown in Table 1.

significant effects: an age difference ($F = 5.44$, $p<.05$), and an age x treatment interaction ($F=9.35$, $p<.01$). The interaction occurs because the aggressive program produced earlier use of the red button than the nonaggressive program among the younger children ($t=2.78$, $p<.01$) but was not influential in this respect for the older participants ($t=1.21$).

Table 4: Mean latency of aggressive responses (only for subjects who aggressed at least once) in all groups

Program shown	5-6 year olds		8-9 year olds	
	Boys	Girls	Boys	Girls
Aggressive	1.17	1.38	2.00	1.43
Number of subjects	12	13	20	14
Nonaggressive	3.91	4.58	1.06	.92
Number of subjects	11	12	17	13

Helping Responses

One possible explanation of the higher total aggression scores shown by the aggressive program group is that these children were simply more aroused than their nonaggressive treatment counterparts. To check on this interpretation, an overall analysis of variance was performed on the total duration of the HELP responses, employing the same square-root transformation described above. Presumably, if general arousal accounted for the effects of the HURT measure, the aggressive program groups should also show larger HELP scores than the nonaggressive program groups. However, contrary to the general arousal hypothesis, the effect of the treatments on this measure was not significant; the overall F comparing the aggressive program subjects' prosocial responses with those of the nonaggressive program observers was only 1.17. The one effect of borderline significance which did appear in this analysis was a program x sex x age interaction ($F = 3.91$, $p \cong .05$). As can be seen in Table 5, which presents these data, the interaction results from the very large helping responses shown by older girls who saw the aggressive program and the relatively large helping responses shown by younger girls who saw the nonaggressive one.

As a second check on the possibility that the longer durations in the aggressive program groups simply reflected a general arousal, a similar analysis was performed on the average duration scores of the HELP responses. In contrast to the comparable measure for aggressive responses, no significant differences for any of the main effects or interactions appeared on this measure (main effect for treatments: $F = 1.24$), although the older girls who saw the aggressive program showed particularly long average durations. The means for all groups are presented in

Table 5: Mean total duration (transformed) of
helping responses in all groups*

Program shown	5-6 year olds		8-9 year olds	
	Boys	Girls	Boys	Girls
Aggressive	10.81	11.66	11.32	19.97
Nonaggressive	10.76	14.12	11.59	10.69

*The number of subjects for each cell in this analysis is the same as that shown in Table 1.

Table 6. Finally, to show from a correlational approach that the overall HELP and HURT scores were not merely alternate measures of the same phenomenon, the product-moment correlation between the two sets of scores was computed. The resulting r of -.24 reflects a weak but significant ($p<.05$, two-tailed) negative relationship. Thus, overall, it appears clear that a specific disinhibition regarding *aggressive* behavior was produced by observing the modeled hostilities which cannot be explained as a general arousal effect.

Table 6: Mean average durations (total duration/number of HELP responses)
of helping responses in all groups*

Program shown	5-6 year olds		8-9 year olds	
	Boys	Girls	Boys	Girls
Aggressive	3.03	3.98	3.75	8.44
Nonaggressive	4.01	4.12	3.67	3.02

*The number of subjects for each cell in this analysis is the same as that shown in Table 1.

Aggression in the play situation

The mean aggressive play scores for all subjects are presented in Table 7. A 2 x 2 x 2 analysis of variance of these data revealed significant main effects for treatment ($F = 8.01$, $df = 1/28$, $p<.01$) and sex ($F = 37.87$, $df = 1/128$, $p<.001$). In addition, the treatment x sex ($F = 4.11$, $df = 1/128$, $p<.05$), treatment x age ($F = 4.28$, $df = 1/128$, $p<.05$) and treatment x sex x age ($F = 4.68$, $df = 1/128$, $p<.05$) interactions were all significant. As is apparent from inspection of Table 7, these interactions arose from the fact that, although children exposed to the aggressive program tended to show a higher level of aggressive play than children exposed to the nonaggressive one in all simple comparisons, the effect was much greater for the younger boys than for any of the remaining groups.

Table 7: Mean number of time-sampled aggressive play responses in
all groups*

Program shown	5-6 year olds		8-9 year olds	
	Boys	Girls	Boys	Girls
Aggressive	7.13	2.94	5.65	3.00
Nonaggressive	3.33	2.65	5.39	2.63

*The number of subjects for each cell in this analysis is the same as that shown in Table 1.

DISCUSSION

The overall results of the present experiment appear to provide relatively consistent evidence for the view that certain aspects of a child's willingness to aggress may be at least temporarily increased by merely witnessing aggressive television episodes. These findings seem to confirm and extend many earlier reports regarding the effects of symbolically modeled aggression on the subsequent imitative aggressive behavior of young observers toward inanimate objects (e.g., Bandura, Ross, and Ross, 1963a; Hicks, 1965; Rosekrans and Hartup, 1967). Likewise, the present data are in accord with other studies which have shown disinhibition of both young children's aggressive play and older viewers' willingness to shock another person after observing symbolic aggressive modeling. As in many earlier studies, subjects exposed to symbolic aggressive models regularly tended to behave more aggressively than control group subjects tested under identical circumstances. Further, the present results emerged despite the brevity of the aggressive sequences (less than four minutes), the absence of a strong prior instigation to aggression, and the clear availability of an alternative helping response.

The various measures obtained from the response box, considered together, provide some clarification of the nature of the effects obtained in the overall analysis. While the younger children tended to show a greater willingness to hurt after observing the aggressive program in every measure employed, the overall effect on the total duration measure appears to stem predominantly from the *average duration* of the subjects' aggressive responses. In fact, as Table 2 shows, the group means on this measure did not overlap; the *lowest* individual cell mean among those who observed the aggressive program was higher than the *highest* mean among those groups who observed the nonaggressive program.

It should also be recalled that the instructions given to all children emphasized that a brief depression of the HURT button would cause only minimal distress to the other child, while longer depressions would cause increasingly greater discomfort. This fact, coupled with the finding that the overall average duration of such responses was more than 75 percent longer in the aggressive program group than in the control group, seems to suggest clearly that the primary effect of exposure to the aggressive program was that of reducing subjects' restraints against inflicting severe discomfort on the ostensible peer victim—that is, of increasing disinhibition regarding the *magnitude* of the hurting response. With the exception of the older girls, this effect was not paralleled by an increment in the corresponding measures of helping; thus it cannot be attributed to simple arousal effects.

It should be noted that the measures of aggressive play response were obtained after all the subjects had been given an opportunity to help or hurt another child. Thus the observed aggressive play effects might reflect an interaction between the programs and some aspect of the hurting/helping opportunity rather than the simple influence of the programs themselves. While the present data do not permit us to address the possibility of such interactions directly, it is clear that the obtained results are consistent with earlier studies which used other types of modeled aggressive scenes and had no such intervening measures.

The present experiment was designed primarily to determine whether children's willingness to engage in interpersonal aggression would be affected by the viewing of violent televised material. Within the context of the experimental situation and dependent measures employed, it appeared that this was indeed the case. However, the findings obtained raise, but leave unanswered, many important issues. For example, it is clear that not all young children will become more aggressive, even temporarily, as a function of observing aggressive programs. It is thus important to determine the antecedents and correlates of such reactions to violence. Initial breakthroughs have begun to be made in that direction, as Ekman, his associates, and the present investigators have reported elsewhere (Ekman, Liebert, Friesen, Harrison, Zlatchin, Malmstrom, and Baron, 1971).

Among the questions raised by the recent findings, the following seem to deserve attention: (1) Do the effects of observed violence upon children's behavior vary as a function of the length and "plot" of the observed sequence? (2) Will the observation of aggressive scenes produce greater effects upon the behavior of young observers when they have been subjected to prior anger arousal? (3) Do the effects of observing aggression change as the child reaches the preadolescent and adolescent years? (4) What particular types of modeled aggression (Western-style gunfights, fist-fights, war scenes) are most and least likely to have such effects? (5) What is the durability of the influence of symbolically modeled aggression and is the effect cumulative? Last, and perhaps of greatest importance, (6) What sort of televised sequences will *reduce* the probability of interpersonal aggression? Extensive experimental analyses in a variety of settings, some of which are already under way, are required to answer these questions.

FOOTNOTES

1. Frustration was also systematically manipulated in this study, but it had no significant effect and did not interact with the modeling factor. However, the frustration manipulation may have been a relatively weak one.

2. This study was supported by a contract from the National Institute of Mental Health to the Fels Institute and was conducted while both authors were affiliated with the institute. (Dr. Liebert is now at the Department of Psychology, State University of New York at Stony Brook. Dr. Baron is now at the Department of Psychology, Purdue University.) The contributions of the coauthors to the project were approximately equal. The authors wish to thank Robert Devine, Joan Kleban, Diane Liebert, Carol Lyons, Cheryl Russell, and Sharon Swenson for their many contributions.

3. Since no specific information could be provided in public announcements or over the telephone, it appeared necessary to have parents accompany their children to the Institute in order to assure that no child participated without the informed consent of his parents. In order to defray the costs of transportation, baby sitters for siblings who remained at home, and the like, and to eliminate economic biases which might otherwise have appeared in the sample, a ten-dollar stipend was given the parent of each participant. No parent who appeared for the interview declined to allow his or her child to participate.

4. It should be noted that similar tasks have gained widespread usage in experiments dealing with human aggression (Baron and Kepner, 1970; Berkowitz and Geen, 1966; Buss, 1966). Moreover, the Mallick and McCandless (1966) apparatus appears to provide subjects with a credible, apparent opportunity to harm a peer without actually jeopardizing a young victim. There is evidence to suggest that behavior on such tasks is related directly to the occurrence of aggressive acts in naturalistic social situations (Wolfe and Baron, 1971; Hartmann, 1969).

5. Nine children, all in the 5-6-year-old age group, were terminated prior to the collection of data because they refused to remain alone, cried, or left the experimental situation. Twenty-three other children participated in the entire experiment but were not included in the sample. Of these, 14 (five in the younger age group and nine in the older group) did not understand or follow instructions for the response box; seven (three younger and four older children) played or explored the room instead of watching television. The data for the remaining two children were not recorded properly due to technical difficulties.

REFERENCES

Bandura, A. Influence of models' reinforcement contingencies on the acquisition of imitative responses. *Journal of Personality and Social Psychology*, 1965, **1**, 589-95.

Bandura, A. *Principles of behavior modification.* New York: Holt, Rinehart, and Winston, Inc. 1969.

Bandura, A., Ross, D., and Ross, S.A. Transmission of aggression through imitation of aggressive models. *Journal of Abnormal and Social Psychology*, 1961, **63**, 575-82.

Bandura, A., Ross, D., and Ross, S.A. Imitation of film-mediated aggressive models. *Journal of Abnormal and Social Psychology*, 1963, **66**, 3-11.(a)

Bandura, A., Ross, D., and Ross, S.A. Vicarious reinforcement and imitative learning. *Journal of Abnormal and Social Psychology,* 1963, **67**, 601-07.(b)

Baron, R.A., and Kepner, C.R. Model's behavior and attraction toward the model as determinants of adult aggressive behavior. *Journal of Personality and Social Psychology,* 1970, **14**, 335-44.

Berkowitz, L. Some aspects of observed aggression. *Journal of Personality and Social Psychology,* 1965, **2**, 359-69.

Berkowitz, L., and Geen, R.G. Film violence and the cue properties of available targets. *Journal of Personality and Social Psychology,* 1966, **3**, 525-30.

Berkowitz, L., and Rawlings, E. Effects of film violence on inhibitions against subsequent aggression. *Journal of Abnormal and Social Psychology,* 1963, **66**, 405-12.

Buss, A. H. Instrumentality of aggression, feedback, and frustration as determinants of physical aggression. *Journal of Personality and Social Psychology,* 1966, **3**, 153-62.

Ekman, P., Liebert, R.M., Friesen, W.V., Harrison, R., Zlatchin, C., Malmstrom, E., and Baron, R.A. Facial expressions of emotion while watching televised violence as a predictor of subsequent aggression. In *Television and social behavior,* Vol. 5. Washington, D.C.: U.S. Government Printing Office, 1971.

Feshbach, S. The stimulating versus cathartic effects of a vicarious aggressive activity. *Journal of Abnormal and Social Psychology,* 1961, **63**, 381-85.

Feshbach, S. and Singer, R.D. *Television and aggression.* San Francisco: Jossey-Bass, 1971.

Flanders, J.P. A review of research on imitative behavior. *Psychological Bulletin,* 1968, **69**, 316-37.

Halloran, J.D. Television and violence. *The Twentieth Century,* 1964, 61-72.

Hanratty, M.A. Imitation of film-mediated aggression against live and inanimate victims. Unpublished master's thesis, Vanderbilt University, 1969.

Hanratty, M.A., Liebert, R.M., Morris, L.W., and Fernandez, L.E. Imitation of film-mediated aggression against live and inanimate victims. *Proceedings of the 77th Annual Convention of the American Psychological Association*, 1969, **4**, 457-58.

Hanratty, M.A., O'Neal, E., and Sulzer, J.L. The effect of frustration upon imitation of aggression. *Journal of Personality and Social Psychology*, in press.

Hartmann, D.P. Influence of symbolically modeled instrumental aggression and pain cues on aggressive behavior. *Journal of Personality and Social Psychology*, 1969, **11**, 280-88.

Hicks, D.J. Imitation and retention of film-mediated aggressive peer and adult models. *Journal of Personality and Social Psychology*, 1965, **2**, 97-100.

Klapper, J.T. The impact of viewing "aggression": studies and problems of extrapolation. In Larsen (Ed.), *Violence and the mass media*.

Larsen, O.N. *Violence and the mass media.* New York: Harper & Row, 1968.

Lövaas, O.I. Effect of exposure to symbolic aggression on aggressive behavior. *Child Development*, 1961, **32**, 37-44.

Mallick, S.K., and McCandless, B.R. A study of catharsis of aggression. *Journal of Personality and Social Psychology, 1966, 4, 591-96.*

Merriam, E. We're teaching our children that violence is fun. *The Ladies' Home Journal*, 1964, **52**.

Rosekrans, M.A., and Hartup, W.W. Imitative influences of consistent and inconsistent responses consequences to a model on aggressive behavior in children. *Journal of Personality and Social Psychology*, 1967, **7**, 429-34.

Savitsky, J.C., Rogers, R.W., Izard, C.E., and Liebert, R.M. The role of frustration and anger in the imitation of filmed aggression against a human victim. *Psychological Reports*, 1971, **29**, 807-810.

Schramm, W., Lyle, J., and Parker, E.B. *Television in the lives of our children.* Stanford: Stanford University Press, 1961.

Siegel, A.E. Film-mediated fantasy aggression and strength of aggressive drive. *Child Development*, 1956, **27**, 365-78.

Walters, R.H. Implications of laboratory studies of the control and regulation of violence. *The Annals of the American Academy of Political and Social Science*, 1966, **364**, 60-72.

Walters, R.H. and Llewellyn-Thomas, E. Enhancement of punitiveness by visual and audiovisual displays. *Canadian Journal of Psychology*, 1963, **16**, 244-55.

Wertham, F. Is TV hardening us to the war in Vietnam? *New York Times,* December 4, 1966.

Wolfe, B.M., and Baron, R.A. Laboratory aggression related to aggression in naturalistic social situations: effects of an aggressive model on the behavior of college student and prisoner observers. *Psychonomic Science,* 1971, in press.

Appendix A: Distribution of economic backgrounds of subjects participating in this experiment

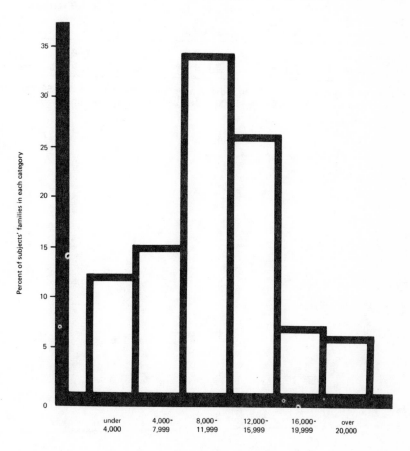

Total family income during 1969

Appendix B: Ranges and <u>means</u> of Economic backgrounds of subjects in this experiment in each group*

Programs	5-6 year olds		8-9 year olds	
	Boys	Girls	Boys	Girls
Aggressive	1–<u>3.0</u>–5	1–<u>3.5</u>–6	1–<u>3.2</u>–6	1–<u>2.9</u>–4
Nonaggressive	1–<u>3.1</u>–5	1–<u>3.1</u>–4	1–<u>3.4</u>–6	1–<u>2.9</u>–5

*Based on assigning the score of 1 to those who reported incomes of less than $4,000, 2 to those reporting incomes between $4,000 and $7,999, and so on (see Appendix A).

Appendix C

This Appendix contains the analyses of variance for each of the seven measures reported in the present paper.

Table C-1: Analysis of variance for total duration of aggressive responses
(transformed: $x' = \sqrt{x} + \sqrt{x + 1}$)

Source	df	MS	F
Program seen: aggressive or sports (A)	1	280.49	4.16*
Sex: male versus female (B)	1	110.05	1.63
Age: 5-6 versus 8-9 (C)	1	30.54	< 1
Interaction: A x B	1	8.89	< 1
Interaction: A x C	1	2.06	< 1
Interaction: B x C	1	56.28	< 1
Three-way interaction: A x B x C	1	4.24	< 1
Error	128	67.33	

*$p < .05$

Table C-2: Analysis of variance of average
durations of aggressive responses

Source	df	MS	F
Program seen: aggressive or sports (A)	1	76.76	3.95*
Sex: male versus female (B)	1	31.34	1.61
Age: 5-6 versus 8-9 (C)	1	3.00	< 1
Interaction: A x B	1	7.83	< 1
Interaction: A x C	1	21.49	1.11
Interaction: B x C	1	3.88	< 1
Three-way interaction: A x B x C	1	3.57	< 1
Error	128	19.45	

*$p < .05$

Table C-3: Analysis of variance of number of aggressive responses

Source	df	MS	F
Program seen: aggressive or sports (A)	1	33.15	1.16
Sex: male versus female (B)	1	68.52	2.40
Age: 5-6 versus 8-9 (C)	1	77.05	2.70
Interaction: A x B	1	5.10	< 1
Interaction: A x C	1	58.81	2.06
Interaction: B x C	1	56.18	1.97
Three-way interaction A x B x C	1	.96	< 1
Error	128	28.57	

Table C-4: Analysis of variance of latency (in trials) of first aggressive response among children who aggressed at least once

Source	df	MS	F
Program seen: aggressive or sports (A)	1	34.14	3.46
Sex: male versus female (B)	1	.06	< 1
Age: 5-6 versus 8-9 (C)	1	53.63	5.44*
Interaction: A x B	1	1.34	< 1
Interaction: A x C	1	92.25	9.35**
Interaction: B x C	1	4.32	< 1
Three-way interaction: A x B x C	1	.00	< 1
Error	104	9.86	

$*p < .05$
$**p < .01$

Table C-5: Analysis of variance for total duration of helping responses (transformed: $x' = \sqrt{x} + \sqrt{x + 1}$)

Source	df	MS	F
Program seen: aggressive or sports (A)	1	91.83	1.17
Sex: male versus female (B)	1	301.53	3.84
Age: 5-6 versus 8-9 (C)	1	81.51	1.04
Interaction: A x B	1	104.57	1.33
Interaction: A x C	1	274.88	3.50
Interaction: B x C	1	26.28	< 1
Three-way interaction: A x B x C	1	306.69	3.91*
Error	128	78.50	

$*p \cong .05$

Table C-6: Analysis of variance of average durations of helping responses

Source	df	MS	F
Program seen: aggressive or sports (A)	1	40.49	1.24
Sex: male versus female (B)	1	45.15	1.38
Age: 5-6 versus 8-9 (C)	1	37.13	1.13
Interaction: A x B	1	69.23	2.11
Interaction: A x C	1	105.55	3.22
Interaction: B x C	1	18.91	< 1
Three-way interaction: A x B x C	1	42.83	1.31
Error	128	32.79	

Table C-7: Analysis of variance of frequency of time-sampled
aggressive play

Source	df	MS	F
Program seen: aggressive or sports (A)	1	47.21	8.01**
Sex: male versus female (B)	1	223.07	37.87***
Age: 5-6 versus 8-9 (C)	1	.77	< 1
Interaction: A x B	1	24.20	4.11**
Interaction: A x C	1	25.25	4.28*
Interaction: B x C	1	.61	< 1
Three-way interaction: A x B x C	1	27.56	4.68*
Error	128	5.89	

*$p < .05$
**$p < .01$
***$p < .001$

Television Content and Young Children's Behavior

Aletha Huston Stein and Lynette Kohn Friedrich
with Fred Vondracek

Pennsylvania State University

The vast amount of experimental study of imitation during the last decade has produced a solid body of information about imitation of aggression. In studies of young children, exposure to aggressive models, whether live or filmed, consistently led to increases in aggressive behavior immediately after exposure (Bandura, 1969). Nevertheless, if one attempts to generalize these findings to the everyday effects of television violence on children, several qualifications must be made. In most of the studies, the children have received one exposure to the modeled behavior and have been observed immediately following exposure. The films have often been specially prepared by the investigator to be a fairly "pure case" of aggression. The behavioral effects have usually been assessed in a setting similar to that observed in the film. The aggression observed has frequently consisted of attacks on Bobo dolls and other inanimate objects rather than on other people.

Survey studies of aggressive behavior in relation to naturalistic viewing of television violence are not subject to these restrictions, but the correlational method used does not permit inferences about causal directions. Such studies have found correlations between preference for television violence and children's aggressive behavior (Eron, 1963; Baker and Ball, 1969), but no relation of aggressive behavior to overall frequency of television viewing. Most survey studies have been focused on children above age ten, who may show less clear effects of television than younger children.

Some combination of the advantages of the experimental and survey methods is needed to provide more information about the actual impact of televised violence on children. One field experiment with adolescent boys did combine experimental control of television exposure with observation of behavior in a natural setting (Feshbach and Singer, 1971). Over a six-week period, the boys who watched aggressive television programs were rated *less* aggressive than a control group exposed to nonaggressive programs. As these results contradict most of the other available data, there is a need for more information on the effects of media exposure on naturalistic behavior.

A second area of behavior that has received attention from imitation researchers is broadly labeled "prosocial behavior." A number of studies have demonstrated that exposure to models can increase children's altruism or generosity to others and can promote the setting of high standards for self-reward (Hoffman, 1970). Other forms of prosocial behavior of concern in the present study are cooperation, nurturance, frustration tolerance, and task persistence. The influence of television on prosocial behavior is almost unexplored in survey studies; yet the potential of this medium for such effect is immense.

The present study was a naturalistic experiment testing the effects of both aggressive and prosocial television programs on the social behavior of preschool children. It differed from most earlier studies by combining experimental manipulation of program content with assessment of behavioral change in a natural setting: the nursery school.

In the learning segment of the theoretical model, two considerations are relevant to the proposed study: what the child learns and what variables influence how much he learns. It is expected that the child will learn aggression *or* prosocial behavior as responses to particular types of stimulus situations, not as "traits" or "motives" which will be manifested regardless of situation.

Background literature. The theoretical basis for the research was Bandura's (1969) theory of observational learning. In that theory, those components which affect learning of the content to which the individual is exposed are conceptualized separately from those which affect performance. Learning is thought to be partially a function of attention to the stimulus and of capacity to cognitively code and retain the stimulus material. Performance of observed behavior is affected by reinforcement and punishment of the model, status of the model, similarity between the model and the observer, and subsequent reinforcement and punishment of the observer. Other variables affecting performance involve direct interpersonal contact between model and subject and are, therefore, not directly relevant to the question of television effects.

On the basis of this model, we expected two variables to influence the amount a child learned from any particular television exposure: attention to the program and capacity for coding and retention. The latter is probably an important component of traditional measures of intelligence, so we expected that brighter children would learn more from a given observational experience. On the other hand, greater learning may not necessarily lead to behavioral effects, because brighter children may also distinguish between fantasy and reality more readily. They might, therefore, be less likely to adopt fantasy content inappropriately from television.

In a natural setting, performance of behavior learned or disinhibited through observation of television programs is undoubtedly influenced by many other variables. One of the most important is the immediate situational context. Many theorists have argued that behavioral dispositions are learned in connection with particular stimulus contexts, not as generalized traits that occur regardless of situation (Mischel, 1968; Wright, 1960). In the case of aggressive and prosocial behavior, it was expected that frustrating or conflict-full situations might be especially prone to elicit these behavioral dispositions. Many television programs present aggression as a mode of problem or conflict solution (Baker and Ball, 1969). One of the goals of prosocial programs is to teach children alternative modes of coping with these situations.

The design of the present study was also directed to two other issues that frequently arise in the media literature: the effects of repeated exposure to televised stimuli, and the duration of effects of a given exposure over time. Two contradictory predictions about the effects of repeated exposure can be made on the basis of current theory. Cumulative effects may be postulated on the assumption that repeated exposure produces overlearning of the frequent themes on television. Some have argued that this overlearning leads children to take for granted the high frequency of violent problems solutions they see each day and, therefore, to be more likely to use such solutions themselves. The contradictory prediction is that habituation to televised violence will occur so that repeated exposures will produce less and less effect. There is some evidence that emotional arousal upon exposure to violence does decline with repeated exposures, but it is unclear whether behavioral responses also are affected less (Stein, in press).

Similarly, there is little evidence concerning the duration of behavioral effects. Most experimental studies have measured behavior immediately following exposure. In one study (Hicks, 1965), children did show retention of imitative aggression when they were returned to the test situation six months after exposure, but this retention may have been due to the fact that the stimulus situation was a unique one with which the child's only previous experience was the earlier modeling and play.

Theoretically, one would expect duration of behavioral effects in a naturalistic context if there were environmental supports and reinforcements for them. One study has demonstrated that aggressive responses in a nursery school receive a high frequency of reinforcements (Patterson, Littman, and Bricker, 1971). Positive reinforcements for prosocial behavior would also be expected to occur frequently in a nursery school. Durable effects might be found if the television exposure triggered some initial increases in aggression or prosocial behavior which were then maintained by environmental reinforcements. Without such supports, most behavioral dispositions would be expected to be extinguished over time.

The discussion thus far has been directed toward the general effects of aggressive and prosocial television on young children .Clearly, the individual characteristics of the children affect the way in which they respond to television as well. Sex, age, intellectual level, patterns of socialization by parents and peers, and the already existing levels of aggressive and prosocial personality dispositions all may influence the ways in which children respond to television.

Boys and girls apparently learn somewhat different content from exposure to the same program. In one study, the children remembered the actions of like-sex characters in a film better than those of opposite-sex characters (Maccoby and Wilson, 1957). Boys are also more likely to imitate some forms of aggression in experimental studies (Bandura et al. 1963a; 1963b), although sex differences have not been found in all studies (Albert, 1957; Mussen and Rutherford, 1961: Rosekrans and Hartup, 1967).

Many authors have hypothesized that the younger the child, the greater the effects that television may have on him or her (e.g., Baker and Ball, 1969; Schramm, Lyle, and Parker, 1961). Preschool children are thought to be especially susceptible because they are less able than older children to separate fantasy from reality or to maintain some distance from their immediate perceptual experience. While many experimental studies of imitation have been conducted with preschool children, there is virtually no survey or naturalistic data with very young children. Further, many of the survey studies with older children were conducted when television was so new that the children studied had not been exposed to television during their own preschool years (e.g., Himmelweit, Oppenheim, and Vince, 1958; Schramm et al., 1961).

A child with a repertoire of alternative behaviors in a given situation is probably less likely to perform a behavior learned from television than is a child with few alternatives. Some authors have suggested that children from violent families or from families of low socioeconomic status are likely to have fewer alternatives to the patterns of behavior learned from television (see Baker and Ball, 1969). There is, in essence, a void in their socialization experiences that is filled with the limited repertoire of current television fare. The concept of a socialization "void" for some children is relevant to both the aggressive and the prosocial television experiences provided in the present study. Children who have learned many alternative and nonaggressive coping responses were expected to be less affected by aggressive television than those who had not. Similarly, children who had relatively little socialization in prosocial means of coping were expected to respond more clearly to the prosocial programs. It was assumed on the basis of previous evidence that children from lower socioeconomic status (SES) families would be less likely to have received training in prosocial alternatives than those from higher SES families (Hess, 1970).

Finally, the child's current level of aggressive or prosocial behavior may affect his response to media presentations. It has been proposed that individuals with high levels of aggression are more likely to adopt aggressive patterns from television than those with low levels of aggression. Evidence with children, however, is equivocal. In situations similar to the one observed, children with different levels of habitual aggression do not differ. Highly aggressive children, on the other hand, are less likely to imitate nonaggressive behavior, and more likely to behave aggressively in situations that are dissimilar to the one observed, than are nonaggressive children. Because of the absence of baseline measures, it is impossible to tell whether the latter finding is a function of the observed aggression or merely a demonstration of a general behavioral tendency to be aggressive in many situations (Bandura et al., 1963a; Meyerson, 1967; Walters and Willows, 1960).

The overall objective of the present study was to determine the effects of repeated exposure to aggressive and prosocial content on the naturalistic behavior of preschool children. In the research reported here, the content of the programs shown to the children was experimentally manipulated in order to provide a basis for the inference of causal relations. The programs were shown repeatedly over a period of time, and evaluation of effects was carried out in a naturalistic setting—the preschool.

The aggressive programs were chosen to be representative of a class of programs commonly viewed by young children. Although many writers have asserted that cartoons are less influential than "real-life" presentations because children perceive them as being less realistic, there is little evidence on this point. For this reason, programs using cartoons of human characters—*Batman* and *Superman*—were chosen as a middle ground between the realistic and animated modes of presentation.

The prosocial programs were selected from *Misterogers Neighborhood*, one of the few programs that stresses social and emotional development rather than cognitive development. Although it is not representative of a large class of programs, it was considered a model which, if effective, might be emulated.

In addition to the obvious practical advantages, the preschool setting was chosen because it was assumed that the effects of the child's everyday television viewing at home would be reduced and that the importance of the programs presented in the study would be enhanced. As children's behavior is somewhat situation-specific, behavior observed in the preschool setting should be more influenced by experiences there than experiences elsewhere.

One specific focus of the study was to determine the effects of television programs on responses to frustration and interpersonal conflict. Frustration was defined very broadly as any interference with ongoing activity either by outside agents or because of the child's own inability to complete an activity easily.

METHOD

The study was a naturalistic experiment conducted during a nine-week summer nursery school program in University Park, Pennsylvania. Observations of aggressive and prosocial behavior were conducted during free play for the entire session. The first three weeks were used to establish observer reliability and baseline levels of behavior. During the middle four weeks of the session, the children were randomly divided into three groups assigned to different types of television viewing: aggressive programs, prosocial programs, and neutral films. Each group saw twelve television programs or films during the four-week period. The final two weeks were considered a postviewing period during which extended effects of television viewing might be evaluated.

Although naturalistic behavior in the classroom was the principal dependent measure, several other measures were collected. These included intelligence test scores, ratings of attention to the television programs shown, observations of social interaction in a dyad immediately after one program, interviews with mothers about the children's home television viewing patterns, a test of knowledge about the content of the television programs, and a projective measure of aggressive and prosocial responses to frustration. The following diagram shows the phases of the study:

Baseline period	Experimental period	Postviewing period
3 weeks	4 weeks	2 weeks
1. Free play observations 2. Intelligence tests	1. Free play observations each day 2. Attention to programs 3. Intelligence tests 4. Mother interview 5. Social interaction in dyad	1. Free play observations 2. Mother interview 3. "Content" of program test 4. Projective measure

Subjects

The subjects were 97 children (52 boys, 45 girls) ranging in age from three years 10 months to five years six months. The children were specially recruited for the summer nursery school program. For most, the program was the first school experience. The mean IQ, mental age, chronological age, and other demographic information about the sample are shown in Table 1. The group was slightly above average in IQ, but there was a wide range of intellectual functioning.

Social class. Considerable effort was expended to enroll children from lower socioeconomic status families—from stable working class families as well as the very poor. For those who could afford it, a token $5.00 in tuition was charged. Bus transportation was provided for 15 rural poor children. Nursery school administrative personnel were also very active in helping parents to make car pool transportation arrangements. As a result, slightly less than half of the sample came from nonstudent families with occupational status below the professional level. Although there were many applications from students and faculty members at Pennsylvania State University for enrollment of their children, preference in admission was given first to families without a university connection (unless they were nonprofessionals), next to undergraduate students, next to graduate students, and finally to faculty members. Priority was given to undergraduate students because at a large state university, they are likely to be more heterogeneous in social class background and in many of the values and attitudes associated with social class than are faculty members or graduate students. All parents were informed about the study before enrolling their children, and they agreed to allow their children to participate in any of the experimental conditions.

The standard scales for evaluating socioeconomic status were inadequate for the population we studied because there were no classifications for students. The occupational status for the nonstudent families was rated by the Duncan scale of occupational prestige (Duncan, 1961). The distribution was negatively skewed, so families with occupations in deciles 1-8 were assigned a rating of 1, and those in deciles 9-10 were

Table 1: Descriptive information about subjects

	Boys		Girls	
	Mean	SD	Mean	SD
IQ	110.3	17.0	114.6	17.3
Mental age (in months)	61.9	8.5	65.8	11.1
Chronological age (in months)	55.1	4.9	54.5	5.8
Local SES	2.5	1.1	2.5	1.1
Father's education (in years)	14.6	5.2	14.8	2.8
Mother's education (in years)	13.9	2.1	15.5	2.1
Occupational status	2.1	0.8	1.9	0.7
Number of children in family	2.1	0.6	2.2	0.6
Ordinal position	1.8	0.9	1.9	0.9
Number of working mothers	21		13	
Numbers of fathers absent	5		4	

assigned a rating of 3. Students were arbitrarily assigned a rating of 2. As this index is not entirely satisfactory, the educational level of each parent was also used. Finally, the investigators formed a socioeconomic status rating of each family based on father's education and student or nonstudent status (local SES). The four levels in this rating were: 1—high school or less; 2—some college or posthigh school training below Bachelor's degree; 3—Bachelor's degree (including *all* graduate students); 4—Master's degree or more and nonstudent.

The principal difference between this rating and father's education was that graduate students with Master's degrees were placed on a lower level than their education alone would indicate. This was done because most students are economically more like families with lower educational levels, even though that economic deprivation may be temporary. The four indices of social class were highly related to one another. The correlations among them appear in Table 2. The local SES index was most highly correlated with the other three. The distribution of families by local SES appears in Table 3.

Other characteristics of the sample about which information was obtained were: birth order, family size, father presence, maternal employment, and the amount of time the father spent at home during the child's waking hours. The means appear in Table 1.

Table 2: Intercorrelations of demographic information

	2	3	4	5	6	7
1. IQ	83	−19	.28	43	41	28
2. Mental age		37	16	31	34	16
3. Chronological age			−16	−14	−07	−16
4. Local SES				75	60	74
5. Father education					53	61
6. Mother education						53
7. Occupational status						——

Subject loss. The nursery school session began with 100 children enrolled. During the first two weeks, five children withdrew either because of poor adjustment by the child or because of changing family plans. These children were immediately replaced from the waiting list with other children who were as close as possible in sex, age, and social class. During the third week, two additional children withdrew, reducing the final sample to 98. They were not replaced because there was not adequate time to obtain baseline data on new children. Five additional children withdrew during the four-week experimental period. Three girls had not adjusted to nursery school; they showed continuing fear of maternal separation and had other problems. Two others (one boy and one girl) were taken on family vacations for two weeks and were disqualified from further participation in the study. Losses due to vacations were small because parents were asked to assure the nursery school that they would not plan vacations that would take the child out of school more than two days. Finally, one boy was absent due to illness during the entire postviewing period (the final two weeks). Therefore, complete classroom observational data were obtained on 92 subjects. Of the subjects lost, three were in the Aggressive condition, three in the Neutral condition, and two in the Prosocial condition.

Table 3: Distribution of subjects in the four
local SES categories

	Number of subjects
1. (high school or less)	29
2. (some college)	17
3. (Bachelor's degree and graduate students)	34
4. (advanced degrees)	17

Setting. The summer nursery school was conducted in the facilities of the Division of Individual and Family Studies at the Pennsylvania State University. There were four classes of 25 children each that met for two and one-half hours three times a week. Two classes met in the morning, two in the afternoon. Each class was conducted in a large room designed as a laboratory preschool facility. An outdoor playground with extensive equipment was available to each.

Two head teachers each taught two classes. Both teachers were advanced graduate students in Child Development and Family Relationships with an emphasis in early childhood education. Each had previous teaching experience. Other personnel in each class included a paid graduate or undergraduate assistant and three to five undergraduate students enrolled in a practicum course for preschool teaching. The overall functioning of the nursery schools was supervised by another advanced graduate student and by the early childhood education faculty. Both classes were conducted in a fairly traditional way with a great deal of freedom for the children to choose activities and to behave spontaneously.

Sex, age, and social class were balanced in making classroom assignments. The classroom means on these variables were generally equivalent except that the afternoon classes were of higher average social class than the morning classes. The biserial correlation of time of day with local SES was .44. This difference was unavoidable for practical reasons: bus transportation for rural poor children could be provided only once a day; and parents generally preferred morning sessions. As lower SES families were more difficult to recruit, it was more often necessary to assign them to their preferred time in order to get them to come at all. Despite these differences between the morning and afternoon sessions, there was a considerable amount of overlap. Within each, children of different SES levels were evenly distributed between the two classrooms (see Table 4).

Table 4: Mean age and SES in each classroom

	CA (in months)	Local SES
Morning		
Teacher 1	54.9	2.2
Teacher 2	55.8	1.8
Afternoon		
Teacher 1	52.8	3.0
Teacher 2	55.8	2.8

Design. Because the two types of television programs were expected to have somewhat antithetical effects, the design was arranged so that children in a given classroom were not assigned to both experimental conditions. Instead, within each classroom, children were divided between one experimental condition and the neutral condition. The design is summarized in the following diagram:

	Condition		
Morning	Aggressive	Neutral	Prosocial
Teacher 1	15	10	
Teacher 2		10	15
Afternoon			
Teacher 1		10	15
Teacher 2	15	10	

This design was intended to provide controls for the possible differences between specific classrooms while avoiding contaminating the effects of one experimental condition with those of the other. Because each teacher had two classes, it was possible to balance teachers and conditions.

Experimental conditions

Aggressive program condition. Six *Batman* cartoons and six *Superman* cartoons were shown on alternate days in this condition. Each cartoon actually consisted of two stories lasting slightly more than ten minutes each. They were shown as they were broadcast on the air with commercials removed. Although detailed content analyses of the cartoons were not made, each contained several instances of physical violence and verbal aggression. Other content analyses indicate that such programs consistently contain high frequencies of aggressive behavior (Gerbner, 1969).

Prosocial program condition. Twelve episodes of *Misterogers Neighborhood* were shown in the Prosocial condition. These episodes were selected from scripts made available by the *Misterogers* staff. They included the following themes: cooperation, sharing, sympathy, affection and friendship, understanding the feelings of others, verbalizing one's own feelings, delay of gratification, persistence and competence at tasks, learning to accept rules, control of aggression, adaptive coping with frustration. Details of the programs appear in Appendix A. Although each program was approximately 28 minutes long, each was divided into two sections: "real life" themes in which Mr. Rogers played a central role, and fantasy themes in which puppets and people portrayed fictional events.

Neutral film condition. The children in the Neutral condition were shown varied films chosen from the extensive library of children's films at Pennsylvania State University. The films were chosen on the criterion that they had little or no aggressive or prosocial content. Each film was previewed and judged by the principal investigator. Aggressive content was almost completely absent from the films, but some prosocial content was inevitable. Films were selected only when such prosocial content was not emphasized and did not form the central theme. For example, a film about children on the farm was selected even though there were occasional references to the fact that the children helped with the chores. On the other hand, a film about an Indian boy and his elephant was excluded because there was a heavy emphasis on kindness and mutual help. A more complete description of the neutral films appears in Appendix B. The films covered widely diverse topics and themes. Each lasted 10-15 minutes; two films were usually shown in one session. Although black-and-white films were preferred, some of the films were in color.

Films were used rather than television programs because of their availability for prior screening. It was considered particularly important in this condition to eliminate stimuli that were similar to either experimental condition. Additionally, previous research indicated comparable effects of stimuli presented on television or on film (Bandura, Ross, and Ross, 1963a and b).

Procedures

Assignment of subjects to conditions. Children were assigned to experimental conditions at the end of the baseline period. The assignment of experimental conditions to classrooms was determined by a coin flip. Within each classroom, boys and girls were assigned randomly to conditions. Adjustments were then made if the mean chronological age or social class ratings differed. All assignments and adjustments were made using the children's identification numbers rather than names.

Mechanics of television viewing. The television programs were shown in three small, windowless rooms located near the children's classrooms. Videotape recorders were used to show the aggressive and prosocial programs. For purposes of viewing, each classroom was divided into two shifts: Group A and Group B. On a given day, the first shift to go to the viewing rooms left 15-20 minutes after nursery school began and returned approximately half an hour later. The second shift left after nursery school had been in session for about an hour. While they were gone, the first shift was observed. When the second shift returned, they were observed for the remaining hour of nursery school. Equipment problems disrupted this schedule on a few days, but it was followed on most days.

A particular group of children alternated between the first and second shift every other day. That is, Group A went first one day, second the next, first the next, and so on. Each group was composed of both experimental and neutral boys and girls—they went to different rooms during the same time period. The viewing groups for the two experimental conditions numbered seven or eight children. As the Neutral condition children from both classrooms in a particular shift were combined, their groups numbered ten.

Children were accompanied to the viewing rooms by the teaching assistant from their classroom. Each assistant remained with the children in the experimental condition from her classroom. Children in the Neutral condition were accompanied by a student nurse whose course involved participation in the nursery school program. These individuals were the only teaching staff who were told which programs the children were seeing, and they were cautioned to secrecy. The head teachers were aware of the need for the teaching staff to remain blind to the experimental assignments of the children and assiduously maintained their own and others' ignorance. In general, they appeared to be relatively unconcerned about the children's television assignments.

Equipment failure in all conditions on one day (the fourth in the experimental period) forced cancellation of nearly all of the film and television showings. Therefore, the experimental treatment was extended one day beyond the original schedule, reducing the postviewing period to five days.

Subject absence. The maximum number of programs missed by any child due to absence was four. Therefore, all children saw at least eight of the twelve programs. The mean number of programs actually seen by children in the three conditions was: Aggressive = 11.14, Neutral = 10.86, Prosocial = 10.75.

Classroom observations

Two categories of stimuli to the child being observed were scored: frustration and commands. Frustration was broadly defined as any interference with an ongoing activity. The interference might result from the actions of an adult or another child or from objects in the environment. It might be intentional or accidental. Frustrations were scored independently of the child's response; that is, an interference with his activity was scored even when he showed no response to it. For example, if all the swings were occupied and a child expressed a desire to swing, frustration was scored even when he walked away to do something else.

Commands and requests by adults and children were scored separately because it was unclear whether they could be considered frustrations. It was decided that they would be combined with the frustration categories if there were substantial correlations between stimulus categories and if both types of stimuli correlated with similar types of behavior. A list of the specific stimulus categories appears in Table 5, and the definitions of each are given in Appendix C.

The behaviors were grouped in the following general categories: aggression, prosocial interpersonal behavior, persistence, self-control, and regression. The subcategories in each are listed in Table 5 and defined in Appendix D. The aggression categories were adopted with very minor revision from those used by Sears, Rau, and Alpert (1965). Aggression was generally defined as an action that was intended to injure another person or an object. Intention was inferred from cues that accompanied the behavior, such as looking directly at the object and failing to terminate the response when the object protested.

During the preliminary development of the categories, it became clear that some behaviors that would ordinarily be scored as aggressive were carried out as a game even when there was no evidence of role playing. For example, two boys sitting next to each other engaged in a game in which one hit the other's arm and both laughed. Then the second child hit the first and both laughed again. For this reason, the fantasy aggression category was extended to include such playful, game-like aggression as well as aggression occurring in role play. Scoring of this category was very conservative—it was scored only when the aggression was *clearly* playful for all participants.

The prosocial interpersonal categories included cooperation, nurturance, mature social skills, and verbalization of feeling. Cooperation was

Table 5: Summary of observation categories

Stimulus categories			Responses which are specific to these stimuli	
Frustration				
FA	C aggressive to S		o	no response
FP	property frustration		pa	persistence for attention
FC	frustration by C		laf	laughs, positive affect
FI	T or C ignores S		al	finds alternative
FT	frustration by T		+	submits
FO	object frustration		−	refuses to comply
Commands				
CT	T commands S		+	S complies
	1	Request, S has choice	o	S ignores
	2	Demand, no choice	−	S refuses or actively
	3	Vigorous command		does not comply
CC	C commands S			
	2	Request or demand, friendly		
	3	Vigorous, loud demand		

Behavior (to be scored regardless of Stimulus)

Aggressive (ax)			Regressive	
ap	physical		cr	crying, pouting
av	verbal		wi	withdrawal, giving
at	teasing (nonverbal)			up
af	fantasy or playful		**Interpersonal (ix)**	
ao	agg to object		ic	cooperation
ac	vigorous commands		im	mature social skills
aa	tattling		in	nurturance,
Persistence (px on tasks)				sympathy
pt	task persistence		iv	stating feelings or
pi	independence - refuses help			reasons
ph	instrumental help seeking		**Rules and self-control**	
			ro	rule obedience
			rd	rule disobedience
			dg	delay of gratification

Others		
=	general indicator that behavior scored immediately before is repeated	
v	=	behavior has verbal component
1	=	low intensity
3	=	hi intensity
d	=	displaced
f	=	fantasy

Social setting		
1	=	alone
2	=	with adult only
3	=	other child only
4	=	child and adult

scored when children engaged in reciprocal role playing (nonaggressive) or when they engaged in behavior directed toward a common goal (Parton, 1933). Nurturance included giving another child help, reassurance, approval, affection, or protection (Hartup and Keller, 1960). Mature social skills included use of adult-like techniques for dealing with another child, often by indirect methods. For instance, when a boy tried to pull a circus wagon away from one little girl, she silently pointed to another wagon on the shelf and he went to play with it. Other examples are given in the Appendix D. Verbalization of feeling included descriptions of emotional states or explanations of reasons for one's own behavior. (The latter two subcategories were developed by the authors during preliminary observations.)

The persistence categories were all designed to tap the child's involvement with and pursuit of tasks, particularly when they were difficult or challenging. "Tasks" were defined as making something with material objects or practicing motor skills. The child's continuing efforts on tasks were scored as well as his attempts to work independently or to obtain instrumental help in order to proceed with a task. These categories were adapted from those used by the Fels Research Institute (Rabson, 1966).

Self-control included voluntary obedience of rules and patient tolerance of delay. Rule obedience was scored when the child behaved in accord with a rule without direct adult supervision. It was scored only when there was a clear choice point for the child. In some respects this category is similar to adult role-taking as defined by Sears et al. (1965), because it often involved voluntarily helping to put away toys, clean up after juice, and so on. Delay of gratification was scored when the child waited patiently for materials or adult help with a project. In later discussions, it is called "tolerence of delay" because it reflects ability to tolerate imposed delays rather than voluntary deferring of pleasures. A third subcategory, rule disobedience, was included as the negative instance of self-control. It was scored when the child disobeyed a rule he clearly knew existed. The category was adopted from Sears et al. (1965).

Regression included instances of crying, pouting, withdrawal, and autoerotic activities.

Following a procedure used by Caldwell (1969), a set of "qualifiers" was developed that could be attached to any of the stimulus or behavior categories. Two qualifiers indicated that the behavior was verbal or fantasy respectively. Qualifiers also indicated intensity level: 1 = minimal intensity; 2 = average intensity; 3 = high intensity. All scores were assumed to be at level 2 unless otherwise indicated.

The place, activity, and social setting for the child were recorded continuously. The place merely indicated whether the child was inside or outside. The activity categories appear in Appendix C. The social setting score indicated whether the child was alone or in the presence of adults, peers, or both.

Observational procedures

A modified time sampling procedure was used in the classroom observations. Each child was observed for five minutes at a time; behavior was scored in one-minute blocks. If two separate instances of a category of behavior were observed during the same minute, two scores were given. If the same behavior was repeated, it was indicated by an "=". Three observers worked in each classroom during each nursery school session. Each observer was given a list of names with instructions to observe the children in the order shown. The lists were established by dividing the two-and-one-half-hour session into three blocks of time. Within each block, children were assigned to the lists in random order. The lists were arranged so that a given child fell in the first time block on one observer's list, in the second time block on another observer's list, and in the third time block on the remaining list. Observations were made in all situations except when the child went to the bathroom or when he participated in an adult-led group activity like group singing. The six observers were rotated between classrooms. Thus, the observations for a given child were spread evenly across observers and across the time period of the nursery school session.

Observer training. Five graduate students and one advanced undergraduate in Child Development and Family Relations served as regular observers. One additional graduate student and one of the investigators were trained as substitute observers. During the latter half of the spring term (1970), the observers spent approximately 15 hours in practice observations. The first six hours were spent alone; the last nine were spent working together and discussing disagreements. Although the number of categories is extensive, the system was not difficult for the observers to learn.

Observer reliability. Formal reliability was assessed during the first two days of the summer nursery school. The eight people who served as regular or substitute observers worked in pairs. Each individual was paired with every other individual (with two exceptions) for one to two hours of observation. Reliabilities for each pair were computed using the formula (from Sears et al. (1965):

$$\frac{2 \times \text{Number of agreements}}{\text{Total number of scores for Observer 1} + \text{Total number of scores for Observer 2}}$$

This method of evaluating reliability is a stringent one because it does not count instances in which both observers assign no score to a behavior. Two sets of calculations are reported: percentage of exact agreement (that is, agreement on the exact subcategory, intensity level, and modifier), and percentage of agreement on categories (that is, the scores fell in the same general category of behavior, but might be different subcategories). In the latter instance, both observers might score aggression but use different subcategories. The mean percent exact agreement among pairs of observers was 74.8; the mean percent agreement on general categories was 79.0. The percentages for all pairs of observers are shown in Appendix E.

Observation scores. Scores were calculated for each of four time periods in the study: baseline, experimental period I (first two weeks of experimental treatments), experimental period II (second two weeks of experimental treatments), and the postviewing period. The number of scores received in each category was divided by the total number of minutes for which the child was observed. Scores with intensity level 1 and 3 were weighted by multiplying them by .5 and 1.5 respectively. Any stimulus or behavior that was repeated ("=") during the same minute was weighted one intensity level higher than the score given regardless of the number of repitions. This procedure raised the maximum intensity level to 4. Scores with intensity 4 were weighted by multiplying them by 2.

Intelligence

The short form of the Stanford-Binet Intelligence Scale was administered to each child during the first six weeks of the nursery school program. The short form was selected in order to reduce testing time. On earlier versions of the Stanford-Binet, correlations between the short and long form were .94 (Brown, 1942). The intelligence tests were administered by two trained clinical psychologists with extensive experience in testing children.

Attention to programs

Attention was rated using a system developed by Smothergill, Smothergill, and Grossman (1969). In that study, relatively inexperienced undergraduates were able to rate as many as three children at one time with reliabilities above .70. The rating was a binary one in which the child was scored attentive or nonattentive. In order to be scored attentive, he had to meet three criteria: "1) maintains orientation of head and eyes toward the screen for most of the time interval, 2) does not speak to or interfere with another child, and 3) does not make gross movements of arms or legs."

Observers were placed in the television viewing rooms facing the children. They scored two children at one time. They watched two children for ten seconds, then scored during the next five seconds. During the next fifteen seconds, they scored two different children, and so on. By this method the behavior of up to eight children was sampled for ten seconds in each minute. Details of the instructions to the observers appear in Appendix F.

Four individuals served as attention observers: one graduate student, two advanced undergraduates, and one college graduate with experience in early childhood education. These individuals were different from the classroom observers; they obviously knew which program the children were seeing. Every group of children was observed for two out of three viewing sessions per week. Reliability among observers was assessed during the initial viewing sessions. The mean percent agreement was

93. All observations for a given child were combined in one index defined as:

$$\frac{\text{Number of "attentive" ratings}}{\text{Total number of ratings}}$$

Mother interview

The purpose of the interview was to obtain detailed information about the viewing habits of children at home—television program preferences and the amount of time spent watching each day. The interview included nine general questions with specific followup questions. Programs on two lists, made up from the television guides of weekend programs and daily programs until 6 p.m., were to be rated for frequency of viewing (see Appendix G).

In order to reduce defensiveness about the amount of television children watch and to minimize generalizations and estimates, the interview began with several brief demographic questions and presented the detailed questions about morning, afternoon, and evening television watching in the context of a description of the child's day. The bulk of the interview elicited details of the child's television viewing, with special attention given to favorite programs and to the frequency of viewing. Information about favorite programs was drawn from a number of specific questions about the child's preferences throughout the day and on the weekend. Frequencies were obtained primarily from the printed television schedules marked by the mother, although hours for programs named as favorites in the evenings (not covered in the schedule ratings) were added as well.

Favorites. Favorite programs (questions 2a, 2e, 2f and 2g) represent the mother's spontaneous naming of these programs. Preferences for *Batman, Superman,* and *Misterogers* were specifically asked, in order to obtain information on home viewing of the programs used in experimental treatments.

Frequencies. Weekday television schedules covered the hours between 7 a.m. and 6 p.m. Each listed program was assigned by the mother to one of four categories of her child's viewing frequency: 1) almost every day, 2) often (three out of five days), 3) seldom (one out of five days), and 4) never. To obtain weekly Monday-Friday a.m. and p.m. viewing time, the hours represented by each frequency category were summed and weighted by 5 for the "almost every day" category, by 3 for the "often" category, by 1 for the "seldom" category, and the results were summed.

Saturday and Sunday schedules covered the hours between 7 a.m. and 11:30 p.m.; the four frequency categories were: 1) almost every Saturday or Sunday (weighted by 4), 2) often, two out of four Saturdays or Sundays (weighted by 2), 3) seldom, one out of four Saturdays or Sundays (weighted by 1), and 4) never. The weighted frequency category sums were totaled and divided by 4, yielding the average Saturday and Sunday viewing time.

Evening weekday totals were obtained from the mother's reports of child's viewing (2g), child's favorites (2g), and number of programs watched with family members (9), and were weighted by frequency of each program per week. Frequency ratings of each evening program (M - F) were not obtained. These evening totals, therefore, represent an underestimation of the child's viewing during this time period. Total viewing time per week was computed by simple summation of weekday totals, Saturday and Sunday totals, and evening totals.

Questions about differences in viewing habits in winter were included (2b, 2g) to ascertain the generality of our computed frequencies. Such differences as did exist were consistently in the direction of more television use during the winter with an attendant reduction in outdoor play. Only current viewing, however, is included in our frequencies, so these frequencies represent an underestimation in terms of yearly viewing patterns during the daylight hours as well as an underestimation of evening viewing.

Content. Scheduled programs (not including ads and news) were placed in four content categories:

1. Children's programs: those directed specifically toward children, exclusive of cartoons (e.g., *Misterogers Neighborhood, Lassie*).

2. Cartoons: any program using entirely animated format, either of people or of animals.

3. Violent programs: noncartoon programs with violence significant to the plot (e.g., horror shows, adventure shows, westerns, crime shows).

4. Miscellaneous: adult or family-oriented programs with violent episodes either nonexistent or incidental to the plot (e.g., soap operas, comedies, quiz shows).

These criteria of violence were developed by Gerbner (1968): 0 = no violence, 1 = violence present, incidental to plot, and 2 = violence present, significant to plot.[1] Violence was defined as the overt expression of force intended to hurt or kill. We rated as violent only those programs Gerbner rated as 2. New programs appearing after his analysis had been made were rated according to his guidelines. Our "miscellaneous" category combined Gerbner's categories 1 and 0 and therefore does include violence, though only when incidental to the plot. (See Appendix G for content-coded schedule).

The weekly frequencies for each category were computed in the same manner as the weekly totals, and proportions of total frequency were calculated. The number of favorites in each category was tabulated, and proportions of total favorites were calculated.

It should be noted that violent programs in our analysis refer only to those whose violence is significant to the plot, but miscellaneous viewing also implies exposure to incidental violence. Since the largest amount of violent and miscellaneous viewing occurred in the evening, which was underrepresented, our estimates of exposure to violence are systematically underestimated.

Exposure to television. The child's waking hours were calculated on the basis of the earliest "getting up" time to the latest bedtime, minus naptimes (questions 2, 2d, 2h). Questions 2c, 2e, 2g, 4, 5, and 7 provided an estimate of the child's control of his own television viewing at different times of the day. Since the location of the television set in the home was known (question 7), patterns of parental viewing (see below) gave additional information about the child's regular exposure to certain kinds of programs, such as soap operas in the afternoon.

Parental viewing and restrictions on child's viewing. To ascertain parental viewing patterns, answers to questions 3, 7, 8, and 9 were tabulated to obtain total parental favorites; those considered violent by our criteria were calculated as a proportion of this total.

Parental attitudes toward and restrictions on the child's viewing were elicited (question 4); on inspection, responses fell into two general classes: restrictions based on program content and restrictions based on time. These were compared with the estimation of the child's control of his own television viewing as an accuracy check.

Another measure of parental firmness about scheduling was obtained from the bedtime question (2h); answers were classified as a) fixed schedule (when a specific bedtime was stated with no indication of variability), b) flexible (when a range of an hour or less was given), and c) no regular time (when larger ranges of time were given).

Procedures. The interview was constructed after lengthy pretesting, centered about determining realistic limits for the number of general questions and frequency ratings that could be administered during one meeting. Since the evening television programs are different each night, the inclusion of five more frequency ratings was found impracticable. For the same reason, frequency ratings for the parents' own viewing were omitted.

Administration

Interviewers. The interviews were given by two female graduate students. The preliminary versions of the interview and frequency charts were also given by these interviewers, and tapes were made and used for training purposes. Both interviewers made tapes of trial administrations of the final interview as well, and differences were discussed by the interviewers and the investigator.

Biserial correlations of interviewer with variables in the interview were calculated to check for interviewer differences. The only significant differences appeared for SES (.21), program restrictions (.28), and proportion of miscellaneous favorites (.24), reflecting the fact that one of the interviewers dealt with more of the lower SES families. This interviewer had initially contacted these families about sending their children by bus to nursery school; in those cases in which there was some reluctance to admit strangers, it was felt that the same person would have better success scheduling the subsequent interview.

Setting. All parents of children enrolled in the nursery school had been advised at the time of recruitment that an interview on home viewing would be scheduled later at their convenience and that they would be paid $2.50 to cover transportation and babysitting fees. All 97 mothers were interviewed in the nursery school building or, in a few cases, at home. The length of the interviews ranged from 35 to 75 minutes; most were completed in 45 minutes.

Reliability of the instrument. One index of the internal consistency of the information obtained in the interview is the relation between favorite programs and frequency of viewing. Most of the frequency information was obtained from the frequency ratings; the information about favorites was taken from another section of the interview in the context of the child's daily habits.

The relations between favorites and frequencies in various categories are shown in Table 6. The highest overall correlations occurred between favorites and frequencies for specific programs. However, there were significant correlations between favorites and frequencies in each content category as well as between total number of favorites and total frequency. One may view these comparisons as supportive of internal reliability.

Table 6: Relationships between home viewing favorites and frequencies

	Correlations between favorites and frequencies	
	Boys	Girls
Misterogers	.50*	.70*
Batman	.70*	.70*
Superman	.80*	.60*
Children's	.20*	.40*
Cartoon	.50*	.60*
Miscellaneous	.50*	.20
Violent	.50*	.50*
Total	.60*	.40*

*$p < .05$

Content tests

For both the Aggressive and Prosocial conditions, sets of items were constructed to measure the children's knowledge about the programs shown. Because the tests were not to be administered immediately following a particular program, they did not tap specific events shown in any one program. Instead, three types of questions were designed: 1) identification of the central characters (from pictures); 2) "Who Am I?" questions in which a behavior was described and the child indicated which character would be likely to exhibit such behavior; and 3) behavior alternatives in which two or three alternative responses to a situation were presented and the child was asked which characters in *Misterogers* (or *Batman* or *Superman*) would choose. The alternatives were aggressive, prosocial, or avoidance. In both the "Who Am I?" and behavior alternative sections, the behavior described was similar to that shown in the programs, but not identical. Thus, the child was required to identify some of the generalized principles of behavior from the programs— e.g., sharing or cooperating in *Misterogers*, counteraggression to wrongdoers in *Batman*.

Construction of the measures. (Copies of the items appear in Appendix H.) For both measures, items were selected from a larger pool through pretesting of children who regularly watched the programs at home. After the test was administered to the study sample, item analyses were performed between the items in each of the three sections and the total scores for the sections. All items correlated significantly with the total scores except one behavior alternative item in the *Misterogers* test and two behavior alternative items in the *Batman* and *Superman* test. Those items were eliminated from the final scores used for analysis. Two subtotals and a total score were computed for each measure. The first subtotal consisted of the character identification and "Who Am I?" questions; the second was the behavior alternatives section. The latter was expected to be more difficult. The final *Misterogers* measure was composed of eight items in the first section and seven in the second. The final *Batman* and *Superman* measure was composed of eight items in the first section and eight in the second.

Administration. The character identification and "Who Am I?" sections of each measure were accompanied by pictures of the characters in the program. In the character identification section, the child was shown the picture and asked to name it. In the "Who Am I?" section, he was asked to choose one (of two or three characters) who would fit the description given verbally by the examiner. In the behavior alternative section, the alternatives were presented verbally. The alternatives were stated slowly and repeated to be sure the child understood them.

All the content tests were administered during the postviewing period. Children were taken to a small testing room near their classroom. The order of the two tests was balanced across subjects. Both tests were administered in one session with a break in the middle. If the child appeared to be tired or restless, he or she was given the second test later in the day. Children who did not give at least two correct answers in the first seven items were discontinued after seven items. Their scores were not included in the analyses. The total time for the two tests was about 25 minutes. Because of time limitations during the postviewing period, not all of the children in the Neutral condition were tested. The two experimental groups were considered more theoretically interesting, and there was a larger number of children in the Neutral group. Tests were administered to 34 children in the Neutral group and to all children in the experimental groups.

The examiners were three graduate students and one of the investigators. All examiners had extensive training in testing of young children.

Picture measure of responses to frustration

Psychological testing of preschool children is a difficult task for a number of reasons. Limited verbal facility and generally short attention spans necessitate the development of largely nonverbal tasks which have high interest value for preschoolers and which require relatively little time for completion. Although a number of investigators have been moderately successful in constructing such instruments, there has been a paucity of reliable instruments, even for research purposes. It was deemed desirable in the present study to complement observational techniques with a picture measure of responses to frustration.

The problems involved in measures of fantasy aggression have been discussed at length in the literature (Mussen and Naylor, 1954; Berkowitz, 1958; Lövaas, 1961; Patterson, 1960; Sears, 1950). These problems revolve about two major issues: the nature of the inferences to be made from the test responses and the predictions that can be made from such responses. The investigators' positions on these issues determine whether they assume test responses to reflect the aggressive drive of the individual, some "disposition" toward aggressive behavior, or the reinforcement history of the subject. Thus, some investigators have suggested that intervening variables such as anxiety (Pittluck, 1950), punishment history (Mussen and Naylor, 1954), parental modeling of aggression (Bandura and Walters, 1963; Becker et. al., 1962), and strength of avoidance behaviors (Lesser, 1957: Miller, 1957; Smith and Coleman, 1956) must be taken into consideration before predictions can be made from test responses to overt, observable behavior. Still other researchers have considered projective test responses to be indicators of motivational states (Atkinson, 1958) and to have complicated relationships with overt behavioral expression.

Although the theoretical and conceptual questions raised above have not been resolved, the present authors, for a number of reasons, have chosen to assume that the child's responses to the stimulus items (to be described in the following pages) directly sample areas of his own observable behavior (Patterson, 1964). Such a position may well represent an oversimplification of what the test responses "really" mean, but for the time being we concluded that empirically determined relationships could lead to the most satisfactory answers to these issues. Furthermore, there appears to be ample precedent for defining aggression behaviorally and to treat motivational constructs separately (Selg, 1968, p.20).

Consistent with this line of reasoning, we made a number of assumptions in connection with the present study. First, we assumed that children learn three basic behavioral solutions to frustrating situations— namely, aggressive, prosocial, and avoidance behaviors. This assumption is supported in the research literature. Since the frustration-aggression hypothesis of Dollard et al. (1939), numerous studies have shown that aggressive behaviors may result from frustration. Although modifications have much refined the basic hypothesis since Miller's (1941) initial addendum, the work of Rosenzweig (1948) has confirmed applicability of the hypothesis in the area of projective measurement.

Prosocial behaviors were thought to include the delay of gratification, persistence in difficult activities, cooperation, self-control, and attempts to understand another's feelings. These behaviors are frequently conceptualized as ego mechanisms (Hartman et al., 1949), and they are socially desirable, highly rewarded alternatives to aggression.

Avoidance behaviors were defined to include such behavior as "crying" or "walking away" from a frustrating situation. Miller (1941) was first to point out the importance of studying the strength of the disposition to avoid in the study of response to frustration, and Patterson (1960) has demonstrated that prediction of overt aggressive behavior is significantly enhanced if both "aggressive response dispositions" and "inhibitory variables" are considered.

A second major assumption was that interpersonal and situational stimuli are conditioned elicitors of aggressive, prosocial, or avoidance behaviors and that eliciting stimuli may vary from child to child (Patterson, 1964). We followed Patterson's lead in recognizing that an adequate assessment device should have a representative sampling of these discriminative stimuli—i.e., the frustrating behavior of peers and adults in various situational contexts. The specific ways in which these stimuli get to be conditioned elicitors of the behaviors under consideration is not crucial in this context: the acquisition of these discriminative stimuli can be explained either on the basis of a theory of observational learning (Bandura, 1969) or on the basis of an operant reinforcement theory (Skinner, 1954; Patterson, Littnan, and Bricker, 1967).

The third assumption was that if the test situation presented an easily recognizable, adequate sampling of the interpersonal and situational contexts within which the elicitors of aggressive, prosocial, and avoidance behaviors were acquired, it would maximize chances that the child's test responses would indeed be representative of his own observable behaviors. This assumption, like the others, was thought to be subject to empirical verification.

Since the present assessment method was to be used primarily with preschool children (ages 4-5), it was felt to be desirable to require no verbal responses from the subjects. Consequently, picture sequences (cartoons) were used to present both the stimuli and the response alternatives. A similar format was first used by Patterson (1960) with a somewhat older population. His procedure entailed the presentation of six different and specific response alternatives; ours was designed with only three response alternatives (aggressive, prosocial, and avoidance) for each set of stimulus pictures. We thought this reduction in the number of choices would reduce the complexity of the situation for the younger subjects; it also permitted the administration of more test items while keeping the time required for administration at a very reasonable 15 minutes.

The total assessment device consisted of 18 sets of pictures, two pictures in each stimulus set and three pictures in each corresponding response set. The method attempted to sample as large a variety of interpersonal and situational contexts as possible. Consequently, of the 18 stimulus sets, six each presented home, playground, and nursery school contexts; three each depicted aggression by adults and by peers, rejection by adults and by peers, and "being difficult" by adults and by peers. To facilitate projection on the part of the subjects, those picture sets administered to boys depicted boys as the protagonists; the girls were shown pictures identical in every respect, except that the protagonists were girls.

All pictures were drawn in ink by an artist according to the investigators' specifications. The initial drawings were drawn on 3 x 5 index cards. For administration, however, the two stimulus pictures were copied on a single piece of paper, as were the three response pictures for each set.

Testing procedure. The order of presentation of the 18 picture sets was randomized and constant for all subjects. The two stimulus pictures for each set were always introduced with a specified commentary by the administrator, which was designed to clarify and emphasize the cues presented in the picture sequences. For example, one of the sets—designated "rejection by peers in the nursery school situation"—depicts on the first stimulus picture two girls playing with a ball. The second stimulus picture shows a third girl who apparently wants to enter the game but is rejected by the other girls. The verbal comment of the test administrator was specified as follows: "These two girls are having a good time playing with their ball. Ronda wants to play with them, but they won't let her. What is Ronda going to do?" Immediately following the presentation of the stimulus pictures, the three response alternatives were presented with the commentary: "Here, Ronda is crying because they don't want her to play with them (avoidance); in this picture she is telling the teacher about it (prosocial); and here, Ronda is kicking the ball so that the other girls can't play either (aggressive)."

The order of the three response alternatives was also randomized. After seeing the response alternatives, the subjects were asked: "Which of these do you think Ronda will do?" The scores for each subject were represented by three numbers indicating the frequency with which he or she had chosen the aggressive, the prosocial, and the avoidance alternatives in responding to the 18 picture sets. Thus, the subject's score on each of these three variables could theoretically range from 0 through 18.

The test administrators were four advanced female undergraduate students in the Division of Individual and Family Studies, who were trained and supervised by a graduate assistant. They reported that the children had little difficulty in comprehending the task and that they cooperated well. Only two children were apparently unable to produce acceptable protocols. Inspection of the test protocols did not reveal systematic differences among administrators.

DESCRIPTIVE INFORMATION

Classroom observations

Final observation categories. In the initial tally, 64 separate categories of stimulus and behavior were identified. The number was large because of the use of the modifiers (verbal and fantasy) on many behavior categories. Scores on these 64 categories during the pretest period were intercorrelated to identify clusters that could be appropriately combined.

The initial stimulus and behavior categories were combined to form 22 categories. The combinations were based both on clustering in the initial correlational analysis and on the theoretical coherence of the subcategories. The final categories are defined in Table 7.

Five stimulus categories and one total were derived. Several categories were combined when they were correlated with one another and with similar behavior patterns. High-intensity commands from other children, for example, were combined with aggressive frustration because they were essentially defined as verbal aggression directed toward the child. Low- and average-intensity commands by other children were not analyzed further because they were uncorrelated with most of the other variables. Commands by adults at average or high intensities were combined with teacher frustration because of similar correlational patterns. Low-intensity teacher commands were excluded from further analysis. Frustration with a "fantasy" qualifier was considered separately because it was correlated with fantasy aggression, not with other

Table 7: Definitions of final observation categories

Stimulus categories

1. Aggressive frustration—FA (C aggressive to S) + CC3 or CC4 (vigorous commands by C to S)
2. Fantasy frustration—Any aggressive or frustrating behavior directed toward S that was qualified as "fantasy"
3. Frustration by child—FP (property frustration) + FC (frustration by C)
4. Object frustration—FO (object frustration)
5. Teacher frustration—FT (frustration by T) + CT2 + CT3 + CT4 (demands and commands by teacher)
6. Total frustration—Sum of 1—5 above

Behavior categories

7. Physical aggression—ap (physical aggression) + at (nonverbal aggression)
8. Verbal aggression—av (verbal) + ac (vigorous commands) + aa (tattling) + any aggressive category with a "verbal" modifier.
9. Interpersonal aggression—Sum of 7 + 8 above.
10. Object aggression—ao (aggression to object) + rd (rule disobediance)
11. Fantasy aggression—af (fantasy) + any aggressive category with a "fantasy" modifier
12. Cooperation—ic (cooperation) + im (mature social skills)
13. Nurturance—in (nurturance)
14. Verbalization of feeling—iv (stating feelings)
15. Prosocial interpersonal—Sum of 12 + 13 + 14 above
16. Rule stating—rov (stating rules)
17. Rule obedience—ro (rule obedience)
18. Tolerance of delay—dg (delay of gratification)
19. Task persistence—pt (task persistence)
20. Instrumental help seeking—ph (instrumental help seeking)
21. Total verbalization—Sum of all categories that are defined as verbal and all with a "verbal" modifier
22. Total interpersonal—Sum of interpersonal aggression and prosocial interpersonal

forms of aggression nor with other frustration categories. The category of "being ignored" was excluded because it was unrelated to other categories and because it seemed too minimal in most cases to be legitimately considered a frustration.

Five aggression categories were derived on grounds of theoretical coherence and correlational clustering. Physical and verbal aggression represented clusters of behavior that correlated more highly within than between clusters, though all were positively related. Interpersonal aggression, the combination of physical and verbal aggression, was included because of the particular concern in the study with separating aggression directed seriously toward people from other forms of aggression. Object aggression included both aggression to inanimate objects and rule disobedience.

The correlational patterns indicated very clearly that fantasy or playful aggression was a separate dimension from the other more "serious" forms of aggression. All those aggression scores qualified as fantasy correlated more highly with one another than they did with the other aggression categories. For this reason, all were combined in a fantasy aggression category.

Most of the prosocial interpersonal categories were retained as separate, because the intercorrelations were generally positive but low. Mature social skills was combined with cooperation because it was too infrequent to analyze separately and was most highly related to cooperation. A summary score, prosocial interpersonal, was also derived.

For the most part, the other subcategories were not combined because they were not intercorrelated. Independence and the regression categories were excluded from further analysis because they occurred very infrequently and were not related to other types of behavior.

Once scores on the final categories were calculated for each child, distributions of these scores during the pretest period were examined for normality. Virtually all the distributions were positively skewed. Therefore, all scores were submitted to a logarithm transformation (log 10 of 10 (X + 1). These logarithms were used throughout the analyses reported.

A second set of intercorrelations among the final categories was calculated for boys and girls separately. These correlations are shown in Table 8.

A number of patterns in these correlations are important to the interpretation of the observational data. First, the frustration and aggression categories were positively related to one another for both boys and girls. More specifically, for boys, all aggression categories except fantasy aggression were positively related to frustrations involving other people. For girls, the pattern was similar, but somewhat less consistent. Fantasy aggression was related specifically to fantasy frustration for both sexes. It seems most appropriate to view these correlations as indicators of the dyadic relations between the child and others around him rather than indicators of unidirectional effects. While frustration from others may lead to increased aggression, it is equally likely that aggression by a child elicits increased frustration from others.

All of the aggression categories were related to one another except fantasy aggression. The correlations among aggression categories were higher for boys than for girls. The separation of fantasy aggression from the other categories was apparent in these correlations, as it was in the initial correlations. The "fantasy" category was scored not only when the aggression occurred in role play, but also when it was clearly playful or gamelike for all children involved. It appears from these findings that this playful form of aggression is a rather different dimension from aggression with more serious intent.

Those prosocial categories that involved interpersonal interaction were expected to be related to one another. For boys, the correlations were generally positive, but low. Cooperation and nurturance were the only categories with high intercorrelations. For girls, the correlations among cooperation, nurturance, and rule stating were positive, but low. Verbalization of feelings was unrelated to the other categories for girls.

The prosocial interpersonal categories were positively related to interpersonal aggression. This finding is consistent with other observational studies (Wright, 1960). It apparently reflects the fact that some children are more socially interactive than others and engage in more of all kinds of social behavior. This pattern was further indicated by high correlations of the two summary categories, verbal total and interpersonal total, with virtually all of the interpersonal subcategories, although these correlations are inflated because they are not independent.

All the patterns discussed were similar for boys and girls, but dissimilar patterns for the two sexes appeared for rule obedience. For boys, rule obedience was negatively related to several indices of frustration, aggression, and prosocial interpersonal behavior; for girls, these correlations were positive. In each case, the correlations were low but formed a consistent pattern. The correlations for boys and girls were significantly different at the .05 level on aggressive frustration, total frustration,

Table 8: Intercorrelations of classroom observ

		1	2	3	4	5	6	7	8	9
Frustration										
1.	Aggressive	--	−09	34	20	50	65	62	58	6
2.	Fantasy	.26	--	13	−18	03	13	03	26	1
3.	By Child	50	.15	--	20	38	73	55	62	6
4.	Object	13	−20	25	--	0	38	12	16	1
5.	Teacher	14	11	21	18	--	81	68	49	6
6.	Total	54	32	80	49	64	--	75	69	8
Aggression										
7.	Physical	06	−05	17	04	38	28	--	73	9
8.	Verbal	34	19	65	17	17	55	40	--	9
9.	Interpersonal	28	15	58	17	27	55	68	94	-
10.	Object	10	−02	20	23	33	36	55	14	3
11.	Fantasy	30	63	21	−22	09	28	02	25	2
Prosocial										
Interpersonal										
12.	Cooperation	09	−03	34	0	27	31	23	51	4
13.	Nurturance	13	23	34	−04	16	30	−17	14	0
14.	Verbalization of feeling	−04	−28	25	03	24	20	11	09	1
15.	Total Prosocial interpersonal	16	03	50	0	35	45	13	45	4
16.	Rule stating	35	22	34	−10	25	35	−08	08	(
Other prosocial										
17.	Rule obedience	23	03	21	−01	21	22	17	25	
18.	Tolerance of delay	−03	−09	23	11	−01	11	0	24	
19.	Task persistence	−23	06	−17	08	−17	−11	−13	09	(
20.	Instrumental help seeking	−24	−15	12	25	27	19	22	0	
21.	Total verbal	39	11	11	74	21	42	72	32	
22.	Total interpersonal	27	14	64	06	40	61	38	72	

Note: Correlations for boys are above median; girls are below Correlations above .27 f boys and .30 for girls are significant at the .05 level and are underlined *except* where the two variables contaminate one another.

verbal aggression, interpersonal aggression, and cooperation. It appears that rule obedience is part of a pattern of high social interaction for girls, but characterizes boys who are more quiet and socially inactive.

Relation of observation categories to sex, age, intelligence, and social class. The mean observation scores for boys and girls during the pretest period are shown in Table 9. Boys were significantly higher than girls on all categories of frustration, except fantasy frustration, and on all categories of aggression. Boys also had higher scores on cooperation, total verbal, and total interpersonal behavior. Girls were significantly higher than boys on nurturance, tolerance of delay, and instrumental help seeking.

The correlations of the behavior categories with IQ, mental age (MA), chronological age (CA), and social class appear in Table 10. Intellectual level, as indicated by IQ or by MA, was unrelated to most of the behavior categories. For both sexes, object frustration was negatively related

n categories during the baseline period

	11	12	13	14	15	16	17	18	19	20	21	22
	12	31	34	-04	31	01	-33	22	-05	-22	46	57
	61	16	03	-04	13	-06	-11	01	-06	25	19	18
	08	20	35	18	28	30	-20	11	-01	-10	61	58
	01	22	31	-05	24	10	-30	09	22	0	19	23
	21	16	25	10	23	04	01	11	-09	-14	46	56
	26	31	47	10	39	16	-22	15	01	-10	65	74
	14	33	37	02	35	24	-12	02	-15	-19	66	80
	38	50	38	13	49	43	-28	05	-14	-07	92	83
	30	43	41	06	44	33	-21	06	-14	-13	83	88
	10	04	21	06	10	26	-04	-25	06	-27	38	41
	--	27	05	12	25	04	-01	08	05	21	36	32
	-07	--	54	26	95	24	-30	13	08	-21	53	75
	22	24	--	09	69	15	-16	-02	06	-32	40	61
	-22	18	15	--	44	25	21	-01	06	10	41	27
	0	83	67	42	--	27	-21	08	09	-21	58	79
	17	25	45	05	44	--	-25	-08	07	12	55	40
	05	27	-03	08	18	-11	--	-34	10	15	-20	-26
	06	21	05	-06	16	-10	04	--	-23	13	0	07
	-02	-06	-12	02	-09	-34	0	-17	--	08	-10	-02
	-21	10	-19	31	07	-09	08	24	-01	--	0	-15
	22	57	34	45	68	40	17	20	0	09	--	85
	17	79	55	35	91	43	23	19	-09	09	86	--

Table 9: Mean baseline classroom observation
scores for boys and girls

	Boys		Girls		
	Mean	SD	Mean	SD	F ratio
Frustration					
Aggressive	.096	.095	.045	.052	9.17***
Fantasy	.026	.051	.023	.058	.06
Child	.229	.114	.140	.099	14.67***
Object	.136	.088	.100	.080	3.78*
Teacher	.236	.148	.128	.092	16.43***
Total	.495	.159	.336	.138	24.23***
Aggression					
Physical	.131	.143	.027	.048	19.76***
Verbal	.131	.140	.069	.085	5.76**
Interpersonal	.223	.199	.093	.104	13.83***
Object	.100	.113	.018	.032	19.91***
Fantasy	.057	.083	.022	.050	6.50**
Prosocial Interpersonal					
Cooperation	.176	.125	.109	.109	7.16***
Nurturance	.062	.057	.087	.077	4.16**
Verbalization of feeling	.041	.050	.045	.045	.10
Total	.242	.139	.210	.125	1.13
Other Prosocial					
Rule stating	.025	.037	.018	.037	.79
Rule obedience	.084	.057	.102	.086	1.50
Tolerance of delay	.036	.052	.056	.071	2.83*
Task persistence	.413	.124	.411	.140	.01
Instrumental help seeking	.082	.076	.107	.078	2.82*
Total verbal	.205	.156	.142	.104	4.92**
Total interpersonal	.394	.206	.277	.161	8.24***

Note: The F ratios were taken from unweighted means analyses of variance of Sex x Condition.

*p < .10
**p < .05
***p < .01

to IQ and MA: brighter children experienced less difficulty in their contacts with the physical environment than lower ability children. For girls, IQ and MA were positively related to fantasy frustration, although there was no relation to fantasy aggression. There were slight trends for the prosocial interpersonal categories to be positively associated with MA, particularly for girls, but in general, the behavior categories were independent of intellectual ability.

Chronological age, by contrast, was positively related to the prosocial interpersonal categories—particularly cooperation and nurturance—for

Behavior category

	IQ			MA			CA			Local SES		
	Boys	Both	Girls	Boys	Both	Girls	Boys	Both	Girls	Boys	Both	Girls
Frustration												
Aggressive Fantasy			.30*			.31*	.24			-.21		
Child							.25					
Object		-.26*	-.35*	-.20	-.31*							.26
Teacher						-.41*				-.21		.31*
Total												.29
Aggression												
Physical												
Verbal							.22					.28
Interpersonal						-.23	.22	.21*				.24
Object									-.21			
Fantasy									.29			
Prosocial												
Cooperation				.20	.20	.30*	.31*	.31*	.30*			.20
Nurturance							.23	.22*	.24			
Verbalization of feeling									-.21			.26
Total prosocial interpersonal					.20	.26	.31*	.29*	.26			.23
Rule stating	.25	.24*	.25			.24	-.21			.35*	.23*	
Rule obedience												
Tolerance of delay			-.23				-.23					
Task persistence												
Instrumental help seeking							-.27					.32*
Verbal total						.28	.23	.20			.23*	.34*
Interpersonal total							.28*	.27*	.25			.27

*p < .05

Note: Correlations not shown were below .20.

both sexes. There were trends toward positive relations between chronological age and aggression for boys, but none of the correlations was significant. Older children were apparently more socially interactive, primarily in the prosocial interpersonal modes of behavior.

Social class was generally unrelated to the observational measures for boys but was positively associated with a number of behavior categories for girls. For boys, rule stating was positively related to social class, but no other correlations approached significance. For girls, there was a trend toward *positive* correlations between social class and both aggressive and prosocial interpersonal behavior. Girls from higher social class families were also more verbal and received more teacher frustration.

Home television viewing

Descriptive data—television preferences and viewing frequency. In Table 12 the means and standard deviations (SD) for favorites and frequency are presented for the four general categories of programs—children's cartoons, miscellaneous, and violent programs.

Table 11: Mean favorites and frequencies* for
television programs viewed at home

	Boys		Girls	
	Mean	SD	Mean	SD
Children favorites	4.46	1.65	4.08	1.74
Children frequency	8.31	4.74	7.58	5.74
Cartoon favorites	6.63	3.48	5.20	3.85
Cartoon frequency	7.71	5.96	6.73	6.05
Miscellaneous favorites	6.87	5.14	7.40	5.40
Miscellaneous frequency	7.35	8.90	6.67	7.50
Violent favorites	1.37	1.30	1.08	1.44
Violent frequency	1.15	2.05	1.09	1.65
Total frequency	34.56	17.64	32.44	16.14
% of waking hours	.38	.19	.36	.18

*Means for favorites refer to the number of favorites named.
Means for frequencies refer to hours per week.

Two patterns of programs in home viewing were identified on the basis of the intercorrelations of favorites and frequencies shown in Table 13. Correlations of each with demographic data show a difference in SES associated with the two patterns.

In Pattern 1 are *Misterogers,* children's programs, and cartoons; in Pattern 2 are *Batman, Superman,* miscellaneous programs, and violent programs.

Viewing Pattern 1. Children for whom *Misterogers Neighborhood* is a favorite also like children's programs and do not like miscellaneous programs, violent programs, or *Superman.* There are no significant correlations with cartoon favorites or *Batman* favorites.

Table 12: Intercorrelations of home viewing variables

	1	2	3	4	5	6	7	8	9	10	11	12	13	14	15	16
			Pattern 1								Pattern 2					
Pattern 1																
Favorite																
Rogers (1)		.39	.00	.64	.17	-.11	.11	-.34	-.34	-.35	-.10	-.33	-.45	-.43	-.19	-.25
Children's (2)			.35	.32	.36	.29	.02	-.03	-.17	-.10	.02	-.04	-.19	-.28	.24	.13
Cartoon (3)				.05	.15	.58	.28	.30	.32	.17	.30	.30	.10	.09	.74	.41
Frequency																
Rogers (4)					.54	.04	-.07	-.25	-.18	-.31	-.19	-.25	-.20	-.30	-.07	.03
Children's (5)						.39	.16	.03	-.07	-.09	.12	.03	.18	.05	.08	.49
Cartoon (6)							.26	.27	.18	.13	.36	.28	.33	.23	.45	.72
Pattern 2																
Favorite																
Batman (7)								.41	.27	.19	.73	.50	.33	.25	.33	.37
Superman (8)									.47	.56	.49	.79	.39	.47	.52	.42
Miscellaneous (9)										.60	.26	.37	.38	.32	.83	.40
Violent (10)											.29	.38	.36	.52	.59	.34
Frequency																
Batman (11)												.63	.44	.38	.35	.46
Superman (12)													.47	.42	.42	.47
Miscellaneous (13)														.69	.30	.79
Violent (14)															.27	.57
Total Favorites (15)																.52
Total Frequency (16)																
Sex	.00	-.11	-.19	.09	-.07	-.08	-.22	-.31	.05	.10	-.35	-.27	-.04	-.02	-.09	-.06
IQ	.40	.35	.09	.31	.10	-.03	-.13	-.05	-.16	-.16	-.17	-.17	-.40	-.24	-.02	-.23
SES	.29	.23	.20	.10	.02	.12	.02	-.13	-.38	-.32	-.09	-.10	-.39	-.33	-.16	-.22
Program restrictions	.17	.23	.15	.10	.05	.14	.01	.03	-.09	-.19	.07	.03	-.08	-.18	.02	-.04
Time restrictions	.19	.04	-.09	.09	.00	-.07	-.20	-.22	-.08	-.09	-.17	-.26	-.12	-.18	-.09	-.13
Parents' favorites																
Number	-.23	-.04	-.02	-.10	-.08	.05	.06	.11	.32	.23	-.02	.06	.16	-.07	.22	.12
% Violent	-.12	-.09	-.04	-.09	-.05	-.03	.17	.10	.20	.24	.10	.13	.05	-.04	.13	.01

Similarly, high frequency of watching *Misterogers* is associated with children's program frequency but not with cartoon frequency. *Rogers* frequency is negatively related to frequency of miscellaneous programs, violent programs, and *Superman*. The negative correlation with *Batman* is near significance (-.19). Additionally, children for whom *Rogers* is a favorite are low television viewers in general.

Children whose favorites are programs primarily aimed at children also like *Misterogers* and cartoons. There is no correlation with *Batman* or *Superman* favorites, and, while the direction is negative with miscellaneous and violent favorites, the correlations are not significant. The correlation between frequency of watching children's programs and frequency of watching other programs presents a similar picture.

The correlation between frequency of watching children's programs and total frequency is .49. However, the correlation of the proportion of frequency devoted to children's programs with total frequency is -.15. So the children who spend a high proportion of their television time watching children's programs are those who have low total frequency scores; they watch much less television.

The correlations between cartoon favorites and frequency with *Rogers* and children's programs have already been discussed. The correlations with miscellaneous programs, violent programs, *Batman*, and *Superman* reveal, however, that cartoons are listed as favorites and watched frequently by many children in the sample no matter what their other viewing preferences might be. There are positive relations between cartoon favorites and *Batman*, *Superman*, and miscellaneous favorites; the relation with violent favorites is near significance. The correlations with cartoon frequency are similar, although the correlations with violent frequency reach significance. Cartoon frequency is highly related to total frequency (.72).

While there are no significant sex differences for *Rogers* or children's favorites or frequencies, boys more often name cartoons as favorites than do girls. There were no sex differences in frequency of cartoon viewing.

The rationale for placing cartoons in Pattern 1 (despite the fact that children who like *Batman*, *Superman*, miscellaneous, and violent programs also like cartoons) is based on three factors:

1.   Cartoons are primarily geared to children, while the other programs in Pattern 2 are geared to all ages or to adults only.

2.   While the correlation between cartoon frequency and total frequency is .72, the correlation of the proportion of cartoon frequency with total frequency is .24. This positive proportion reveals that both low television viewers who like children's programs and high viewers who like miscellaneous and violent programs watch cartoons.

Additional support comes from the correlations between the proportion of cartoon frequency and other variables examined later in this section. The proportion of cartoon frequency correlates positively with

SES level and parental restriction of television programs (like the other programs in Pattern 1). Proportions of miscellaneous and violent frequency are negatively correlated with SES level and with parental restriction of viewing.

3. Children's favorites and frequencies correlate with cartoons but do not correlate with the other programs classified in Pattern 2.

Cartoons belong to the Pattern 1 viewing preference group, and for this group they represent the most violent programs watched. Cartoons also correlate positively with the viewing preferences of pattern 2, but in this case they represent one more category of violent content.

It must be noted as well that Gerbner's rating of cartoons reports variations in amount of violent content in cartoons themselves. For our sample, the cartoon versions of *Batman* and *Superman* do not correlate (either for favorites or for frequency) with children's programs. However, they do correlate with each other and with miscellaneous and violent programs.

Viewing Pattern 2. Children for whom *Batman* is a favorite like cartoons, *Superman*, miscellaneous, and violent programs. Boys more often list *Batman* as a favorite than do girls. Children who frequently watch *Batman* also frequently watch cartoons, *Superman*, miscellaneous, and violent programs. *Batman* favorites and frequency are not related to those for *Rogers* and children's programs. The rationale for placing *Batman* (and *Superman)* with Pattern 2, although they are cartoons, is based on the positive correlations between these programs and miscellaneous and violent programs. The following comparison of *Batman* frequency with the proportion of total frequency for the content categories sheds further light on the way in which *Batman* fits into the total viewing pattern:

Proportion of category frequency	*Batman* frequency
Cartoon	.19
Miscellaneous	.50
Violent	.24

The r of Batman frequency and total frequency is .46.

The correlations between *Superman* favorites and frequency are similar to those reported for *Batman*. There are positive correlations with cartoons, miscellaneous, and violent programs. Boys also prefer *Superman* more than girls. However, the correlations with cartoons are slightly lower, while those with miscellaneous and violent programs are somewhat higher, suggesting a closer relationship with the latter two categories. The proportions of time spent viewing different kinds of television also support this difference between *Batman* and *Superman:*

Proportion of category frequency	*Superman* frequency
Cartoon	.05
Miscellaneous	.42
Violent	.38

So for the high viewers of *Superman,* relatively more of their television time is spent watching miscellaneous and violent programs and less watching cartoons than is true for high viewers of *Batman.*

The miscellaneous category is an extremely heterogeneous lumping of programs which range from quiz programs with no reported violence to family comedies which frequently have violence incidental to the plot (Gerbner, 1968). The limitations of this category were two. A miscellaneous program was not one directed primarily at children; it had to be either adult and child-oriented or adult-oriented. It was not a crime, western, or action-adventure program (rated 2 by Gerbner with violence principal to the plot) or a horror show. So while it is difficult to assess the content of what high viewers of miscellaneous programs actually see, one may judge that there is a good deal of violence in the mixture.

The correlations between miscellaneous favorites and frequencies and other categories support this judgment. Children who list a high number of miscellaneous programs as favorites do not like *Misterogers* or children's programs. There are positive correlations with cartoons, *Batman,* and *Superman,* and a very high correlation with violent favorites.

All of the programs discussed up to this point have been shown on daytime television. The frequency ratings were made from the lists the mother filled out as well as from her comments during the interview. Since miscellaneous programs occur often during the evening and since we do not have frequency lists for Monday through Friday evening, the frequency scores include daytime, Saturday and Sunday evening, and whatever programs the mother named in response to questions about weeknight viewing. So there is very clearly an underestimate of frequency in this category, despite the fact that the mothers had an evening television schedule for the five nights for reference.

Nevertheless, the correlations of miscellaneous frequency with other programs and categories are as follows:

Frequency	Miscellaneous frequency
Rogers	.20
Children's	.18
Cartoon	.55
Batman	.44
Superman	.47
Violent	.69
Total	.79

The correlation of the proportion of miscellaneous frequency with total frequency is .54. Children who are frequent watchers of miscellaneous programs, therefore, are high in television viewing. They also spend a high proportion of their time viewing television programs with violent content.

It is also interesting to note that there were no sex differences in miscellaneous favorites or in frequency.

Violent programs. Crime programs, westerns, action-adventures, and horror shows—with violence significant to the plot—are placed in the violent category. The frequency ratings for these programs are the most severely limited and underestimated ratings we obtained, for, while some miscellaneous programs occur during the day, most violent programs are shown at night. The frequencies are, therefore, based primarily on weekend evenings and on those weeknight programs spontaneously mentioned by the mother in response to questions about weeknight viewing.

It might be argued that since children are in bed in the evenings during the week, claims of underestimation are not valid. Other evidence indicates, however, that many preschool children watch television during the evening hours when such programs are shown (Baker and Ball, 1969). Further, there is a significant correlation (-.28) between lack of rules about bedtime and proportion of violent favorites. The correlation is not significant for violent frequency.

It may be helpful to summarize again the preference pattern and frequency pattern for violent programs:

Violent favorites

Rogers	.55
Children's	.10
Cartoon	.17
Batman	.19
Superman	.56
Miscellaneous	.60

Violent frequency

Rogers	.50
Children's	.05
Cartoon	.25
Batman	.58
Superman	.42
Miscellaneous	.69
Total	.57
Proportion	.52

These correlations show that children who like and watch violent programs also prefer other programs with some violent content and are high television viewers. One cannot estimate how much the violence frequency, the total frequency, and the proportion of violent programs would change if frequency ratings were available for Monday-Friday evenings, but it is clear that all three frequency measures would increase.

There is no sex difference for violent favorites or frequency. One can, therefore, summarize the information on violent programs by stating that the boys and girls who like violent programs are watching a great deal of television and that the other programs they watch have violent content as well.

Differences in SES, IQ, parental regulation of television, and parental television preferences. We have divided the home viewing habits of children into two patterns. Pattern 1 is characterized by low viewing of violent television, preference for programs geared primarily for children, and low television viewing in general. Pattern 2 includes more violent television, programs aimed at child and adult audiences or primarily at adult audiences, and high television viewing in general.

SES level is positively correlated with the program favorites in Pattern 1 and negatively correlated with program favorites in Pattern 2 (except for *Batman* favorite, which is uncorrelated). Frequency of viewing programs in Pattern 1 is not correlated with SES, but SES is positively related to the proportion of total viewing time spent watching children's programs (r=.19) and cartoons (r=.50).

In Pattern 2, SES is negatively correlated with frequency of viewing miscellaneous and violent programs. *Superman* trends are in the same direction, but are not significant. *Batman* frequency is uncorrelated. The proportions of miscellaneous and violent frequency are also negatively related to SES (rs=-.39 and -.35 respectively). Total frequency of television viewing also correlates negatively with SES.

In Pattern 1, IQ is positively correlated with both *Rogers* favorites and frequency. IQ correlates positively with children's favorites but not with children's frequency, although the correlation with proportion of children's frequency is significant (.24). IQ does not correlate with cartoon favorites, frequency, or the proportion of cartoon frequency.

In Pattern 2, there are negative trends between IQ and favorites, but none reaches significance. *Batman* and *Superman* frequency also show negative trends, but only miscellaneous frequency and violent frequency are significant in a negative direction. The proportions of miscellaneous frequency (-.41) and violent frequency (-.26) are also negatively related to IQ. Total television frequency is negatively related to IQ.

Parental restrictions of programs and time. Parents who restrict the programs their children are allowed to watch belong to the Pattern 1 group. In Table 13, one sees that restriction of programs correlates positively with children's favorites and that the trends are in a positive direction for *Rogers* favorites and cartoon favorites. There are no correlations with frequency in Pattern 1, although cartoon frequency is in a positive direction. The proportion of frequency for cartoons is correlated with program restrictions (.23).

In Pattern 2, parents do not restrict programs, and the lack of restrictions is most pronounced with programs containing violence. While parental restriction of programs is uncorrelated with *Batman*, *Superman*, and miscellaneous favorites, the negative trend nearly reaches significance with violent favorites (-.19). The propostion of miscellaneous and violent favorites are both significantly correlated with parental restriction.)-.24) (-.26).

The frequency ratings in Pattern 2 do not reach significant levels with parental restriction, although aggressive frequency (-.18), proportion of aggressive frequency (-.19), and proportion of miscellaneous frequency (-.13) are in a direction consistent with the information on favorites.

Parental restrictions of television time are not significantly correlated with favorites or frequency in Pattern 1 programs. There are, however, positive trends for both *Rogers* favorite (.19) and children's favorite (.15).

In Pattern 2, parental time restrictions correlate significantly with *Batman* and *Superman* favorites and are in a negative direction for miscellaneous and aggressive favorites. These findings are true for frequency ratings as well. The proportions of frequency are all in a negative direction.

As discussed earlier, parental viewing frequency lists were not obtained because of the length of the interview and the quantity of information requested. We did, however, obtain an estimate of parental favorites and made a violence classification of the named favorites.

The only significant correlation between parents' favorites and Pattern 1 favorites and frequency is with *Rogers* favorites (-.25), although all of the correlations are in a negative direction. In Pattern 2, however, there are significant positive correlations between parental favorites and miscellaneous favorites, violent favorites and total favorites for children.

Parents' proportion of violent favorites does not correlate with favorites or frequency in Pattern 2, although all trends are negative. In Pattern 2, parents' proportion of violent favorites correlates positively with miscellaneous favorites and violent favorites for children.

Summary. The picture which emerged from the discussion of viewing favorites and frequency is one of two viewing patterns associated with children's use of television at home. The first pattern was characterized by low television viewing in general and by preference for programs directed at children. The second pattern was associated with high television viewing and preference for programs directed at all ages and containing violence.

The findings on SES, IQ, parental regulations of television, and parental television preferences support the formation of the two patterns. These variables consistently correlate in opposite directions for each pattern. Children in Pattern 1 are from higher SES families and have higher IQ scores. Their parents tend to restrict the programs they are allowed to watch and have fewer television favorites themselves.. Children in Pattern 2 are from lower SES families, have lower IQ scores, and are not limited by parents in either the kind or the amount of television they watch. In addition, the information on parental viewing suggests that there is more family viewing of television programs high in violent content. Parents who like violent television have children who like violent television.

RESULTS

Effects of experimental treatments on classroom behavior

Experimental effects were assessed by examining the changes in behavior from the baseline period to the experimental and postviewing periods. The four-week experimental period was divided into two-week blocks (called experimental periods 1 and 2) in order to assess differences in effects early and late in the television viewing series. For each child, the scores for experimental periods 1 and 2 and for the postviewing period were subtracted from the baseline score. The mean number of minutes of observation on which the scores in each period were based was: Baseline—90.8, Experimental 1—58.4, Experimental 2—56.5, Postviewing—79.6.

Table 13: Mean baseline scores for measures where conditions differed

Aggressive		Condition			F ratios
		Aggressive	Neutral	Prosocial	
Frustration	Boys	.09	.14	.04	Condition = 5.66**
	Girls	.06	.048	.028	Sex x Condition = 2.67*
		.075	.094	.033	
Object	Boys	.088	.160	.145	Condition = 2.85*
frustration	Girls	.102	.124	.067	Sex x Condition - 2.49*
		.095	.142	.106	
Physical	Boys	.114	.171	.090	Condition = 2.27#
aggression	Girls	.020	.045	.014	
		.067	.108	.052	
Interpersonal	Boys	.205	.273	.170	Condition = 1.58#
aggression	Girls	.107	.106	.064	
		.156	.189	.117	
Cooperation	Boys	.191	.189	.145	
	Girls	.152	.092	.086	Condition = 1.77#
		.171	.141	.116	
Verbalization of feeling		.055	.034	.042	Condition = 1.59#
Rule obedience		.115	.086	.080	Condition = 2.20#
Tolerance of delay		.061	.033	.048	Condition = 1.62#
Task persistence		.388	.442	.394	Condition = 1.61#

**p < .05
*p < .10
#p < .25

The baseline scores for each variable were submitted to an analysis of variance of Sex x Condition in order to check for any initial differences. The results of these analyses appear in Table 13. Means are given for all variables where effects reached the .25 level of significance.

The children in the Neutral groups in all four classrooms were combined. Inspection of the means indicated that there were not meaningful differences between those in classrooms with Aggressive condition children and those in classrooms with Prosocial condition children.

In the analyses of variance of classroom behavior, three variables were considered in addition to sex and experimental condition: IQ, SES, and (for the interpersonal categories) initial levels of the behavior studied. For the analyses of variance, the children were classified into two IQ and two SES groups by dividing them at the group medians. Similarly, for interpersonal aggression and prosocial interpersonal behavior, the boys and girls were divided at their respective group medians to form two groups. The sample size made it impractical to include all these variables in a single analysis, so separate analyses were carried out. When the results were significant, they are reported. Where IQ, SES, or initial level are not mentioned, it can be assumed that there were no significant main effects or interactions associated with these variables. All analyses of variance followed the unweighted means procedure for unequal cell frequencies (Winer, 1962).

Secondary correlational analyses were performed to determine the relationship between home viewing experiences and behavior change in the three experimental conditions. Correlations were computed separately for each condition. The number of subjects was too small to warrant separating each condition by sex, but biserial correlations of all variables were examined, and sex was partialed out of any correlations to which it might have made a contribution. These correlations appear in Table 14.

Aggressive behavior

In the analyses of the three interpersonal aggression scores—physical, verbal, and total interpersonal aggression—boys and girls were divided at their respective baseline medians into High and Low Initial Aggression groups. Differences between children who were initially high or low in aggression were of theoretical interest, and this division was intended to control for any possible effects of the small initial differences between conditions. The principal finding of these analyses was that children who were initially high in aggression showed greater interpersonal aggression when they were exposed to the Aggressive condition than when they were exposed to the Neutral and Prosocial conditions. Children who were initially low in aggression did not respond differentially to the television conditions.

Table 14: Correlations of home television viewing with behavior change in the three experimental conditions

Home viewing	Physical aggression			Verbal aggression			Interpersonal aggression			Cooperation			Nurturance		
	A	N	P	A	N	P	A	N	P	A	N	P	A	N	P
Pattern 1															
Favorites															
Rogers	-06	15	-10	15	09	27	02	15	19	31	13*	04	25	09	-21
Childrens	02	19	-21	25	03	-13	20	15	-16	21	32*	01	20	22	-04
Childrens (prop.)	27	07	-18	-02	-01	-01	12	06	-10	31	21	-11	28	-18	-18
Cartoon	-05	31	05	05	-01	03	07	17	07	16	-01	23	14	05	-04
Cartoon (prop.)	06	20a	-33a	-05	-08	13	02	08	-07	37	0	0	34	-03	-06
Frequencies															
Rogers	01	-04	14	02	-08	13	01	-06	03	26	-02	11	07	0	-10
Childrens	-03	-28	10	-06	-10	16	-06	-20	21	28	10	11	25	25	-07
Cartoon	-14	10	-04	20	-03	0	08	07	-04	27	-12	11	27	20	-03
Pattern 2															
Favorites															
Miscellaneous	-25	08	19	15	14	-04	-04	10	07	-24	-28	19	-31	03	09
Miscellaneous (prop.)	-14	-14	26	11	04	-06	0	-09	08	-39*	-41*	-03	-41*	-05	12
Violent	-36a	-04	26a	-04	05	05	-24	03	20	-36a	0	50a*	-26	15	15
Violent (prop.)	-29a	-19	31a	-12	-01	-06	-23	-09	13	-38a*	-04	35a	-21	18	19
Frequencies															
Miscellaneous	-22	-23	28	23	-05	0	0	-12	17	29	-02	23	05	01	25
Violent	01	-23	15	08	0	14	04	-08	21	03	-11	32	15	09	10

Table 14: Correlations of home television viewing with behavior change in the three experimental conditions—Continued

Home viewing	Verbalization of feeling			Prosocial interpersonal			Rule obedience			Tolerance of delay			Interpersonal total		
	A	N	P	A	N	P	A	N	P	A	N	P	A	N	P
Pattern 1															
Favorites															
Rogers	03	02	45*	29	08	10	-02	08	17	-62*	-31	-12	31	14	10
Childrens	-22	-05	-04	12	33*	-02	01	03	13	04	-19	20	16	36*	-09
Childrens (prop.)	02	34*	21	28	20	-08	16	18	12	-29	-03	-06	35	21	-17
Cartoon	20	-08	-23	19	01	08	07	-16	04	-08	-12	03	14	12	13
Cartoon (prop.)	47*	13	03	49*	07	03	07	-21	-16	-50*	-01	-26	46*	09	02
Frequencies															
Rogers	-04	05	42*	13	02	16	07	13	0	-33	-22	-09	14	-04	15
Childrens	-06	-07	-13	18	22	03	24a	-09	-40a*	-14	02	-26	15	-06	11
Cartoon	-12	-02	-36	20	02	-01	02	-04	01	-09	07	-17	17	05	02
Pattern 2															
Favorites															
Miscellaneous	-11	-14	-28	-29	-27	05	-13	-12	08	33	09	20	-34	-14	12
Miscellaneous (prop.)	-25	-11	-11	-46*	-42*	-04	-13	-19	06	47*	16	18	-48*	-35*	02
Violent	-31	-08	-34	-40a*	05	27a	-14	-13	06	42*	-07	25	-43a*	02	33a
Violent (prop.)	-36	-11	-19	-40a*	0	27a	-13	-24	-10	40*	01	11	-42a*	-10	28a
Frequencies															
Miscellaneous	-09	02	-15	18	0	22	-11	-09	-20	32	07	-08	12	-12	28
Violent	-11	-11	-08	-06	-08	22	08	-19	-13	49*	07	-02	-07	-13	29

Note: The abbreviations A, N, P stand for the Aggressive, Neutral, and Prosocial Conditions.

aCorrelations for different conditions are significantly different (p < .05).
*p < .05.

Two analyses of variance were performed on the interpersonal aggression scores. The first included Condition x Initial Agression x Time Period; the second included sex as well as the other three variables. In each, there was an interaction of Conditions x Initial Aggression, but the interaction was significant beyond the .05 level only in the first analysis (F = 3.26, 2,86 *df;* p < .05). It was of borderline significance in the second (F = 2.71; 2,81 *df;* p < .08). The difference is probably due to the fact that an unweighted means analysis was used; when sex was added as a variable, the smaller number of girls was given equal weight to the larger number of boys. The means for the interaction are shown in Table 15. Among High Initial Aggression children, the Aggressive condition was associated with higher levels of interpersonal aggression than the Neutral condition. The Prosocial condition was close to the Neutral condition. Children in the Low Initial Aggression group showed similar levels of aggression in the three conditions.

Table 15: Mean change scores for interpersonal, physical, and verbal aggression

Level of initial aggression	Condition		
	Aggressive	Neutral	Prosocial
		Interpersonal aggression	
Low	.039	.079	.046
High	−.019[a]	−.123[a]	−.088
		Physical aggression	
Low	.017	.037	.022
High	.002	−.072	−.027
		Verbal aggression	
Low	.019	.052	.029
High	−.029	−.071	−.071

[a]Means are significantly different (p < .05) according to Newman-Keuls tests.

The only other significant finding in either analysis was a main effect of Initial Aggression (F = 29.76; 1,81 *df*, p < .001). Children who were initially high decreased in aggression, and those who were initially low increased. These trends may be partly due to regression to the mean, but they may also reflect the effects of nursery school experience.

When physical and verbal aggression were analyzed separately, the patterns were similar to that for interpersonal aggression, but the only effect that reached significance was the main effect of Initial Aggression (F = 8.72, 1,81 *df, p* < .01 for physical aggression; F = 22.08, p < .001 for verbal aggression).

These results suggest that children who are initially high in aggression respond to aggressive television programs with higher levels of aggression than they would under neutral conditions. These effects occurred in naturalistic behavior that was removed both in time and environmental setting from the viewing experience. They occurred with a small amount of exposure, particularly in relation to the amount the children received at home, and they endured during the postviewing period.

One reason for the difference between children who were initially high and those who were low in aggression may be differences in their previous socialization experiences. Children who were initially low in aggression may be those who have been more effectively socialized to exert control over aggressive impulses. When exposed to aggression-arousing stimuli, their controls may be sufficient to prevent behavioral effects, while the weaker controls of the highly aggressive children are not sufficient.

Children who are initially low in aggression may also have more aggression anxiety than those who are highly aggressive. Berkowitz's work with adults suggests that aggression anxiety may be aroused by violent films, with a resulting decline in aggressive behavior (see Baker and Ball, 1969). It is possible that children with low levels of aggressive behavior may have responded more frequently with anxiety than the highly aggressive children. As we have no direct information on socialization experiences or aggression anxiety, these interpretations must remain tentative. Whatever the reason for the difference between these two groups of children, however, it is of particular social importance that the highly aggressive children were those who were responsive to the aggressive programs.

Object aggression. Because of wide discrepancies in the variances of the change scores for boys and girls, analyses of object aggression were conducted separately for the two sexes. The mean scores for boys and girls who were initially high and low in interpersonal aggression appear in Figure 1. Although there appear to be large differences for boys, none of the main effects or interactions was significant in an analysis of Conditions x Initial Aggression x Time Period. In the analysis for the girls, there was a significant interaction of Condition x Initial Aggression x Time Period ($F = 2.51$; 4,72 $df;$ p $< .05$). For girls who were initially low in aggression, those exposed to aggressive television showed an initial rise in object aggression, but returned to their former levels in experimental period 2. Among girls high in initial aggression, those in the Aggressive condition rose slightly during experimental period 2, while those in the Prosocial condition dropped slightly. Both returned to about the same level during the postviewing period. Generally, these effects are quite small and suggest that the television conditions had little effect on object aggression.

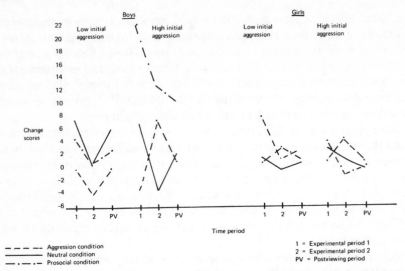

Figure 1: Object aggression scores for boys and girls divided by initial level of aggression

Fantasy aggression. The mean fantasy aggression scores for boys divided by condition and initial aggression are shown in Figure 2. There was a significant interaction of Condition x Initial Aggression x Time Period ($F = 2.78$, 4, 88 df, $p < .05$). The interaction does not lead to any clear interpretation. For girls, there were no significant effects or interactions involving initial aggression.

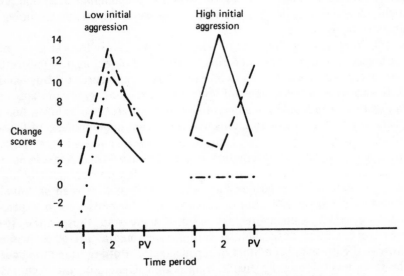

Note — All scores are shown without decimal points. Decimal points belong two places to the left.

Figure 2: Fantasy aggression scores for boys divided by initial aggression

When fantasy aggression scores were divided by sex, conditions, and IQ, there were significant main effects of sex and IQ ($F = 5.29$; 1,81 df; p $<.05$) ($F = 4.68$; 1,81 df; p $<.05$). Boys increased in fantasy aggression more than girls, and low IQ children increased more than high IQ children. There was a borderline trend toward a Condition x IQ interaction. The means appear in Table 16. For low IQ children, fantasy aggression increased most in the Aggressive condition, slightly less in the Neutral condition, and very little in the Prosocial condition. For high IQ children, the pattern was reversed, though the differences among conditions were considerably smaller. These differences were primarily true for boys.

In summary, for children of both sexes who were above average in initial interpersonal aggression, exposure to aggressive television programs led to higher levels of interpersonal aggression than similar children showed under neutral conditions. This pattern did not hold for object and fantasy aggression.

Table 16: Mean fantasy aggression change scores
for children divided by condition and IQ

	Condition			
	Aggressive	Neutral	Prosocial	All
Low IQ	.078	.039	.014	.044
High IQ	−.011	.008	.020	.006

Conditions x IQ $F = 2.51$, 2, 81 df, p $<.10$.

Intelligence was a predictor of fantasy aggression, but not of interpersonal and object aggression. Low IQ children, particularly boys, increased in fantasy aggression following the aggressive television programs and, to a lesser extent, following the neutral programs. Fantasy aggression was quite low among these children after the prosocial programs. High IQ children showed lower increases in fantasy aggression and smaller differences between conditions.

Prosocial classroom behavior

The prosocial behavior categories were divided into two groups—those that involve social interaction with other children and those that do not. The former have been called *prosocial interpersonal* and include cooperation, nurturance, verbalization of feeling, and the total prosocial interpersonal score. Although rule stating is also interpersonal in nature, it was considered separately because it can have aggressive overtones. This category corresponds closely to the behavior Sears et al. (1965) called "prosocial aggression." The remaining prosocial categories—rule obedience, delay tolerance, persistence, and instrumental help seeking —have been called *prosocial self-control* behavior. Although they were not intercorrelated, all appear to involve some degree of self-control and independent effort, but none necessarily involves interaction with other children.

Prosocial interpersonal behavior

For prosocial interpersonal behavior, SES was an important determinant of responses to the television conditions. The results of the analyses of variance of Sex x Conditions x SES x Time period appear in Table 17. Inspection of the patterns of scores indicates that the patterns during the postviewing period were different in some ways from the experimental period, so a second set of analyses of the experimental period alone was performed. The score for each child was the sum of his change scores during experimental periods 1 and 2. The results of these analyses appear in Table 18.

During the experimental period, the interaction of Conditions x SES was significant for the total prosocial interpersonal scores. The means appear in Table 19. For lower SES children, prosocial interpersonal behavior increased markedly in the Prosocial television condition and remained stable or dropped slightly in the Neutral and Aggressive conditions. For higher SES children, prosocial interpersonal behavior increased most in the Aggressive condition, increased moderately in the Neutral condition, and dropped very slightly in the Prosocial condition. Although this pattern occurred to some extent for each of the three individual measures composing the prosocial interpersonal total, it was statistically significant only for the total score. When the means for boys and girls were examined separately, it was apparent that the pattern described was more characteristic of boys than of girls.

These findings suggest that exposure to the prosocial television programs resulted in increased prosocial interpersonal behavior for lower SES children in comparison to the patterns shown by similar children in the Neutral and Aggressive conditions. For higher SES children, on the other hand, exposure to the aggressive programs led to the relatively high levels of prosocial interpersonal behavior, while exposure to the prosocial program led to no increases. These patterns were more pronounced for boys than for girls. (Possible reasons for these differences are discussed below.)

In the analyses that included the postviewing period, the major difference from the experimental period occurred for girls, particularly in the aggressive condition (see Figure 3). These changes occurred primarily on the cooperation measure. During the postviewing period, lower SES girls in the Aggressive condition increased markedly in cooperation while higher SES girls in the same condition declined sharply. Boys' scores remained relatively constant across time periods.

Table 17: Analyses of variance of cooperation, nurturance, verbalization of feeling, total prosocial interpersonal scores for all time periods by sex, condition, and SES

Source of variance	df	Cooperation		Nurturance		Verbalization		Total	
		MS	F	MS	F	MS	F	MS	F
Sex (S)	1	.0207	—	.0001	—	00	—	.0149	—
Condition (C)	2	.0031	—	.0065	—	.0102	—	.0076	—
SES	1	.0275	—	.0087	—	.0056	—	.0005	—
S x C	2	.0190	—	.0046	—	.0156	—	.0008	—
S x SES	1	.0046	—	.0217	—	.0048	—	.0464	—
C x SES	2	.0217	—	.0312	2.01	.0270	1.86	.1401	2.29
S x C x SES	2	.1861	3.91**	.0018	—	.0006	—	.1285	2.10
Error (between $\underline{S}$s)	80	.0476		.0190		.0145		.0611	
Time period (T)	2	.0044	—	.0034	—	.0379	—	.0308	—
S x T	2	.0498	2.95**	.0062	—	.0182	6.81**	.0582	3.66*
C x T	4	.0092	—	.0076	—	.0043	2.13	.0050	—
SES x T	2	.0220	—	.0118	2.04	.0009	—	.0309	—
S x C x T	4	.0090	—	.0057	—	.0029	—	.0077	—
S x SES x T	2	.0582	3.46**	.0006	—	.0096	—	.0278	—
C x SES x T	4	.0355	2.11*	.0021	—	.0024	—	.0306	—
S x C x SES x T	4	.0254	—	.0122	2.11*	.0067	—	.0103	—
Error (within $\underline{S}$s)	160	.0168		.0058		.0056		.0159	

*p < .10
**p < .05

Table 18: Analyses of variance of cooperation, verbalization of feeling, total prosocial interpersonal scores for experimental period by sex, condition, and SES

Source of variance	df	Cooperation		Verbalization of feeling		Total	
		MS	F	MS	F	MS	F
Sex (S)	1	.1368	1.82	.0022	—	.0373	—
Condition (C)	2	.0164	—	.0358	1.85	.0245	—
SES	1	.0764	—	.0100	—	.0166	—
S x C	2	.0300	—	.0244	—	.0103	—
S x SES	1	.0300	—	.0342	1.77	.1109	—
C x SES	2	.0869	—	.0552	2.86*	.3333	3.76**
S x C x SES	2	.1093	1.45	.0117	—	.1184	—
Error	81	.0753		.0193		.0886	

Note: The scores analyzed were the sum of experimental periods 1 and 2 for each S, so all MSs are double the value that would be obtained if means for each S were used. F ratios are, of course, identical so the MSs have not been changed. Means reported in other tables have been corrected by dividing by 2.

*p < .10
**p < .05

Table 19: Mean prosocial interpersonal scores for the experimental period for subjects classified by sex, condition, and SES

	Condition		
	Aggressive	Neutral	Prosocial
Lower SES			
Boys	−.072	−.046	.093
Girls	.058	−.006	.092
Both sexes	−.007	−.026	.093
Higher SES			
Boys	.115	.027	−.019
Girls	.026	.066	−.014
Both sexes	.071	.047	−.017

The significant interaction of Sex x Condition x SES for the cooperation scores reflects the changes described. Among boys, the patterns were similar to those in the experimental period. Lower SES boys became more cooperative in the Prosocial condition and dropped in the Neutral and Aggressive conditions. Higher SES boys increased in cooperation in the Aggressive condition and remained unchanged in the Neutral and Prosocial conditions (see Table 20). Girls, for whom the changes in the experimental period were less clear, showed marked shifts in cooperation during the postviewing period.

Overall, it appears that exposure to the prosocial programs resulted in increased prosocial interpersonal behavior, particularly cooperation, for lower SES children. Exposure to the aggressive programs resulted in increased prosocial behavior for higher SES children. The effects were more marked and more lasting for boys.

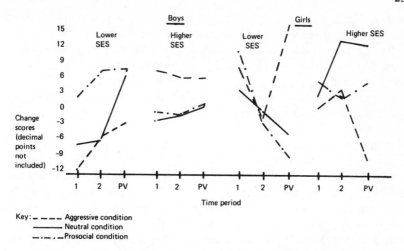

Key: — — — — Aggressive condition
———— Neutral condition
—.—.— Prosocial condition

Figure 3: Cooperation change scores for boys and girls in two SES groups

Table 20: Mean cooperation and prosocial interpersonal scores for all time periods
for subjects classified by sex, condition, and SES

	Cooperation condition		
	Aggressive	Neutral	Prosocial
Lower SES			
Boys	−.069	−.023	.055
Girls	.068	−.012	−.014
Both sexes	0	−.017	.020
Higher SES			
Boys	.058	−.002	−.007
Girls	−.035	.079	.035
Both sexes	.011	.038	.014
	Prosocial interpersonal		
Lower SES			
Boys	−.045	−.005	.093
Girls	.090	−.005	.085
Both sexes	.022	−.005	.089
Higher SES			
Boys	.106	.038	−.012
Girls	.009	.077	.012
Both sexes	.057	.058	0

Home viewing correlates. Lower SES children in the Prosocial condition increased in all categories of prosocial interpersonal behavior more than higher SES children. For two of the prosocial interpersonal categories—cooperation and verbalization of feeling—however, the home viewing correlates differed. Children who increased most in cooperation had relatively high numbers of miscellaneous and violent favorites at home; those who increased most in verbalization of feeling has relatively low preferences for miscellaneous and violent programs. Instead, they were frequent viewers of *Misterogers* (see Table 14).

By contrast, children with "child-oriented" viewing preferences were more likely to show increased prosocial behavior in the Aggressive and Neutral conditions. In the Aggressive condition, particularly, the greatest increases in prosocial behavior were shown by children with low preferences for "all-age" programs and relatively high preferences for cartoons.

Total interpersonal behavior. The correlates of prosocial behavior change are similar to those for the total interpersonal score (which includes aggression). As there is ample evidence that aggressive and prosocial interpersonal behaviors are positively associated, this parallel is not surprising. Lower SES children with miscellaneous and violent home viewing patterns appear to have responded to the prosocial programs with general increases in social interaction. While much of this increase followed the prosocial patterns stressed in *Misterogers,* some increases in aggression were apparent as well. Higher SES children with child-oriented viewing patterns, on the other hand, showed increased interpersonal behavior including both aggressive and prosocial patterns in the Aggressive and Neutral conditions.

SES differences. The SES and home viewing differences are consistent with the socialization "void" hypothesis. Lower SES children whose principal television interests fall in the miscellaneous and violent program categories have fewer opportunities to learn and practice skills in social interaction through either family or media. At least for girls, there is some evidence from the baseline behavior that such skills were less common among lower SES children. Exposure to either the neutral or aggressive program provides no additional training in these skills. Exposure to the prosocial program provides some information about prosocial skills that evidently stimulates some of the children to practice and increase their abilities in interacting cooperatively with others. With increased social interaction, a certain amount of aggression results. The latter may be merely a function of the increased interaction, or it may reflect a behavioral response to the themes of expression of anger in the prosocial television series. One reason for the greater response of lower SES children to *Misterogers* may be its greater novelty. Although many lower SES children watch *Misterogers* at home, the fact that it is less often named as a favorite program suggests that it is less salient in their home viewing experience. Exposure in the controlled, relatively nondistracting conditions used in the study may increase its salience.

The response of the higher SES children to the Aggressive condition suggests that it may have had a generalized stimulating effect that led to increased social interaction in general. The home viewing patterns for these children indicate that they were less accustomed to the types of violence in "all-age" programs; they were cartoon fans. They may then have been particularly likely to be excited by the fast-moving, high noise-level method of presentation in the aggressive programs. As the higher SES children may already have been somewhat more skilled in prosocial modes of social interaction, the generalized stimulation may have led to greater likelihood of prosocial interaction. These interpretations must, however, remain quite tentative because the Neutral group showed some trends in a similar direction.

Sex differences. The patterns described were generally more clear for boys than for girls. In both the aggressive and the prosocial programs, the principal characters were male. Consequently, boys may have been more likely to identify with the characters and to adopt some of their behavior.

Postviewing period changes. The marked shifts for girls in the Aggressive condition during the postviewing period raise questions about the factors affecting the children's behavior during that period. The postviewing period was originally intended to measure possible continuing effects of the television viewing. There are, however, a number of other factors which should be considered in evaluating the results of this period. It represented a shift for all children from a pattern in which they watched programs for a half-hour each day to a full two and one-half hours of regular nursery school activity. It appeared, from watching the children during the programs, that the quality of the viewing time differed across conditions. Those watching *Misterogers* seemed to be experiencing a quiet, rather soothing half hour, while those in the Aggressive condition were more active as they were bombarded with high noise and rapid action. The films in the Neutral condition appeared to fall somewhere between the two experimental conditions on the dimensions of noise level and rapidity of action. It is possible that part of the postviewing changes were responses to the *discontinuation* of these experiences rather than continuation of effects. This interpretation appears most reasonable in cases where the changes were considerably larger than those in the experimental period and different in direction. The exact mechanism operating in these effects is not clear, however.

Rule stating. The television conditions had no effect on the rule stating scores of boys, but there were some differences for girls (see Figure 4). For lower SES girls, there were no differences among conditions during the experimental period, but a sharp increase for girls in the Aggressive condition during the postviewing period paralleled the increases in cooperation. Higher SES girls, on the other hand, showed an increase in rule stating when first exposed to the aggressive television but dropped back to the levels of the other conditions by experimental period 2. For girls in the Aggressive condition, patterns of rule stating during the postviewing period were parallel to those in other forms of prosocial interpersonal behavior, particularly cooperation. As verbalizing of rules

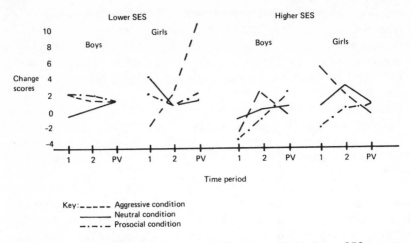

Figure 4: Change scores for rule stating for boys and girls in two SES groups

seems likely to occur during organized cooperative activity, it appears reasonable that similar changes occurred on the two measures. The differences discussed are reflected in a significant four-way interaction of Sex x Condition x SES x Time period (Table 21).

Prosocial self-control behavior

Predicted differences among experimental conditions appeared on rule obedience, tolerance of delay, and task persistence, but not on instrumental help seeking. On all three measures, children in the Aggressive condition generally declined, and children in the Prosocial condition generally increased. These patterns were more pronounced for high IQ children than for low IQ children. Analyses of variance of the three measures for the experimental period only (Sex x Condition x IQ) and for all time periods (Sex x Condition x IQ x Time period) are shown in Tables 22 and 23.

Rule obedience. During the experimental period, there was a main effect of conditions at borderline significance ($p < .06$). Children in the Prosocial condition increased ($\overline{X} = .014$), those in the Neutral condition dropped slightly ($\overline{X} = -.014$), and those in the Aggressive condition dropped most ($\overline{X} = -.039$). These differences did not continue during the postviewing period, as indicated by the significant four-way interaction in the analysis including that period. The patterns are shown in Figure 5.

Independent of the experimental treatments, there was an interaction of Sex x IQ. Boys in the high and low IQ groups showed little overall change in rule obedience, but low IQ girls' scores dropped and high IQ girls' scores increased markedly.

Table 21: Analysis of variance of rule stating scores
for all time periods by sex, condition, SES

Source of variance	df	MS	F
Sex (S)	1	.0069	—
Condition (C)	2	.0033	—
SES	1	.0177	3.23*
S x C	2	.0025	—
S x SES	1	00	—
C x SES	2	.0019	—
S x C x SES	2	.0003	—
Error (between $\underline{S}$s)	80	.0055	
Time period (T)	2	.0040	—
S x T	2	.0011	—
C x T	4	.0007	—
SES x T	2	.0040	—
S x C x T	4	.0024	—
S x SES x T	2	.0085	3.40*
C x SES x T	4	.0081	3.27*
S x C x SES x T	4	.0083	3.32*
Error (within $\underline{S}$s)	160	.0025	

*p < .10
**p < .05

Table 22: Analyses of variance of rule obedience, delay tolerance, and
task persistence scores across all time periods

Source of variance	df	Rule obedience		Tolerance of delay		Task persistence	
		MS	F	MS	F	MS	F
Sex (S)	1	.0064	—	.0149	—	.1074	2.07
Condition (C)	2	.0292	1.48	.0564	3.66**	.1417	2.73*
IQ	1	.0911	4.62**	.0604	3.91**	.0430	—
S x C	2	.0152	—	.0094	—	.0694	1.32
S x IQ	1	.0990	5.03*	.0023	—	.0047	—
C x IQ	2	.0197	1.00	.0461	2.99*	.1705	3.28**
S x C x IQ	2	.0183	—	.0027	—	.0384	—
Error (between $\underline{S}$s)	80	.0197		.0154		.0519	
Time period (T)	2	.0212	3.72**	.0132	—	.1581	9.03**
S x T	2	.0154	2.70*	.0094	—		
C x T	4	.0077	—	.0131	—	.0124	
IQ x T	2	.0059	—	.0084	—	.0028	—
S x C x T	4	.0084	—	.0103	—		
S x IQ x T	2	.0129	2.28	.0016	—		
C x IQ x T	4	.0047	—	.0042	—	.0125	—
S x C x IQ x T	4	.0171	3.03**	.0062	—		
Error (within $\underline{S}$s)	160	.0057		.0078		.0175	

*p < .10
**p < .05

Note: On task persistence, the MS for the main effect and interactions including Time
period were obtained from an earlier analysis that combined sexes. Inspection indicated no interactions involving Sex and Time period, so additional analyses were
not done.

Table 23: Analyses of variance of rule obedience, delay tolerance,
and task persistence for the experimental period only

		Rule obedience		Tolerance of delay		Task persistence	
Source of variance	df	MS	F	MS	F	MS	F
Sex (S)	1	.0007	–	.0062	–	.2221	2.73
Condition (C)	2	.0783	2.96*	.1026	4.16**	.2154	2.65*
IQ	1	.0606	2.29	.0796	3.23*	.0614	–
S x C	2	.0141	–	.0277	1.12	.1076	1.32
S x IQ	1	.2111	7.96**	.0004	–	.0017	–
C x IQ	2	.0518	1.96	.0489	1.98	.3826	4.71**
S x C x IQ	2	.0347	1.31	.0046	–	.0516	–
Error	81	.0265		.0247		.0813	

Note: The scores analyzed were the sum of experimental periods 1 and 2 for each subject,
so all MS are double the value that would be obtained if means for each *S* were used.
F ratios are, of course, identical, so the MSs have not been changed. Tables of means
have been divided by 2 to give accurate means.

*p < .10
**p < .05

Tolerance of delay. There was a significant main effect of conditions
on tolerance of delay. The differences persisted during the postviewing
period, although they were slightly less pronounced than during the experimental period. Children in the Aggressive condition dropped in delay tolerance, while those in the Neutral and Prosocial conditions increased. The means appear in Table 24. High IQ children increased
more than low IQ children, and there was an interaction of Condition x
IQ. Both IQ groups showed the greatest drop in delay tolerance in the
Aggressive condition. The low IQ groups, however, also dropped slightly in the Prosocial condition while increasing in the Neutral condition.
The high IQ children increased most in the Prosocial condition.

It appears from these findings that exposure to the aggressive programs led to decreased tolerance of delay relative to the neutral and prosocial programs. The correlational analysis indicated that this decline

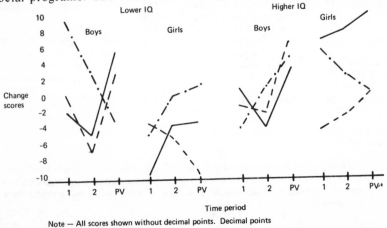

Note — All scores shown without decimal points. Decimal points
belong two places to the left.

Figure 5: Change scores for rule obedience for boys and girls in two IQ groups

was greatest for higher SES children whose home viewing patterns were high in the child-oriented programs and low in violent and miscellaneous programs (Table 14). This is a reversal of the pattern found on prosocial interpersonal behavior. It appears that higher SES children with a child-oriented home viewing pattern may be stimulated by the aggressive television programs to increased interpersonal behavior, much of which is prosocial; but, perhaps because of increased activity level, their delay tolerance is sharply decreased. Lower SES children with all-age viewing patterns, on the other hand, seem to be less affected by the aggressive programs shown them in the study. They appear to be less stimulated to both aggressive and prosocial interpersonal behavior and to be less likely to drop in tolerance of delay.

Table 24: Mean scores on rule obedience, tolerance of delay, and task persistence for the experimental period and for all time periods

	Experimental period			All time periods		
	Rule obedience					
	Aggressive	Neutral	Prosocial	Aggressive	Neutral	Prosocial
Lo IQ	−.045	−.052	.017	−.042	−.033	.008
Hi IQ	−.034	.024	.011	−.006	.038	.017
All Ss	−.039	−.014	.014	−.024	.002	.013
	Tolerance of delay					
Lo IQ	−.051	.034	−.012	−.034[a]	.045[ba]	−.020[b]
Hi IQ	−.007	.028	.053	.002[c]	.027	.057[c]
All Ss	−.030[ab]	.026[a]	.020[b]	−.016[ab]	.036[a]	.019[b]
	Task persistence					
Lo IQ	−.015	−.123	−.064	0	−.101	−.032
Hi IQ	−.121[a]	−.055	.055[a]	−.078[a]	−.035	.060[a]
All Ss	−.068	−.089	−.004	−.039	−.068	.014

Note: Within each set of three means, those with the same superscript are significantly different ($p < .05$) according to Newman-Keuls tests.

These findings suggest that children who have had a lot of exposure to the television fare included in the violent and miscellaneous categories and who come from families who may be more aggressive are somewhat habituated to high levels of excitement and aggression on television. For them the *Batman* and *Superman* cartoons shown in the study are relatively mild compared with many of the programs with which they have extensive experience. Children with more child-oriented viewing experiences and from middle-class homes, on the other hand, may be less habituated to the excitement and violence shown. They apparently view fewer programs in the miscellaneous and violent categories (to which

Batman and *Superman* are most similar). Thus, their greater reaction may reflect less habituation to television violence.

Task persistence. The main effect of conditions on task persistence was at a borderline level of significance. Children in the Prosocial condition had the highest change scores, and those in the Neutral condition had the lowest change scores. Again, responses to the television conditions differed for children at the two IQ levels. There was a significant interaction of Condition x IQ. The means appear in Table 24. Among low IQ children, there was little difference among the three conditions. For high IQ children, however, there was an increase in persistence in the Prosocial condition, a drop in the Neutral condition, and a larger drop in the Aggressive condition.

Despite the fact that rule obedience, delay tolerance, and persistence were independent dimensions of behavior, there are some parallels in the results for the three measures. Children in the Aggressive condition generally declined on these indices, and children in the Prosocial condition generally increased. These patterns were more pronounced for high IQ children than for low IQ children. Following the procedure of using the Neutral group as the comparison point for evaluating effects of the experimental treatments, it appears that the aggressive programs had a deleterious effect on children's willingness to tolerate delay and, to a lesser extent, on rule obedience—that is, it apparently resulted in some decrease in self-control. The Prosocial condition had its primary impact on high IQ children. For them, it apparently led to increased task persistence and, to a lesser extent, to increased rule obedience.

The results for these behaviors are in marked contrast with those for prosocial interpersonal behavior. While lower SES children were most likely to show increased prosocial interpersonal behavior in response to the prosocial programs, higher IQ children showed the most positive response in self-control and persistence. Although the lower SES children were not identical to the low IQ children, the two characteristics were correlated. Thus, it appears that different themes in the *Misterogers* programs reached different groups of children. The themes of self-control and persistence were less often stressed in the programs shown; they may be more cognitively complex the themes of interpersonal relations. Perhaps, also, persistence results in more environmental rewards for high IQ children so that they are more likely to continue such behavior once it is started. Some support for this argument is provided by the fact that low IQ children were more likely to encounter object frustration during the baseline period.

Responses to frustration

In the initial conceptualization of the study, we expected the child's responses to frustration to be modified by exposure to the television programs. The analysis originally planned involved comparing the frequency of different types of responses to frustration. Such an analysis was carried out, but it did not yield meaningful results for two reasons: the number of frustrating stimuli was so small for some subjects that the calculation of frequencies of response was impractical, and the number of frustrating stimuli differed widely across subjects. On the basis of the initial correlations of stimuli with behavior, it was obvious that these individual differences were at least partly dependent on the child's own behavior. It appeared unrealistic to consider responses to frustration in a stimulus-response model that implied a one-way effect from the environment to the child. For these reasons, some additional information on the relation of the frustration and behavior categories is presented.

Responses to frustration. Following the original plan, the number of stimuli and the number of responses that immediately followed the stimuli in each category were tabulated. For aggressive and fantasy frustration no analyses were performed, because approximately half of the subjects had fewer than two stimuli during the baseline period. For the other stimulus categories, children with fewer than two stimuli in either the baseline period or the following periods combined were excluded. (For these analyses, the experimental and postviewing periods were combined to maximize the number of stimuli and responses.) For those children with two or more stimuli, the proportion of responses in particular behavior categories was calculated. Changes from baseline to the combined experimental and postviewing periods were calculated. The following combinations of stimuli and responses were tabulated in this way: frustration by child with interpersonal aggression, no response and negative response; frustration by teacher with no response and negative response; total frustration with total verbal. There was not sufficient variability in other possible combinations to provide useful analyses. None of these analyses resulted in significant differences among conditions. In view of the earlier discussion, this absence of findings is not surprising. By calculating the proportion of responses to a stimulus category, the number of stimuli is in effect rendered constant across children. Thus, one part of the real variability in the child's encounter with the environment has been removed.

Correlations of changes in frustration with behavior changes. The correlations of changes in frustration with changes in behavior reflect all the behavior scored, even when no frustration was immediately involved, but they may provide indicators of the overall pattern of the children's behavior. If such correlations differ in different conditions, this may imply at least a different constellation of interaction patterns.

The correlations between changes in four of the six stimulus categories and changes in behavior during the experimental period appear in Table 25. For children in the Aggressive and Neutral conditions, increases in aggressive frustration and, to some extent, in other forms of interpersonal frustration were associated with increased interpersonal aggression. In the Aggressive condition, there were negative correlations between frustration and prosocial interpersonal behavior, while there were generally no correlations in the Neutral group. In fact, nurturance was positively correlated with frustration for the Neutral group. Thus, the expected pattern of frustration-aggression correlations was present for both groups, but the Aggressive group showed an additional trend toward declining prosocial behavior in conjunction with increased frustration.

Table 25: Correlations of frustration changes with
behavior changes during the experimental
period for the three conditions

Behavior Category	Condition	Frustration categories			
		Aggressive	Child	Object	Total
Physical aggression	Agg	29	05	−11	24
	Neut	46*	29	−10	31
	Pro	−08	17	32	17
Verbal aggression	Agg	41*	19	−11	25
	Neut	45*	52*	06	38*
	Pro	−02	31	−09	04
Interpersonal aggression	Agg	42*	14	−09	32
	Neut	50*	49*	01	45*
	Pro	02	36	12	18
Object aggression	Agg	−42*	21	26	09
	Neut	26	15	26	26
	Pro	35	07	46*	39*
Cooperation	Agg	30	−.27	−38*	−12
	Neut	−03	−06	−23	−22
	Pro	−07	41*	22	33
Nurturance	Agg	−10	−43*	−32	−32
	Neut	0	30	30	41*
	Pro	52*	37	−01	44*
Verbalization of feeling	Agg	−07	22	−16	19
	Neut	−19	0	−22	−25
	Pro	17	28	−04	31
Total prosocial interpersonal	Agg	19	−23	−38*	−09
	Neut	−10	05	−20	−13
	Pro	30	56*	13	56*

*p <.05

In the Prosocial condition, by contrast, interpersonal aggression was not associated with aggressive frustration, and there were weaker associations with other types of frustration than was the case in the other conditions. By contrast, increases in frustration for children in the Prosocial condition were positively associated with increased prosocial interpersonal behavior and with object aggression.

These patterns of correlations cannot be interpreted as showing changes in children's immediate responses to frustration, but they do suggest that children in the different experimental conditions had evolved somewhat different patterns of social interaction. Children in the Aggressive and Neutral conditions manifested patterns of frustration and aggression that would be expected, but children in the Prosocial condition did not show increased aggression with increased frustration to the same extent. Instead, children in the Prosocial condition manifested increased prosocial behavior in conjunction with increased frustration; children in the Aggressive condition showed reduced prosocial behavior with increased frustration.

Attention to the programs

According to the model of observational learning used in the study, attention to the programs should affect the amount learned from the programs. Learning in turn is one determinant of behavioral effects. It was expected, therefore, that attention would be correlated with the "content" test and with behavioral change in the Aggressive and Prosocial conditions. None of the predicted relations of attention to content or to behavior change appeared with consistency. Attention to the aggressive programs was positively related to the characters identification section of the content test for *Batman* and *Superman* ($r = .41$) but not to the behavioral alternatives section. There were no correlations of attention to the prosocial program with the content test for *Misterogers.*

None of the correlations of attention with behavior change was significant, and there were no trends in the predicted direction. Attention to the programs was unrelated to behavioral change in the classroom.

The relative absence of relations of attention to the content tests and to behavior change may be due to the fact that both of the latter measures were some distance in time and setting from the television viewing sessions. The content test does not represent the child's immediate learning or memory of specific programs, but represents what he can recall or generalize from several programs one or two weeks after he has seen them. It may still be true that attention is related to more immediate learning and memory, although there are no data to support that proposition in this study. Even if attention were related to more immediate learning from the programs, behavior change is probably affected by factors other than learning. Such factors may dissipate any correlations of attention with behavior.

It is also possible that exposure to the aggressive and prosocial programs was sufficiently repetitious that children were able to "get the message," or much of it, even without high levels of attention. The aggressive themes in *Batman* and *Superman* are quite repetitous and may be learned to some asymptote even by the child who attends only half the time. Although the themes in the *Misterogers* program are more complex, they were also repeated.

Finally, the observations taped only visual attention, not auditory. As the children were a captive audience, it is quite likely that they were listening to the programs during many of the instances when they were not watching. The themes in both programs are conveyed through auditory presentation, so it would be possible to learn much of the content through listening. This is especially true for *Misterogers*, because much of the theme material is verbally explained both by the fantasy characters and by Mr. Rogers himself.

Even though the attention measure was not related to the measures of learning or behavior change, it may be an indicator of the children's immediate interest and involvement in the programs. Therefore, the attention scores were subjected to an analysis of variance of Sex x Condition x IQ. The means for boys and girls in the three conditions appear in Table 26. There was a significant Sex x Condition interaction ($F = 8.33$; 2, 79 df, $p < .001$) as well as main effects of Sex ($F = 8.33$, 1,79 df, $p < .005$) and Condition ($F = 42.3$, 2, 79 df, $p < .001$). Children were most attentive in the Neutral condition and least attentive in the Prosocial condition. The means for boys and girls in those two conditions were almost identical. In the Aggressive condition, however, boys were much more attentive than girls. The mean for boys was similar to that in the Neutral condition, while the girls' attention scores were approximately equal to those in the Prosocial condition. There was also a main effect of IQ ($F = 4.68$, 1, 79 df, $p < .05$), but no interactions with IQ. Children with IQs above the group median were more attentive ($X = .71$) than those with lower IQs ($X = .65$).

Table 26: Mean attention scores for boys and girls in three experimental conditions

	Condition		
	Aggressive	Neutral	Prosocial
Boys	.79	.85	.53
Girls	.53	.87	.51

There are a number of differences in both program content and mode of presentation between the neutral films and the television conditions that might have affected the children's attention. First, the Neutral group saw movies rather than television. Films may have been slightly more novel to them, and the image was larger. Some of the films were in color, though as many black-and-white films as possible were included. Second, the content and themes of the neutral films were much more variable than either of the television programs. A third difference was that the viewing groups for the Neutral films were slightly larger (ten children) than those for the experimental conditions (seven or eight children). One would expect, however, that the larger group would make attention more difficult rather than easier.

Initial behavior and home television viewing

Two major patterns of program types were identified in the home viewing habits of the subjects. Pattern 1 ("child-oriented" programs) contains *Misterogers,* children's programs, and cartoons. Pattern 2 (all-age programs) includes *Batman, Superman,* miscellaneous, and violent programs. For the most part, where correlations between baseline behavior and home viewing occurred, the directions were consistent for the different components within each viewing pattern. Correlations between baseline behavior and home viewing patterns were computed for boys and girls separately. The results for those behavior categories in which significant correlations appeared are shown in Table 27.

In general, there were relatively few significant correlations, particularly for boys. For girls, there were some patterns of significant correlations which were probably not due to chance. For girls, relatively high Pattern 1 home viewing and low Pattern 2 home viewing were associated with high levels of verbal and interpersonal aggression, verbalization of feeling, total verbalization, and total interpersonal behavior. It appears, therefore, that girls who watched relatively few miscellaneous and violent television programs and who preferred child-oriented programs were more socially interactive than girls with high Pattern 2 viewing frequencies. More socially interactive girls were also from higher SES families, but SES did not entirely account for the relations between home viewing and behavior.

The only behavior negatively related to Pattern 1 viewing for girls was fantasy aggression, but fantasy aggression was also negatively related to Pattern 2 viewing and to total frequency ($r = .26$).

These correlational results do not, of course, necessarily reflect causal effects of home television viewing. It is quite possible that more quiet, inactive girls are more prone to sit quietly in front of the television set and therefore watch a greater variety of programs than do more active children. Further, home viewing was correlated with verbal aggression, but not physical aggression. For girls, high levels of verbal aggression may often reflect assertiveness as well as hostility.

Studies with older children have found correlations between home television viewing and aggression for boys. The experimental portion of the present study indicated some behavioral effects of small exposures to aggressive programs, yet virtually no relations between behavior and

Table 27: Correlations of home viewing patterns with baseline behavior

Home viewing	Behavior category					
	Verbal aggression	Interpersonal aggression	Fantasy aggression	Verbalization of feeling	Total verbal	Total interpersonal
Pattern 1						
Favorites						
1. Rogers	20			30*(24)a	35*(27)a	20
2. Children's			−30*(−38*)b	39*(34*)a	24	23
3. Cartoons						
Frequencies						
4. Rogers				30*		
5. Children's			−32*	30*		
6. Cartoons				[35]*a		
Pattern 2						
Favorites						
7. Miscellaneous	−30*(−24)a		−21		−27	
8. Violent	−31*(−27)a				−30*	−22
Frequencies						
9. Miscellaneous	−32*(−24)a	−32*(−26)a			−34*(−25)a	−27
10. Violent	−39*(−33*)a	−41*(−36*)a			−38*(−30)a	−26

Note: All correlations are for girls except those in brackets. Correlations below .20 are not shown.

aSES partialled out   *p < .05
bMA partialled out

home viewing were found for boys. One reason for the absence of findings may be the fact that the children were in a new setting in which their behavior was shaped more by the setting than by their home experiences. The situation-specificity of children's behavior has been mentioned earlier and may partially account for the absence of relationships. Another possible reason may be that children's responses to television programs depend on individual differences in variables such as initial aggression. If different children responded to home television in different ways, these changes would not be reflected in overall correlations of the kind presented in this report. Finally, of course, it is possible that exposure to television at home does not have any clearcut directional effects on children's behavior.

Content tests

The purpose of the content tests was to determine the children's knowledge about the programs shown. For the *Misterogers* show, knowledge could be gained from viewing in the study or from home viewing. For *Batman* and *Superman,* these sources exist, but there are others as well. Both characters are presented to children in a variety of contexts in the popular culture, including *Sesame Street.* Therefore, although some differences as a function of viewing in the study were expected, these were not expected to be large because of other sources of knowledge, particularly for the aggressive programs.

Experimental conditions. There were no differences among the three conditions in scores on either content measure. Thus, the overall knowledge of the programs was not differentially affected by the viewing that occurred in nursery school. There were differences between children at different IQ levels. For the *Misterogers* content test, higher IQ children had higher scores than lower IQ children in each condition (rs ranging from .42 to .46 ps < .05), possibly because of more frequent home viewing. There were no correlations of IQ with performance on the *Batman* and *Superman* content test.

Home viewing. Correlations between the *Misterogers* content test and the mothers' reports of the children's preferences for and frequency of watching *Misterogers* appear in Table 28. High preference for *Rogers* was related to total test score only for children in the Prosocial condition. Those in the Neutral condition who liked *Rogers* at home also did better on the character identification-Who Am I (hereafter called "character") section of the test than those who did not prefer *Rogers.*

Rogers frequency was positively related to character scores for all children and to behavior alternative and total scores for children in the Aggressive and Prosocial conditions. These findings, particularly for the "*Rogers* favorite" variable, suggest some additive effect of liking *Rogers* with being exposed in the nursery school. The differences are more

Table 28: Correlations between content tests and home viewing

| Home viewing category | Misterogers content test | | | | | | | | |
| | Character | | | Behavior alternative | | | Total | | |
	A	N	P	A	N	P	A	N	P
Rogers favorite	11	45*	47*	20	−20	43*	18	17	51*
Rogers frequency	35	34	45*	34	−09	36	40	17	46*
	Batman-Superman content test								
Batman favorite	−03	20	15	10	27	50*	02	28	42*
Superman favorite	10	26	−11	32	29	21	29	33	08
Batman frequency	03	30	12	16	30	49*	10	35	40*
Superman frequency	35	23	02	39	35	18	54*	36	13

Note: A=Aggressive condition; N=Neutral condition; P=Prosocial condition.

*$p < .05$

apparent on the more difficult section of the test—the behavior alternatives—than on the section requiring mere identification of characters.

Batman and Superman measure. The correlations of home preferences and frequencies of viewing of *Batman* and *Superman* with scores
on the content test appear in Table 28. The correlations between home
viewing and the character section of the test were nonsignificant, possibly because many children are exposed to *Batman* and *Superman* in other contexts. The correlations between the behavior alternative section
and total scores were positive for the most part, indicating greater knowledge for children who are high viewers of the programs at home. The
differences among conditions, however, did not fit any predicted pattern.

Relation of content scores to behavior change. On the basis of the
original model, it was expected that scores on the content tests would be
related to behavior change in the Aggressive and Prosocial conditions
respectively. That prediction was based on the assumption that the content test would measure learning during the experimental sessions. The
results discussed above indicate, however, that the content tests reflect
more clearly the knowledge the child has gained from his home viewing
experiences and other sources. Nevertheless, the correlations between
content tests and behavior change in the three conditions were examined. Those for the *Misterogers* content test appear in Table 29. There
were significant positive relations between total content score and increases in cooperation, prosocial interpersonal behavior, persistence,
and total interpersonal behavior during the experimental period for children in the Neutral condition. These correlations suggest that children
who were more familiar with *Misterogers* and who experienced neutral

viewing in nursery school were prone to increase in these prosocial forms of behavior. In the Prosocial condition, however, there were no correlations; in the Aggressive condition, knowledge of *Rogers* was positively associated with increased rule obedience and decreased fantasy aggression. While some of these correlations may be due to chance, they are suggestive of positive effects in nursery school from viewing *Misterogers* at home.

Table 29: Correlations of Misterogers content test with behavior change during the experimental period

| Behavior category | Condition | | |
	Aggressive	Neutral	Prosocial
Physical aggression	02	12	−26
Verbal aggression	−10	02	20
Interpersonal aggression	0	07	01
Object aggression	05	01	0
Fantasy aggression	−55*	0	19
Cooperation	0	45*	04
Nurturance	16	24	−25
Verbalization of feeling	11	20	15
Prosocial interpersonal	01	48*	−03
Rule stating	26	34	−22
Rule obedience	.51*	03	08
Tolerance of delay	−40	−17	24
Task persistence	−20	43*	−03
Instrumental help seeking	0	−16	22
Total verbal	01	26	0
Total interpersonal	06	45*	−05

* $p < .05$

None of the correlations between the *Batman* and *Superman* content test and behavior change reached significant levels.

Picture measure of responses to frustration

Strictly speaking, obtained reliabilities (Table 30) were not sufficiently high to warrant further use of the technique, except for research purposes. The present reliabilities were computed using the analysis of variance method described by Winer (1962, p. 124). Reliabilities for prosocial responses were acceptable, especially if one keeps in mind that the subjects were only four and five years old. Reliability of the aggression responses was marginal, and the reliability for the avoidance responses was not acceptable. It is hoped that refinement and weighting of the items will substantially improve these reliabilities in future studies.

In spite of the relative lack of sophistication of the assessment method, expected relationships among aggressive, prosocial, and avoidance

Table 30: Reliability coefficients for picture measure
of responses to frustration

Sample	Aggressive	Prosocial	Avoidance
Total (N=91)	.55	.75	.37
Boys (N=50)	.45	.74	.44
Girls (N=41)	.63	.75	.29

choices on the one hand and among individual difference variables, mother interview variables, and observed behaviors on the other hand were generally obtained. One noticeable exception was the fact that sex differences on the assessment technique were not statistically significant.

The correlations reported below were highest for the prosocial and aggressive choices, and relatively low for the avoidance choices. Inspection of all results suggests that the avoidance choices may not have been sufficiently distinct from some of the other choices as they were perceived by the subjects. Furthermore, they tended to correlate positively with the aggressive choices. The implications of this relationship are unclear at this point.

Tables 31 and 32 report Pearson correlation coefficients between some of the mother interview variables and the aggressive and prosocial choices on the picture method. Correlations with the avoidance choices are not reported, since none of them were significant. Although most of

Table 31: Correlations between aggressive choices on picture measure
and mother interview variables

Interview variable	Total items			Adult items			Peer items		
	All Ss	Boys	Girls	All Ss	Boys	Girls	All Ss	Boys	Girls
Frequency M−F evening	.25*	.13	.37*	.25*	.12	.43**	.15	.09	.22
Frequency Saturday	.23*	.05	.44**	.22*	.05	.39**	.13	.03	.30*
Batman favorite	.22*	.07	.37*	.33**	.21	.43**	0	−.13	.18
Superman favorite	.25*	.21	.23	.25*	.14	.31*	.14	.19	.08
Batman frequency	.17	0	.28	.22*	−.04	.33*	.03	.05	.13
Superman frequency	.26*	.23	.23	.26*	.15	.30*	.15	.22	.07
Violent favorites	.34**	.22	.43**	.29**	.08	.48**	.29**	.27*	.31*

*p < .05;   **p < .01

the correlations are relatively low, most are significant and in the expected direction: amount of television watching, as reported by the mother, is related positively to aggressive choices and negatively to prosocial choices; if the mother reported that aggressive programs were the child's favorite programs (especially *Batman* and *Superman* cartoons), the child picked aggressive choices significantly more often than proso-

Table 32: Correlations between prosocial choices on picture measure
and mother interview variables

Interview variable	Total items			Adult items			Peer items		
	All Ss	Boys	Girls	All Ss	Boys	Girls	All Ss	Boys	Girls
Frequency M–F evening	−.20	−.11	−.30*	−.19	−.09	−.30*	−.16		−.09	−.24
Frequency Saturday	−.20	−.01	−.46**	−.16	0	−.33*	−.17		−.03	−.39**
Batman favorite	−.23*	−.12	−.33*	−.26*	−.24	−.24	−.12		.03	−.33*
Superman favorite	−.21*	−.20	−.18	−.21*	−.19	−.13	−.18		−.19	−.17
Batman frequency	−.15	0	−.28	−.21*	.09	−.25	−.05		−.08	−.23
Superman frequency	−.26*	−.23	−.23	−.24*	−.20	−.19	−.20		−.20	−.20
Violent favorites	−.26*	−.17	−.33*	−.20	−.02	−.36*	−.30*		−.35*	−.26

*$p < .05$; **$p < .01$

cial choices; the more often the child watched *Batman* and *Superman* cartoons, according to the mother, the more likely the child was to pick aggressive instead of prosocial choices. Typically, the correlations were higher for those choices involving adults as the frustrating agents than for those involving peers as the frustrators. The most important fact apparent from inspection of Tables 31 and 32 is that all significant correlations between the aggressive choices and the interview variables are positive, while those between the interview variables and prosocial choices are negative. Provided the above assumptions about the present picture method are valid, this would give some support to the conclusion that children whose mothers report that they watch a lot of television and that they favor and frequently watch aggressive shows, tend to be more aggressive in their everyday behavior.

Relationships between the individual difference variables Age, IQ, and MA (mental age) were quite consistent. All three of these variables correlated negatively with aggression and avoidance and positively with prosocial choices (Table 33). The correlations are most pronounced for MA, suggesting that age and IQ interact in their contributions to the variance. It is also noteworthy that these correlations cannot be accounted

Table 33: Correlations of age, IQ, and MA with aggressive,
prosocial, and avoidance choices on picture measure

Var.	Aggressive choices		Prosocial choices		Avoidance choices	
	Boys	Girls	Boys	Girls	Boys	Girls
Age	−.08	−.27	.31*	.34*	−.41**	−.25
IQ	−.27*	−.25	.20	.36*	−.03	−.31
MA	−.33	−.36*	.39**	.48**	−.26	−.38*

*p < .05
**p < .01

for on the basis of socioeconomic status differences; only the girls' aggressive scores correlated slightly with socioeconomic status ($r = .30$).

In order to test the possibility that sex, IQ, and treatment condition (Aggressive, Prosocial, and Neutral) interacted to produce certain patterns of test choices, a three-way analysis of variance was performed for the nine variables: aggressive, prosocial, and avoidance choices on all 18 picture sets, on the nine sets involving adults as the frustrating agents, and on the nine sets involving peers as the frustrating agents. None of the interactions was found to be significant, and, among the main effects, only IQ produced significant F-ratios (Table 34).

Table 34: Aggressive, avoidance, and prosocial choices
on picture measure for high and low I.Q. subjects

Variable	High I.Q.	Low I.Q.	F	P
Aggression (total)	4.86	6.15	4.49	.05
Prosocial (total)	9.18	6.59	10.24	.01
Avoidance (total)	3.96	5.27	7.35	.01
Aggression (adults)	2.01	2.72	3.46	.07
Prosocial (adults)	4.66	3.64	4.45	.05
Prosocial (peers)	4.37	2.98	9.22	.01
Avoidance (peers)	1.71	2.59	8.39	.01

These results are in agreement with the positive correlations reported between IQ and prosocial choices, and the negative correlations between IQ and aggressive and avoidance choices. The fact that the treatment conditions did not produce significant differences in picture choices, combined with the fact that mother interview variables correlated highly with the same picture choices, leads to the not surprising finding that the long-term effects of television content are more easily measured than the short-term exposure effects.

Cautious optimism for the use of the present assessment method may be gained from the fact that one category of aggressive choices (those involving adults as the frustrating agents) were found to correlate significantly with the extensive behavior ratings performed in connection with the overall study (Table 35). These relationships were found to be of much larger magnitude for the boys than for the girls. Interestingly, the opposite was true for the relationship between the mother interview variables and the picture method choices.

Table 35: Correlations between aggressive and prosocial choices on picture measure and observed aggressive behavior

Variable	Aggression (adults)			Prosocial (adults)		
	All Ss	Boys	Girls	All Ss	Boys	Girls
Physical aggression	.27**	.23	.16	−.17	−.14	−.06
Verbal aggression	.22*	.19	.04	−.21*	−.20	−.08
Interpersonal aggression	.26*	.24	.07	−.21*	−.20	−.06
Object aggression	.24*	.21	−.10	−.17	−.11	−.11
Serious aggression	.27**	.24	.07	−.21	−.17	−.11

*$p < .05$
**$p < .01$

SUMMARY AND CONCLUSIONS

The major purpose of the study was to determine the effects of television programs with aggressive and prosocial content on the naturalistic behavior of preschool children. After a baseline period of classroom observation, 97 preschool children were exposed to one of three experimental treatments: aggressive programs (*Batman* and *Superman* cartoons), prosocial programs (*Misterogers Neighborhood*), or neutral films (various children's films). Each group saw 12 programs over a four-week period. Observations were continued during a two-week postviewing period during which no television was shown.

The classroom behavior fell into three broad categories: aggression (physical and verbal), prosocial interpersonal behavior (cooperation, nurturance, and verbalization of feeling), and prosocial self-controlling behavior (rule obedience, tolerance of delay, and task persistence).

The clearest main effects of the television programs appeared on the self-controlling behaviors. Children exposed to the prosocial television programs showed higher levels of rule obedience, tolerance of delay, and persistence than children exposed to the aggressive programs. Those in the Neutral condition generally fell between the two television groups. The differences among conditions were greatest for high IQ children.

There were no overall effects of conditions on prosocial interpersonal behavior, but children in different SES groups responded differently. Lower SES children showed increased prosocial interpersonal behavior in the Prosocial television condition but not in the Neutral and Aggressive conditions. Higher SES children showed higher levels in the Aggressive condition than in the Prosocial condition. As in previous studies, prosocial interpersonal behavior was positively correlated with aggression.

There were not overall effects of conditions on interpersonal aggression, but children who were initially above average in aggression did show more aggressive behavior after being exposed to the aggressive programs than they did in the Neutral condition. Children who were initially below average in aggression did not respond differentially to the three television conditions.

Other measures of condition effects included a picture measure of fantasy responses to frustration administered during the postviewing period. There were no differences among conditions in the likelihood of giving aggressive or prosocial responses to frustration on this measure.

On the basis of imitation theory, two variables were expected to influence the amount learned from the programs and, as a result, the behavioral effects of the programs: attention to the program, and intelligence. Although there were differences in attention to the three types of programs, there were no relations of attention to behavior change or to understanding the content of the program. Intelligence was related to changes in self-control but not to changes in aggression or prosocial interpersonal behavior.

The home viewing habits of the children were assessed from a detailed mother interview. The children in the sample watched television, on the average, slightly more than 30 hours per week, or 37 percent of their waking hours. Two patterns of viewing were identified. In the first, viewing was concentrated primarily on child-oriented programs, including cartoons. The second pattern included cartoons as well as extensive viewing of programs oriented to all ages, many of which were violent. Overall frequency of viewing was higher for children with the second pattern. The first pattern was associated with relatively high social status, high IQ, parental regulation of television viewing, and low parental viewing of violent programs; the second pattern correlated with these variables in the opposite direction.

The home viewing patterns were not associated with the baseline period behavior of boys in the study, and the correlations with girls' behavior were small. Girls with high child-oriented viewing preferences and low preferences for violent and miscellaneous adult programs were more verbally aggressive and higher in general social interaction than those with opposite viewing patterns. For the most part, however, the data provided little evidence for relating home television viewing to initial behavior in nursery school.

From the experimental part of the study, it appears that the prosocial programs were most effective in helping children to develop increased self-control and task persistence. Children functioning at relatively high intellectual levels responded most in these areas of behavior, perhaps because these themes are more subtle and were stressed less in the programs shown. For lower SES children, however, it appeared that the themes of cooperation and verbalization of feeling had an impact on behavior. It is particularly interesting to note this response to the *Misterogers* program by lower SES children, as critics have frequently suggested that the appeal of the program was limited to middle-class children.

The aggressive programs had an impact on the aggressive behavior of children who were already relatively high in aggression. At the same time, self-controlling behavior—particularly tolerance for minor frustrations—declined for all children exposed to the aggressive condition. This reduction in self-control was accompanied, for higher SES children, by increased social interaction that was primarily cooperative. It appears, therefore, that the aggressive programs had a general stimulating effect for the higher SES children that led to higher social interaction and lower levels of personal control. For those who were already aggressive, it led to aggression as well.

These effects occurred despite the fact that the study included only 12 programs spread over four weeks and that the behavior observed was distant in both time and stimulus setting from the viewing experience. All of these factors would be expected to dilute the obtained effects.

If the effects in the study represent in miniature those that occur in home viewing, correlations of initial behavior with home television viewing would be expected. The absence of such relations may be due to the situation-specificity of children's behavior. The observations were conducted while the children were entering a new setting with many differences from home. If the behavior were observed at home, in the setting where viewing occurs, stronger relations might be found.

The question of the cumulative or declining effects of repeated exposures to television content is relevant to possible home viewing effects. If children became less responsive with repeated exposure, then effects might be dissipated in extensive home viewing. Over the short span of programs shown in the study, no trends toward increasing or decreasing responses appeared. Further, although children with extensive experience viewing violent television showed less response to the aggressive programs than those without such experience, they still responded, for example, with reduced tolerance of delay. Correspondingly, children with high previous experience with child-oriented programs responded less to *Misterogers* in some ways (e.g., cooperation) but were not unaffected. Thus, the data suggest some reduction in response with repeated exposure, but not a complete loss of responsiveness.

The duration of television effects was tested in a modest way during the postviewing period. Although the condition effects on some of the prosocial behaviors declined slightly during this period, the effects on aggression and task persistence continued. The duration of these effects suggests that the television programs may have played a role in initiating patterns of behavior that were then maintained by the school environment.

There was a notable absence of sex differences in most of the findings. Although boys and girls began with different levels of many behaviors, the changes that occurred in response to the experimental conditions were quite similar. This effect is even more striking in view of the fact that girls liked the aggressive programs shown less than boys did.

Television critics have frequently pointed out the one-sided nature of the current viewing fare. Violent solutions to problems, whether by villain or hero, have been standard in endless series of programs. The findings of this study are consistent with the views of critics: there are behavioral effects associated with viewing violence. Such viewing has an impact not only on aggressive behavior, but also on other aspects of behavior like self-control.

But the equally important implications which can be drawn from the data are those that support the belief that television can play an important role in the positive social development of children. *Misterogers Neighborhood* is essentially the only program now on television which has as its prime concern the emotional and social growth of the child. Our findings indicate that the themes of cooperation, persistence in difficult tasks, tolerance of frustration and delay, and verbalization of feelings are understood by children and alter their behavior. Since *Misterogers* appears only on educational television in most localities, it is not available to many children, particularly those from lower social status families who have fewer socializing experiences that promote self-esteem and social skills. The program is also limited in appeal to very young children. All these factors suggest the need for more programs of this type with wider availability to children and with appeal to a variety of age levels.

FOOTNOTES

1. Corinne Nydegger and Francine Deutsch made major contributions to the development of the measurement techniques, the data analyses and many other aspects of the project. Nancy McCarrell, Jeanette Coufal, Alan Rappaport, Anthony Jurich, and Carol Vernon served as classroom observers. Dr. Sarah Vondracek and Mr. Stephen Schlein administered the Stanford-Binets and some other individual tests. Joyce Pattison, Florence Hammonds, Margo Rubin, Susan Ewing, Patrick Lingafelt, Sarah Adler served as interviewers and observers in the television sessions. The nursery school program was supervised by Dorothy Gish. The two head teachers were

Barbara Bieler and Roslyn Green. Others who served as assistant teachers were Sarah Adler, Carol Quarton, Gwendolyn Harries, Linda Krumrine, and Virginia Powell. The authors extend their thanks to all of these people and to many others who contributed their time and efforts to the completion of the project.

2. Violence significant to the plot was defined as violence that would have to be mentioned in a brief (200-word) plot description.

3. All correlations mentioned are significant at the .05 level and above.

REFERENCES

Albert, R. S. The role of mass media and the effect of aggressive film content upon children's aggressive responses and identification choices. *Genetic Psychology Monographs,* 1957, **55,** 221-85.

Atkinson, J.W. *Motives in fantasy, action, and society.* Princeton, N.J.: Van Nostrand, 1958.

Baker, R. K., and Ball, S. J. (Eds.) *Mass media and violence:* a report to the National Commission on the Causes and Prevention of Violence, Vol. 9. Washington, D.C.: U. S. Government Printing Office, 1969.

Bandura, A. Social-learning theory of identificatory processes. In Goslin, D.A. (Ed.) *Handbook of socialization theory and research.* Chicago: Rand McNally, 1969.

Bandura, A., Ross, D., and Ross, S.A. Imitation of film-mediated aggressive models. *Journal of Abnormal and Social Psychology,* 1963, **66,** 3-11. (a)

Bandura, A., Ross, D., and Ross, S.A. Vicarious reinforcement and imitative learning. *Journal of Abnormal and Social Psychology,* 1963, **67,** 601-07. (b)

Berkowitz, L. *Aggression: a social psychological analysis.* New York: McGraw-Hill, 1962.

Brown, F. A comparison of the abbreviated and complete Stanford-Binet scores. *Journal of Consulting Psychology,* 1942, **6,** 240-42.

Dollard, J., Doob, L.W., Miller, N.E., Mowrer, O.H., and Sears, R.R. *Frustration and aggression.* New Haven, Conn.: Yale University Press, 1939.

Eron, L.D. Relationship of TV viewing habits and aggressive behavior in children. *Journal of Abnormal and Social Psychology,* 1963, **67,** 193-96.

Feshbach, S., and Singer, R. *Television and aggression.* San Francisco: Jossey-Bass, 1971.

Hartman, H., Kris, E., and Lowenstein, R. Comments on the formation of psychic structure. In *The psychoanalytic study of the child,* Vol. 2. International Universities Press, 1962.

Hartup, W.W., and Keller, E.D. Nurturance in preschool children and its relation to dependency. *Child Development*, 1960, **31**, 681-89.

Hess, R.D. Social class and ethnic influences on socialization. In Mussen, P. (Ed.) *Carmichael's manual of child psychology*, 3rd ed., Vol. 2. New York: Wiley, 1970.

Hicks, D.J. Imitation and retention of film-mediated aggressive peer and adult models. *Journal of Personality and Social Psychology*, 1965, **2**, 97-100.

Himmelweit, H.T., Oppenheim, A.N., and Vince, P. *Television and the child*. London: Oxford Press, 1958.

Hoffman, H.L. Moral development. In Mussen (Ed.) *Carmichael's manual of child psychology*, 3rd ed., Vol. 2. New York: Wiley, 1970.

Kagan, J. The measurement of overt aggression from fantasy. *Journal of Abnormal and Social Psychology*, 1956, **52**, 390-93.

Livson, N., and Musses, P.H. The relation of ego control of overt aggression and dependency. *Journal of Abnormal and Social Psychology*, 1957, **55**, 66-71.

Lövaas, C.I. Effect of exposure to symbolic aggression on aggressive behavior. *Child Development*, 1961, **32**, 37-44.

Maccoby, E., and Wilson, W.C. Identification and observational learning from films. *Journal of Abnormal and Social Psychology*, 1957, **55**, 78-87.

Maccoby, E., Wilson, W.C., and Burton, R.V. Differential movie-viewing behavior of male and female viewers. *Journal of Personality*, 1958, **26**, 259-67.

Meyerson, L.J. The effects of filmed aggressive responses on high and low aggressive subjects. Paper delivered at the biennial meeting of the Society for Research in Child Development, New York, 1967.

Miller, N.E. The frustration-aggression hypothesis. *Psychological Review*, 1941, **48**, 337-42.

Miller, N.E. Experiments on motivation: studies combining psychology, physiology, and pharmacological techniques. *Science, 126*, 1271-78.

Mischel, W. *Personality and assessment*. New York: Academic Press, 1968.

Murphy, L.B. *Social behavior and child personality*. New York: Columbia University Press, 1937.

Mussen, P.H., and Naylor, H.K. The relationship between overt and fantasy aggression. *Journal of Abnormal and Social Psychology*, 1954, **49**, 235-40.

Parten, M.B. Social play among preschool children. *Journal of Abnormal and Social Psychology*, 1933, **28**, 136-47.

Patterson, G. A nonverbal technique for the assessment of aggression in children. *Child Development*, 1968, **31**, 643-53.

Patterson, G.R. *Manual, the NOT* (Nebraska-Oregon Test). University of Oregon Child Study Laboratory, 1964 (mimeo).

Patterson, G.R., Littman, A.A., and Bricker, W. Assertive behavior in children: a step toward a theory of aggression. *Monographs of the Society for Research in Child Development*, 1967, **32,** Serial No. 113.

Pittluck, P. The relation between aggressive fantasy and overt behavior. Unpublished doctoral dissertation, Yale University, 1950. (Quoted by Patterson et al., 1967.)

Rabson, A. Rating manual for Fels Nursery School and Day Camp behavior variables. Unpublished manuscript, Fels Research Institute, Yellow Springs, Ohio, 1966.

Rosekrans, M.A., and Hartup, W.W. Imitative influences of consistent and inconsistent response consequences to a model on aggressive behavior in children. *Journal of Personality and Social Psychology,* 1967, **7,** 429-34.

Rosensweig, S. *The Rosensweig P-F study.* Copyright 1948 by Saul Rosensweig.

Schramm, W., Lyle, J., and Parker, E.B. *Television in the lives of our children.* Stanford, Calif.: Stanford University Press, 1961.

Sears, R.R. Social behavior and personality development. In Parsons, T., and Shild, E.A. (Eds.) *Toward a general theory of action.* Cambridge, Mass.: Harvard University Press, 1951.

Sears, R.R., Rau, L., and Alpert, R. *Identification and child rearing.* Stanford, Calif.: Stanford University Press, 1965.

Selg, H. *Diagnostik der aggressivitat.* Gottingen: Veriag fur Psychologie, 1968.

Skinner, B.F. *Science and human behavior.* New York: Macmillan, 1953.

Smothergill, D.W., Smothergill, M.L., and Grossman, S. Improvement of group attending behavior in disadvantaged preschool children. Paper given at the biennial meeting of the Society for Research in Child Development, Santa Monica, Calif., 1969.

Stein, A.H. Mass media and young children's development. *Yearbook of the National Society for the Study of Education,* 1972 (in press).

Terman, L.M., and Merrill, M.A. *Stanford-Binet intelligence scale* (third revision, Form L-M). Boston: Houghton Mifflin, 1960.

Walters, R.W., and Willows, M.A. Imitative behavior of disturbed and nondisturbed children following exposure to aggressive and nonaggressive models. *Child Development,* 1963, **39** 79-85.

Wright, H.F. Observational child study. In Mussen (Ed.) *Handbook of research methods in child development.* New York: Wiley, 1960.

Appendix A:
Misterogers Neighborhood Programs

Themes

1. Cooperation
2. Sharing
3. Sympathy and help
4. Affection and friendship
5. Understanding feelings of others
6. Verbalizing own feelings (frustration, anger, sadness, etc.)
7. Delay of gratification
8. Persistence and competence
9. Learning to accept rules
10. Learning to control aggressive impulses
11. Coping with frustration—finding alternative courses of action

Misteroger's Neighborhood Selections for Summer Session
Monday, Wednesday, and Friday for 4 Weeks

Pgr. No.	Guests	Puppets	Songs	Description & Content
27 (M)	Maxine Miller David Newell	LEF Edgar Daniel	"I'd Like to be Like Dad" "I'd Like to be Like Mom" "Please Don't Think It's Funny"	Edgar's pillow is threatened by LEF Themes: N.O.M.: 3;2;6;5;4;5
28 (W)	Marchl, M.D. Judy Rubin	Daniel King Edgar LEF	"I Think I'm Going to Like Today" "Please Don't Think It's Funny"	Edgar sad about pillow, but LEF gives it back. Themes: H.R.: 2:4 N.O.H: 6;3;4;5
195 (F)	Clemmons Aberlin	King Queen	"Children Can" "You Are My Friend"	H.R. cools off in pool and Clemmons joins him. Try to understand Robert Troll's feelings. Themes: W.R.: 4;2 N.O.M.: 5;3
188 (M)	Negri Newell	King, Queen Corney, LEF Dr. & Mrs. P.	"You Are My Friend"	King gives rules for Rocket Themes: M.R.: 9;8;4 N.O.H.: 9;8
189 (W)	Negri W. Saunders Mr. & Mrs. Clemmons	King, Queen LEF Dr. and Mrs. P.	"Sometimes People Are Good" "You've Got to Do It"	Rocket lands at Platypus home. Themes: M.R.: 6;8;9 N.O.M.: 4;3;6;8
190 (F)	Negri Clemmons Aberlin	King LEF, Donkey Dr. & Mrs. P.	"You're Growing" "I Like to be Told"	Successful launching. Themes: M.R.: 7;8;9 N.O.M.: 8;9;7;4

Pgr. No.	Guests	Puppets	Songs	Description & Content
172 (M)	Trow Saunders	King Corney Donkey Platypusses	"You Are My Friend" "To Go Someplace Else" "Just for Once"	Troll wants to play noisy grames— goes Someplace Else. Themes: M.R.: 4;11 N.O.M.: 11;9;7;3
223 (W)	Aberline Sculptor	King Daniel X	"What Do You Do" (variation of above at end?) "It's Great to be Able to Stop"	M.R. and Lady Aberlin frustrated — how to handle feelings. Themes: M.R.: 6;11;1 N.O.M.: 6;5;11;4
199 (F)	Clemmons	Platypusses LEF	"Sometimes People Are Good"	Cooperate to make pie. Themes: H.R.: 4 N.O.M.: 1
202 (M)	Negri Clemmons	King Platypusses LEF	"You're Growing"	Upset about money matters. Tell when angry. Themes: M.R.: 7;6;10 N.O.M.: 4;6;9;1;10
204 (W)	Negri Trow (as dog)	X Men LEF Elsie Platypus	"Fences"	LEF puts Bob Dog in cage. Themes: M.R.: 11 N.O.M.: 10;11;5;6;3;1
205 (F)	Aberlin Trow (as dog)	Daniel King, Queen LEF Platypusses Monkey Modie Daniel	"Everybody's Frog" "Just for Once"	Parts on inside. When dog isn't scared, doesn't need his cage. Themes: M.R.: 6 N.O.M.: 1;10;5;3;6;4

Appendix B:
Contents of Neutral Films

Day 1. *Children in Summer*—color. Features young children exploring plants and other natural phenomena of summer.
Frog Went a Courtin'—color. Series of still drawings illustrating story while narrator sings. Then children are asked to sing
with the narrator.

Day 2. *Children in Spring*—color. Young children and mother explore
woods looking at budding plants and picking flowers. Focus
on natural phenomena of spring.
A Helicopter Carries Mail—black and white. Shows a helicop-
tor carrying mail into an airport, the unloading and sorting in
the post office.

Day 3. *Children in Autumn*—color. Focus on natural phenomena in
autumn. Children walk in woods looking at fall flowers and
changing leaves.
Milk—black and white. Shows modern milk production and
processing. Begins with large dairy, shows transportation to
processing plant, pastuerizing, and homogenizing.

Day 4. *Children in Winter*—color. Features natural phenomena of
winter.
Airport in the Jet Age—black and white. Shows airport con-
troller in control tower with discussion of importance of air
safety.

Day 5. *Dairy Farm*—black and white. Features a boy and girl who
live on a dairy farm. Shows variety of activities on a farm.
Three American Ballads—color. Narrator sings ballads such
as "John Henry" while still photographs and drawings are
shown.

Day 6. *Circus Day in Our Town*—black and white. Shows arrival and
setting up of a large circus, then shows the circus in operation
with various side shows and acts.

Day 7. *Farmyard Animals*—black and white. Shows various chores
around farm focusing primarily on feeding of various animals
and milking cows.
Fire Boat—black and white. Shows the firefighting boat in the
Los Angeles harbor. Shows men cleaning boat and drilling,
then shows practice spraying of hoses.

Day 8. *Let's Build a House*—black and white. Shows a father and
two children building a playhouse. Focuses on the procedures
involved in building such as pouring concrete into molds.

Little Blue and Little Yellow—color. Pictures are abstracts—blue and yellow dots which play together, blend into one another to become green, and separate again.

Day 9. *Norwegian Children*—black and white. Features life of children on a Norwegian farm who take the cattle to the mountains during the summer.

Our Post Office—color. Two children send a present to their mother. Procedures for addressing and mailing shown, then the package is followed through the postal system.

Day 10. *One Rainy Day*—color. Focus on the functions of rain. Features a boy who does not like and a girl who does.

Toccata for Toy Trains—color. Using models of old-fashioned trains and towns, shows a train running through towns and countryside with musical accompaniment.

Day 11. *Pride, the Saddle Horse*—black and white. Follows a baby horse growing up; shows training of the horse, ends with his winning a prize at a horse show.

Summer is an Adventure—color. Features children who go to a lakeside cabin with their family. Brief pictures of various vacation activities.

Day 12. *A Visit to the Waterworks*—color. Shows a group of children being taken on a tour through a waterworks with an adult explaining operations.

What the Frost Does—black and white. Features a boy who is waiting for a pumpkin to ripen. Describes changes in nature brought about by the first frosts.

Appendix C:
Observation Categories

General instructions: Behavior and certain types of stimulus situations will be recorded sequentially as they occur. The codes appear on a single sheet. Definitions of each category follow.

Each child will be observed for 5 minutes at a time.

S = child observed
C = any other child
T = teacher

For each observation, the place, activity, and social setting will be noted. Codes for place and activity are not included in the present set of categories, but will be provided later. Social setting is coded as shown on the summary sheet.

When a child repeats a behavior already coded once, the symbol "=" will be used to indicate repetition of same behavior just coded, e.g., if he yells six times: "I'm shooting you, bang, bang," code afv= = = = =.

Place: Just indicate inside (i) or outside (o)
Activities (to be designated by brief beginning of word)

When the following categories describe the major activity in which S is engaged, use them. If he is engaged in some activity not listed, write it if you can do so without losing the behavior ratings. If you can't write it, score Misc.

veh	Vehicle. Any riding activity—trikes, More-Pla, etc.
cli	Climb. Any climbing on bars or other equipment.
sli	Slide.
san	Sand—in sand box and using sand (don't score this if he is doing something like painting on a table which happens to be in the sand box.)
wat	Water—when principal activity.
swi	Swings.
art	Art—any artistic activity such as painting, cutting and pasting, clay, or others where materials are basically unstructured.
blo	Blocks.
rol	Role play—principal activity is playing house, cowboy, fireman, etc. Include dress-up if that is the principal activity.
con	Construction—putting together materials which are at least partially structured such as snap-blocks, puzzles, tinker-toys, Lincoln logs.

sho   Shopwork. Use of tools such as hammer, saw, etc.

man   Manipulative. All small toys such as doll furniture, toy garages, etc.

gro   Group. A demonstration or other group activity led by adult.

rea   Read. Use of books or listening to story.

mus   Music.

jui   Juice.

mis   Misc.—S is engaged in an activity that doesn't fit above categories.

non   None.—S is wandering, going between tasks, or just doing nothing.

Social setting
1 = *S* alone
2 = *S* with adult (S) only; no other children present
3 = *S* with other children only; no adults present
4 = *S* with both children and adults

Appendix D:
Definitions of Observation Categories

STIMULUS CATEGORIES

Frustrating situations

FA   C aggressive toward S—any action defined in aggression scoring categories which is directed toward S.

FP   With no aggressive intent, C takes a piece of equipment (property) or position which S has just had. e.g., S leaves a bucket in sand while he goes to get a shovel. C picks up bucket when S gone without appearing to be deliberately taking from S.

FC   C interferes with ongoing activity. Any occasion on which the actions of another child interrupt or interfere with the activity of S. Stands in S's path, moves in front of S to get on slide or other equipment, other child occupying toy or equipment that S wants, even when no intention to interfere. (Do not score when FA or FP approp.) When in doubt about whether to score FA or FP, use FC.

FI   T or C rejects or ignores friendly overtures by S or ignores requests and commands by S, e.g., S asks to play with other child and is refused or ignored, S attempts to join one or more others and is refused, S asks C to pass the butter and C does not, S shows T something he made and T ignores.

FT   T interferes with ongoing activity or prevents child from action he wants to take, e.g., teacher stops child physically or verbally; teacher terminates group activity S is involved in; teacher requires S to do something he does not want to do. T scolds S. (Do not score when CT is scored). See addition.

FO   Impersonal source of interference, e.g., Child has difficulty with completion of a task such as a puzzle or something he is building; piece of equipment or toy does not work, he does not get it to do what he is apparently trying to do.

Commands

CT   1 -   any request by T to S directly (given to S individually or S is named along with other Cs). This level includes requests by the teacher which are not requirements. That is, S has a choice about whether or not to comply. e.g., "Johnny, would you like to put the napkins around the table for juice." This judgment must be made on basis of whether or not the T is likely to insist that the child comply.

2 - any request by T to S directly for which compliance is demanded either explicitly or implicitly. That is, if the S does not comply, T will follow up to be sure he does. e. g., "Johnny, sit down. It's not time to leave the table." Or "Johnny, don't bring that toy outside." (Note: this category includes only directions to the child for action, not scolding for misbehavior. If he has already broken a rule and T scolds him, score that FT.)

CT_2 is distinguished from CT_1 when a command is given in imperative language (e.g., "Put your shoes on, please") or when clear that T intends to follow up. Save CT_1 for instances that clearly involve a choice by S. In other words, when in doubt, score CT_2.

3 - rarely used. Includes criteria for 2 plus loud, angry or vigorous tone by T.

CC 2 - request or command by C to S in friendly manner and normal tone of voice. "Give me the hammer." "Put yours here."

3 - vigorous tone of voice, loud, often angry sounding. Uses imperative language. e.g., "Get out of my way." (Shouted). "Put that back."

If commands from C occur in the context of role playing (e.g. Susie is playing Mommy and tells Sally to go to bed in context of mother-child role play), do not score CC at all. Just score for the role playing and any other behavior categories appropriate.

Double scoring

Stimulus categories are usually not double scored. In a few instances however, a frustration may occur concurrently with a command (e.g. T takes S's clay and puts in jar, says to S "Go wash your hands.") In this case, both FT and CT_2 should be scored because the T has provided a frustration (stopping play) which is clearly separate from the command.

Responses specific to frustration (score only as response to frustrating stimulus)

o   No response. Score this when child shows no scorable reaction to frustration of any child. e.g., S tells C to stop at sign, C goes through, S shows no reaction.

pa   Persistence for attention. This scored primarily after FI. S repeats bids for attention or attempts to get T or C to comply with his requests. E.g., S calls T to see picture, T pays no attention, S calls again.

laf   Laughs. S laughs, smiles or shows other signs of positive affect after a frustration.

al   Alternative activity. S finds alternative activity after being prevented from engaging in one. This scored only if he shows no signs of pouting, crying, or anger. That is, this is supposed to be an adaptive response. E.g., S wants to roller skate and C has skates, then goes over to paint instead and appears fairly happy. (Score FC al). Score only when S does this alone, not an adult suggestion.

+   Submits. This applied when the frustrating agent is trying to get the S to do something (e.g. T fairly forcibly leading S and he follows). If situation does not permit distinction between + and o score o.

−   Refuses to comply. This used particularly in response to FA and FP. Used to indicate nonaggressive resistance (e.g., C grabs toy S playing with, S hangs on to toy. e.g., T restrains S and S struggles without striking out).

Responses to commands

+   S complies

o   S does not respond by complying or by refusing

−   S actively refuses either verbally or by performing action which is in direct opposition to command. e.g., T tells S to come here, and S runs other way. C tells S to give him a toy and S refuses either verbally or by actively pulling the toy away from C. (In this instance, if S merely ignored C, would score o).

Note: in some cases, more than one of the above may apply to one response or to a sequence of responses. e.g., Child may say, "No" and comply with request. This would be scored − v +.

BEHAVIOR

Aggression

ap   Physical assault—hitting, banging, throwing, pulling, etc., at other person or toys C is playing with. Include *clear* threatening gestures.

av   Verbal aggression—name calling, jeering, threatening, angry talk to other, derogation.

at   Teasing, nonverbal—withholding object from C, taking things C playing with, interfering in other's play. (Score these only when aspects of S's behavior indicate intention).

af   Playful and fantasy aggression. Aggression occurring as part of role playing or aggression in clear playful way. Conservative scoring here. (If in doubt, don't score.) Include fantasy about aggression, e.g., "I've been stabbed."

ao   Injury to objects—score only where not interpersonal and is intentional; banging, hitting, throwing inappropriate objects.

ac   Commanding vigorously—yelling at other to do something. Definition same as CC3 in Stimulus categories.

aa   Tattling. Telling adult about C's misbehavior or threatening to tell adult. May occur in C's presence. Include generalized protest to no one in particular, e.g., child sitting alone yelling, "He tried to knock down my blocks."

Persistence

pt   *Task persistence.* Score this under two circumstances.
> a. S engaged in task or activity for one minute. Shows signs of intense involvement during most of that time: doesn't look away from task much, continuously manipulates object or materials involved. *Task* here is activity involving making something or playing with physical objects or practicing motor skills (climbing, riding, etc.) *Do not score* for involvement in social activity. *Do not score* where ic appropriate because 2 children are cooperatively involved in a task. In this case, pt is scored only once each minute.
> b. S makes repeated efforts to accomplish a task in which a series of discrete trials can be observed. This will usually involve an FO stimulus. If the S tries 3 or more times, score pt even if his efforts do not last the entire minute. If this type of pt is unusually long or intense, use pt_3.

pi   *Independence.* Score when S does something for himself under two conditions:
> a. He has asked or indicated need for help, then does it himself (usually after being ignored).
> b. The activity is normally one which requires adult help.

ph   *Instrumental help seeking.* Score only when help sought in completing or continuing a task (as defined under pt). *Do not score* when help asked for something which is not part of an ongoing task such as asking to button a piece of clothing.

Interpersonal

ic   *Cooperation.*

        a. S interacts with one or more other children in such a way that behavior of both is directed toward a common goal. Often will involve taking turns or *mutual* sharing. The essence of this category is a 2-way interchange, not one-way. (e.g., one child pushes and other steers the "Mor-Pla" vehicle.) Can be formal game, but does not have to be.

        b. S and one or more other children engage in role playing in which roles are related to each other. They exchange remarks and actions in these roles.

        Under both conditions, the activity must last 10-15 seconds (roughly). That is, it must be more than a fleeting instance.

im   Mature social skills—use of social skills which are adult-like or mature for manipulation of someone else; e.g., "Sally, get off the swing for just a minute, just to show you can do it." E.g., C1 takes paper crown off S's head. C refuses to give it back to S. S tells him to put it on her toy animal.

        Often involves use of indirection or distraction from true purpose of S's behavior. E.g., S tells T she wants to make something. T lets her go to sink to wash a bowl to make something. S then tries to get soap suds which she has previously been told she can't have now. Score when S says, "Excuse me" or uses other "polite" terms to get someone to do something.

in   Nurturance or sympathy—giving C approval, help, comfort, reassurance, affection, protection. Asking adult to help other child. Any statements about other child's feelings or the reasons for C's behavior, e.g., "She wants to swing." Sharing when it is "one-way" giving. *Do not score* when T is object.

        This category is distinguished from ic by the fact that it is one-way. (E.g., During clay work, S gives C some clay. This scored in. If, however, S and C exchange pieces of clay over a period of 10-15 seconds, score ic.)

iv   Verbal statements giving reasons for own behavior or about own feelings, e.g., "I hate him." "No, I don't want to. I just started doing this."

Rules and self-control

ro   Rule obedience. Any evidence of S's awareness of and spontaneous attempts at compliance with rules.

a. Spontaneous obedience of rules when there is some clear choice point. This scored when group directions given such as time to clean up but not when CT or CC scored. (e.g., waiting to drink juice until T starts.)
b. Any statements of rules, either those made by adults or those made by children in games (score rov).
c. Questions about rules, e.g., "Is it time to clean up now?" "Can we play outside?"
d. Spontaneous doing of adult work in nursery school, e.g., putting away the sawing equipment without being asked. Taking the dishes from the table to the clean-up cart.

If T tells S to do something, and S not only complies but carries on the activity into the next minute (well beyond what he was asked to do), score ro in second and succeeding minutes (one per minute). (E.g., T asks S to help put away blocks. He not only puts away a few in her presence, but continues putting away many blocks during succeeding minutes.)

rd   Rule disobedience. Clear that child knows rule and disobeys mischievously, with awareness of what he is doing, e.g., boy climbs over fence out of play yard. Score this only when behavior not covered in other categories. If T has given command, score negative response (−). If behavior of child is aggressive, score there and do not score rd also.

       If T tells S to do something, and in a succeeding minute, he disobeys the earlier command, score rd. (E.g., T tells S to leave slide and sit down for juice. He does so. A minute later, he runs back to the slide.)

dg   Delay of gratification. S voluntarily waits patiently for something he has indicated he wants. Score once per minute *only* when *S* waits the whole minute. e.g., boy sits down at table where other children are blowing through straws into bowls of sudsy water. He sits patiently while T helps other C although he has no bowl to play with.

Regression

cr   Emotional outburst. Crying, pouting, whimpering.
wi   Withdrawal without constructive alternative, giving up on task readily, e.g., going to locker, sitting doing nothing, engaging in self-stimulation such as thumb sucking or masturbation. S tries to cut paper and it doesn't cut. S puts down and leaves table

Qualifiers

These are symbols which can be added to any stimulus or response categories to indicate that the action has a particular component. These *not* to be used alone.

v	Behavior has verbal component.
1	Low intensity. Behavior is minimal, but scorable.
3	High intensity. Unusually intense or long-lasting. This can be used for all stimulus and behavior categories.
d	Displaced. An aggressive response is directed toward a different object than the one that frustrated S.
f	Fantasy. Indicates that response occurred in the context of fantasy or role play. Already defined for aggression. Apply also to prosocial, e.g., if S nurturant in role as nurse to patient, score inf.

Appendix E:
Reliability of Classroom Observations

Observer pair	% exact agreement	% agreement on general categories
A - B	58%	65%
A - C	51	56
A - D	73	82
A - E	43	54
A - F	62	65
A - G	46	51
B - C	65	73
B - D	94	94
B - E	76	76
B - F	88	88
B - G	84	87
B - H	68	81
C - D	76	83
C - E	72	71
C - F	91	94
C - G	62	67
D - E	68	74
D - G	100	100
D - H	91	92
E - F	100	100
E - G	66	72
E - H	64	72
F - G	96	97
F - H	97	97
G - H	47	53

Appendix F: Instructions for Observations of Attention to Television Programs and Films

1. Criteria for attention.

The rating for attention is made on the basis of three criteria:
A. Child maintains orientation of head and eyes toward screen during most of time interval.
B. Child does not speak to or interfere with another child.
C. Child does not make gross movements of arms or legs (except where these involve participation in the program). If the child meets *all three* criteria, check "Yes" on scoring sheets. If he does not meet all three criteria, check "No".

2. Method of rating.

Using a stopwatch, observer will watch 2 children for 10 seconds. He will then score the 2 children according to the above criteria during the next 5 seconds. Next, he will go on to 2 different children, observe them for 10 seconds and score them during the next 5 seconds.

Children in the two television groups will watch the programs in groups of 7 or 8. If we designate them by the letters A through G, you will observe A and B for the first 15 seconds (10 seconds of observation and 5 for scoring), C and D for the second 15 seconds, E and F for the third 15 seconds, and G (when there is one) for the fourth 15 seconds in any minute. You will then return to A and B at the beginning of the next minute. The scoring sheet is arranged in blocks of 5 minutes for each child.

The children in the film group will watch the films in groups of 10. You will observe, however, only 7 on any given day using the same arrangement as that described for the television programs.

3. The children and observers will be alternated each day. You will be given a schedule of which room you are to be in each day. You will be responsible for putting the tape on the recorder and turning on the equipment in the television groups or, in the film groups, for running the projector. Another adult will bring the children to the room and stay with them. That adult will be responsible for handling any necessary interactions with the children. You should try to avoid interacting with the children unless some emergency arises.

Appendix G:
Mother Interview

"We see lots of children in nursery school and see them playing with other children there, but we are interested in a broader picture of each child and knowing more about the things he does at home with you and the rest of the family. As you know, we're also especially interested in children's reactions to television at home—which program they like best, when they like most to watch, and so on."

1. First of all, we'd like to get a picture of the family. How many children do you have?

   a. How old are they?
   b. Do you have a job? If yes:

      1. What hours are you usually at home during the week? What about the weekend?
      1.a If part time: days and/or hours
      2. When do you usually leave the house for work?

   c. What's your husband's job?
      1. What hours is he usually at home during the week? (What time does he leave a.m.? Comes home p.m.?) After supper what does he usually do? What about the weekend? What hours is he usually home then?
      2. If student: part time or full time? Does he study in the evenings at home?

2. Now would you tell me about ----'s day: What time does he usually get up? (Give mother *T V Guide*)

   a. What are his favorite TV programs in the morning? (If mother works in the a.m. ask the following:

      a.1 Where does ----- go when you go to work?

      a.2 What kinds of things does he like to do there?

      a.3 Does he watch any of these favorite morning TV programs there?

   b. Sometimes children like spending the morning inside, especially on rainy days or when they're a little tired. Does ---- play more

frequently inside or outdoors in the mornings now? What about
during the winter? (Does he watch more TV then?)

c. What time does he usually eat lunch?

d. Does he take a nap? When? How long?

e. Where does he play in the afternoon? (Indoors or outdoors.)
When he plays in the house what room does he usually play in?

f. What are his favorite afternoon TV shows?

g. What time do you usually eat dinner? Where does he most often
play after dinner? Are there any programs he likes to watch then?
How about during the winter?

h. In the summer some families let children more less go to bed
when they want to and other families have a regular bedtime. Do
you have any special rules about when he is supposed to go to
bed?

i. Does he have morning programs he likes to watch on Saturdays?

    1) Which are his favorites?

    2) How long does he watch?

    3) What about Saturday afternoon programs? "Underdog,"
       "Superman," or "Johnny Quest?" How often?

    4) What about Sunday morning? Does he watch "Batman,"
       "Tom and Jerry," or "Fantastic Voyage?" How often?

    5) Sunday afternoon favorites?

    6) Are there any evening programs on the weekend he usually
       watches? Saturday night? Sunday night?

3. What are your own weekend favorites? What about your husband?
Who else usually watches?

a. Here is the list of weekend programs: (give out Saturday and
Sunday frequency lists) Could you mark how often ----- watches
these programs and also make sure to include the ones which he
likes to watch with you or others in the family? (Take lists from
mother when she finishes: be sure she keeps *TV Guide*)

4. Can ----- turn on the TV when he wants to? Now could you tell me
something about the other rules you have about -----'s TV watching?
Are there some programs you don't let him watch? What? How does
he react?

5. Sometimes people in the family want to watch different programs at
the same time. What is -----'s reaction when his program is changed?
Are there any regular quarrels and arguments about particular programs? How do you handle this?

6. Could you describe (name) as he watches his favorite programs? Is
he very quiet and attentive or does he get up from time to time or
play with other things while he is watching?

Finally, I'd like some general information about how the whole family enjoys and uses TV.

7. Where is the TV set?

8. Do you have any favorite daytime programs up until 6 p.m.? (Consult the TV Guide here). Who usually watches with you? Do you turn off the set in between programs or just leave it on?

9. What about evening programs (after 6)? (Consult TV Guide) Do you have any favorites (probe about movies, etc.) Who usually watches? What does (name) do while you watch? What programs does your husband like to watch regularly? Are there any others he watches occasionally?

10. Give out TV sheets for a.m. and p.m. daily viewing.

   a) "Here is the list of weekday programs. Could you mark how often ----- watches these programs and also make sure you include the ones which he likes to watch with you or others in the family?"

11. Nurses may want to visit some homes.

Evening Television Schedule—Summer 1970

(* Programs shown Monday through Friday)

Program Content Code:
   1 Children's program
   2 Cartoon
   3 Violent program
   4 Miscellaneous program

Monday

6:00 4 *McHale's Navy**
      4 *The Munsters**
      4 *Gilligan's Island**

6:15 4 *Farm, Home and Garden**

6:30 4 *Joyce Chen Cooks*
      4 *My Favorite Martian**
      4 *Dick Van Dyke**

           4   *Huntley—Brinkley**
           4   *F Troop**

7:00   4   *What's My Line**
           1   *Misterogers Neighborhood**
           4   *Truth or Consequences**
           4   *I Love Lucy**
           4   *Please Don't Eat the Daisies**

7:30   4   *Beat the Clock**
           4   *Truth or Consequences**
           4   *Know Your Antiques*
           3   *Gunsmoke*
           4   *My World and Welcome to It*
           3   *It Takes a Thief*

8:00   4   *To Tell the Truth**
           4   *Baseball**
           4   *Can You Top This?**
           4   *World Press*
           3   *Laredo*

8:30   4   *He Said, She Said**
           4   *Here's Lucy*
           4   *David Frost**

9:00   4   *Mayberry R. F. D.*
           3   *N.Y.P.D.*
           4   *NET Journal*

10:00   4   *Carol Burnett Show*

10:30   4   *Bridge with Jean Cox*
           4   *All American College Show*

11:00   4   *Sound of Progress**
           3   *Perry Mason**
           4   *Peyton Place**

11:30   4   *Merv Griffin**
           4   *Johnny Carson**
           4   *Dick Cavett**

Tuesday

6:30   4   *The Dangerous Years*

7:30 4   *Man Against His Environment*
      4   *I Dream of Jeannie*
      4   *Divorce Court*
      3   *The Mod Squad*

8:00 4   *Firing Line*
      4   *Debbie Reynolds Show*

8:30 4   *Julia*

9:00 4   *Dr. Kildare*
      4   *NET Symphony*

9:30 4   *The Governor and J. J.*
      4   *Win With the Stars*

10:00 4   *Marcus Welby, M. D.*

10:30 4   *Something Else*

Wednesday

6:30 4   *Safety First*

7:30 4   *Hee Haw*
      4   *The Place*
      4   *Nanny and the Professor*

8:00 4   *Courtship of Eddie's Father*
      3   *Laredo*

8:30 4   *Room 222*
      4   *Beverly Hillbillies*
      3   *Twilight Zone*

9:00 4   *Johnny Cash Show*
      4   *Kraft Music Hall*
      4   *Medical Center*
      3   *N. Y. P. D.*

9:30 4   *Win with the Stars*

10:00 3   *Hawaii Five O*
      4   *Engelbert Humperdinck Show*
      3   *Then Came Bronson*

Thursday

6:30   4   *French Chef*

7:30   4   *Man in the Middle*
       4   *Family Affair*
       4   *Divorce Court*
       3   *Daniel Boone*
       1   *Animal World*

8:00   4   *Virginia Graham Show*
       4   *Happy Days*
       4   *That Girl*

8:30   3   *Ironside*
       4   *Bewitched*

9:00   4   *Dr. Kildare*
       4   *This is Tom Jones*

9:30   4   *Win with the Stars*
       3   *Dragnet 1970*

10:00 4   *Dean Martin*
       3   *Perry Mason*

Friday

6:30   4   *Passport to Education*

7:00   1   *Superman*

7:30   3   *Get Smart*
       4   *TV Garden Club*
       4   *Divorce Court*

8:00   4   *He and She*

8:30   4   *Hogan's Heroes*
       4   *The Name of the Game*
       4   *Temple Music Festival*

10:00 4   *Love American Style*
       4   *Bracken's World*

10:30 4   *Know Your Antiques*

Child _____   Are you on the cable? _____
Mother _____
Date _____
Place _____

MORNING TV SCHEDULE
(M-F)

Time		Name of Programs	Almost Every Day	Often (3 out of 5 Days)	Seldom (once a week)	Never
7:00	4	Today Show	1	2	3	4
	4	News	1	2	3	4
7:15	4	News	1	2	3	4
7:30	2	Popeye	1	2	3	4
	2	Cartoon Clubhouse	1	2	3	4
7:50	2	Adventures of Gulliver	1	2	3	4
8:00	3	Cisco Kid	1	2	3	4
	1	Captain Kangaroo	1	2	3	4
	4	Loretta Young	1	2	3	4
8:20	2	Mr. Magoo	1	2	3	4
8:30	4	Fireside Theatre	1	2	3	4
	3	Tales of Wells Fargo	1	2	3	4
8:50	4	Fashions in Sewing	1	2	3	4
9:00	1	Timmie and Lassie	1	2	3	4
	4	Dialing for Dollars Movie	1	2	3	4
	4	Beat the Clock	1	2	3	4
	1	Romper Room	1	2	3	4
	1	Sesame Street	1	2	3	4
	4	My Little Margie	1	2	3	4
	4	Movie	1	2	3	4
9:30	4	Gilligan's Island	1	2	3	4
	4	Gomer Pyle	1	2	3	4
	2	Huckleberry Hound and Friends	1	2	3	4
10:00	4	Jack LaLanne Show	1	2	3	4
	4	Fashions in Sewing	1	2	3	4
	4	Lucy Show	1	2	3	4
	2	Pixanne	1	2	3	4
10:10	4	Jack LaLanne	1	2	3	4
10:15	4	Fashions in Sewing	1	2	3	4

MORNING TV SCHEDULE (Continued)
(M-F)

Time		Name of Programs	Almost Every Day	Often (3 out of 5 Days)	Seldom (once a week)	Never
10:25	4	News	1	2	3	4
10:30	4	Beverly Hillbillies	1	2	3	4
	4	Tell Me Dr. Brothers	1	2	3	4
	4	Concentration	1	2	3	4
	4	Best of Everything	1	2	3	4
11:00	4	Gourmet with David Wade	1	2	3	4
	4	Bewitched	1	2	3	4
	4	Andy of Mayberry	1	2	3	4
	4	Truth or Consequences	1	2	3	4
	4	Sale of the Century	1	2	3	4
	4	V.I.P. Travel Guide	1	2	3	4
11:30	2	The Gumby Show	1	2	3	4
	4	Love of Life	1	2	3	4
	4	The Hollywood Squares	1	2	3	4
	1	Bozo	1	2	3	4
	4	Queen for a Day	1	2	3	4
	4	That Girl	1	2	3	4
12:00		News	1	2	3	4
	1	Romper Room	1	2	3	4
	4	Jeopardy	1	2	3	4
	4	Where the Heart Is	1	2	3	4
	2	Underdog	1	2	3	4
	3	Route 66	1	2	3	4

Child _____   Are you on the cable? _____
Mother _____
Date _____
Place _____

AFTERNOON TV SCHEDULE
(M-F)

Time		Name of Programs	Almost Every Day	Often (3 out of 5 Days)	Seldom (once a week)	Never
12:25	4	News	1	2	3	4
12:30	4	The Who, What or Where Game	1	2	3	4
	4	The World Apart	1	2	3	4
	4	Search for Tomorrow	1	2	3	4
	4	Noonday on 8	1	2	3	4
	2	Rocky and His Friends	1	2	3	4
12:50	4	Fashions in Sewing	1	2	3	4
12:55	4	Weather	1	2	3	4
1:00	4	All My Children	1	2	3	4
	4	Movie	1	2	3	4
	4	Big John Riley Show	1	2	3	4
	4	News	1	2	3	4
	4	Dear Julia Meade	1	2	3	4
	4	Burns and Allen Show	1	2	3	4
1:30	4	Let's Make a Deal	1	2	3	4
	4	The Millionaire	1	2	3	4
	4	Life with Linkleletter	1	2	3	4
	4	As the World Turns	1	2	3	4
2:00	4	Days of Our Lives	1	2	3	4
	4	Black Pride	1	2	3	4
	4	Love is a Many Splendored Thing	1	2	3	4
	4	Newlywed Game	1	2	3	4
2:25	4	News	1	2	3	4
2:30	4	The Doctors	1	2	3	4
	4	Patty Duke	1	2	3	4
	4	The Guiding Light	1	2	3	4
	4	Dating Game	1	2	3	4
3:00	4	General Hospital	1	2	3	4
	3	Strange Paradise	1	2	3	4
	2	Popeye	1	2	3	4
	4	Another World	1	2	3	4
	4	Secret Storm	1	2	3	4
	4	Della	1	2	3	4

AFTERNOON TV SCHEDULE (Continued)
(M-F)

Time		Name of Programs	Almost Every Day	Often (3 out of 5 Days)	Seldom (once a week)	Never
3:30	4	Bright Promise	1	2	3	4
	4	Edge of Night	1	2	3	4
	2	Felix the Cat	1	2	3	4
	2	The Flintstones	1	2	3	4
	4	Mike Douglas	1	2	3	4
4:00	4	Another World—Somerset	1	2	3	4
	4	Gomer Pyle	1	2	3	4
	1	Wonderama	1	2	3	4
	1	The Little Rascals	1	2	3	4
	3	Dark Shadows	1	2	3	4
	1	Sesame Street	1	2	3	4
	4	The Movie Game	1	2	3	4
4:30	4	I Love Lucy	1	2	3	4
	4	F Troop	1	2	3	4
	3	Dark Shadows	1	2	3	4
	1	Superman	1	2	3	4
	4	Stump the Stars	1	2	3	4
		Movie	1	2	3	4
5:00	4	Addams Family	1	2	3	4
	4	The Munsters	1	2	3	4
	1	Eastside Comedy	1	2	3	4
	2	Flintstones	1	2	3	4
	4	Beat the Clock	1	2	3	4
	1	Misteroger's Neighborhood	1	2	3	4
	3	Perry Mason	1	2	3	4
5:30	4	What's New?	1	2	3	4
	4	Stump the Stars	1	2	3	4
	1	Abbott and Costello	1	2	3	4
	4	Movie	1	2	3	4
	4	Hazel	1	2	3	4

Child _____   Are you on the cable? _____
Mother _____
Date _____
Place _____

SATURDAY TV SCHEDULE

Time		Name of Program	Almost Every Day	Often (3 out of 5 Days)	Seldom (once a Week)	Never
7:00	4	Eye on Agriculture	1	2	3	4
7:30	4	Across the Fence	1	2	3	4
	4	Faith to Faith	1	2	3	4
	4	The Christophers	1	2	3	4
7:45	2	Davey and Goliath	1	2	3	4
7:55	4	News	1	2	3	4
	4	Congressman Dan Flood	1	2	3	4
8:00	4	Across the Fence	1	2	3	4
	2	The Jetsons	1	2	3	4
	2	Heckle and Jeckle	1	2	3	4
	2	Prince Planet	1	2	3	4
	4	En France	1	2	3	4
8:26	4	News	1	2	3	4
8:30	2	The Smokey the Bear Show	1	2	3	4
	1	Fireball XL-5	1	2	3	4
	2	Bugs Bunny/Road Runner	1	2	3	4
	4	Insight	1	2	3	4
	4	This is the Life	1	2	3	4
9:00	2	Here Comes the Grump	1	2	3	4
	2	The Chattanooga Cats	1	2	3	4
	2	Marine Boy	1	2	3	4
	4	The Government Story	1	2	3	4
	4	Aprenda Ingles	1	2	3	4
9:30	2	Dastardly & Muttley in Their Flying Machines	1	2	3	4
	2	The Pink Panther	1	2	3	4
	4	Connecticut Report	1	2	3	4
	4	My Little Margie	1	2	3	4
	4	The Puerto Rican New Yorker	1	2	3	4
10:00	2	H. R. Pufnstuff	1	2	3	4
	2	Wacky Races	1	2	3	4
	1	Hot Wheels	1	2	3	4
	4	Suburban Closeup	1	2	3	4
	4	New Jersey Report	1	2	3	4
	3	Cisco Kid	1	2	3	4

SATURDAY TV SCHEDULE (Continued)

Time		Name of Program	Almost Every Day	Often (3 out of 5 Days)	Seldom (once a Week)	Never
10:30	1	The Hardy Boys	1	2	3	4
	2	Scooby Do Where Are You	1	2	3	4
	2	The Banana Splits	1	2	3	4
	4	Movie	1	2	3	4
	4	The Green Thumb	1	2	3	4
	4	Wagon Reels	1	2	3	4
11:00	2	Sky Hawks	1	2	3	4
	2	Archie	1	2	3	4
	4	Focus: New Jersey	1	2	3	4
11:30	4	Insight	1	2	3	4
	2	George of the Jungle	1	2	3	4
	2	The Flintstones	1	2	3	4
12:00	4	Continental Miniatures	1	2	3	4
	3	Death Valley Days	1	2	3	4
	1	Jambo	1	2	3	4
	4	The Monkees	1	2	3	4
	4	Get It Together	1	2	3	4
12:30	2	The Perils of Penelope Pitstop	1	2	3	4
	2	Underdog	1	2	3	4
	3	Sherlock Holmes Theater	1	2	3	4
	4	American Bandstand	1	2	3	4
	4	Survival	1	2	3	4
	3	Tales of Wells Fargo	1	2	3	4
1:00	2	Superman	1	2	3	4
	4	Black News	1	2	3	4
	4	Burns and Allen Show	1	2	3	4
	4	The World in Which We Live	1	2	3	4
1:30	4	Seaway	1	2	3	4
	2	Johnny Quest	1	2	3	4
	4	The Willburn Brothers	1	2	3	4
	4	Get It Together	1	2	3	4
	3	The Westerners	1	2	3	4

SATURDAY TV SCHEDULE (Continued)

Time		Name of Program	Almost Every Day	Often (3 out of 5 Days)	Seldom (once a week)	Never
2:00	2	Thunderbirds	1	2	3	4
	4	Movie	1	2	3	4
	4	Baseball	1	2	3	4
2:30	4	Movie	1	2	3	4
	3	Big Attack	1	2	3	4
3:00	3	Battlefield	1	2	3	4
3:30	4	NET Jazz	1	2	3	4
4:00	4	Scene Seventy	1	2	3	4
	4	Joyce Chen Cooks	1	2	3	4
	4	Movie	1	2	3	4
4:30	4	Race of the Week	1	2	3	4
	4	World Press	1	2	3	4
	4	Now Explosion	1	2	3	4
5:00	4	Wide World of Sports	1	2	3	4
	3	Combat	1	2	3	4
	1	Animal World	1	2	3	4
	4	Movie	1	2	3	4
5:30	4	Jim Thomas Outdoors	1	2	3	4
	4	NET Journal	1	2	3	4
	4	Big Picture	1	2	3	4
6:00	4	McHale's Navy	1	2	3	4
	3	Judd for the Defense	1	2	3	4
	4	Gilligan's Island	1	2	3	4
	4	Cross Section	1	2	3	4
6:30	4	News	1	2	3	4
	4	Dick Van Dyke	1	2	3	4
	4	My Favorite Martian	1	2	3	4
	4	The Show	1	2	3	4
	4	Star Time	1	2	3	4
7:00	3	Perry Mason	1	2	3	4
	3	Death Valley Days	1	2	3	4
	4	Sing Along with Mitch	1	2	3	4

SATURDAY TV SCHEDULE (Continued)

Time		Name of Program	Almost Every Day	Often (3 out of 5 Days)	Seldom (once a week)	Never
7:00	4	I Love Lucy	1	2	3	4
cont'd.	4	Hugh X. Lewis Country Club	1	2	3	4
	4	Country Music Jubilee	1	2	3	4
7:30	4	Jackie Gleason	1	2	3	4
	4	Andy Williams Presents the Ray Stevens Show	1	2	3	4
	4	Let's Make a Deal	1	2	3	4
	3	The Prisoner	1	2	3	4
	4	Folk Guitar	1	2	3	4
8:00	4	Forsyte Saga	1	2	3	4
	4	Now Explosion	1	2	3	4
	3	The Avengers	1	2	3	4
	4	Newlywed Game	1	2	3	4
8:30	4	My Three Sons	1	2	3	4
	3	Creature Feature	1	2	3	4
	4	Lawrence Welk	1	2	3	4
	3	Adam 12	1	2	3	4
9:00	4	Green Acres	1	2	3	4
	4	Speaking Freely	1	2	3	4
	4	Movie	1	2	3	4
	4	News	1	2	3	4
9:30	4	Petticoat Junction	1	2	3	4
10:00	4	News	1	2	3	4
	3	Mannix	1	2	3	4
	4	NET Playhouse	1	2	3	4

Child _____   Are you on the cable? _____

Mother_____

Date _____

Place _____

SUNDAY TV SCHEDULE

Time		Name of Program	Almost Every Day	Often (3 out of 5 Days)	Seldom (once a week)	Never
7:00	4	Faith for Today	1	2	3	4
	4	Cathedral of Tomorrow	1	2	3	4
7:30	4	Bishop Sheen	1	2	3	4
	4	This Is the Life	1	2	3	4
7:55	4	Jot	1	2	3	4
8:00	2	Alvin Show	1	2	3	4
	4	Insight	1	2	3	4
	2	Popeye Show	1	2	3	4
	4	Sacred Heart	1	2	3	4
	2	The Christophers	1	2	3	4
8:15	4	Time for Joya	1	2	3	4
	2	Davey and Goliath	1	2	3	4
8:30	4	Pattern for Living	1	2	3	4
	1	Wonderama	1	2	3	4
	2	Davey and Goliath	1	2	3	4
	4	Sunrise Semester	1	2	3	4
	2	Captain Noah	1	2	3	4
8:45	2	Popeye and Friends	1	2	3	4
9:00	4	Dialogue	1	2	3	4
	2	Tom and Jerry	1	2	3	4
	4	Right Now	1	2	3	4
	4	Camera III	1	2	3	4
9:30	2	Batman	1	2	3	4
	2	The Christophers	1	2	3	4
	4	Mass for Shut-Ins	1	2	3	4
	4	New York Report	1	2	3	4
9:55	4	News	1	2	3	4
10:00	4	The Story	1	2	3	4
	2	Fantastic Voyage	1	2	3	4
	4	Lamp Unto My Feet	1	2	3	4
	4	Point of View	1	2	3	4
	2	Captain Noah	1	2	3	4

SUNDAY TV SCHEDULE—Continued

Time		Name of Program	Almost Every Day	Often (3 out of 5 Days)	Seldom (once a week)	Never
10:30	4	Roller Derby	1	2	3	4
	4	Look Up and Live	1	2	3	4
	2	The Christophers	1	2	3	4
	2	Speed Racer	1	2	3	4
	2	Spiderman	1	2	3	4
	4	American's Favorite Hymns	1	2	3	4
10:45	4	Inside USA	1	2	3	4
11:00	4	The Munsters	1	2	3	4
	4	Rev. Rex Humbard	1	2	3	4
	1	Superman	1	2	3	4
	4	Camera Three	1	2	3	4
11:30	4	Face the Nation	1	2	3	4
	4	Movie	1	2	3	4
	2	Flintstones	1	2	3	4
	3	Time Tunnel	1	2	3	4
	4	Movie	1	2	3	4
12:00	4	Life of Triumph	1	2	3	4
	4	Eastside Comedy	1	2	3	4
	4	This Is the Life	1	2	3	4
12:30	4	Oral Roberts	1	2	3	4
	4	Insight	1	2	3	4
	4	News	1	2	3	4
	4	Wrestling	1	2	3	4
	4	News Conference	1	2	3	4
1:00	4	5 Star Movie	1	2	3	4
	4	Meet the Press	1	2	3	4
	4	You and the Law	1	2	3	4
	4	Movie	1	2	3	4
	4	Baseball	1	2	3	4
	4	Meet Model Cities	1	2	3	4
1:30	4	Blue Ridge Quartet	1	2	3	4
	4	Movie	1	2	3	4
	4	Issues and Answers	1	2	3	4
	4	Faith and the Bible	1	2	3	4

SUNDAY TV SCHEDULE (Continued)

Time		Name of Program	Almost Every Day	Often (3 out of 5 Days)	Seldom (once a week)	Never
2:00	4	Georgetown Forum	1	2	3	4
	4	Baseball	1	2	3	4
	4	Changes In the Unchanging	1	2	3	4
2:10	4	Baseball	1	2	3	4
2:30	4	Flying Nun	1	2	3	4
3:00	4	Metromedia movie	1	2	3	4
	4	Movie	1	2	3	4
3:30	4	Your Dollars Worth	1	2	3	4
4:30	4	Bookbeat	1	2	3	4
	4	NFL Action	1	2	3	4
	4	100,000 Pennsylvanians	1	2	3	4
5:00	4	Movie	1	2	3	4
	4	Big Picture	1	2	3	4
	3	The Baron	1	2	3	4
	4	The World We Live In	1	2	3	4
	4	Here Come the Brides	1	2	3	4
	3	International Zone	1	2	3	4
5:30	4	Folk Guitar	1	2	3	4
	4	Amateur Hour	1	2	3	4
	4	Roller Derby	1	2	3	4
6:00	3	Judd for the Defense	1	2	3	4
	4	All American College Show	1	2	3	4
	4	Barbara McNair	1	2	3	4
	4	Festivals of Pennsylvania	1	2	3	4
	3	Death Valley Days	1	2	3	4
6:30	3	The Brady Bunch	1	2	3	4
	4	News	1	2	3	4
7:00	4	He Said, She Said	1	2	3	4
	1	Wild Kingdom	1	2	3	4
	1	Lassie	1	2	3	4
	4	The Stakes in Asia	1	2	3	4
	4	Judy Garland Theatre	1	2	3	4
	4	Movie	1	2	3	4

SUNDAY TV SCHEDULE (Continued)

Time		Name of Program	Almost Every Day	Often (3 out of 5 Days)	Seldom (once a week)	Never
7:30	4	To Rome with Love	1	2	3	4
	1	Wonderful World of Disney	1	2	3	4
	4	Can You Top This	1	2	3	4
8:00	4	NET Festival	1	2	3	4
	4	Ed Sullivan	1	2	3	4
	3	The F. B. I.	1	2	3	4
	4	The Honeymooners	1	2	3	4
8:30	4	Bill Cosby	1	2	3	4
9:00	4	Glen Campbell Goodtime Hour	1	2	3	4
	3	Bonanza	1	2	3	4
	4	The Forsyte Saga	1	2	3	4
	3	Perry Mason	1	2	3	4
	4	Movie	1	2	3	4
10:00	4	News	1	2	3	4
	3	The Advocates	1	2	3	4
	3	Mission Impossible	1	2	3	4
	3	The Bold Ones	1	2	3	4

Appendix H:
Content tests

MISTEROGERS

"I'd like to ask you to help me find out about people in the Misterogers neighborhood.

"Do you know these people? (Show photographs of LEF, King Friday, Mr. Daniel, Lady Abelin)

"Now, try to guess who says this. Who's talking?" (Begin who am I questions)

*1. "I always like to make good rules and have people listen to them. Who am I?"

     a. Queen Sara
  *b. King Friday

2. "When I feel like biting someone, I put myself in a cage. Who am I?"

  *a. Bob Dog
   b. Daniel

3. "I always like things to happen fast. When they don't happen fast, it makes me feel angry. Who am I?"

  *a. LEF (Lady Elaine Fairchild)
   b. Bob Dog

4. "I'm learning to use rules to help me do hard things better. Who am I?"

     a. Robert Troll
  *b. Handyman Negri

5. "I go to Some Place Else when there is too much noise at the Castle. Who am I?"

    *a. Robert Troll
     b. King Friday

"Now, I am going to ask you a different kind of question." (give illustra-
tion with hands, using 3 possible choices)

  6. Lady Aberlin gets angry at her drawing. What does she do?

      a. Does Lady Aberlin tear it up?
      b. Does Lady Aberlin ask Mr. Rogers for help?
     *c. Does Lady Aberlin sing about how mad she feels?

  7. Handyman Negri has trouble building a house. What happens?

     *a. Does he try to do it again?
      b. Does he give up?

 *8. Lady Elaine Fairchild takes Robert Troll's ball. What does Daniel
     do?

      a. Does Daniel lock her in the castle?
     *b. Does Daniel give her something that is better for her?

  9. King Friday tells Queen Sara that he wants to be alone. What hap-
     pens?

      a. Does Queen Sara yell at King Friday?
     *b. Does Queen Sara tell King Friday she understands his feelings,
         and go for a walk?
      c. Does Queen Sara cry?

 10. Daniel finds Misteroger's book. What happens?

      a. Daniel keeps the book.
     *b. Daniel gives the book to Misterogers

 11. Misterogers is eating cookies. Then Officer Clemens walks by. What
     does Misterogers do?

      a. Misterogers tells Officer Clemens he can't have a cookie.
     *b. He gives Officer Clemens half of the cookies.
      c. He doesn't say anything to Officer Clemens.

 12. Lady Aberlin sees her friends fighting. What happens?

*a. Does Lady Aberlin talk to her friends and try to help?
 b. Does Lady Aberlin walk away?
 c. Does Lady Aberlin tell the king?

13. The people in Neighborhood of Make Believe have trouble making a bridge. What do they do?

    a. Do they give up?
    b. Do they fight?
  *c. Do they go to King Friday for rules?

BATMAN AND SUPERMAN

"I'd like to ask you to help me find out about the *Batman* and *Superman* programs"

"Do you know these people?" (show pictures of Batman, Robin, Superman, and Jimmy Olsen)

"Now try to guess who says this."

1. "I am the person who opened the animal cages at the circus and let all the animals out. Who am I?"

    a. Robin
  *b. The Joker
    c. Cat Woman

*2. "Some people call me the 'boy wonder.' Who am I?"

    a. The Joker
    b. Batman
  *c. Robin

3. Batman and Robin catch someone in a fish net, from a boat. Did they catch:

    a. Simon Pieman
  *b. Cat Woman

"Now I'm gonna ask you a different kind of question." (instructions)

4. When Batman finds a person in his car what happens?

    *a. Does Batman tell him to get out fast?
    b. Does Batman throw him out on the ground?
    c. Does Batman ask him if he wants a ride?

5. When the Penguin goes to Bruce Wayne's birthday party, what happens?

    a. Does the Penguin blow out Bruce's candles?
    *b. Does the Penguin get in a fight with Bruce?
    c. Does the Penguin give Bruce a present?

6. What happens when Cat Woman locks Batman and Robin in a high tower?

    *a. Do Batman and Robin throw something at her?
    b. Do Batman and Robin ask her if they can get out?

7. When a flying saucer comes over Gotham City, what happens?

    *a. Do Batman and Robin fly up and shoot it down?
    b. Do Batman and Robin fly up and help it land?
    c. Do Batman and Robin fly up and talk to the people?

8. When the Joker invites Bruce to a Halloween party, what happens?

    a. Bruce gets a prize at the party.
    b. Bruce doesn't go to the party.
    *c. Bruce's pumpkin blows up.

"Now I'd like to ask you about Superman."

9. Superman has trouble getting off his coat. What happens?

    a. Superman rips off the buttons.
    *b. Superman asks someone to help him.
    c. Superman tries to undo the buttons carefully.

10. "Superman is my friend. I can always call him for help when I'm in trouble. Who am I?"

    *a. Jimmy Olsen
    b. The Japanese Sandman

11. When the giant bees attack the city, what does Superman do?"

    a. Does he get stung by the bees?
  *b. Does he hit them and capture the queen?

12. When the flying saucers attack the city, what happens?

    a. Does Superman go to bed?
  *b. Does Superman fly up and knock them down?
    c. Does Superman tell them to go back where they came from?

13. When two men take the money from the bank, what happens?

  *a. Does S knock them out and give the money back?
    b. Does S get the police?
    c. Does S try to explain they shouldn't take the money?

14. Mr. X has a radio. Jimmy tells Mr. X he needs the radio for a while. What happens?

    a. Mr. X gives Jimmy a turn with the radio.
  *b. Mr. X says "no," it's mine.

Reality and Fantasy in Filmed Violence

Seymour Feshbach

University of California, Los Angeles

The present series of studies[1] was undertaken to clarify the role of one dimension of filmed violence—its real or fictional basis—upon the subsequent aggressive behavior of children who have been exposed to these films. The medium utilized for the presentation of the stimulus material is a television screen. Consequently, while the theoretical arguments apply to films as utilized in several media, the studies bear most directly upon children's reactions to violence observed on television.

The functional relationship between the depiction of violence in the media and children's aggressive behavior has been and continues to be a source of controversy and sharp disagreement. A number of factors contribute to the controversy: the different methods used to draw inferences about the effects of violence in the media (clinical, laboratory, and field studies); the variety of measures that have been employed; and the many parameters that must be considered before the effects of exposure to an aggressive display upon an audience's response can be predicted (Feshbach, 1970; Feshbach and Singer, 1971; Hartley, 1964).

There is clearly substantial laboratory evidence of facilitation of aggressive behavior by such processes as modeling (Bandura and Huston, 1961; Bandura, Ross, and Ross, 1961, 1963a, 1963b) and reduced inhibition or stimulation (Hartmann, 1969; Lövaas, 1961; Mussen and Rutherford, 1961; Walters, Thomas, and Acker, 1962; Walters and Thomas, 1963). The results of field studies either are ambiguous or fail to support the proposition that exposure to the media enhances children's aggressive behavior (Bailyn, 1959; Eron, 1963; Schramm, Lyle, and Parker, 1961). For example, an extensive field study in Great Britain by Himmelweit, Oppenheim, and Vince (1958) failed to yield any significant differences between television "viewers" and "nonviewers" on measures of aggression, delinquency, and maladjustment, although a number of the "viewers" did report having been frightened by television fare.

The findings of a recently published field study (Feshbach, 1968; Feshbach and Singer, 1971) in which laboratory methods were employed in a naturalistic setting indicated that exposure to aggressive content in television may serve to modulate rather than stimulate aggressive behavior in certain groups of preadolescent and adolescent boys. These results provided the immediate stimulus for the present series of experiments.

In this experimental field investigation, television contest was experimentally varied over a six-week period so that the influence of differential exposure to aggressive stimuli upon aggressive attitudes and behavior could be assessed. Six hundred sixty-five boys in seven different institutional settings (five in Southern California and two in New York City) served as subjects. The boys were randomly assigned within each institution either to a television schedule containing predominantly aggressive programs or to a control treatment of predominantly nonaggressive programs. The institutional settings included three private schools (one a military school) and four boys' homes. The latter were residential settings for boys from a predominantly low socioeconomic background whose families were unable to take care of them. The students at the private schools were from predominantly upper middle to lower upper class backgrounds. The boys ranged in age from ten to 17 years old; with the exception of those in two institutions, they volunteered for the project. The subjects and the cottage supervisors who were to record and rate their behavior were informed that the study was concerned with the relationship between the evaluation of different types of television programs and the personality and attitudes of the viewer. A rationale for viewing the same program series and similar types of programs was also provided. Questionnaire measures of overt and covert hostility, aggression-anxiety, impulsiveness, and aggressive values, peer ratings of aggression, and a thematic apperception test (TAT) measure of fantasy aggression were administered before and after the six-week experimental period. In addition, daily behavior ratings were submitted for each boy by his immediate supervisor. The boys also rated each television program they observed, in part as a check on the effectiveness of the experimental manipulation. All subjects were required to watch a minimum of six hours of television a week and were permitted to view as much television as they wished, provided they observed programs from the designated list or "diet."

The most impressive differences were yielded by the behavior ratings, which essentially recorded aggressive incidents. The frequency of verbal aggression and physical aggression, whether directed toward peers or toward authority figures, was consistently higher in the control group exposed to the nonaggressive programs than in the experimental group placed on the aggressive "diet." This effect was significant for the subjects in the boys' homes, but not for the private school subjects. Similar trends were observed for the elementary, junior high, and high school samples. The difference between the control and experimental groups in aggressive behavior directed toward peers was greatest in boys who were initially aggressive, especially boys above the mean on the questionnaire measures of hostility. Significant effects on two measures of aggressive values and on the sociometric rating scale were obtained for subsamples initially predisposed to aggression. The TAT fantasy measure was the only one in which the aggressive television group increased relative to the control group. This difference is readily attributable to the subjects' generalization of the television content to the TAT stories they were asked to construct.

Of considerable interest is the one exception to the general finding of a stronger experimental effect in the boys' homes sample for boys high on the premeasures of aggression; boys who were initially low in aggressive fantasy (as assessed by a TAT-type measure) displayed less aggression in the aggressive television condition then in the control condition, while a much weaker effect was obtained for boys initially high in aggressive fantasy. These data suggest the possibility that fantasy expression of aggression serves as a means of "controlling" overt aggressive expression, and that boys who lack internalized fantasy resources may utilize the external fantasy of aggressive television content for this purpose. This explanation assumes that fantasy in the narrow "fictional" sense may have some of the properties of fantasy in the broader cognitive sense of internal ideational activity. Fantasy in this sense is not so much a substitute goal activity as a "binder" or means of cognitive control.

This analysis suggests a functional equivalence between the generation of a TAT story with aggressive content and the more passive exposure to aggressive content in the media. They are both cognitive activities, they are both concerned with "unreal" elements, and (we would argue) they both may help mitigate the instigation to action. A quotation from J.C. Singer's (1966) excellent monograph on daydreaming is pertinent: "The adolescent who cannot provide himself pleasure through internal fantasy, contemplation, or manipulation of daydream images is compelled more directly to an overt motor imitation of the adult pattern." There are obvious gaps between daydreaming, TAT fantasy, and fantasies presented through the mass media. Most particularly, the media content has the capacity to stimulate imitation, a function not shared by self-generated fantasies. At the same time, most dramatic content in television and in other media is also fantasy—a fact or dimension which has not been adequately considered in the body of research and theory on media effects. The specific problem this study addresses is determining the empirical consequences of the fantasy (as opposed to "real") presentation of aggressive content in the media. It is our contention that the "message" of fantasy is different from the "message" of reality.

Fantasy is a realm of ideational activity in which the child (or adult) can freely engage in flights of imagination without the concomitants associated with real events that cannot readily be detached from one's own life. While fantasy activity can be preparatory to action, it also functions to delay action and substitute for it (Feshbach, 1960; Singer, 1966). Children are taught to discriminate between fantasy and reality, between thought and action, between the wish and the deed. Fantasy, in the form of play and drama, becomes a means of expressing impulses and ideas for which neither author nor audience need assume personal attribution. There is a qualitative difference between playfully "burying" one's sibling on a sandy beach and actually burying one's sibling, and both children and parents are aware of this difference.

The depiction of real violence in the media, by definition, describes the world as it is. It serves as a direct source of information about how people behave and about the kinds of behavior that are reinforced and socially sanctioned. The feelings elicited by a television news program or documentary cannot easily be discarded when a child leaves the television set for the "real" world, since he has been exposed to a clearly labeled mirror of the real world. When he watches a drama, however, the child can more readily restrict his experience to the television viewing situation and, in some circumstances, can freely engage in vicarious aggressive expression without fear of punishment.

These considerations lead to the proposition that a child's acting out of aggressive tendencies should be lessened or unaffected to the extent that dramatic content functions as fantasy in the larger, cognitive sense and is perceived as fantasy in the narrower, fictional sense. If the dramatic content is perceived as "real," the possibility of facilitating aggression through such processes as imitation, instruction, and disinhibition should be considerably enhanced.

METHOD

General design. All the experiments to be described involve the presentation on television of a six-minute film stimulus, the assessment of affective changes through an adjective check list, a behavioral measure of aggression, and a measure of aggresive values. These procedures were formally pretested as part of a master's dissertation by Berkovici (1970). One hundred two boys and girls, varying in age from six to 14, were involved in this study. Although this experiment was primarily concerned with other issues than the effects of the fantasy-reality variable, one of the several findings bore directly upon the procedures to be employed here. The effects of a six-minute baseball sequence, which we had intended to use as a control film, were compared with those of a highly aggressive sequence of comparable length from the movie *Prince Valiant.* Children in the older age group (12-14 years olds) who had observed the *Prince Valiant* sequence were significantly less aggressive afterward than children who had observed the baseball film. Since it could not be determined from this experiment whether witnessing the aggressive sequence had lowered aggression or whether the baseball stimulus had stimulated aggression, it was decided to supplement the baseball film with additional control groups for the present series of studies.

EXPERIMENT 1

Subjects. One hundred twenty-nine children from a large elementary public school in the Los Angeles area participated in this experiment. The subjects ranged in age from nine to 11 and were from the fourth, fifth, and sixth grades. Half the children were from middle-class backgrounds; half came from low income groups. The children from the families of low socioeconomic status were predominantly black, while a majority of the middle-class children were caucasian.

Design. Subjects were randomly assigned to one of three experimental conditions—Real Aggression, Fantasy Aggression, and Control —and were randomly assigned to treatment groups within each condition. Half the children in the Fantasy Aggression and Real Aggression conditions witnessed a war sequence, while half witnessed a police action sequence. In addition, the control group was divided into three subgroups. One group of children watched a sequence from a baseball game, one watched a sequence from a circus film, and the third group was not exposed to any television stimulus. All cells were balanced for sex, socioeconomic status, and age group (fourth graders in one group and fifth and sixth graders in the other). In essence, the design resembles a replicated 2 x 3 factorial design (sex by experimental condition, socioeconomic status by experimental condition, and age by experimental condition). The replicated part of the design substituted the police action sequence for the war sequence.

Reality and Fantasy film stimuli. An effort was made to select and edit the reality and fantasy versions of the campus riot to be comparable; a similar procedure was followed for the two war films. However, fiction does not neatly mirror reality. Structural and technical, as well as content, differences in the filming of fantasy and reality are almost impossible to eliminate. Nevertheless, each film was analyzed for aggressive and related content. The descriptive data for the two war films are presented in Figure 1. A time sequence analysis was used in which the presence of a particular category was scored for each fifteen-second interval. The row totals indicate that although there is more gunfire in the Vietnam newsreel and more shouting and running in the war film, the amount and type of aggressive interactions depicted were generally comparable. In other respects, however, the films were quite different.

The reality war film shows soldiers fighting in and around Saigon. There is a counterattack by the Viet Cong and the soldiers and newsmen are forced to retreat. The film cuts to a U.S. patrol in the jungle using grenades and rifles to attack two Viet Cong in caves. The officer in charge can be heard directing the troops. Bombing scenes, patrols with narration, and very heavy firing end the segment.

The fantasy war film is taken from *Walk in the Sun.* The scene opens with a grenade and machine gun attack against a German half-track. A U.S. soldier kills the surviver of a crash. The next scene shows U.S. troops moving through a field up to a stone wall which is near a farm house. The soldiers crawl toward the house, are attacked, and are forced to retreat back behind the wall. They counterattack with the help of additional troops, rush the house against German machine gun fire, enter the house, killing the soldiers inside, and leave victorious.

The descriptive data for the campus riot films are presented in Figure 2. The row totals indicate that much more physical aggression by the police occurred in the news report than in the dramatic films. In contrast to the fantasy war film, which looked like a movie, the segments from the movie *The Whole World is Watching* looked quite real and may have been difficult to discriminate from the reality versions.

The reality campus riot film opens with a scene of a demonstrator lowering an American flag, then cuts to scenes of police arresting demonstrators and demonstrators throwing rocks. Tear gas is thrown into

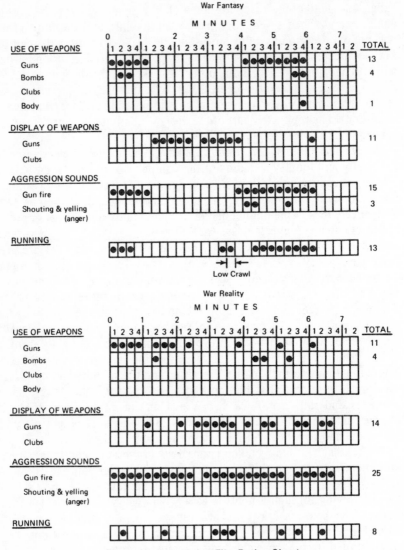

Figure 1:   Aggression Film Rating Sheet

the crowd by the police, and the demonstrators throw it back. Leaders of the demonstration attempt to control and direct the crowd, urging them to avoid confrontation with the police. The police march in formation to attack the demonstrators with their clubs. There are several scenes of injured demonstrators. Police order those who are not part of the demonstration to cross the street to avoid arrest. There is chanting from the crowd and much use of clubs by the police. The last scene of this segment is an interview with a policeman about campus demonstrations while scenes of campus violence and arrests are shown.

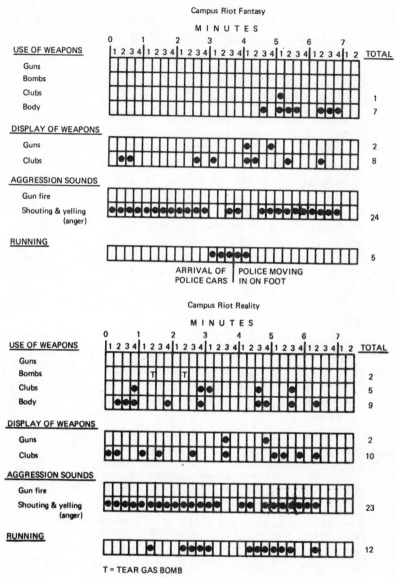

Figure 2:   Aggression Film Rating Sheet

The fantasy campus riot film opens with a scene of an angry crowd. The police escort a man into a campus building. A policeman in charge suggests to the man that the police could clear out the demonstrators; the man replies that he does not want them to do so until he gives instructions to disperse the crowd. The demonstrators have established a "sit-in" in the building, and police watch outside as a crowd chants. After nightfall, a large number of police arrive, enter the building, and arrest those inside. As the arrested demonstrators are taken to waiting police cars, the crowd outside chants, "Pigs off campus."

Procedure. The experimenter escorted each subject individually from his classroom to the experimental room where, on arrival, the subject was given the adjective check list (see Appendix B) and was asked to check those items which most closely described his mood. Following the administration of the adjective check list, the subject was exposed to one of the experimental film conditions, unless he had been assigned to the No Television condition. The experimenter preceded the viewing of each film with a brief introduction. Viewers of the reality-war film sequence were told, "You are now going to see a newsreel of the Vietnam war photographed by some NBC cameramen who were right on the scene." Viewers of the reality-riot film were told, "You are now going to see a newsreel of a campus riot photographed by some NBC cameramen who were on the scene." Viewers of the fantasy-war film were told, "You are now going to see a war film made by a Hollywood studio." Viewers of the fantasy campus riot film were told, "You are now going to see a film of a campus riot made by a Hollywood studio." Viewers of the baseball and circus film sequences were told, "You are now going to see a film of a baseball game or circus."

After viewing one of the six-minute films, the subjects were given the adjective check list a second time. They were asked to indicate how they felt while viewing the television film. After the second administration of the adjective check list, the subjects were asked to play a guessing game with one of the two experimenters, using an "aggression machine." Each child was told that one of the experimenters would have to match colored lights to 3 x 6-inch colored cards which were placed in front of the child. The following instructions were given:

> We are now going to play a guessing game with Mr. J. We want to see if Mr. J., sitting behind a screen, can guess the color of the card you have in front of you. If Mr. J. guesses correctly, you press the button marked "right" which will turn on a light on Mr. J.'s side telling him his guess is correct. If Mr. J. makes an incorrect guess, you can press any one of these noise buttons. The higher the number, the louder the noise. Number "1" is very soft, number "3" is a little louder, number "5" is still louder, and number "7" is very loud and painful.

The experimenter then proceeded to demonstrate to the child the different noise levels. When he reached the highest level, number 7, the experimenter said, "This noise is so loud and painful that I am not even going to show it to you." The experimenter-accomplice then came from behind the screen, placed the earphones on his head in front of the child, returning to take his seat behind the screen. Unseen to the subject, the accomplice removed the earphones from his head and turned off the noise generator.

For each trial the subject "presented" a colored 3 x 6-inch card to the accomplice. The accomplice made 15 errors in 22 trials. The intensity of the noise level administered by the subject on each incorrect trial was recorded by the accomplice. The average intensity of sound administered over the 15 error trials constituted the primary measure of aggression.

After completing the behavioral aggression measure, each subject was given a questionnaire which included one item referring to his enjoyment of the television film, one item referring to his identification with the main characters, and six items assessing his aggressive values.

The subject was then thanked for his participation and escorted back to his classroom.

Apparatus. The details of the "aggression machine" can be seen in Figure 3. The four different colored lights on top of the machine indicate the accomplice's "guess" to the child. The four buttons on the lower half of the machine give the child an opportunity to administer sounds of varying intensities. The noise generator in the right half of the photograph is not visible to the child but is situated near one of the experimenters who is separated from the subject by an opaque screen. The unpleasant sound stimuli are derived from a general purpose audio generator capable of delivering a maximum audio signal of 1.5DBM at 1350 hertz. A resistive load from the generator output terminal to common ground provides sound intensity levels of .1DBM, .5DBM, and 1.5DBM, which correspond to positions one, three, and five respectively on the control panel. Position seven is internally wired to position five, providing an equal intensity signal for positions five and seven. The actual signal is delivered to the subject via a stereo headset which delivers the same signal to both ears.

Results

The average level of sound intensity employed by each subject over the fifteen "error" trials was determined; the means of these averages

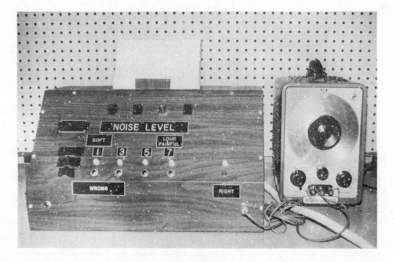

Figure 3: Apparatus

for each of the experimental groups are presented in Table 1. Initially two analyses of variance were carried out, one based on the two war films and the three control conditions, the other based on the two campus riot films and the same control conditions. Subsequent analyses of variance, taking into account age, sex, and socioeconomic variables, failed to yield any significant effects—with the exception of an age x experimental condition interaction (F=3.2, p<.05) for the war films. This interaction reflects similar mean aggression scores for the reality (M=3.6) and fantasy (M=3.4) conditions in the younger group and an experimental difference in the older group, with a reality mean of 3.6 and a fantasy mean of 2.8.

Table 1 (Experiment 1): Mean level of aggressive response

| | Aggressive TV | | Control TV | | |
	Reality	Fantasy	Baseball	Circus	No TV
War	3.62 (N=18)	3.02 (N=16)			
			4.24 (N=20)	2.86 (N=20)	3.33 (N=20)
Campus Riot	3.38 (N=17)	3.91 (N=18)			

War	Campus Riot
Main effect: F=4.1, p < .01	Main effect: F=3.1, p < .05
Reality vs. fantasy: F=2.1, N.S.	Reality vs. fantasy: F=1.4, N.S.
Reality vs. circus: F=3.8, p < .10	Fantasy vs. circus: F=5.7, p < .05

Baseball vs. circus: F=13.3, p < .01
Baseball vs. No TV: F=5.8, p < .05
Circus vs. No TV: F=2.2, N.S.

The data presented in Table 1 yield a number of interesting findings. However, with respect to the central hypothesis of the study—the predicted differences between the fantasy and reality conditions—the results are, at best, inconclusive. The behavior difference between viewers of the reality and viewers of the fantasy war films is in the predicted direction and is significant at the .10 level (two-tailed test) for the older age group. The difference in subsequent aggression for viewers of the two campus riot films, although statistically insignificant, is in a direction opposite to that predicted.

The differences between the aggression films and the three control conditions must be understood in terms of differences among the control treatments. Consistent with previous findings, exposure to the baseball film tended to stimulate aggressive behavior. The children who had seen the baseball film displayed significantly greater aggression than the children who had seen the circus film or who had not been exposed to any television program. There is some suggestion that the circus film tended to produce a decrement in aggressive behavior, but this trend was not statistically significant. The fact that neither the war reality nor the campus riot fantasy group mean is significantly greater than the no television group mean (while both means are significantly greater than the circus group mean) suggests that contrasting effects may have been operating in the circus group and in the two aggressive film groups—one real and the other fantasy. However, the data do not permit drawing such a conclusion with any reasonable degree of confidence.

As we have previously noted, no significant main effects were found for sex, age, and economic status, and only one significant interaction was found—between the experimental treatments and age. The younger children were apparently more aggressive on the behavior measure than the older children, though the differences were vitiated by the stimulating effects of the war reality and baseball films. Although there were no significant main or interaction effects for ages when the effects of the campus riot films were analyzed, the differences were sufficiently large to warrant comment. Younger children exposed to the campus riot reality film had a mean aggression score of 3.9, while older children had a mean aggression score of 2.9. This difference was reversed for the campus riot fantasy film, the means for the younger group being 3.7 and for the older group 4.1. For the older children, then, the campus riot fantasy film apparently had a greater stimulating effect than the campus riot reality film. The variance for the groups exposed to the campus riots was larger than the variance for the war film groups; as a consequence, the difference between the campus riot fantasy and campus riot reality conditions for the older children is not statistically significant (F contrast of only 1.8).

Table 2 (Experiment 1): Enjoyment of TV

Question:	Did you like the television program?
Response:	"very much" (Scored 3)
	"a little" (Scored 2)
	"not at all" (Scored 1)

	Reality	Fantasy	Baseball	Circus
War	1.81$_b$ (N=18)	2.54$_a$ (N=16)		
			2.55$_a$ (N=20)	2.75$_a$ (N=20)
Campus Riot	2.00$_b$ (N=17)	2.06$_b$ (N=18)		

(War films & controls) $F=7.5$, $p < .01$
(Campus riot films & controls $F=5.7$, $p < .01$

Means with different subscripts significantly differ at the .05 or .01 levels.

The analysis of the several verbal measures administered provides additional insights into the effects of films on the children's aggressive behavior. Thus, one might reasonably hypothesize that variations in the degree to which the children liked the various films could account for the experimental differences in aggression. However, the data in Table 2 indicate that the degree of liking was unrelated to the degree of aggression. The children liked both the circus and the baseball films. Yet there was much more aggression in the baseball film than in the circus film. They also liked the war fantasy film. They were less pleased with the two campus riot films and most especially displeased with the Vietnam war sequence. This pattern held over age, sex, and socioeconomic status; no main effects or significant interactions were found for any of these variables.

Table 3 (Experiment 1): Mean changes in dysphoric mood

	Reality	Fantasy	Baseball	Circus
War	$+7.5_a$* (N=18)	$+2.0_{bc}$ (N=16)		
			$+.8_{cd}$ (N=20)	$-.1_d$ (N=20)
Campus riot	$+4.5_{ab}$ (N=17)	$+3.6_{ab}$ (N=18)		

*Means that do not share a common subscript are significantly different at the .05 or .01 levels.

Comparable data were obtained for the assessment of mood changes. The number of positive affects checked were subtracted from the number of negative affects checked, and the after-before difference was then determined for each subject. An increase on this measure reflects an increase in dysphoric feelings (anger, annoyance, fear) and/or a decline in positive feelings (cheerfulness, friendliness). It may be noted, parenthetically, that the great majority of the children checked predominantly positive adjectives before presentation of the films.

The mean changes in dysphoric mood as a function of each of the film conditions are presented in Table 3. Very little change was recorded in the baseball and circus groups; subjects in each of these conditions maintained their essentially pleasant moods. The aggressive films, however, produced an increase on the dysphoric index, with the most marked change occurring in the war reality group. The difference between the war reality and the war fantasy groups is statistically significant (p< .05). Analyses of variance of the effects of the war films compared with the controls, and of the campus riot films compared with the controls, yielded significant main effects. Due to differences in variance, nonparametric procedures were used; these yielded comparable findings.

Table 4 (Experiment 1):   Mean changes in aggressive mood

	Experimental		Control	
	Reality	Fantasy	Baseball	Circus
War	1.2_a* (N=18)	0.4_b (N=16)		
			0.05_c (N=20)	0.05_c (N=20)
Campus riot	0.8_{ab} (N=17)	1.3_a (N=18)		

*Means that do not share a common subscript are significantly different at the .05 or .01 levels.

Similar findings were obtained when the aggressive mood adjectives of the larger check list were analyzed (Table 4). However, in the case of changes in aggressive affect, there was an interaction between exposure to the war films and the age of the sample.The younger boys reported essentially no change in aggressive affect in response to either war film. Among the older boys, the mean increment in aggressive adjectives in the war reality group was 2.0, while the mean increment in the war fantasy group was only 0.6; the difference is significant at the .05 level. A separate analysis of the positive affect adjectives yielded a significantly greater decline (-3.2) among the army reality viewers than among the army fantasy viewers (-1.6), there being no interaction with age.

At the end of the experiment, after the behavioral aggression measure, the subjects were administered an aggressive value scale and were asked several questions about the television program. The questions included the "like-dislike" measure, the results of which have been described. The means for the aggressive value measure are presented in Table 5. Since six items are included in this measure, and the score for each item can vary from 1 to 4, the total possible range is from 6 to 24; the higher score reflects a more favorable attitude toward aggressive options. The means are presented separately for each age group. The data for the war film groups are indicated in 5A, and those for the campus riot films are indicated in 5B. There is a consistent age effect in Table 5A (F=7.4, p <.01); the younger children display stronger aggressive values than the older group. As Table 5B indicates, this difference does not hold for the groups exposed to the campus riot films, there being a suggestion of a reversal (nonsignificant) for the campus riot reality film group. The most important finding noted in Table 5 is the lower mean aggressive value reported by the war reality groups. This mean is significantly lower than the war fantasy mean (p< .01), the no television group means (p < .05), and the circus group mean (p < .10).

Observing scenes from the Vietnam war on television apparently resulted in some disenchantment with the desirability of aggressive

Table 5: Mean aggressive values as a function of experimental conditions

Table A

	War films		Control films		
	Reality (N=18)	Fantasy (N=16)	Baseball (N=20)	Circus (N=20)	No TV (N=20)
Younger	13.0	16.7	14.2	15.5	17.0
Older	11.0	14.1	12.8	11.6	12.8

Table B*

	Campus Riot films		Control films		
	Reality (N=17)	Fantasy (N=18)	Baseball (N=20)	Circus (N=20)	No TV (N=20)
Younger	12.2	14.9	14.2	15.5	17.0
Older	15.0	14.9	12.8	11.6	12.8

War films — younger vs. older: $F=7.4, p < .01$
War reality vs. war fantasy: $F=6.4, p < .01$
War reality vs. no TV: $F=5.8, p < .05$
War reality vs. circus: $F=3.9, p < .10$
War fantasy vs. no TV: $F=1.2$, N.S.
War fantasy vs. circus: $F=1.7$, N.S.

*None of the mean differences in Table B are statistically significant.

actions. This finding holds for the value items dealing significantly with war but also holds for other aggressive actions. For example, in response to the statement, "Teenage hoodlums or troublemakers should be punished severely," 11 of the 18 subjects in the war reality group expressed strong disagreement, in contrast to three of the 16 subjects in the war fantasy group and two of the 20 subjects in the no television group who disagreed. Thus the war reality group, which reported the greatest increase in aggressive feeling and dysphoric mood and which tended to use more unpleasant noise than the war fantasy groups, displays a decrement in aggressive values compared with the war fantasy and control groups.

The responses to the additional questions asked about the films are of some interest. Fourteen of the war reality viewers and ten of the war fantasy viewers indicated that they did not want to be like one of the soldiers. Twelve of the campus riot reality viewers and seven of the campus riot fantasy viewers stated that they did not want to be like one of the police, while the great majority (15) in each of these groups said they did not want to be like one of the students. Sixteen subjects in the campus riot reality group and 17 in the campus riot fantasy group thought the police were in the right, while only one person in each group thought the students were in the right.

EXPERIMENT 2

The first experiment yielded several interesting findings: the aggression stimulation produced by exposure to the baseball sequence; the opposite effects suggested by value, affective, and behavioral measures of aggression; and the dependence of the reality-fantasy variable upon the stimulus content of the film. It is apparent that the central issue with which this study is concerned—the differential effects of real versus fantasy depiction of violence—should be investigated by a design different from that employed in the first experiment. We noted earlier that the campus riot fantasy film looked much too real. More important, the investigators could not separate the effects of the fantasy-reality dimension from the many content differences between real and fantasy depictions of violence.

In designing these experiments, the difficulty of matching the content of reality and fantasy films dealing with similar themes was anticipated. In order to resolve these difficulties, in the second experiment we employed the same violent film but under clearly different set conditions. In one experimental treatment, the subject believed he was seeing a film of a real event; in another treatment, the subject was shown the same film but was led to believe that it was fictional. In all other respects, the experimental procedures followed were the same as in Experiment 1.

We had initially planned to carry out this second experiment after the first had been completed. Due to a reorganization of the grade schools in the community in which we were carrying out our studies, the number of children in the grade levels from which our sample was drawn was substantially augmented. It was then possible to assign subjects at random to the experimental conditions in this study from the same population used in Experiment 1 and at the same time. Experiment 1 was essentially completed before the set conditions were implemented. The two additional groups in Experiment 2 can be considered additional conditions in Experiment 1. The control data obtained in Experiment 1 were used in the same manner in Experiment 2.

Film. This six-minute film combines elements of the campus riot reality and campus riot fantasy films in Experiment 1. It opens with part of a scene shown in the news-police violence segment, showing arrests and a massed police line facing the demonstrators. Leaders of the demonstration attempt to control and direct the crowd, urging them to avoid confrontation with the police. The police march in formation to attack the demonstrators with their clubs. The film cuts to a scene from the campus violence movie *The Whole World is Watching.* The demonstrators have established a "sit-in" in the building and police watch outside as a crowd chants. After nightfall, a large number of police arrive and enter the building and arrest those inside. As the arrested demonstrators are taken to waiting police cars, the crowd outside chants, "Pigs off campus."

In order to compare this film with the films in Experiment 1, the following marginal totals are provided: Use of weapons: bombs—1, clubs —1, body—1; Display of weapons: club—13; Shouting and yelling—19; Running —11 (including police cars and police on foot moving in).

Method. Forty subjects, from the same school as Experiment 1 and balanced for sex, socioeconomic status, and age group, were randomly assigned to a reality set or a fantasy set condition. In the reality set condition, subjects were told that they would be shown a newsreel of a campus riot, while subjects in the fantasy set condition were told that the film sequence they would view was a part of a movie made by a Hollywood studio about a campus riot. The same film sequence was used for both conditions; only the instructions were different. The verbatim instructions given the subjects were:

(1)   (Reality Set Condition):
We are going to show you a newsreel of a student riot which was photographed by NBC news photographers who were right on the scene. You might have seen some of this on the news on television before.

(2)   (Fantasy Set Condition):
We are going to show you a film that was made in a Hollywood studio. The story is about a student riot. You might have seen some of the actors on television before.

Results

The aggressive behavior means for the reality set and fantasy set conditions are presented in Table 6. The reality set mean is almost twice the level of the fantasy set mean, the difference between the two conditions being highly significant ($p < .001$). Comparisons of these means with the

Table 6 (Experiment 2): Mean level of aggression response
as a function of fantasy versus reality set

Reality set (N=20)	Fantasy set (N=20)
4.30	2.29

t=3.7; p < .001

no television group mean are instructive. Analyses of variance were carried out to determine the effects of sex, socioeconomic status, and age. These data are presented in Table 7. The F values for the principal contrasts are enumerated at the bottom of the table. The main effect for experimental conditions is highly significant, and the main effect for age is significant at the .05 level. The difference between the fantasy and reality sets is highly significant ($p < .01$) for boys, for girls, for each age level, and for each socioeconomic level. Particularly revealing is the finding that the reality and fantasy set means are significantly different from the no television mean as well as from each other. These data indicate that the reality set condition stimulated aggression, while the fantasy set condition reduced aggressive behavior.

Table 7 (Experiment 2): Mean level of aggressive response

	Reality set (N=20)	No TV (N=20)	Fantasy set (N=20)
Boys	4.60	2.94	2.40
Girls	4.00	3.72	2.19
H-SES	4.25	3.10	2.28
L-SES	4.35	3.56	2.31
Younger	4.77	3.98	2.77
Older	3.99	3.05	1.98

Main effect	$F=11.51, p < .01$
Reality vs. fantasy	$F=23.05, p < .01$
Reality vs. no TV	$F= 5.39, p < .05$
Fantasy vs. no TV	$F= 6.14, p < .05$
Younger vs. older	$F= 5.69, p < .05$

The fantasy and reality set means for the other measures administered are presented in Table 8. As Table 8A indicates, there is a small but reliable effect of the reality set variable upon the degree to which the subjects liked the film. Sixteen of the 20 subjects in the fantasy set group (compared with ten of the 20 in the reality set group) liked the film at least a little. The reality set condition also elicited a greater change in dysphoric affect than the fantasy set condition, but this difference is not significant. The mean change in aggressive affect is also nonsignificant. In order to further explore possible differences in dysphoric affect changes, the experimenters separately analyzed changes in responses to the two adjectives "afraid" and "upset," which directly reflected fear and tension. The mean change for the reality set group was +.85, while the corresponding mean for the fantasy set group was +.40 ($t=1.69, p<.10$).

As Table 8D indicates, there was no difference between the reality set and fantasy set means in aggressive values (the means being comparable to the Control means reported in Experiment 1). In response to another question asked, about half the subjects in each group indicated some preference to be like the police. None of the subjects in the reality set condition and only three of the fantasy set group stated they would want to be like the students. Seventeen of the 20 subjects in each group felt that the police were in the right.

Table 8 (Experiment 2)

8A. Mean liking of television

Reality set (N=20)	Fantasy set (N=20)
1.80	2.20

$t=1.99$; $p < .05$

8B. Mean change in dysphoric affect

Reality set (N=20)	Fantasy set (N=20)
+6.1	+4.6

p: N.S.

8C. Mean change in aggressive affect

Reality set (N=20)	Fantasy set (N=20)
+1.2	+.9

p: N.S.

8D. Mean aggressive values

Reality set (N=20)	Fantasy set (N=20)
2.4	2.4

EXPERIMENT 3

The investigators carried out an additional experimental variation in order to explore the relationship between the fantasy and reality natures of the responses. It was hypothesized that aggression seen as fantasy would, through generalization, result in an increase in "play" or imaginary aggressive behavior. A weaker hypothesis suggested that aggression seen as real might have a greater influence on "real" than on imaginary aggressive behavior. Thirty subjects from the same school participated in this exploratory experiment. Ten were randomly assigned to the reality set condition, ten to the fantasy set condition, and ten to the no television condition. The experimental procedure used in Experiment 2 was followed—with one critical deviation. After the unpleasant noise was demonstrated, the child was told that the apparatus would be disconnected and that, when pressing the different buttons, he was to imagine that the machine was working and that pressing the various buttons would produce the designated sounds.

The means of these three groups, along with the corresponding means of the comparable groups run previously under "real" response conditions, are presented in Table 9. The table shows, under fantasy response (as compared to real response) conditions, a small decrease in aggression among the reality set group and a larger increase among the fantasy set group. These trends are in accordance with expectation. However, there was also an aggression increase among the no television condition group, and none of the group means under the fantasy response orientation is significantly different from one another. The fantasy response orientation tended to raise (as expected) the aggressive response level but at the same time obscured possible effects of exposure to the aggressive film stimuli. Nevertheless, the trends reflected in the data are sufficiently promising to warrant additional investigation of the relationship between the real and fantasy natures of the film stimuli and between the real and fantasy natures of the aggressive response that is assessed.

Table 9 (Experiment 3): Effects of reality-fantasy set variation in the aggressive response

| | | Stimulus | | |
		Reality set	Fantasy set	No TV
RESPONSE	Real	4.30 (N=20)	2.29 (N=20)	3.33 (N=20)
	Fantasy	3.82 (N=10)	4.06 (N=10)	3.89 (N=10)

DISCUSSION

These experiments have yielded diverse findings. The results of the first experiment are ambiguous. There is some indication that the war reality film stimulated more aggressive behavior than the war fantasy film in the older age group. However, the differences were not significant for the campus riot film and, moreover, were in an opposite direction. Further complicating the interpretation is the evidence of a significant reduction or suppression of aggressive values in the group exposed to the war reality film which, at the same time, elicited more negative feeling than any of the other film stimuli. Still other issues are raised by the incidental finding in the first study of an increment of aggressive behavior in the children who observed the baseball film. Finally, in contrast to the complexity of the results of the first experiment, the findings obtained in the second experiment are more clearly consistent with the expectation of greater aggression following exposure to aggressive television content depicted as real than when the same content is depicted as fantasy.

The results of these experiments carry a number of important methodological and theoretical implications. Methodologically, the data underline the proposition that different response measures of aggression can yield diametrically opposite results bearing upon the influence of direct or vicarious participation in an aggressive act (Feshbach, 1964). The measure of aggressive values indicates that exposure to a film of the Vietnam war produces a decrement in "aggression." The measures of aggressive affect and of behavioral aggression indicate that exposure to films of the Vietnam war stimulates aggression, especially in the older group. Reliance on one of these measures, to the exclusion of the others, would have led to an erroneous conclusion. It must also be emphasized that these diverse findings are not theoretically inconsistent. "Aggression" is a complex construct with affective, drive, attitudinal, and instrumental components. Previous theoretical statements by the author (Feshbach, 1964; Feshbach, 1970) have proposed varying but predictable effects of the same aggressive experience upon different aggressive response systems.

In the case of the Vietnam war sequence, the avoidance properties of the stimulus were not anticipated, although they probably should have been. Too much is already known about the war, even by these children; it cannot be glorified by one newsreel exposure. In addition, the newsreel did not portray soldiers in the process of obvious victory. The children were upset by the film and reacted less favorably on a verbal level to war and other aggressive options after viewing it. However, their anger was also stimulated by the film, and the increment in aggressive behavior in the older children suggests a displacement effect. The children exposed to the war fantasy film also reported an increase in aggressive affect but did not displace. Since the increment in that group was smaller than in the war reality group, it is possible to argue that the degree of anger aroused was below the threshold for displacement.

It would be difficult to invoke the displacement hypothesis to account for the effects of the baseball film. The children did not appear to be upset or particularly excited by the one-inning sequence they observed, and their affective reports reflect little emotional change. It is of course possible that the mechanism mediating the effects of the baseball film are different from those mediating the effects of the Vietnam war film or the effects of the reality set conditions in Experiment 2. Baseball, by virtue of its competitive nature, its particular implements (bats, spikes, a ball directed toward the batter) and aggressive concomitants ("Kill the ump!") may stimulate aggressive associations in the observer and facilitate aggressive behavior. Perhaps the fact that only one inning rather than a longer sequence was shown explains the increase in aggression. But this explanation does not seem likely in view of Foulkes's (1967) finding of a significantly greater amount of aggressive dream content among boys who had seen a baseball film in which baseball was depicted and described than among boys who had seen a "cowboys and Indians" film. The reality nature of the baseball film (as compared with the cowboy film) could be a critical parameter. The stimulating effects of baseball may in part be due to its reality component. Winning and losing in sports has very real consequences for the players' self-evaluation and attitudes toward others. It is not simply a "game" isolated from other aspects of their lives. The implements employed in baseball can be used to inflict injury as well as to compete in the game, and the difference between the two can on occasion become quite blurred.

It would be desirable to assess the effects of other baseball sequences in which the outcome varied and of other sports sequences as well. The stimulating effect of the baseball film suggests a further disturbing possibility. Perhaps the depiction of violence is not the most relevant aggression-instigating stimulus presented on television. This possibility opens a Pandora's box of potential stimuli. If competition proves to be a possible potent stimulus, for example, it will then be necessary to evaluate the effects of the many different forms in which competition finds expression on television.

The effects of the baseball film and of the aggression films used in Experiment 1 suggest that there are structural as well as content characteristics of film stimuli—characteristics that may be relevant to their aggression-stimulating or aggression-reducing properties and that have been ignored by behavioral scientists. Dramatic films have an aesthetic dimension. They can illuminate an experience as well as portray it (Bentley, 1965). They have a climax, a beginning, a middle, and an end. The dramatic tension typically rises to a high point and then falls as a result of some resolution. The war fantasy sequence had some of these structural characteristics. The campus riot fantasy sequence was more episodic. (The campus riot fantasy film might have been better, from the point of view of reducing audience aggression, had more incidents of physical aggression been depicted in the beginning of the film, as they were in the campus riot reality sequence. The end of the film might then more readily have been perceived as resolving the violent conflict.) In any case, we know much too little about the effects of these structural parameters, which, from the dramatist's perspective, are critical to a film's or play's dramatic qualities.

Drama critics have also suggested that the fictional nature of drama is essential to the dramatic experience (Olson, 1961). The view expressed by Coleridge when he said that the proper response to fiction requires a "willing suspension of disbelief" is not descriptive of the behavior of audiences who are all too quick to notice improbabilities in plot or incident (Olson, 1961). The audience, however, by exercising its imagination, contributes to the creation of drama (Hamilton, 1910; Olson, 1961). These conjectures by drama theorists point to psychological processes that require empirical study. One such speculation, on the psychological differences between fiction and reality, was the principal focus of the present investigation.

The results of the second experiment are striking in their consistency over age, socioeconomic status, and sex; they reflect powerful psychological differences between the reality and fantasy depictions of a violent event. Subjects who thought the film depicting violence was a newsreel became significantly more aggressive than a control group; subjects who thought this same film was fictional displayed significantly less aggressive behavior than the controls. A displacement hypothesis might be offered to explain the stimulation effect. The children were more upset when they thought that the events depicted actually happened; they might have expressed their tension in the form of displaced aggression toward the experimenter. We noted, however, an increase in anger arousal without an increase in aggressive behavior when they believed the film was fictional. We suggest that when an event is fictional, subjects can "leave their feelings in the theater," as it were; or, if these feelings linger, they are focused on the dramatic event. The "message" of a newsreel, however, goes beyond the context in which the film is observed. By definition, the newsreel has meaning for events beyond the theater or living room. As an alternate to the displacement hypothesis, we suggest that the observation of socially approved or otherwise reinforced "real" violence, through secondary reinforcement, reduction in anxiety, and imitation, generalizes to "real" aggressive behavior. The reactions to the war reality film in Experiment 1 suggest a process similar to that which occurred when nursery school children witnessed the reinforced misbehavior of an aggressive model (Bandura, Ross, and Ross, 1963). They disapproved of the model's behavior but nevertheless imitated him.

Considering the fact that there is very little relationship between affect arousal and aggressive behavior, the displacement hypothesis is less tenable than an explanation of the increased aggression produced by the reality set in terms of the socially sanctioned character of the aggression depicted. Additional research is required before a choice can be made among these two alternatives and others that have been suggested. The decrement in aggression produced by the fantasy set condition must also be accounted for. The reality-fantasy set variable not only functioned as a discriminative stimulus (so that children in the fantasy set group did not manifest the increase resulting from the reality set) but also produced opposite behavioral effects. The fantasy set condition, we suggest, gives the child an opportunity to exercise his imagination and to engage vicariously in harmless aggressive fantasy and express aggressive affect without the fear of punishment. Fantasy may have a cathartic effect and actually reduce aggressive motivation or, as suggested by Feshbach and Singer (1971), it may act as a cognitive control over the expression of aggressive impulses. The difference between these two hypotheses is subtle but can be operationally specified. In the case of a reduction in aggressive motivation, the aggressive tendency should remain at a low level unless some additional aggression-arousing event occurs. In the case of the cognitive control explanation, the aggressive tendencies should eventually return to a higher level unless the child engages in additional vicarious or self-initiated cognitive activity pertinent to these aggressive dispositions.

Research resolving this theoretical distinction is less important at this stage of knowledge than is additional investigation of the effects of fantasy violence in the media on children's aggression. The reality set-fantasy set findings need to be replicated with other film stimuli. Of equal relevance, studies attempting to describe more precisely the psychological effects of the fantasy set orientation are required. There is a considerable gap between exposure to an aggressive film, whether under a reality or a fantasy orientation, and the measures of the child's subsequent aggressive behavior. To fill that gap requires a more profound and detailed knowledge of the dramatic experience than is currently available.

FOOTNOTES

1. This study was supported by research contract HSM 42-70-78 from the National Institute of Mental Health, United States Public Health Service. The author wishes to acknowledge the energy, care, and thoughtful assistance rendered by Antonia M. Bercovici and Yoram Jaffe. In addition, the author wishes to express his gratitude to the National Broadcasting Company and to Universal Studios for their cooperation in providing several of the critical stimulus films and for their help in the editing of these films.

REFERENCES

Bailyn, L. Mass media and children: A study of exposure habits and cognitive effects. *Psychological Monographs,* 1959, **73,** No. 471.

Bandura, A., and Huston, A. Identification as a process of incidental learning. *Journal of Abnormal and Social Psychology,* 1961, **63,** 311-18. (a)

Bandura, A., Ross, D., and Ross,S. Imitation of film-mediated agressive models. *Journal of Abnormal and Social Psychology,* 1963, **66,** 3-11.

Bandura, A., Ross, D., and Ross, S. Transmission of aggression through imitation of aggressive models. *Journal of Abnormal and Social Psychology,* 1961, **63,** 575-82. (b)

Bentley, E. *The life of the drama.* New York: Atheneum, 1965.

Bercovici, A. The influence of aggressive and non-aggressive television and cognitive style on elementary and junior high school children. Master's thesis, University of California at Los Angeles, 1970.

Eron, L. Relationship of TV viewing habits and aggressive behavior in children. *Journal of Abnormal and Social Psychology,* 1963, **67**, 193-96.

Feshbach, S. The influence of drive arousal and conflict on fantasy behavior. In Kagan, J., and Lesser, J., (Eds.), *Contemporary issues in thematic apperceptive methods.* Thomas, 1960, 119-40.

Feshbach, S. The function of aggression and the regulation of aggressive drive. *Psychological Review,* **71**, 257-72.

Feshbach, S. Effects of exposure to aggressive content in television upon aggression in boys. (Proceedings of the XVI International Congress of Applied Psychology, Copenhagen, 1968.)

Feshbach, S. Aggression. In Mussen (Ed.) rev. Carmichael. *Manual of Child Psychology,* Vol. 2. New York: John Wiley & Sons, 1970.

Feshbach, S., and Singer, R. *Television and Aggression.* San Francisco, Calif.: Jossey-Bass, Inc., 1971.

Foulkes, D. Dreams of the male child: an EEG study. *Journal of Abnormal Psychology,* 1967, **72**, 457-67.

Hamilton, C. *The theory of the theatre.* New York: Henry Holt & Co., 1910.

Hartley, E.R. The impact of viewing aggression: studies and problems of extrapolation. *In A Review and Evaluation of Recent Studies on the Impact of Violence.* Office of Social Research, CBS, Inc., 1964.

Hartmann, D.P. Influence of symbolically modeled instrumental aggression and pain cues on aggressive behavior. *Journal of Personality and Social Psychology,* 1969, II (3), 280-88.

Himmelweit, H. T., Oppenheim, A. N., and Vince, P. *Television and the child.* Toronto: Oxford University Press, 1958.

Lövaas, O. Effect of exposure to symbolic aggression on aggressive behavior. *Child Development,* 1961, **32**, 37-44 (2).

Mussen, P.H. and Rutherford, E. Effects of aggressive cartoons in children's aggressive play. *Journal of Abnormal and Social Psychology,* 1961, **62**, 461-64.

Olson, E. *Tragedy and the theory of drama.* Detroit: Wayne State University Press, 1961.

Schramm, W., Lyle, J., and Parker, E.B. *Television in the lives of our children.* Stanford: Stanford University Press, 1961.

Singer, J.L. *Daydreaming: an introduction to the experimental study of inner experience;* New York: Random House, 1966.

Walters, R.H., and Llewelyn–Thomas, E. Enhancement of punitiveness of visual and audio–visual displays. *Canadian Journal of Psychology,* 1963, **17**, 244-55.

Walters, R.H., Llewelyn-Thomas, E. and Acker, C.W. Enhancement of punitive behavior by audio displays. *Science,* 1962, **136**, 872-73.

Appendix A:
Aggressive values items

INSTRUCTIONS: People have different opinions about the following statements. Check how much you agree or disagree with each. You can either agree a lot, agree a little, disagree a little, or disagree a lot. The choice is yours. Please circle the answer that is best for you.

Used in "No TV" and all Film Conditions:

It is very seldom right to hit
another person.
- a. agree a lot
- b. agree a little
- c. disagree a little
- d. disagree a lot

It would be O. K. for a person to
kill someone if the nation would be
better off without him.
- a. agree a lot
- b. agree a little
- c. disagree a little
- d. disagree a lot

It is the tough guy who always
comes out on top
- a. agree a lot
- b. agree a little
- c. disagree a little
- d. disagree a lot

A nation has to go to war once
every generation to keep its self-respect.
- a. agree a lot
- b. agree a little
- c. disagree a little
- d. disagree a lot

Teenage hoodlums or troublemakers should be punished severely.
- a. agree a lot
- b. agree a little
- c. disagree a little
- d. disagree a lot

War is sometimes good for a country
- a. agree a lot
- b. agree a little
- c. disagree a little
- d. disagree a lot

Used in all Film Conditions:

Did you like the television
program?

    a. very much
    b. a little
    c. not at all

Used in War Film Conditions:

Would you like to be like one
of the soldiers?

    a. very much
    b. a little
    c. not at all

Used in Campus Riot Film Conditions:

Would you like to be like one
of the STUDENTS?

    a. very much
    b. a little
    c. not at all

Would you like to be like one
of the POLICE?

    a. very much
    b. a little
    c. not at all

Do you think what the
STUDENTS or what the
POLICE did was right?

    a. the POLICE
    b. the STUDENTS

Used in Baseball Film Condition:

Would you like to be a baseball
player like one of the players you saw?

    a. very much
    b. a little
    c. not at all

Used in Circus Film Condition:

If you could, would you like to
join a circus?

    a. very much
    b. a little
    c. not at all

Appendix B:
Adjective Check List

Angry	Upset
Happy	Nice
Annoyed	Good Natured
Friendly	Feel like hitting someone
Afraid	Cheerful
Good	Grouchy
Mad	Ready to fight
Glad	

Television and the Behavior of Preschool Children

Harold W. Stevenson
University of Minnesota

*Every new medium of communication has in its time aroused anxiety—
the cinema, radio, and at one time (a chastening thought) even reading.
Now it is the turn of television* (Himmelweit, Oppenheim, and Vince,
1958).

The influence of television on the behavior of preschool children is a
topic of great social concern. It has, nevertheless, received only minimal
attention in the research of social scientists. Reviews of research on television's effects on social behavior contain relatively few studies using
preschool children as subjects (Chu and Schramm, 1969; Maccoby,
1964; Schramm, 1964; Atkin, Murray, and Nayman, 1971). As a result,
much of what can be said must be inference and conjecture. Results are
frequently suggestive but seldom definitive. When we are able to make
firm statements, they tend to be of a low order—such as "young children are able to learn through television" or "the amount of learning

that occurs through television viewing is dependent upon the frequency with which the material is viewed."

In many ways, therefore, this is not a good time to attempt to discuss the effects of television on the behavior of preschool children; we know before we begin that the number of questions we raise far exceeds the number we will be able to answer. Even so, it is important to make an attempt. By exposing our own ignorance, social scientists may be motivated to undertake more extensive explorations of this extremely important topic.[1]

Difficulties in research

An obvious question is why so little research has been conducted. The answer is that research on the effects of television is excruciatingly difficult and very costly. James Halloran, a leading British researcher, has summarized the problems in an effectively depressing way:

> The student is confronted by a veritable avalanche of relevant variables (predispositions, subjective perception, retention, selection, contextual organization, image of source, group membership, activity of opinion leaders, class membership, level of frustration, family background, educational level, availability of social mechanisms and nature of the media to name a few) and it is perhaps not surprising that a preliminary survey of the field leaves one with the impression that we have not advanced very far (Halloran, 1965, p. 29).

Three major approaches have been used in this area of research: *laboratory studies, research in naturalistic situations,* and *survey research.* Each of these approaches has serious methodological problems, and it is useful to review them before we begin our discussion of the studies that have been done.

Laboratory studies typically are short-term investigations conducted under controlled conditions. Such experiments are probably the most efficient means of obtaining information, but they may be criticized on the grounds that the laboratory represents an artificial situation that seriously restricts the possibility of generalizing the experimental findings to the everyday world. Statistically significant effects may be obtained from events that occur in the laboratory, but will they have any relation to the behavior of the young child in his everyday life and over long periods of time? Will effects manifest one minute after viewing the program persist one month or one year later? Will the child's ability to repeat or remember the content of a short film seen under the discrete, isolated conditions of a laboratory study represent anything approaching what he can repeat or remember from the rush of material seen during several hours of television? Laboratory studies give us insight into cause-effect relationships that exist under specified conditions, but they are incapable of providing conclusive evidence about what happens in the everyday world.

Research in naturalistic situations does carry us into the everyday world of the child. But such research is very time-consuming and seldom leads to more than a set of correlations, where causality is difficult to assess. Ordinarily it is impossible to control all the variables that are of potential relevance, because relatively few constraints can be introduced into most naturalistic situations. For example, the vocabulary of children who watch television may be above that of children who have not watched television. We are unable, however, to control the number of questions they ask about the program, the number of new activities they may undertake which were demonstrated on television, or how much they may engage other members of their families in discussions about what they have seen. It is difficult to be sure that the effects would be comparable for children who do not choose this sedentary, indoor type of activity. It would be appropriate to conclude that television viewing is related to a child's level of vocabulary development, but cause-effect relations are difficult to assess. A comparable degree of verbalization, question-asking, and new activities may, in the absence of television, produce comparable effects.

Surveys obviously cannot be easily conducted with young children as respondents. Discrepancies between what young children say and what they do are notorious. When parents serve as respondents, the investigator is taken one step away from the subjects under consideration. Some parents may be able to describe quite accurately the child's viewing habits and the apparent effects viewing has on the child's behavior, but we cannot expect all parental reports to be so reliable. Parents who are away from home much of the time or continuously engaged in work while at home are not likely to be able to report reliably on children's activities.

Each approach, therefore, has serious methodological problems. As we begin to impose the controls necessary for unambiguous conclusions, we move away from natural conditions of viewing and thereby restrict the number of generalizations that can be made from our data. As we begin to approximate natural conditions of viewing, we lose control of variables that may play an important role in determining our results. As is so often the case in investigating phenomena of the real world, we probably never will obtain information as satisfactory as we would desire. Nevertheless, it is only through research that we will be able to make statements on the basis of what we *know* rather than on the basis of what we may *believe*—or, worse, what we wish to believe.

The extent of viewing

By 1970 over 95 percent of American homes were equipped with at least one television set. Estimates of the number of hours these sets are on varies, but we know that televison has come to play a significant role in the daily life of most American families. Although data are limited, several surveys indicate something about the viewing habits of pre-school children. It has been estimated that children actively begin watching television at the average age of 2.8 years. Viewing increases very rapidly during the next four years; by age five, 82 percent of the children are viewing television regularly; by age seven, 94 percent (Schramm, Lyle, and Parker, 1961). There are indications that among both school-age (Schramm et al., 1961) and preschool-age children (Ball and Bogatz, 1970), brighter children tend to be heavy rather than light viewers of television. Boys tend to watch television more than girls; approximately 65 percent of boys aged three to five watch television more than two hours a day, while somewhat less than 60 percent of pre-school girls watch television frequently (Ball and Bogatz, 1970).

The extent to which preschool children watch television can be seen in Table 1. It is evident that the vast majority of children—in this case mostly disadvantaged children—watch television more than two hours a day.

Table 1: Percentage of children viewing television
for various amounts of time each day

Age	Hours viewed	Quartile*			
		Q_1	Q_2	Q_3	Q_4
3	6 or more	0	3	9	13
	4 or 5	31	14	27	21
	2 or 3	38	46	50	54
	2 or less	31	27	14	13
4	6 or more	10	6	6	14
	4 or 5	11	15	16	14
	2 or 3	36	34	31	38
	2 or less	37	45	40	34
5	6 or more	6	0	0	6
	4 or 5	12	38	34	14
	2 or 3	33	38	25	39
	2 or less	33	23	38	42

*Quartiles determined by frequency with which parents report children viewed Sesame Street. From Ball & Bogatz, 1970, p. 127-39.

Content viewed

What do preschool children watch on television? They do not have a great deal of opportunity to watch programs designed specially for them. In 1970, national networks produced four programs for preschool children: *Captain Kangaroo* (one hour on weekdays), *Misterogers Neighborhood* (one-half hour on weekdays), *Romper Room* (one-half hour on weekdays), and the highly successful *Sesame Street* (one hour five days a week, in some cities two hours). But even if a child wanted to watch all these programs every day, he probably could not do so; in many cities several of them may be broadcast at the same time.

Local children's programs, while more numerous than nationally produced programs, tend to be of poor quality. Producing programs for children has generally been considered a low-prestige job in local television studios; children's programs have been used as a training ground for producers and technicians who want to work on adult programs. Staff members of children's programs often have no special qualifications for working with young children. The programs have been characterized by relatively little preparation, little live action, and large numbers of old cartoons.

Since good children's programs are infrequent, preschool children spend a good deal of time viewing programs designed for more mature audiences. What is the content of these programs? One obvious element of content is violence. In a survey of typical Saturday morning programs, Gerbner (1969) found that of the popular cartoon programs, 94.3 percent in 1967 and 92.8 percent in 1968 contained violence. (Violence was defined as an overt expression of force with the intent to hurt or kill.) The percentage of programs containing violence was greater in children's cartoons than in any other type of program except crime-western-adventure.

In a study of cartoons presented on a typical Saturday in 1968, Zusne (1968) found that cartoons occupied a total of 3.6 hours on each of two networks. Violent incidents occupied from 4.2 to 7.3 percent of the time these cartoons were on the air. "Monster" or horror cartoons were found to be less violent than the seemingly more benign "Bugs Bunny" or "Tom and Jerry" types of cartoons.

Dramatic programs on the air between 4 and 10 p.m. were also found to contain a high frequency of violence (Gerbner, 1969). Of 455 leading characters in these programs over two weeks, 241 had committed some violence, 54 had killed an opponent, and 24 had died violent deaths. A count of the injured and dead in all of these programs during the two weeks was 790. Violence was perpetrated by "good" guys in the programs as often as by "bad" guys, and nearly half of all killers achieved a clearly happy ending in the plays. Most of the violence was individual and selfish, often directed against strangers and victims who could not resist. Other studies (Dillon, 1968; Osborn and Hale, 1969) have found that during evening television acts of violence occurred once every 16.3 minutes , and killings once every hour.

It is likely that preschool children view at least some of these programs, especially in homes where the television is on for large numbers of hours during the evening. First graders, for example, spend 40 percent of their viewing time watching such programs (Schramm et al.,

1961). During most evenings, therefore, preschool children can be prevented from viewing violence only when programs are carefully selected or the set is turned off. Violence could not be avoided on Saturday mornings in 1968 if the three major networks were watched; depending on the network, there were from 17.3 to 24.6 acts of violence every hour (Gerbner, 1969).

Networks have attempted to reduce the number of cartoons depicting violence, but current data showing their success are not available. Cartoons have frequently been replaced by fantasy programs involving witches, grotesque characters, and animals conducting human-like activities. The content of these programs and their possible effects have not been studied.

Violence has been a dominant theme of cartoons and dramatic programs on American television. Few programs have been produced specially for preschool children, and the majority of these have been improvisations presented by persons with little or no experience with preschool children. The content of children's television has been summarized by a leading news magazine: "Vulgarity and violence dominate children's video: mice endlessly bombing cats, family "comedies" and dumb daddies, mischievous kids and dogs who wend their way into your heart, all accompanied by commercials as intense as the Chinese water torture" *(Time,* November 23, 1970).

Why do children like television?

Children say they like television because it is "interesting" or "fun to watch." Their answers give us little insight, however, into what it *is* about the constantly changing images on the screen that makes television such an attractive and compelling medium of communication. Although there are many possible reasons for children's enjoyment of television, only one hypothesis has been investigated: that children may gain satisfaction from watching television because they identify with the fictional characters on the television screen when they are frustrated. This hypothesis suggests that children who are likely to be frustrated in their home lives should be the most frequent viewers of television.

Maccoby (1954) attempted to investigate this possibility through analysis of data obtained from interviews of 379 mothers who were part of a larger study on child rearing practices and personality development. The mothers were asked how much time their children spent watching television. The major part of the interview consisted of questions related to the home training of the child. The sample of children was divided into upper-middle class families and upper-lower class families.

Relatively few differences were found in the television viewing time among upper-lower class children subjected to different child rearing practices. Among the upper-middle class children, however, seven of the nine measures related to child rearing were associated significantly with the amount of time the child spent each day watching television. Children from the more punitive and less permissive families viewed television more frequently. Among the child rearing practices associated with high television viewing were punishment for aggression toward parents, permissiveness of sex behavior in the child, mother's reaction to dependent behavior in the child, demands for obedience and quiet, neatness, good table manners, going to bed on time, extent of physical punishment, and emotional relationship of the mother toward the child.

A possible explanation of the differences in the findings according to social class was offered. Lower-class children may escape to television when they are frustrated, but when they are not frustrated they do what their parents do—watch television. Upper-middle class families, on the other hand, watch television less; thus the effects of frustration in increasing viewing time on the part of the child may be more apparent in these families.

This is an isolated study. It is, however, the only one which has investigated the dynamics of television watching in preschool children. Until we become more aware of the functions that television viewing serves for the young child, we will be unable to understand the underlying bases for television's influence on their behavior.

Parental response to television

What do parents think about television as a force in the lives of their young children? Relatively little evidence is available; our major source of information is a study by Hess and Goldman (1962) in which information was obtained from 99 mothers of children between five and ten years of age in the metropolitan area of Chicago. The authors summarized their results in the following way: "Television is seen as both an educational, enlightening influence and a habit-forming source of nightmares. The responses of the group indicate the prevalence of a concept of television as a learning experience even though virtually none of the programs that children watch could be called educational in any formal sense" (p. 413). The detailed evaluations upon which these conclusions were reached may be found in Table 2.

Children were more often in control of the television set than were the parents. When the families were asked who decided to turn the television on, the answer was the child in 49 percent of the families, the mother in 32 percent, mother or child in 13 percent, and the father in three percent. The degree to which parents prohibited specific programs or set general restrictions on the types of programs the children could view differed according to socioeconomic class. Sixty-three percent of the upper-class families placed such restrictions on their children's viewing, while only 34 percent did so in the low-status families. (It is of interest

Table 2: Parental response to television

Statement	% of mothers agreeing
1. Television is too violent for children	63
2. Television is not responsible for behavior problems	55
3. Television is a great educational influence	91
4. Television opens the world to the child	89
5. Television-viewing tends to become a habit	89
6. The more the child watches television, the less he reads	80
7. Television programs influence the child temporarily and have no lasting effect	76

Data from Hess and Goldman, *Child Development*, 1962, p. 413-14.

that so small a percentage of all parents attempted to restrict what their children watched.)

Further indications that parents of different social classes handle the use of television differently are found in a study of Michigan families by Blood (1961). Over 100 families were categorized as lower-lower, upper-lower, lower-middle, and upper-middle class, according to socioeconomic status. The families selected had children between two and 18 years of age; no analyses were presented separately for preschool children.

Class differences were found in the average amount of television viewing, ranging from 3.8 hours during each weekday for lower-lower class children to 2.3 hours for upper-middle class children. On the weekend days the comparable averages were 6.4 and 3.3 hours. The most marked differences were between the upper-middle class families and the other three. The results also indicated that, even though their children watched television more, the lower-lower class parents did not believe television led their children to neglect other activities. Only 16 percent of the lower-lower class families thought this was the case—contrasted with 41 percent of the upper-middle class families who thought so.

The location of the television set and its potential for disrupting family life also differed according to social class. The television set was in the living room in nearly all of the lower-lower class homes (partly because of the smaller number of available rooms) and in only two-thirds of the upper-middle class homes. One-quarter of the upper-middle class families and three-quarters of the lower-lower class families maintained a laissez-faire attitude in controlling the use of television. When controls over the use of television were applied, the techniques differed by social class. Distraction was never used by the lower-lower class parents, but 40 percent of the upper-middle class parents attempted to lure their children from television by distracting them. Upper-middle class parents also used reasoning more frequently than did parents in the other groups. Lower-lower class parents more typically used a direct form of control—they turned the set off.

Whatever effects television may have on the behavior of young children probably differ according to the socioeconomic status of the children's families. Lower-class children apparently have greater control over their own television viewing, view television more frequently, and are less subject to parental concern over the frequency and content of what they view.

Sesame Street

In testimony before the Kefauver Committee in 1955, Paul Lazarsfeld talked about what a "good" children's television program might look like:

> Let me draw your attention to the fact that everyone talks about bad television programs and the effects which they have; but actually it would be much more constructive and enlightening to experiment with good programs. Why shouldn't it be possible to get reformers and writers together, and have them devise programs which everyone thinks would be desirable, and beneficial? Would children listen to them? Would they have good effects? And even prior to that, do we really know what we mean by a good program? Are there people around who could write them? It is such a simple idea, but consider what has to be done to carry it out. You have to get psychologists and writers to meet and work together. You have to have funds to provide programs for experimental purposes, regardless of whether a television station or network is willing to put them on the air. But the aridity and the negativism of much of the discussion which takes place today can be overcome only if it is shown that there is something like a good program, that there are people who can be trained to write and produce them, and that children are willing to listen to them (Lazarsfeld, 1955, p. 246).

No one would have been able to give responsible answers to Lazarsfeld's questions before the advent of *Sesame Street.* While Joan Ganz Cooney, the producer of *Sesame Street,* may not have read Lazarsfeld's comments, she and her staff have shown that psychologists, educators, and writers can collaborate successfully in the production of a popular and beneficial program for preschool children. After a year of preparation, *Sesame Street* was first presented on television in the fall of 1969. It rapidly became one of the most talked-about programs in the history of television, with a daily audience of approximately seven million children. An initial grant of $8 million provided the financial resources of the most carefully planned children's program in American television. Before the program was begun, a detailed catalogue of goals was written, and the program has been structured to try to accomplish these goals.

With a clear prospectus of what was to be attempted in *Sesame Street,* Samuel Ball and Gerry Ann Bogatz of the Educational Testing Service were able to undertake an extensive study of the effects of the program on the behavior of preschool children. Their study is the most comprehensive published investigation of preschool children's responses to television (Ball and Bogatz, 1970).

A battery of 240 questions that dealt directly with the content of the program was constructed. Before the program went on the air, 1,124 preschool children, mostly from disadvantaged homes, were tested in five communities in the United States. Six months later 943 of these children were located for retesting. In addition to the data obtained from these tests, parents and teachers were interviewed about children's viewing of television and about their viewing of *Sesame Street* in particular. The children were divided into quartiles (fourths) according to the amount of time they watched *Sesame Street*: Q_1, never or rarely; Q_2, two or three times a week; Q_3, four or five times a week; and Q_4, more than five times a week.

Generally, the children who were most in need of the types of information conveyed by *Sesame Street* viewed the program least often. They were from the most disadvantaged families. Their homes had the fewest books, their parents had the smallest amount of education, their mothers read to them least often, and their families represented the least positive educational climate. These children also had the lowest mental ages and the lowest pretest scores.

This problem is illustrated by the test results. Children in Q_1, for example, increased their knowledge of the alphabet by an average of 1.5 letters over the six-month period. Children in Q_4 increased their knowledge, on the average, by 7.9 letters. Ability to sort objects by function ("Which one doesn't go with the others?"), a more general cognitive task, improved ten points among Q_1 children and 43 points among Q_4 children. Ability to write one's own name (which was not taught specifically on *Sesame Street*) improved by eight percent among Q_1 children and by 30 percent among Q_4 children. At the pretest, two percent of children in Q_1 and four percent of children in Q_4 knew the whole alphabet. By the end of six months nine percent in Q_1 and 55 percent in Q_4 knew the whole alphabet.

According to these data, degree of improvement in performance depended upon how frequently the child viewed the program. The more often the child viewed *Sesame Street* each week, the greater the improvement. Developing a good television program for preschool children is a major task, but the program's effectiveness will be restricted until techniques are developed to insure that the children who need it most view it most.

When divided by age, the youngest children showed the greatest gains in scores. For example, the gain for three-year-olds in Q_4 was 57 points, while for five-year-olds in Q_4 it was 37 points. (These figures take on increased significance when it is noted that the gains for children in Q_1, who rarely viewed the program, were only 12.4 among three-year-olds, but were 23.1 among five-year-olds.)

The ETS study showed what we all know but need to be reminded of: children can learn a great deal from viewing television. It is impossible to summarize briefly all the findings of this extensive study. Perhaps the most efficient means of conveying its contributions would be to quote from the conclusions of the report:

> From this evaluation of *Sesame Street*, television has been shown to work extremely well as a teaching medium. It achieved this result not only in learnings that involve simple association (for example, naming letters) but also in learning that involves complex cognitive processes (sorting and classifying), and even verbalization of these processes. In open competition with other television shows, it achieved this result through a program that attracted and held the attention of the viewers (Ball and Bogatz, 1970, p. 373).

This is an important study, but one study cannot answer all our questions. Would children who did not watch *Sesame Street* frequently have shown comparable gains if some external motivation existed for watching it? Were children more expressive in their use of language after watching *Sesame Street?* How critical were variables such as parental interest and the home's educational environment in producing the gains found from viewing *Sesame Street?* What effect has *Sesame Street* had on children's performance in kindergarten and first grade? Are these effects lasting? Will attendance at preschool coupled with viewing *Sesame Street* produce greater gains than either alone? Does the cognitively oriented content of *Sesame Street* influence the child's social behavior and personality development? Is racial tolerance influenced by viewing the interracial cast of *Sesame Street?* Answers to these and many other questions will await further research.

The Rural Appalachia program

A different (though related) type of project has been conducted by the Appalachia Educational Laboratory in West Virginia (Alford, 1969). Rural Appalachia is characterized by shortages of teachers, classrooms, teaching equipment, and money for education. One-third or fewer of the region's children under six were enrolled in kindergarten in 1967. To offset these difficulties in the education of young children, the Appalachia Educational Laboratory began a television program for three-, four-, and five-year-olds. The use of television in alternative educational programs for children of kindergarten age did not originate with this project; similar programs have been produced on educational television in cities like Albuquerque and Pittsburgh.

The core of the program was a television show broadcast five times a week for one-half hour a day. Since 94 percent of the homes in the area were equipped with television, it was assumed that this would be an effective means of contacting the children. These children ordinarily watched television quite frequently; 45 percent watched two or three hours each day, 24 percent watched four to five hours each day, and some children were reported to spend eight or more hours a day watching television.

In addition to the television show, the study used two other methods: home visits by trained paraprofessionals once each week for one-half hour; and a weekly one and one-half hour program with ten to 15 children , held in a mobile classroom and supervised by a teacher and an aide. The objective of the program was teaching orienting and attending skills, motor activities, and language and cognitive materials. The children were divided into four groups: Group 1 participated in television, home visits, and mobile classroom; Group 2 in television and home visits; Group 3 in television only; Group 4, control.

There was no tendency for the average intellectual level to increase more in the experimental groups than in the control group. However, on the Illinois Test of Psycholinguistic Abilities test of verbal expression, gains were as follows: Group 1, 4.4 points; Group 2, .05 points; Group 3, 1.41 points; Group 4, 1.63 points. Thus only when the three components of the program were combined was there a significant improvement in verbal expression. On a 95-item test of cognitive activities involving the ability to recognize numbers and symbols correctly and to make appropriate associations, the members of Group 1 were correct on 45 percent of the items, while the scores for Groups 2 and 3 were approximately 33 percent correct.

This study found that the three experimental groups (like the viewers of *Sesame Street*) differed in several important ways. Children in Group 1 came from families that differed from those in the other three groups on such factors as parents' level of schooling and number of parents owning or renting a home. The actual frequency with which children viewed the television program also differed among the three experimental groups. The number of children who watched the program four or five times a week in Group 1 was 83 percent of the group; in Group 2, 82 percent; and in Group 3, 44 percent. The proportion of parents who watched the program with their children was 64 percent in Group 1, 56 percent in Group 2, and 27 percent in Group 3. Differences like these in parental characteristics and in actual viewing time make it impossible to reach firm conclusions about the influence of the television program on the children's behavior.

Recall of material

We know very little about how much preschool children remember after viewing typical television programs. What we do know leads us to believe that they retain only a very small part of what they see after a single viewing. For example, Halloran (1969) has reported the results of studying young children's responses to *Patrik and Putrik*, the program that won the Prix Jeunesse in 1966. (Of incidental interest is the fact that even though the program was judged by adults to be the best of the entries, children interviewed in various countries did not evaluate the program very highly. Thus we cannot be confident that children's judgments about the attractiveness of a program will be in high concordance with the judgments of adults.) The film contained 127 incidents. Five-year-old British children were able to recall an average of only six of the incidents; children aged six to eight recalled an average of 12 incidents. Data from America revealed that children between the ages of five and eight recalled an average of 12 incidents.

A further indication of the difficulties preschool children have in remembering what they have seen is found in a study by Leifer, Collins, Gross, Taylor, and Andrews (1970). Children at three age levels were shown a twenty-minute fairy tale of the type commonly seen on television. The average ages of the children were 4.3, 7.4, and 10.3 years. After viewing the film, the children were presented with four series of photographs (of three, five, seven, and nine photos, respectively) showing central incidents in the film and were asked to lay them down in the order they had happened in the film. Only 20 percent of the four-year-olds were able to place three photographs in the proper sequence; their performance was even more impoverished when larger numbers of photographs were used. In contrast, all the seven-year-olds were able to place three photographs in proper order, and 55 percent were able to place five photographs in their proper order. When the preschool children were asked questions about the feelings or motivations of the characters in the film, their responses were "vague at best." Preschool children were unable, therefore, either to remember what they had seen with any fidelity or to interpret accurately why the characters had acted the way they did.

More novel materials were presented to children in a study by Coates and Hartup (1969). Four-year-olds were shown a movie of a man performing a series of novel acts—for example, building a tower of blocks in a unique way, putting a toy on top of the tower, and walking backward four steps from the tower. A total of 20 critical behaviors were displayed in the film. Unlike those in other studies, the children were told before they viewed the film that they would later be asked to show what the man in the movie had done. Four-year-olds did not learn a great deal from their observation of the film. They were able to reproduce an average of only six of the model's responses.

A second group of four-year-olds was tested using the same procedure, but the experimenter viewed the film with the child, described each of the critical responses as they were performed, and asked the child to repeat his descriptions. This procedure proved to be effective in increasing the children's ability to remember the content of the film. Now they were able to recall 12 of the 20 critical behaviors. This study seems to show the advantages of parental discussion of television programs to improve children's retention of what they have seen.

All these films were seen once. How much more the children would have remembered had they seen the materials more frequently is unknown. If these studies are a valid indication of what preschool children retain from television programs, we would expect enduring effects only when the themes are presented repeatedly, when their content is discussed by another person, or when the material results in emotional responses of some magnitude.

Another study tested children's retention of frequently repeated commercials. The frequent repetition of printed words in television commercials apparently has little influence on children's ability to remember the meaning of the printed word. LaPlante (1969) presented preschool children with 24 of the words most frequently shown and spoken on the most popular television show in three formats: (a) the unique typography as shown on television; (b) the unique typography in color as shown on packaging; and (c) conventional typography. Over 60 percent of the children could recognize one word, but when it was presented in conventional typography the percentage dropped to 13 percent. Casual observation is not an easy road to reading.

Emotional response

Is there any evidence that preschool children become emotionally aroused while viewing television violence? Endsley and Osborn (1970) sought to answer this question by showing to four- and five-year-olds some television film episodes containing violence and others containing no violence. Two films of each type were shown, one a cartoon and the other depicting real human characters.

The results indicated that children responded more emotionally (as reflected by increased palmar sweating) to the two films containing violence, especially when human characters were involved. Children selected the film with human violence as the "scariest" and judged the nonviolent cartoon "best liked." A week later the children recalled more about the film portraying human violence than about the other three. When asked if the children thought the grandmother in one of the films, *Billy Goats Gruff*, really had been killed or whether it was just pretend, about half expressed the belief that she really had been killed.

Aggression

The most frequently cited studies dealing with television and the behavior of preschool children are those concerned with aggression. Critics of television have used these studies as evidence that television violence may increase young children's tendencies to display violence and aggression. Others have regarded the studies as valid indications that under *some conditions* televised violence may have this effect but that it has not yet been demonstrated that the effects carry over to the child's everyday behavior in social settings. The studies have been performed in the laboratory for short periods of time and have involved aggression toward inanimate objects rather than toward other people. The types of aggression studied have tended to be somewhat unusual (hitting a Bobo doll in a certain way, making certain verbalizations while performing aggressive acts). We have learned from these studies that the observation of televised aggressive material does increase the child's expression of aggression in the laboratory immediately after viewing the film. Whether this carries over into his everyday behavior is still a matter for experimental investigation.

The basic objective of this aggression research was to determine: (a) whether children learn to imitate specific acts of aggression from seeing them performed in a film; and (b) whether viewing the film produces an increase in general, nonimitative aggression. The initial study was conducted by Bandura, Ross, and Ross (1963a); since this study has become the basis for much of the ensuing research, it should be described in some detail.

Three groups of preschool children were used. Some children saw an adult display a series of aggressive responses. Others saw the same behavior demonstrated by an adult in a film. For a third group, the aggressive model was an adult dressed in the costume of a cartoon animal. After the viewing of the different aggressive models by the three groups, the same procedure was followed for all three groups of children. The behavior of these children was contrasted with that of children in a control group who did not witness a display of aggression.

In order to distinguish between generalized or nonimitative aggression and the aggression that might be a direct imitation of the model, the aggressive responses performed by the model were very distinctive. After spending a minute playing with some tinker toys, the model began to pommel a Bobo doll, hit it with a mallet, sit on it, and engage in other distinctive forms of physical and verbal aggression for ten minutes.

The children then were subjected to mild frustration. The experimenter allowed each child to play with a variety of attractive toys; once the child had become engrossed in play, the experimenter abruptly told him he no longer could play with these toys but could play with some in an adjacent room. (The use of this mild form of frustration was found in later studies to be an unnecessary component of this procedure.) The child's aggression was measured by determining the numbers and types of responses he made while in the experimental room. This room contained the toys used by the model in displaying aggression, as well as other aggressive and nonaggressive toys. Each child remained in the room for 20 minutes.

All three groups of children displayed more imitative physical and verbal aggression than did the children who had not seen the film. While imitative aggression was greater following exposure to a real-life model than to a cartoon character, the incidence of imitative aggression did not differ between children who had been exposed to aggressive adults in person and in film. Boys displayed more imitative and nonimitative aggressive responses than did girls. Nonimitative aggression scores were higher for children who had observed the films than for those in the control group that had not observed aggression.

The results indicated, therefore, that viewing aggression served to heighten the children's general tendencies to be aggressive and to offer them examples of specific forms that aggression could take. This has been considered an important finding, for it offers evidence against a "cathartic" view of observing aggression (the view that observing aggression will reduce the child's need to display aggression himself) and demonstrates that aggressive responses observed by a child can become incorporated into his own behavior.

In the study just described, the aggressor was neither rewarded nor punished for his aggression. Would not the consequences of aggression influence the likelihood that the child would display such aggression? In a subsequent study (Bandura, Ross, and Ross, 1963b), preschool children were allowed to watch one of three five-minute programs on a television set. The central characters were two men, Rocky and Johnny. Rocky approached Johnny, who was playing with some attractive toys, and asked if he could play. Johnny refused. Rocky then exhibited a series of aggressive responses directed at the toys and at Johnny. In one film, Rocky emerged the victor and departed with Johnny's toys. In a second film, Johnny was victorious and Rocky fled to a corner of the room. In a third (control) film, the two adults engaged in vigorous, nonaggressive play.

Children displayed more imitative aggression after watching an aggressive adult rewarded for his aggression than after seeing the aggressor punished. Interestingly, however, seeing a model aggressor punished did not reduce the children's tendency to display imitative aggression to a point below that tendency in a control group. Thus seeing an aggression rewarded increased the likelihood that the children would display such aggression, but punishment did not suppress this tendency.

How are we to interpret these results? Do they mean that the children learned less through observation when they saw the aggressive adult defeated than they learned when he was successful? This seems unlikely, for the children did not see the consequences of the adult's aggression until after the aggression had been displayed. The consequences of the aggression must have influenced only the children's willingness to display what they had learned, not the amount they had learned.

This possibility could be demonstrated rather easily by offering a child a reward for each aggressive incident he could recall. The reward should increase the child's motivation to translate what he knows into action. New films were made in which an adult performed four novel aggressive responses to the Bobo doll, each accompanied by a distinctive remark

(Bandura, 1965). The sequence of responses was repeated twice; afterwards the adult either was rewarded lavishly for his aggression or was described as a bully and told to quit acting aggressively. Some of the children saw the film without either ending. After ten minutes in the experimental room, where the child was free to perform aggressive acts spontaneously, the experimenter asked the child to "show me what Rocky did in the TV program" and promised a reward for each response demonstrated.

There were no differences among the three conditions when the child was rewarded for reproducing the adult's aggression. The children had learned equivalent amounts from viewing the three films, even though they had shown less spontaneous imitative aggression after seeing the adult punished than after seeing him rewarded. Sex differences in imitative aggression also were reduced when the children were rewarded for displaying aggression. We have no reason to believe that girls learn less from observing aggression than do boys; we need only assume that they are less willing, without direct reward, to display the aggression they have observed.

One complaint lodged against these studies is that they demonstrate only short-term effects and fail to reveal any lasting influences. Hicks (1965) has responded to this criticism by testing children six months after they had observed aggression displayed in a film. The procedure was the same as that of the Bandura (1965) study, except that the aggressive models were peers as well as adults. Six months after viewing the films, the children were brought back to the experimental room where they were observed for a second twenty-minute period.

All four types of models (female adult, male adult, female peer, male peer) were found to be highly effective in shaping the children's aggressive responses. Children who had viewed a male peer as the model showed the highest frequency of imitative aggression. Six months later, the amount of imitative aggression among the subjects had decreased, but it still was notably above that shown by children who had not seen the films. In the six-month retest the highest frequency of aggression was found among children who had observed an adult male. As in the earlier study, a promise of a reward during the retest period resulted in the recall of more aggressive acts than children displayed spontaneously in their free play.

No one knows whether the effects demonstrated in these studies would be obtained if the focus of aggression were another person rather than inanimate objects. (It is of incidental interest to note that the children in the previous studies never displayed aggression toward the experimenter who remained in the room with the children during the testing period.) Only one small study (Hanratty, Liebert, Morris, and Fernandez, 1969) has used a human, rather than an inanimate, object as the focus of aggression. Four- and five-year-old boys were shown a brief film in which aggression was displayed toward a clown. During the testing period the clown was either a large plastic toy or a human dressed as a clown. Much more aggression was displayed toward the plastic clown than toward the human, although some aggression was shown toward the human.

These are important studies. In contrast to the "single-shot" studies that fill most of the literature we have been discussing, this whole series of studies has dealt with the observational learning of aggressive responses. The evidence is remarkably consistent: children are capable of learning novel aggressive responses through observation of adult aggression; aggressive responding increases with observation; the effects of observation endure over at least a six-month period; children learn more from observing aggression than they ordinarily are willing to display. There is a need for further research in this area—especially research in which the aggressive responses are less contrived and in which the effects are assessed in ordinary environments.

Characteristics of preschool children

Although our knowledge about the effects of television viewing on the behavior of preschool children is limited, we do know a great deal about the psychological characteristics of preschool children that may be relevant for our discussion. Some of the characteristics which appear most relevant are:

1. *Habituation.* The world contains an infinite array of objects to which the child could respond. The child must have some protective mechanism that enables him or her to ignore aspects of the environment that are constant and to attend to those that are capable of providing new and useful information. Habituation is such a mechanism. Habituation refers to the phenomenon whereby stimuli which initially are effective in producing a particular form of behavior become ineffective with repeated presentation. Habituation has been demonstrated with a wide variety of organisms, including the young child. It has obvious relevance for the viewing of television. Charges have been made, for example, that the recurrence of violence on television leads to habituation: the emotional and cognitive responses produced by the initial displays of violence cease to occur. While this may reduce the impact of violence viewed on television, does it lead the child to be less responsive to violence encountered in his everyday life? The question must be explored methodically.

2. *Learning.* The efficiency with which learning occurs is dependent upon maturation and experience. The more mature the organism, ordinarily, the less experience is required to master a particular task or skill. Young children typically require frequent exposure and extensive practice in order to learn. This is especially true in situations like television

viewing, in which the material is highly dependent upon language. Preschool children are just beginning to master language and have difficulty both in expressing themselves and in directing their own behavior on the basis of words. Verbal instructions and explanations unaccompanied by concrete examples are difficult for preschool children to follow.

Preschool children learn most readily by doing. Materials that elicit active response and can be incorporated into the child's limited past experience are those that will be learned most effectively. There are several reasons, therefore, why preschool children may learn little from watching television. Typical television programs elicit passive rather than active response, infrequently repeat specific content, and represent a highly verbal medium of communication.

3. *Retention*. Preschool children not only learn complex material more slowly than do older children but also retain less of what they learn. Retention is dependent, in part, upon the ways in which information is coded and stored. Coding and storage can be done most effectively through the use of language. Young children, with their limited language facility and conceptualization difficulties, are closely bound to the here and now. When the child becomes capable of using words as substitutes for objects and actions, he is freed from his dependence upon the immediate physical world as a means of organizing his behavior. Learning and retention occur with increased speed and efficiency. We might expect, therefore, that any detrimental effects that occur from watching a single incident on television may not last as long when children are young as when they are older. Similarly, beneficial effects also may dissipate more rapidly among young children.

4. *Selective attention*. Preschool children seem to have difficulty determining what is relevant and what is irrelevant to a specified goal; they respond to many salient features in a restricted fashion. As the child grows older, he appears to sample the stimuli in his environment more broadly and becomes capable of attending selectively to those stimuli that have the greatest potential utility or value. What young children may acquire from viewing materials on television may, therefore, be decidedly different from what older children and adults respond to and learn. Preschool children are readily distracted from the central content of a program by irrelevant details. Older children, on the other hand, are able to disregard irrelevant or incidental aspects of the materials and concentrate their attention on what is central and of critical importance. When we know that preschool children have difficulty making such discriminations and attending selectively, we must be careful to emphasize or make salient those aspects of the situation to which we wish the child to direct his response.

5. *Reality*. A clear sense of what is real and possible—as opposed to what is fanciful and imaginary—develops relatively late in a child's life.. Preschool children are highly dependent upon immediate perception,

while older children are capable of differentiating between what they may perceive and what may be true. That actors are playing roles, that scenes are artificial renderings of real situations, that the active characters in cartoons are not alive—these are difficult, if not impossible, discriminations for the young child to make. All events have an immediate reality, and only with greater experience or a developed capacity for abstract thought can the child, without help, realize that all he sees is not necessarily real.

6. *Individual differences.* We tend to speak of the preschool child as if all preschool children shared the same characteristics. But children of the same age and sex differ in the rate at which they learn, the amount they retain, their verbal facility, their understanding of abstract concepts, their identification with adults, and in many other ways. While such characteristics may be found more frequently at one developmental level than at another, all children do not share them equally. It is dangerous, therefore, to attempt to talk of the effects of television on preschool children as a group. What may frighten one child may amuse another. What is fascinating to one may bore another. The best we can do is attempt to find the types of experiences that are most likely to be useful to the greatest number of children of particular ages. Generalizations about the effects of this experience will not be equally valid for all children no matter how careful we may be.

Many other characteristics could be mentioned, but these five seem to be the most important for the present discussion. Responsible producers of television programs for preschool children should capitalize on such factors in planning their programs. Repetition, simple language, vivid materials devoid of many irrelevant features, sequences of events clearly demonstrating causal relations among events, and distinguishing what is real from what is "pretend" would seem to be important attributes of television programs that seek to impart information to the preschool child. The merit of such suggestions can be better understood with further research.

Conclusions

We have much to learn. Television viewing consumes large numbers of hours in the lives of preschool children, and an investment of this amount of time must influence their intellectual, social, moral, and personality development. At this time, however, we have only a modest idea of what these influences are. Generally, our conclusions after reviewing the research with preschool children are the same as those summarizing an earlier discussion of television and children's behavior:

We know a great deal about children's viewing habits. We know something of the effects of television on children—not as much as we need to know, but enough to say that facts are learned, attitudes acquired, and behavior patterns adopted by means of television and film. Which children are influenced, the extent of the effects, the circumstances under which they occur, the relation with primary socializing forces of family, friends, and school are far from known (Carskadon et al., 1967, p. 26).

Perhaps the most important results are those from the study of *Sesame Street*. We now know (although there never really was reason to doubt) that television programs can be designed both to be attractive to preschool children and to lead to positive effects on their cognitive development. Much of the social concern about television has been directed to its possible harmful effects, especially in the domain of aggression and violence, and many studies have sought to determine whether behavior like aggression can be learned through observing its occurrence on television or film. Expanded efforts to discover how the *beneficial* effects of television can be increased would be of much greater value. Not all television programs will be designed to foster cognitive or social development, but when the goal is to entertain children, researchers and television producers might ask how the entertainment can be a positive force in the child's life.

Television probably has not had as negative an influence on the lives of preschool children as some of its severest critics have suggested. Young children are limited in their ability to direct their attention, to learn and retain complex materials, and to follow verbal discourse; programs aimed at older children and adults probably do not have the impact on their lives that programs at their own level of comprehension would have. We can be sure, however, that television has not been as positive a force as it could have been. Few programs have been presented for the preschool child; of these programs, most have been designed by persons with little knowledge about young children.

The television viewing of many preschool children is unsupervised, especially in disadvantaged homes. However valuable certain programs might be, the benefits will be unrealized until we learn how to motivate parents to become interested in what their children are viewing and in directing their children toward the most appropriate programs.

While our knowledge of the effects of television on the behavior of preschool children is still at a primitive state, research in developmental psychology is not. Psychologists have a relatively good understanding of many aspects of the behavior of preschool children; with a reasonable amount of effort, many of these ideas could be applied to the study of television. Although there are difficulties in conducting research on the mass media, we need the guidance of sound research if television is to meet the needs of the nation's young children.

Future research

Past efforts to investigate television's influence on the lives of young children have given us, as we have seen, only a rudimentary understanding of this complex problem. Many relevant research problems are amenable to investigation; the results of such studies would be suitable for immediate application. Many lists of problems could be proposed, but the following includes some of the questions that would seem to be most fruitful to investigate.

1. *What makes a program good?* It seems unlikely that television producers purposely expend their funds to create poor programs for children. Their goal is to present programs that appeal to large numbers of children. What appears on television is, in the judgment of the networks, what the public will support. It is easy to criticize many present programs; it is much harder to describe how good programs could be created. The "wasteland" of television for young children is due in part to our inability to define the components of television programs that are most appealing to children of different ages . Knowing what *has* been appealing is not knowing all that *can* be appealing. Nevertheless, analyzing the programs that children of different ages do like will provide clues about where to begin. We need to know which programs are appealing and what it is about these programs that attracts children's interest and attention. Why do cartoons capture children's attention so well? Which techniques used in *Sesame Street* best sustain children's interest? What kinds of fantasy do children like most? Answers to such questions will enable us to offer useful suggestions about how to develop new and more appropriate programs. Unless programs interest children, they will not be watched.

2. *What do children remember about what they view?* From what we know, preschool children appear to remember relatively little of the specific content of what they see on television. While we may be pleased that much of the content of current television programs may not be retained by young children, ultimately our hope is to provide information that children do remember. Psychologists have done much research on learning that occurs through passive observation, but few of these studies deal with retention of substantive material. What conditions can be introduced which improve learning and retention of the content of television programs? Are adults the most effective persons to present information to young children? How much of what children *hear* (compared with what they see) do they remember? What is the optimal length of programs, and how frequently must the materials be repeated? Does active involvement improve young children's retention?

3. *Will children perform what they know?* Demonstrations have repeatedly shown that children are capable of performing in a laboratory the responses they have observed in films. Nothing is known about the degree to which this behavior is carried over into their everyday lives. All adults carry with them a large amount of knowledge that they never translate into action. Even young children, as we have seen, do not

demonstrate all the aggressive responses they have observed and can describe. If young children fail to demonstrate responses in the protective environment of the laboratory, how readily will they perform such acts in their ordinary environments? Does repeated observation of filmed aggression increase the aggressiveness of children in group play? Are children who observe aggressive episodes on televison less responsive to the display of aggression by other children? Does observation of altruistic, sympathetic, or tolerant behavior in films increase the likelihood that children will display such behavior at home, at school, and at play? Can interracial and intercultural tensions among young children be reduced by observing harmonious interactions on television? Questions like these can be researched quite readily; the findings would give us a more enlightened perspective for evaluating the ways television may influence the lives of young children.

4. *What do children think about television?* Abundant anecdotes are told about young children who think animals in cartoons are alive, that people are inside the television set, and that the people on television see *them* but fail to respond to them. How representative are these anecdotes? We know that young children sometimes have a difficult time separating reality from fantasy. How does this difficulty extend to their viewing of television? Do young children mistake what is real for fantasy, and what is fantasy for reality? Do they recognize programs that are designed for them and distinguish these programs from those created for older children and adults? Do children believe claims that are made in television advertising? Do young children understand the news presented on television? Besides knowing that young children enjoy television, we have little idea of their attitudes and beliefs about this medium of communication.

5. *Who watches what?* Social class and parental values influence the manner in which television is used by young children, but few other characteristics of young viewers or their parents are known. We need to know more about such characteristics if we are to persuade families to get their young children to view programs like *Sesame Street* or to introduce programming correctives that will produce desirable outcomes. Do aggressive children prefer to watch aggression? Do asocial young children prefer to watch fantasy programs? If so, could the content of these programs be changed so that prosocial forms of aggression are enhanced and fantasy is employed to improve skills for social interaction? Can programs be constructed to meet the needs of the ghetto child, the fatherless child, the child living in a family under great tension?

Closely related to these questions are those dealing with television viewing and personality development. Are children who view a great deal of television less active socially and physically at other times during their daily lives? How does television influence the family life of preschool children? Does television viewing lead to isolation or does it form a basis for improved social interaction? How do young children respond to the display of emotion by adults on television? Are other forms of stimulation, such as being read to or being taken on excursions, diminished by the presence of television? Can television viewing by preschool children become a habit? How frequently do parents use television as a source of reward and punishment for controlling the behavior or preschool children? What kinds of parents exert controls on their children's television viewing? Knowledge about the personal and social characteristics of those who watch television will lead to a better understanding of the dynamics of television viewing.

6. *Does television influence school work?* As television programs become more cognitively oriented and as more preschool children begin watching such programs, children will be better prepared for the tasks of kindergarten and first grade. How does television influence their work in school? How do children who have learned their alphabet and numbers from the fast-paced and exciting *Sesame Street* adapt to the routines of elementary school? Further improvement in television programming for young children will require changes in elementary school practices and curricula if schools are to sustain children's interest and challenge their abilities. The early school years can be a time for innovation if we know how to make such changes. To do this most wisely, we must know more about how extensive and useful the acquisitions from television are for school learning.

When we begin to compare what we need to know with what we do know, our past efforts at research seem puny indeed. Television is a powerful medium, capable of introducing enormous change. A vast amount of research must be conducted before its power can result in positive influences on children's lives rather than stultifying and eroding influences on the creativity and vitality of the young children of the nation.

FOOTNOTES

1. The studies reviewed in this paper, although small in number, represent a comprehensive survey of the information we have about television and the behavior of preschool children. The goal was to include all relevant studies; any omissions are those that were unavailable from standard bibliographic sources.

The author is now at the University of Michigan.

REFERENCES

Alford, R. W., Jr. *Evaluation Report: Early childhood educational program, 1969 field test.* Charleston, W. Va.: Appalachia Educational Laboratory, March, 1970.

Atkin, C. K., Murray, J. P., and Nayman, O. B. *Television and social behavior: an annotated bibliography of research.* Washington, D.C.: National Institute of Mental Health, 1971.

Ball, S., and Bogatz, E. A. *The first year of Sesame Street: an evaluation.* Princeton: Educational Testing Service, 1970.

Bandura, A. Influence of model's reinforcement contingencies on the acquisition of imitative responses. *Journal of Personality and Social Psychology,* 1965, 1, 589-95.

Bandura, A., Ross, D., and Ross, S. A. Imitation of film-mediated aggressive models. *Journal of Abnormal and Social Psychology,* 1963, 66, 3-11. (a)

Bandura, A., Ross, D., and Ross, S. A. Vicarious reinforcement and imitative learning. *Journal of Abnormal and Social Psychology,* 1963, 67, 601-07. (b)

Blood, R. O., Jr. Social class and family control of television viewing. *Merrill-Palmer Quarterly,* 1961, 7, 205-22.

Carskadon, T. P., et al. *Television for children.* Boston: Foundation for Character Education, 1967.

Chu, G. C., and Schramm, W. *Learning from television: What the research says.* Washington, D. C.: National Association of Educational Broadcasters, 1967.

Coates, B., and Hartup, W. W. Age and verbalization in observational learning. *Developmental Psychology,* 1969, 1, 556-62.

Dillon, J. Violence dominates U. S. summertime TV. *Christian Science Monitor* July 25, 1968.

Endsley, R. C., and Osborn, K. Children's reactions to TV violence. *Young Children,* 1970, 26, 4-11.

Garry, R., Rainsberry, F. B., and Winick, C. *For the young viewer.* New York: McGraw-Hill, 1962.

Gerbner, G. The television world of violence. Baker, R. K. Baker, and Ball. S. J. (Eds.) *Mass media and violence:* A staff report to the National Commission on the Causes and Prevention of Violence. Washington, D. C.: U. S. Government Printing Office, 1969.

Halloran, J. D. *Patrik and Putrik: Reports on international evaluations of children's reactions to the Swedish television programme.* Munich: Internationales Jentralinstitut für das Jugend und Bildungsfernsehen, 1969.

Halloran, J. D. *The effects of mass communication.* Leicester: University of Leicester Press, 1965.

Hanratty, M. A., Liebert, R. M., Morris, L. W., and Fernandez, L. E. Imitation of film-mediated aggression against live and inanimate victims. *Proceedings, 77th Annual Convention, American Psychological Association,* 1969, 457-58.

Hess, R. D., and Goldman, H. Parents' views of the effect of television on their children. *Child Development,* 1962, 33, 411-26.

Hicks, D. J. Imitation and retention of film-mediated aggressive peer and adult models. *Journal of Personality and Social Psychology,* 1965, 2, 97-100.

Himmelweit, H., Oppenheim, A. N., and Vince, P. *Television and the child: An empirical study of the effects of television on the young.* London and New York: Published for the Nuffield Foundation by the Oxford University Press, 1958.

LaPlante, W. A. Investigation of the sight vocabulary of preschool children as measured by their ability to recognize words shown frequently on commercial television. *Dissertation Abstracts International,* 1969, **30**, 930-31.

Lazarsfeld, P. F. Why is so little known about the effects of television on children and what can be done? *Public Opinion Quarterly,* 1955, **19**, 241-51.

Leifer, A. D., Collins, W. A., Gross, B. M., Taylor, P. H., Andrews, L., and Blackmer, E. R. Developmental aspects of variables relevant to observational learning. *Child Development,* 1970.

Maccoby, E. Effects of mass media. In M. L. Hoffman & L. W. Hoffman (Eds.), *Review of child development research,* Vol. 1. New York: Russell Sage Foundation, 1964.

Maccoby, E. Why do children watch television? *Public Opinion Quarterly,* 1954, **18**, 239-44.

Osborn, D. K., and Hale, W. Television violence. *Childhood Education,* 1969, **45**, 505-09.

Schramm, W. *The effects of television on children and adolescents.* Paris: UNESCO, 1964.

Schramm, W., Lyle, J., and Parker, E. B. *Television in the lives of our children.* Stanford: Stanford University Press, 1961.

Zusne, L. Measuring violence in children's cartoons. *Perceptual and Motor Skills,* 1968, **27**, 901-02.